HERBERT MARCUSE

Herbert Marcuse: A critical reader is a collection of brand new papers by sixteen Marcuse scholars, which provides a comprehensive reassessment of the relevance of Marcuse's critical theory at the beginning of the twenty-first century.

Although best known for his reputation in critical theory, Herbert Marcuse's work has had impact on areas as diverse as politics, technology, aesthetics, psychoanalysis, and ecology. This collection addresses the contemporary relevance of Marcuse's work in this broad variety of fields and from an international perspective.

In Part I, veteran scholars of Marcuse and the Frankfurt School examine the legacy of various specific areas of Marcuse's thought, including the quest for radical subjectivity, the maternal ethic, and the negative dialectics of "imagination." The second part of this collection documents Marcuse's reception among a new generation of critical theorists, on subjects including philosophical anthropology and technology, and Marcuse's relation to thinkers such as Heidegger and Habermas. Part III focuses on a new trend in Marcuse scholarship: the link between Marcuse's ideas and environmental thought. The final section of the book contains recollections on Marcuse's person rather than his critical theory, including a look back over his life by his son, Peter.

Contributors: John Abromeit, Stephan Bundschuh, Detlev Claussen, W. Mark Cobb, Angela Y. Davis, Andrew Feenberg, Samir Gandesha, Douglas Kellner, Andrew Light, Tim Luke, Peter Marcuse, John O'Neill, Gérard Raulet, Carl E. Schorske, Steven Vogel, Michael Werz.

John Abromeit is a Ph.D. candidate in history at the University of California, Berkeley. He is the co-editor of *Herbert Marcuse: Heideggerian Marxism* (2004).

W. Mark Cobb is Professor of Philosophy at Pensacola Junior College, and a Ph.D. candidate in the history of consciousness at the University of California, Santa Cruz.

HERBERT MARCUSE

A critical reader

Edited by
John Abromeit and W. Mark Cobb

Routledge
Taylor & Francis Group
NEW YORK AND LONDON

First published 2004
by Routledge
29 West 35th Street, New York, NY 10001

Simultaneously published in the UK
by Routledge
11 New Fetter Lane, London EC4P 4EE

Routledge is an imprint of the Taylor & Francis Group

© 2004 Selection and editorial matter, John Abromeit and W. Mark Cobb;
individual chapters, the contributors

Typeset in Garamond by Taylor & Francis Books Ltd
Printed and bound in Great Britain by MPG Books Ltd, Bodmin

All rights reserved. No part of this book may be reprinted or
reproduced or utilized in any form or by any electronic,
mechanical, or other means, now known or hereafter
invented, including photocopying and recording, or in any
information storage or retrieval system, without permission in
writing from the publishers.

Library of Congress Cataloging in Publication Data
A catalog record for this title has been requested

British Library Cataloguing in Publication Data
A catalogue record for this book is available from the British Library

ISBN 0–415–28909–2 (hbk)
ISBN 0–415–28910–6 (pbk)

CONTENTS

Notes on Contributors   viii
Acknowledgements   x

Introduction   1
    JOHN ABROMEIT AND W. MARK COBB

Part I
Veteran Scholars' Reflections on Marcuse's Theoretical Legacy   41

  1 Marcuse's Legacies   43
      ANGELA Y. DAVIS

  2 The American Experience of the Critical Theorists   51
      DETLEV CLAUSSEN

  3 Heidegger and Marcuse: the Catastrophe and Redemption of Technology   67
      ANDREW FEENBERG

  4 Marcuse and the Quest for Radical Subjectivity   81
      DOUGLAS KELLNER

  5 Marcuse's Maternal Ethic   100
      JOHN O'NEILL

CONTENTS

  6 Marcuse's Negative Dialectics of Imagination   114
      GÉRARD RAULET

Part II
New Critical Voices Interpret Marcuse   129

  7 Herbert Marcuse's Critical Encounter with Martin Heidegger 1927–33   131
      JOHN ABROMEIT

  8 The Theoretical Place of Utopia: Some Remarks on Marcuse's Dual Anthropology   152
      STEPHAN BUNDSCHUH

  9 Diatribes and Distortions: Marcuse's Academic Reception   163
      W. MARK COBB

10 Marcuse, Habermas, and the Critique of Technology   188
      SAMIR GANDESHA

11 The Fate of Emancipated Subjectivity   209
      MICHAEL WERZ

Part III
Marcuse and Contemporary Ecological Theory   225

12 Marcuse's Deep-social Ecology and the Future of Utopian Environmentalism   227
      ANDREW LIGHT

13 Marcuse's Ecological Critique and the American Environmental Movement   236
      TIM LUKE

14 Marcuse and the "New Science" 240
STEVEN VOGEL

Part IV
Recollections 247

15 Herbert Marcuse's "Identity" 249
PETER MARCUSE

16 Encountering Marcuse 253
CARL E. SCHORSKE

Index 260

CONTRIBUTORS

John Abromeit is a Ph.D. candidate in history at the University of California, Berkeley. He is the co-editor of *Herbert Marcuse: Heideggerian Marxism* (2004).

Stephan Bundschuh holds a Ph.D. in philosophy from the J.W. Goethe University in Frankfurt am Main, Germany. He has published essays on the topics of National Socialism and aesthetics.

Detlev Claussen is a professor of social theory and cultural sociology at the Institute for Sociology at the University of Hannover, Germany.

W. Mark Cobb is Professor of Philosophy at Pensacola Junior College, and a Ph.D. candidate in the history of consciousness at the University of California, Santa Cruz.

Angela Y. Davis is a professor in the department of History of Consciousness and the University of California Presidential Chair in African American and Feminist Studies at the University of California, Santa Cruz. She is the author of five books including *Angela Davis: An Autobiography* and *The Angela Davis Reader*.

Andrew Feenberg holds the Canadian Research chair in Philosophy of Technology in the School of Communication at Simon Fraser University. His most recent book is *Transforming Technology: A Critical Theory Revisited* (Oxford, 2002)

Samir Gandesha is Assistant Professor of Modern European Thought and Culture in the Department of Humanities at Simon Fraser University. His work concerns the relation between art and ethics in modern philosophical discourse.

Douglas Kellner is George F. Kneller Chair in the Philosophy of Education at UCLA. He is the editor of Marcuse's collected papers, published by Routledge in six volumes.

CONTRIBUTORS

Andrew Light is Assistant Professor of Environmental Philosophy and Director of the Environmental Conservation Education Program at New York University. His most recent book is *Moral and Political Reasoning in Environmental Practice* (MIT, 2003)

Tim Luke is University Distinguished Professor of Political Science at Virginia Polytechnic Institute and State University in Blacksburg, Virginia.

Peter Marcuse is a lawyer and Professor for Urban Planning at Columbia University in New York. He is the author of *Missing Marx* (1991). He is also Herbert Marcuse's son.

John O'Neill is Distinguished Research Professor of Sociology at York University, Toronto, a Member of the Centre for Comparative Literature at the University of Toronto, and a fellow of the Royal Society of Canada.

Gérard Raulet is Professor of German Intellectual History at the University of Paris-Sorbonne and Research Program Director at the Maison des Sciences de l'Homme in Paris.

Carl E. Schorske is Professor Emeritus of History at Princeton University. He is the author of *German Social Democracy, 1905–1917*, *Fin-de-siècle Vienna*, and *Thinking with History*.

Steven Vogel is Professor of Philosophy at Denison University in Granville, Ohio. He is the author of *Against Nature: The Concept of Nature in Critical Theory* (1996).

Michael Werz received his Ph.D. in philosophy from the J.W. Goethe University in Frankfurt am Main, Germany. He is now Assistant Professor at the Institute for Sociology at the University of Hannover, Germany.

ACKNOWLEDGEMENTS

The original inspiration for this volume came from the international conference on "The Legacy of Herbert Marcuse" that was held at the University of California, Berkeley, on 6–7 November 1998 to commemorate the 100th anniversary of Herbert Marcuse's birth. Although many of the papers that appear here have been modified or completely replaced in the meantime, it remains true that this volume would not have been possible without the support of various people and organizations who made the conference possible. Foremost among them was Martin Jay, who made a generous contribution of research funds from his endowed professorship, provided invaluable aid and advice on organizing the conference, and also delivered the opening remarks. Other individuals who helped with the conference include Lisa Walker, Ania Wertz and Sam Moyn. Other organizations at the University of California, Berkeley, who supported the conference include the Department of History, the Center for Western European Studies, the Center for German and European Studies, and the Townsend Center for the Humanities. The History of Consciousness Department at the University of California, Santa Cruz, also made a financial contribution to the conference.

For their help in the production of the volume we would like to thank our editors at Routledge, Adrian Driscoll, Tony Bruce, Faye Kaliszczak, and Zoe Drayson. We would also like to thank our skillful copy-editor, Mark Ralph. Finally, we would like to thank the contributors to this volume for their patience and cooperation. It has taken us longer than expected to bring this volume to fruition, but our Marcusean obstinacy in seeing the project through to completion has never wavered. We are certain that the extra time we have taken and the changes that have been made along the way have improved the quality of the volume.

We would like to thank the German publishing house Neue Kritik for granting us permission to publish the essays by Angela Davis, Detlev Claussen, Carl E. Schorske, John Abromeit, and Michael Werz. They published the original versions of the papers given at the conference in either German translation, or, in the case of Claussen and Werz, in their

ACKNOWLEDGEMENTS

original German form. With the exception of Schorske's essay, these essays have all been updated for publication in the present volume. We would like to thank Les Éditions de Minuit for granting us permission to reproduce the poem by Samuel Beckett which appears in the introduction. We would also like to thank the Herbert Marcuse Archive, in Frankfurt Germany, for permission to quote unpublished materials. Finally we would like to thank Eric Oberle, who translated the articles by Detlev Claussen and Michael Werz, and Matt Erlin, who translated the article by Gérard Raulet.

INTRODUCTION

John Abromeit and W. Mark Cobb

    pas à pas   step by step
    nulle part   nowhere
    nul seul   not a single one
    ne sait comment knows how
    petits pas   tiny steps
    nulle part   nowhere
    obstinement   stubbornly[1]

Samuel Beckett,
dedicated to Herbert Marcuse
on his 80th birthday

The Anglo-American Reception of Herbert Marcuse's Critical Theory

Herbert Marcuse was certainly the most famous member of the so-called Frankfurt School, particularly in the United States, but his thought may be the least understood of any of the Frankfurt critical theorists. Marcuse's contemporary reputation, which is still largely determined by his active engagement in the protest movements of the 1960s, tends to conceal the fact that he spent over five decades engaged in critical theoretical work. The mere mention of Marcuse's name today often provokes an array of responses that reveal more about the respondents' attitudes toward the 1960s than about Marcuse or his critical theory. These responses range from wistful smiles and an open admission of a nostalgic yearning for the 1960s, when radical social change still seemed possible, to heated denunciations of Marcuse as the intellectual agent behind a vaguely Marxist program of political correctness alleged to have overtaken higher education in the US. The striking emotional responses that Marcuse still evokes are testimony to the admiration and attraction, the anger and hostility that Marcuse's thought and activity as a public intellectual produced in the 1960s and early 1970s.

During the 1960s Marcuse was christened alternatively as the father, grandfather, or guru of the New Left. Marcuse's books, particularly *Eros and Civilization* (1955) and *One-Dimensional Man* (1964), resonated deeply with students in the 1960s who were disturbed by the destructive nature of advanced industrial society and longed for a freer, more erotic society and existence. Eric Hobsbawm, characterizing the global nature of the New Left during this period, writes: "The same books appeared, almost simultaneously, in the student bookshops in Buenos Aires, Rome, and Hamburg (in 1968 almost certainly including Herbert Marcuse)."[2] Furthermore, in discussing Che Guevara's importance for activists during this period, Hobsbawm writes: "No name (except that of the philosopher Marcuse) is mentioned more often than his in a well-informed survey of the global 'New Left' of 1968…"[3] In retrospect, given Marcuse's age and the density of his prose, the fact that students in the New Left discussed Marcuse alongside Guevara, the embodiment of the romantic revolutionary, is astounding. That Marcuse, an elderly German-Jewish émigré philosopher living and teaching in the US, had attracted such worldwide attention with his formidable theoretical texts is a testament to the depth and power of his critique of contemporary capitalism. As one leading Marcuse scholar puts it: "During the 1960s, Herbert Marcuse was more widely discussed than any living philosopher.…Almost alone among contemporary philosophers, Marcuse's ideas became topics of debate not only in scholarly journals, but in the popular press as well."[4] But one effect of Marcuse's sudden popularity was that his critical theory was often treated in a grossly simplistic way. Due to the political pressures and tensions of the time, some radicals were too quick to read their own immediate political and cultural concerns into Marcuse's work, while most critiques of Marcuse's thought tended to be specious and shrill.

Marcuse was undoubtedly an important influence on many involved with the New Left and the protest movements of the 1960s. Angela Y. Davis, an activist on a variety of fronts since the 1960s, said of her former mentor: "Herbert Marcuse taught me that it was possible to be an academic and an activist, a scholar and a revolutionary."[5] But while some students, such as Davis, had the intellectual background necessary to understand Marcuse, many students, particularly in the US, where Hegel and Marx were not standard fare on the syllabi of most academic institutions during the Cold War, lacked the background to understand all the implications of Marcuse's richly philosophical and dialectical texts. Even when students were willing to read Marcuse seriously, the tenor of the times was not always conducive to prolonged theoretical contemplation.[6] As John Bokina writes: "For better and worse, New Left ideas and actions were characterized more by emotion, circumstance, and improvisation than they were by any self-conscious theoretical orientation."[7] Thus, even among those constitutionally and intellectually inclined toward Marcuse's positions, a number of factors complicated the tasks of fully comprehending Marcuse's critical theory. Before Marcuse's critical theory could be assimilated – a substantial task since Marcuse began to produce theoretical texts in the late 1920s – the New Left began to disintegrate and with it the political impulse that had fueled Marcuse's precipitous rise in popularity. While scholars interested in the Frankfurt School continued to explore the context out of which Marcuse's theory had emerged, their attention turned increasingly to his former colleagues at the Institute for Social Research, Theodor Adorno, Walter Benjamin, and Max Horkheimer. Adorno and Benjamin, in particular, continued to attract serious attention throughout the 1980s and 1990s, as did Jürgen Habermas, who served as an assistant to Adorno in the late 1950s, took over Horkheimer's professorship in Frankfurt in 1965, and viewed his own work as a critical reformulation of their project. While many scholarly works were produced that considered these figures, interest in Marcuse lessened considerably. An unfortunate tendency to relegate Marcuse's thought to the New Left and the 1960s developed and, as a result, Marcuse has been largely ignored since the early 1970s. As Mike Davis put it: "Unwonted media celebrity first 'guruified' Marcuse...then stamped his thoughts with the killing censorship of a fad whose time had passed."[8]

There have been some exceptions to this general waning of interest. The political Right in the US has long attempted to demonize Marcuse, beginning with the efforts of California governor Ronald Reagan and Vice-President Spiro Agnew in the late 1960s while Marcuse was teaching at the University of California at San Diego.[9] In 1987, Allan Bloom's influential *The Closing of the American Mind* sparked a huge debate about the state and curricula of higher education. Bloom offers several typically distorted characterizations of Marcuse such as the following: "Marcuse began in Germany in the 1920s by being something of a serious Hegel scholar. He ended up here writing trashy culture criticism with a very heavy sex interest in *One-Dimensional Man* and other well known books."[10] One can imagine the disappointment and frustration Bloom's credulous readers felt as they pored through *One-Dimensional Man* in search of non-existent sexual passages.

In 1990 Roger Kimball weighed in with another right-wing polemic, *Tenured Radicals: How Politics Has Corrupted Our Higher Education*. Kimball also views Marcuse as a malevolent figure and in a section of his book entitled "Gender, Race, and Class," Kimball takes issue with a remark made by Cornel West at a public symposium at Yale in 1986. West called Herbert Marcuse and the post-Second World War French Marxists "the best of Western Civilization."[11] Ignoring Marcuse's critique of advanced industrial society and his alternative vision of a less repressive and more humane civilization, Kimball challenges West's characterization of Marcuse by focusing superficially on his controversial essay "Repressive Tolerance" and the "Political Preface" Marcuse added to the 1966 edition of *Eros and Civilization*. Conveniently overlooking the arguments and content of every major text Marcuse wrote, Kimball characterizes Marcuse's critical theory as "nearly universal mendacity."[12] While such "critiques" of Marcuse might seem to represent new lows in fairness and responsible scholarship, unfortunately Bloom and Kimball have plenty of company. They also illustrate how irritating Marcuse has always been to the political Right and how reluctant his critics have been to confront his arguments directly.[13]

Fortunately there has been a small number of scholars who have produced some important studies of Marcuse in English during the past few decades.[14] In 1980 Morton Schoolman published *The Imaginary Witness: The Critical Theory of Herbert Marcuse*. His study offers a substantial critical interpretation of Marcuse's thought as a whole and is distinguished by its emphasis on the work Marcuse produced prior to 1933, and its contention that Max Weber was Marcuse's most important theoretical precursor. In 1982 Barry Kātz published an intellectual biography, *Herbert Marcuse and the Art of Liberation*, which highlights the aesthetic dimension of Marcuse's thought. Kātz also provides an informative discussion of Marcuse's US government service during and after the Second World War in the Office of Strategic Services (OSS) and the State Department. In 1984 Douglas Kellner's *Herbert Marcuse and the Crisis of Marxism* appeared; it presents Marcuse's theoretical project as a provocative and valuable attempt to think through the crises of Marxism. Kellner's study is the most comprehensive survey of Marcuse's critical theory to appear in English to date.

In the following year, 1985, two insightful studies focusing on particular aspects of Marcuse's theoretical project were published. Timothy J. Lukes' *The Flight into Inwardness* offers a lucid explication and thoughtful political critique of Marcuse's aesthetics. C. Fred Alford's *Science and the Revenge of Nature: Marcuse and Habermas* offers a critical appraisal of Habermas and Marcuse's views of nature and science, while suggesting that Marcuse's treatment of these subjects contains virtues that have been overlooked. In 1988 Alford's *Narcissism: Socrates, the Frankfurt School, and Psychoanalytic Theory* was published. The study includes an astute discussion of Marcuse's radical reinterpretation of Freud, Marcuse's conceptions of "Eros" and repression, and the problems and promise involved in Marcuse's attempt to offer Narcissus and Orpheus as models of non-repressive sublimation. Also appearing in 1988 was an excellent anthology entitled *Marcuse: Critical Theory and the Promise of Utopia* – edited by Andrew Feenberg, Robert Pippin, and Charles P. Webel. The contributors include such luminaries as Jürgen Habermas, Martin Jay, Richard J. Bernstein, Claus Offe, and Alfred Schmidt. Habermas's essay, "Psychic Thermidor and the Rebirth of Rebellious Subjectivity," provides important insights into the ethical commitments underlying Marcuse's critical theory.

INTRODUCTION

The most important event in Marcuse scholarship in the mid-1990s was the publication, in 1994, of *Marcuse: From the New Left to the Next Left*, which was edited by John Bokina and Timothy J. Lukes. The anthology re-examined Marcuse's work at a time when "postmodern" theoretical approaches were heavily influencing academic discourse, and the logic of the Cold War had been rendered obsolete due to the events of 1989. The anthology includes a host of provocative essays, including Ben Agger's "Marcuse in Postmodernity," that encourage reading Marcuse to engage postmodern concerns with the body, discourse, and domination in ways that were less cynical and more informed by social theory. Trudy Steuernagel's "Marcuse, the Women's Movement, and Women's Studies" and Gad Horowitz's "Psychoanalytic Feminism in the Wake of Marcuse" both argue, in distinctive ways, for the importance that Marcuse's texts and some of his strategies still have for gender and women's studies. The anthology also includes a provocative section entitled "Ecofascists and Cyberpunks," in which Andrew Feenberg and Timothy J. Lukes discuss the relevance of Marcuse's theory of technology in the age of cyborgs, hyperindividuality, and virtual reality. The final essay in the collection is Douglas Kellner's "A Marcuse Renaissance?". Using the example of the technologically anaesthetized human and environmental destruction of the first Gulf War, Kellner argues for the ongoing relevance of Marcuse's analysis of the transformation of the welfare into the "warfare" state. In his article Kellner also announces the existence of a wealth of previously unpublished works by Marcuse, housed in the Marcuse archive in Frankfurt.[15]

Marcuse's critical theory began to receive additional popular notice as a result of an intriguing documentary film released in 1996, *Herbert's Hippopotamus: Marcuse and Revolution in Paradise*, which was written, directed, and produced by Paul Alexander Juutilainen. Juutilainen's film has won more than a dozen awards and festival prizes in Canada, Europe, and the US. Juutilainen first read about Marcuse as a student in Denmark and in 1992 he enrolled in a graduate program in visual arts at the University of California at San Diego (UCSD), where Marcuse had become embroiled in controversy in the late 1960s. At UCSD Juutilainen began to research Marcuse's life, focusing on the California period and battles with Ronald Reagan. Juutilainen interviewed numerous former students and colleagues of Marcuse's, including Angela Y. Davis, Fredric Jameson, and Reinhard Lettau. The film is culled from over sixty hours of archival footage and provides a close and revealing look at the odd assortment of characters and forces that fiercely opposed both Marcuse and what they took or mistook for his message. The film also sheds light on the historical preconditions of current attacks on affirmative action and public education by the political Right, and asks important questions about the current practices and social role of the university in the contemporary world.

The year 1998 marked not only the 30th anniversary of the revolts of 1968, the 150th anniversary of the *Communist Manifesto*, and the 75th anniversary of the founding of the Institute for Social Research, but also the 100th birthday of Herbert Marcuse. At least five conferences were held around the globe – in Frankfurt, Rio de Janeiro, Rome, Genoa, and Berkeley – to commemorate the occasion and to reflect upon Marcuse's work. The Berkeley conference, which was entitled "The Legacy of Herbert Marcuse," attracted an impressive international and intergenerational array of speakers who paid tribute to Marcuse while assessing the various ways in which his work may still be relevant today. The same year also witnessed the publication of the first of a projected six-volume edition of mostly unpublished writings by Marcuse, edited by Douglas Kellner. *Technology, War, and Fascism*[16] focuses on the years 1942–51, when Marcuse worked for the US government in the fight against fascism and the post-war reconstruction of Germany. The volume includes several important essays that Marcuse wrote on Nazi Germany, as well as Marcuse's revealing correspondences during this time with Max Horkheimer and Martin Heidegger. This volume and those that follow should greatly increase our understanding of Marcuse and his critical theory and should deepen debates about Marcuse's legacy as a philosopher, critical social theorist, and public intellectual.[17]

In 2000, Charles Reitz published a full-length study of Marcuse's theory of education, entitled *Art, Alienation and the Humanities: A Critical Engagement with Herbert Marcuse*.[18] Reitz divides Marcuse's work into an early period, which lasts until the publication in 1932 of Marcuse's essay on Marx's *Philosophic-Economic Manuscripts*,[19] a middle period, which comes to an end in 1970 after the appearance of *Essay on Liberation*, and a final period, which culminates in Marcuse's final work, *The Aesthetic Dimension*. Reitz characterizes the first and last periods in terms of "art as alienation," which he defines as an emphasis on an idealist notion of aesthetic education that focuses on the formal aspects of art.[20] He characterizes the middle period in terms of "art against alienation," which he explains in Lukácsian terms as aesthetic education as a form of praxis directed to overcoming reification.[21] In both periods, however, Reitz argues that Marcuse ultimately falls prey to a "reduction of social theory to aesthetic theory."[22] Reitz's loyalty to a certain interpretation of Marx leads him to the conclusion that Marcuse's work as a whole is best characterized as an "aesthetic ontology"[23] and a "philosophical anthropology"[24] that has more in common with Nietzsche, Dilthey, and Heidegger than Marx.

Overview of Marcuse's Life and Work

Despite the fact that he has been given some scholarly attention in the past few decades, the dominant understanding of Marcuse is still largely determined by his critical support of the student movement and the New Left in the 1960s. This understanding has created myths which continue to hinder an adequate reception of his theoretical work. For Marcuse's theoretical production was, of course, not limited to the writings which influenced, or were influenced by, the political events of the 1960s. Already in 1922, at the age of 24, Marcuse wrote a substantial study of the German artist-novel, which traced the development of this sub-genre of the novel of development (*Bildungsroman*) throughout the long nineteenth century.[25] Drawing on the aesthetic theory of Hegel and the early Lukács, Marcuse analyzed the ways in which these artist-novels – from Karl Phillip Moritz's *Anton Reiser*, to Thomas Mann's *Death in Venice*, by way of Goethe's *Wilhelm Meister*, Gottfried Keller's *Green Henry*, and several others – illustrated the fate of the individual and art in a society being transformed by capitalist modernization. Following Lukács, Marcuse argued that in a society characterized by "transcendental homelessness" the novel assumes the role of preserving the ideal of a less alienated existence.[26] The marginal social position of the anti-heroes of the artist-novel embody the fate of art in a world that has become prosaic, and their mostly unsuccessful attempts to overcome their alienation highlights the "problematic" nature of society as a whole. Marcuse's dissertation introduces several themes that would figure prominently in his later work, such as the importance of the aesthetic dimension as a source of transcendent social critique, or the search for new forms of critical subjectivity among marginal social groups.

After a five-year interlude in Berlin, during which time he worked on an extensive bibliography of Schiller and immersed himself in the Weimar cultural scene, Marcuse returned to Freiburg to study philosophy with Martin Heidegger, who had just published his magnum opus, *Being and Time*. Like many others of his generation, Marcuse was deeply impressed with *Being and Time*, which he saw as a breakthrough beyond the sterile positivism and neo-Kantianism that had dominated philosophical debates in Germany for several decades. Marcuse viewed Heidegger's existential analytic of *Dasein* as the most advanced attempt to bring the individual subject, in its full concreteness, back to the center of philosophical debate. He was also fascinated by Heidegger's stress on the historicity of *Dasein*, and his argument that *Dasein* could be authentic only if its actions were guided by full awareness of its historical possibilities. But Marcuse never became a Heideggerian himself; his purpose from the beginning was to use the most advanced aspects of Heidegger's project to revitalize the reified Marxist theory of his day. Frustrated with the economist orthodoxy of the Second International, which provided ideological justification for the Social Democratic reformism, and no less satisfied with the vanguardism of the Bolsheviks, Marcuse wrote a series of essays while studying with Heidegger which sought to re-establish the importance of subjectivity and historicity in Marxist theory. His efforts eventually led him down the same path Lukács had followed a few years before in *History and Class Consciousness*, namely to a re-examination of the philosophical origins of Marx's theory, particularly in the work of Hegel. Marcuse's *Habilitationsschrift*,[27] which he wrote under Heidegger's guidance, was an attempt to recover the concepts from Hegel's work, such as labor, doing (*Tun*), and historical self-reflexivity, that he believed were necessary to put Marxist theory back on the right track. In this, his first full-length study of Hegel, and in his essays from this period, Marcuse developed a highly original and often trenchant interpretation not only of several of Marx's and Hegel's central concepts – such as labor, alienation, and the dialectical method – but also of *Being and Time*. Marcuse's *political* interpretation and subsequent rejection of Heidegger sheds important light on the much debated link between *Being and Time* and Heidegger's enthusiastic embrace of National Socialism.[28]

Heidegger's own political reading of *Being and Time*, which led him to pin his hopes on the National Socialists as the potential saviors of "fallen" German *Dasein*, came as a shock to Marcuse and forced him to rethink his relationship to Heidegger's philosophy. Marcuse had the good fortune of being able to pursue this self-critical re-evaluation of Heidegger, and to contribute more broadly to the development of critical theory, through his collaborative work with Max Horkheimer's Institute for Social Research in the 1930s. After a brief stint at the Institute's branch office in Geneva, Marcuse emigrated to New York to join Horkheimer and the other members of the relocated Institute, whose former headquarters in Frankfurt had been confiscated by the National Socialists. In the interdisciplinary division of labor established by Horkheimer at the Institute, Marcuse played the role of the house philosopher. Marcuse published several lengthy essays, including a commentary on Horkheimer's programmatic essay, "Traditional and Critical Theory," as well as numerous reviews of philosophical works in the Institute's remarkable journal, the *Zeitschrift für Sozialforschung*.[29] Marcuse also wrote a lengthy philosophico-historical preface for the Institute's major empirical social research project in the 1930s, the *Studies on Authority and Family*.

Marcuse's essays from the 1930s, which repay close reading to the present day, analyzed the ambivalent legacy of the bourgeois era whose demise in the first decades of the twentieth century the Institute had diagnosed. Marcuse argued that, on the one hand, the historical triumph of the bourgeoisie had created the conditions that had made fascism possible: the division of society into antagonistic classes; structural unemployment and periodic crises; increasing concentration of social wealth and power in the hands of large monopolies; repressive forms of socialization that instilled uncritical submission to authority; and affirmative forms of culture that glossed over real social contradictions. On the other hand, Marcuse maintained that the bourgeoisie had also developed in its historical struggle against feudalism and absolute monarchy critical cultural forms that could still serve as a guide to building a more humane society. Bourgeois art was not just affirmative, it also preserved – albeit in a transcendent form – humanist ideals that pointed beyond capitalist social domination. Bourgeois philosophy in its rationalist form was not only an expression of increasingly abstract social relations, or *Seinsvergessenheit*, as Heidegger would have it. In Marcuse's dialectical interpretation, the affirmative and metaphysical concept of reason of the rationalists is transformed into a transcendent regulative idea that serves as an indispensable component of the critical theory of society: the real must be judged in terms of rational standards that have not yet been attained.[30] Marcuse's post-1933 critical re-evaluation of the rationalist tradition culminated in *Reason and Revolution*, a study of Hegel and the rise of modern social theory. The purpose of the book, which Marcuse wrote in English and published in New York in 1941, was to outline historically the theoretical origins of critical theory and to counter the then widespread belief in England and America that Hegel was a precursor of the irrationalism or the authoritarian statism of the National Socialists.

In the late 1930s and early 1940s, financial troubles forced the Institute to discontinue publication of the *Zeitschrift für Sozialforschung*. Since Horkheimer had chosen to collaborate with Adorno on writing the *Dialectic of Enlightenment* and closed down, for all practical purposes, the Institute's New York office, Marcuse decided to take up the fight against fascism at a more practical level, by accepting a research and analysis position in the intelligence branch of the US government.[31] For nearly a decade Marcuse worked side by side with several other prominent leftist émigré scholars – including some who were affiliated with the Institute for Social Research, such as Franz Neumann and Otto Kirchheimer – on projects such as identifying groups that would potentially support post-war democracy or developing policy recommendations for denazification programs. While Marcuse's stay in Washington was not the most theoretically productive period of his life, it was not a period of intellectual dormancy either, as has often been assumed. This myth has been put to rest by the recent publication of several previously unavailable texts from the Herbert Marcuse Archive.[32] Among these are two lengthy articles on National Socialist Germany, which contain the core of Marcuse's analysis of fascism. Marcuse's complex, insightful, and provocative analysis of the economic and cultural factors that made Nazism possible offers an important corrective to one-dimensional theories that see only breaks, but no continuities, between capitalist modernization and fascism, or that treat fascism as a product of pathologies unique to German history or culture. Although his practical activities in the service of the Allied war and reconstruction efforts did not leave him much time to pursue his philosophical and aesthetic interests, he did not abandon them altogether. In an essay on Louis Aragon's novel *Aurelien*, written in 1945, Marcuse developed his ideas on the autonomy of the aesthetic dimension, and in a lengthy review of Sartre's *Being and Nothingness*, published in 1948, he pointed out the fatal flaws of existentialism.[33]

Marcuse had been interested in remedying the relative neglect of subjective factors in Marxist theory for quite some time, but in contrast to Horkheimer, Adorno, and Eric Fromm, he had approached this problem via Heideggerian phenomenology not Freudian psychoanalysis. Although his interest in materialist theories of subjectivity grew in the 1930s, it was not until after the war that Marcuse seriously studied Freud. The result was *Eros and Civilization*, which was published in 1955. It was Marcuse's attempt to draw out the emancipatory undercurrent of Freud's thought through a historicizing, immanent critique. But *Eros and Civilization* was much more than simply a reinterpretation of Freud. It was at the same time a self-reflexive theory of social and individual development on the same massive historical scale as Horkheimer and Adorno's *Dialectic of Enlightenment*. As the scattered references to Auschwitz throughout the text make clear, *Eros and Civilization* must also be seen as Marcuse's attempt to understand and critique the social conditions that had made the recrudescence of barbarism in the heart of the "civilized" West possible. Marcuse had, in the meantime, like Horkheimer and Adorno, become more critical of the Western rationalist tradition. He no longer stressed reason's ability to identify the objective possibilities of liberation latent in the bad immediacy of the present, but rather its complicity with domination. But unlike later post-structuralist critics, Marcuse did not fall into the performative contradiction of abandoning reason altogether.[34] He also went beyond Horkheimer and Adorno's efforts to make reason self-reflexive again, insofar as he sought to identify a foundation for a qualitatively different concept of reason – what he called "erotic rationality" – in the human instinctual structure. But Marcuse's position was neither an essentialist defense of a static concept of human nature, nor a Rousseauian diatribe against civilization per se, nor a celebration of free love, to name just a few of the common misinterpretations.[35] Marcuse argued that the capitalist development of the means of production and technology had made it possible to eliminate surplus repression and to replace, to a large extent, alienated labor with new forms of non-repressive sublimation. At a time when technological advances are eliminating jobs at an unprecedented rate, and discussions about the "end of work" and the "obsolescence of the production paradigm" abound, Marcuse's arguments seem more timely than ever. Marcuse's critique of Freud's theory of phylogenetic and ontogenetic development, which posit patriarchy and heterosexuality as the norm of social and individual maturity, could also still contribute to current discussions in feminist and queer theory.

In his next book, *Soviet Marxism*, on which he had also been working throughout the 1950s, and which was published a few years after *Eros and Civilization*, Marcuse outlined an immanent critique of real-existing socialism. He made clear just how far the Soviet Union had strayed from Marx's critique of political economy with the ideological doctrine of "Diamat" that was used to legitimate authoritarian statism and arbitrary, massive violence against its own population. On the other hand, Marcuse was far from being just another voice in the hysterical chorus of anti-communism in the US in the 1950s. Marcuse viewed Soviet Marxism as a form of forced economic development which, in its emphasis on industrial and technological development at all costs, displayed certain similarities with Western capitalist societies. Although Marcuse was critical of the then popular "convergence" thesis, he did believe that the instrumental logic of technological rationality underlay both systems. He also believed, however, that development of this logic would lead to economic and social contradictions that would force a liberalization of the Soviet command economy. Although he was writing at a time when the Soviet economy seemed stronger than ever, and Khrushchev was introducing certain reforms at the political level – both tendencies that would be reversed in the following decades – Marcuse's analysis of Soviet Marxism still offers many insights into the structure of so-called real-existing socialism and the tendencies which led to its collapse its 1989.[36]

Marcuse's next book, *One-Dimensional Man*, which he published in 1964 at the age of 66, catapulted him out of the relative obscurity of scholarly life to the forefront of the burgeoning protest movements of the 1960s. Within the next five years, 100,000 copies of *One-Dimensional Man* were sold in the US alone. *One-Dimensional Man* provided a trenchant critique of advanced industrial society that resonated with students frustrated by the stultifying conformity and complacency generated by contemporary capitalist technocracy.[37] In the introduction to the text, Marcuse emphasized "the vital importance of the work of C. Wright Mills,"[38] the maverick sociologist and author of *The Power Elite*, which exposed the ruling caste behind the putatively pluralist democracy in the US. Mills had already found many enthusiastic readers among critical students, in part because of the accessibility of his powerful prose and the empirical evidence he used to substantiate his arguments. Marcuse's texts were, in contrast, highly abstract and densely dialectical and thus posed a greater challenge to readers accustomed to the Anglo-American theoretical tradition. Marcuse's version of Hegelian-Marxist critical theory provided the New Left with an alternative theoretical basis for their political critique and introduced students to a philosophical tradition that was marginalized in the positivist-dominated intellectual climate in the US in the post-war period.[39] While Marcuse had garnered considerable attention in Europe prior to the publication of *One-Dimensional Man*, the text unexpectedly thrust Marcuse into the political spotlight in the US. Shortly thereafter, Marcuse emerged as a truly international public intellectual whose works were translated and read in many languages.

The sudden prominence Marcuse attained was due to the provocative nature of the argument developed in *One-Dimensional Man*. The text delineated the more subtle, but effective forms of social control found in Western capitalist societies. Marcuse argued that these societies produced false needs while dramatically reducing the capacity for critical thought and resistance. Thus Marcuse offered a theoretical explanation for the alienation and frustration many felt but found difficult to articulate in a society in which even language itself had been distorted to serve the interests of the ruling powers.[40] While the overall mood of the text was pessimistic, Marcuse did suggest some possibilities for resistance. For example, Marcuse pointed to historical memory as a force with the potential of subverting the compulsory amnesia of technological reason: "Remembrance of the past may give rise to dangerous insights, and the established society seems to be apprehensive of the subversive contents of memory."[41] In addition, Marcuse advocated the preservation and recovery of the critically transcendent dimension of language, found in universal philosophical concepts or poetry, against the dominant tendency to subordinate language to operational imperatives. Because the working class in Western capitalist societies had been effectively integrated through consumerism and the culture industry, Marcuse looked to new social groups, those outside the system and radical students, as potential catalysts of change. But these possibilities, Marcuse lamented, were no more than a hope.

The following year Marcuse published "Repressive Tolerance,"[42] his most controversial essay. At this time the liberal establishment in the US was demonstrating its willingness not only to tolerate but to actively support authoritarian neo-colonial and military regimes in Vietnam, Brazil, and many other countries in Latin America, Asia, Europe, and Africa.[43] On the domestic front, the civil rights movement was becoming increasingly militant following the "freedom summer" of 1964, during which several activists were brutally killed in their attempts to secure basic constitutional rights for Blacks in the South. Marcuse's essay was a spirited defense of those rebels and activists at home and abroad who were putting their lives on the line for freedom and justice. In the essay, Marcuse points out that the liberal concept of tolerance had developed historically in the bourgeoisie's struggle against absolutism; it had used the concept to win acceptance for ideas which would ultimately contribute to the overthrow of the feudal order. But in the present, according to Marcuse, the concept has lost its critical thrust, and has acquired a primarily ideological character insofar as the informed and the uninformed, the progressive and the reactionary, the humane and the cynical are "tolerated" equally. While Marcuse insists that pure tolerance is desirable and necessary in certain spheres, such as religion or science, when it comes to society as a whole, he argues that there are rational criteria that should determine what should and should not be tolerated.[44] Marcuse concludes that tolerance should be extended to those persons and groups actively opposing the repressive status quo and denied to those intent upon the perpetuation of unnecessary toil, misery, and domination. Marcuse's problematic advocacy of denying civil rights to persons deemed politically reactionary and his refusal to counsel strict non-violence to oppressed groups drew widespread criticism from many quarters. But his essay was well received by some factions of the New Left and by many members of the burgeoning student movement, who cited his arguments to defend their increasingly militant positions of the next few years.

In addition to participating in dialogues and speaking throughout the world during the late 1960s, Marcuse also joined the students and various politically active leftist coalitions in the streets. During the famous protests and strikes of 1968, when his name was invoked in Paris, Rome, and Berlin, Marcuse was present alongside the protestors. That Marcuse was almost 70 years old during this activity lent credence to the heady and hopeful atmosphere at the time, as students shouted "Demand the impossible!" In addition to such activity, Marcuse also began to deepen positions he articulated earlier regarding the importance of women's active participation in any movement aimed at a radical and liberative transformation of society and the necessity for developing a new ecological consciousness. Feminism and ecology, along with aesthetics, would remain key components of Marcuse's thought until his death in 1979.[45]

In 1969, *An Essay on Liberation* was published, which Marcuse had written before the events of May 1968. The text is by far Marcuse's most optimistic and provides utopian speculation for a socialism rooted in the instinctual structure of men and women whose needs and sensibilities demand a break with the status quo. The extended essay also includes Marcuse's broadest embrace of the counter-culture and a variety of revolutionary struggles throughout the world. The resistance that Marcuse had referred to as the "Great Refusal" in *One-Dimensional Man* had materialized and Marcuse did not hide his hopefulness. On the other hand, he continues to castigate contemporary capitalist society as wasteful, destructive, and "obscene in the words and smiles of its politicians and entertainers; in its prayers, in its ignorance, and in the wisdom of its kept intellectuals."[46] While Marcuse's blistering response to his intellectual critics might seem extreme, recent scholarship carefully documents the ways in which much of the academy, including many of Marcuse's detractors, were sustained by the very forces that were the target of Marcuse's critique.[47]

Marcuse's next book, *Counter-Revolution and Revolt* (1972), shifts tone dramatically in reaction to the dissolution of the lofty aspirations and demands of May 1968. By this time the liberation movements had been torn apart internally by factional conflict and thrust onto the defensive by a powerful and dangerous conservative backlash. Marcuse begins the text by arguing that a new stage of development had been reached in which "the defense of the capitalist system requires the organization of counterrevolution at home and abroad. In its extreme manifestations, it practices the horrors of the Nazi regime."[48] Massacres and torture have become standard operating procedures in what Marcuse characterizes as largely preventive counter-revolution. In the US, students and black militants had been killed and "the murder of the Kennedys shows that even liberals are not safe if they appear as too liberal."[49] The brutal realities of this backlash led Marcuse to articulate new and longer-range strategies intended to expand the power and social influence of those remaining committed to the goals of the liberation movements. Despite the disintegration of the emancipatory movements of the 1960s, Marcuse realized that the system's ideological hold over the populace had loosened significantly during the period since the publication of *One-Dimensional Man*. As a consequence, the internal tensions within capitalism had increased, creating the potential for resistance from *both* inside and outside the system. These developments led Marcuse to place renewed emphasis on political education and the subversive potential inherent in art; he also stressed the radical potential of the nascent feminist and environmental movements. However, Marcuse also consistently pointed out throughout the text, as he had earlier, that the present period was not yet ready for revolutionary change and that anti-intellectual "radicalism" was counter-productive in the face of the enormous power of the opposition.[50] Marcuse concludes the text by stressing the importance of sustaining a long process of education because "the next revolution will be the concern of generations, and 'the final crisis of capitalism' may take all but a century."[51]

Aesthetics had played a crucial role in Marcuse's theory from the very beginning, so it should come as no surprise that he returned to art in his final theoretical work. *The Aesthetic Dimension: Toward a Critique of Marxist Aesthetics* represented an unmistakable shift in emphasis vis-à-vis Marcuse's earlier writings on aesthetics. When Marcuse had addressed aesthetics in his earlier writings – such as in the essay "The Affirmative Character of Culture" in 1937, or in *An Essay on Liberation* – he had stressed not only the emancipatory but also the ideological character of autonomous art. By removing art from everyday life and the material sphere of production and reproduction, aesthetic form preserves humanist ideals and an unmutilated sensibility. But its refusal to take an explicit political stance also contributes to the mystification and perpetuation of real-existing domination: every document of culture is at the same time a document of barbarism, as Marcuse's former colleague Walter Benjamin once put it. But in *The Aesthetic Dimension*, Marcuse placed much more emphasis on art's potential to prevent barbarism, which lies precisely in its ability to transcend immediate reality through aesthetic form:

> In contrast to orthodox Marxist aesthetics I see the political potential of art in art itself, in the aesthetic form as such. Furthermore, I argue that by virtue of its aesthetic form, art is largely autonomous vis à vis the given social relations. In its autonomy art both protests these relations, and at the same time transcends them. Thereby art subverts the dominant consciousness, the ordinary experience. ...

> The more immediately political the work of art, the more it reduces the power of estrangement and the radical, transcendent goals of change. In this sense, there may be more subversive potential in the poetry of Baudelaire and Rimbaud than in the didactic plays of Brecht.[52]

In addition to his defense of aesthetic form and autonomy, Marcuse also emphasized the emancipatory potential of other "bourgeois" concepts, such as the individual, interiority, and beauty.[53] Although these concepts were developed historically by the bourgeoisie, they point beyond the society it has created, according to Marcuse.

Marcuse spent his final months in 1979 campaigning for East German dissident Rudolf Bahro's release from prison, as he had battled for the release of his student Angela Y. Davis from prison years earlier. Bahro was the author of the influential *Die Alternative*, which Marcuse considered a valuable contribution to Marxian theory.[54] Marcuse died in Starnberg, Germany, on 29 July 1979. Bahro was released a few days later.[55] Throughout his life Marcuse fused an enormous intellectual creativity and productivity with the obstinate commitment to emancipation, which he had identified in an essay in the late 1930s as a prerequisite for critical theory. Marcuse's laudable example as a politically engaged critical theorist speaks volumes not only for his ideas, but also for liberatory dreams that obstinately refuse to die.

Marcuse's Relevance to Contemporary Discussions

Critical Theory

From the beginning Marcuse refused to confine his thought within disciplinary boundaries, and this tendency was reinforced during his collaboration on the interdisciplinary projects of the Institute for Social Research in the 1930s. Although his version of critical theory is heavily indebted to Max Horkheimer and his other colleagues at the Institute, he was an original thinker in many respects, and he developed positions which can still contribute to discussions in a wide variety of fields. Contemporary discussions in critical theory, for example, could certainly benefit from a reconsideration of Marcuse's work. Marcuse's version of critical theory could serve as a reminder that not all theorists in the twentieth century took a pragmatic or linguistic turn, and those who did may have left something essential behind. Marcuse and his colleagues at the Institute for Social Research developed a critique of pragmatism, which focused on its acceptance of efficacy as a standard of truth, its unwillingness to conceptualize society as a totality, and its rejection of transcendent rational norms.[56] Although they are at odds on most issues, Habermas and the post-structuralists have both taken the linguistic turn, even if it has led them in opposite directions.[57] Marcuse's lifelong efforts to develop a materialist theory of subjectivity offers an alternative to both the post-structuralist jettisoning of subjectivity as well as the Habermasian model,[58] which eliminates the somatic components of subjectivity and stresses the unifying force of discursive consensus and the internalization of social norms over the negative power of critique, non-conformist dissent, and the development of new forms of emancipatory subjectivity. Similarly, Marcuse's efforts to rethink Marx's critical theory in light of the catastrophic developments of the twentieth century could contribute to developing an alternative to the post-structuralist retreat from social theory, as well as Habermas's attempt to reconceptualize critical social theory in terms of the "systemic" imperatives of bureaucracy and markets, and the countervailing forces of communicative reason and the lifeworld.[59]

Politics

> If fear and destructiveness are the major emotional sources of fascism, eros belongs mainly to democracy.
> The authors of *The Authoritarian Personality*

One of the most noticeable and deeply troubling effects of the terrorist attacks on the World Trade Center and the Pentagon on 11 September 2001 has been the "closing of the political universe,"[60] not only in the US, but also around the globe. The Bush administration's reaction to the attacks has been to declare a state of emergency, which it has used to justify a wide variety of repressive measures, both at home and abroad. But as Marcuse's friend and colleague Franz Neumann reminded us in his analyses and critiques of National Socialism and its theoretical apologists, such as Carl Schmitt, the state of emergency does not justify the suspension of basic constitutional rights or the disregard of domestic or international law. On the domestic front, basic democratic principles have been violated by the widespread arrest and detention of citizens and non-citizens of the US – simply because they had affiliations with countries in which al-Qaida was suspected of operating – as well as by the Bush administration's willingness to rely on military courts in these cases and others. Although the Bush administration was initially concerned to build a broad international alliance for its war against al-Qaida and the Taliban, the manner in which it conducted itself soon alienated many of its partners: for example, its use of carpet bombs, which make no pretense of being "smart" enough to avoid civilians,[61] or its shameful treatment of war prisoners in Guantanamo Bay, not to mention its subsequent threats to act unilaterally against Iraq and other members of the so-called "axis of evil."[62] But among the general population of the US these extraordinary measures favored by Bush, Rumsfeld, and Ashcroft were initially met with widespread approval. The more brutally and arbitrarily Bush, Rumsfeld, and Ashcroft proceeded against the "evil" represented by the internal and external "enemy," the higher their ratings in popularity polls climbed. This state-of-emergency climate, and the Manichean friend-foe logic that has accompanied it, were also reflected in the widespread incidences of discrimination and racial profiling against Arabs and Muslims, or those who were mistaken for them (Sikhs, for example), as well as the hostile response to critical or dissenting voices in American universities and in the American public sphere in general.

Marcuse unambiguously rejected sectarian violence as means of achieving political goals, not only by religious fundamentalists of any type, but also in the name of allegedly revolutionary ends.[63] Murder cannot be a political weapon, according to Marcuse, because the *telos* of emancipatory politics – the pacification of existence and the liberation of the universal individual – must already be present in the means used to attain it.[64] So while Marcuse would of course have condemned the 11 September terrorist attacks as a nihilistic and barbaric act,[65] he most certainly would also have criticized the repressive state-of-emergency climate that has developed in the US (and elsewhere) since then. Marcuse's negative experiences of "bourgeois" democracy in Weimar made him extremely sensitive to the fragility of democratic principles in capitalist societies, particularly those, like Weimar or the contemporary US, with an entrenched power elite, a weak welfare state, and a large underclass into which the lower-middle class is deathly afraid of (and in increasing real danger of) "falling down."[66] Marcuse was also extremely wary of situations in which demagogic political leaders begin to play upon the patriotism and the conscious and unconscious authoritarian attitudes of large sections of the population in order to introduce "new forms of control"[67] into a society already characterized by high levels of surplus repression and by far the highest rates of imprisonment and executions of any industrialized Western country.[68] Unlike Horkheimer and Adorno, Marcuse chose to stay in the US after the war and, by all accounts, he usually felt quite comfortable living there, and was quick to adopt typically American mannerisms.[69] But he also consistently remained one of the most radical critics of the US. A recently published manuscript from the Herbert Marcuse Archive, bearing the title "The Historical Fate of Bourgeois Democracy,"[70] illustrates that he was particularly concerned about the political climate in the US following the landslide re-election victory of Richard Nixon in 1972, who was swept into office by the "silent majority" who supported the backlash against the progressive social movements of the 1960s at home, and the futile and barbaric attempt to "bomb Vietnam back into the Stone Ages" abroad.[71] While Marcuse's fears about authoritarian tendencies in the US may seem exaggerated to many, at a time when demagogic political leaders are using a state of emergency to play fast and loose with constitutional rights as well as domestic and international law, Marcuse's "critical pessimism" deserves to be taken seriously.[72]

But, as is well known, the pessimistic, negative current in Marcuse's critical theory was dialectically related to an even deeper utopian and obstinately hopeful current, which carried him – for better or worse – "Beyond One-Dimensional Man"[73] and beyond the metaphysical pessimism and negative dialectics of the late Horkheimer and Adorno as well. But this strong "warm current"[74] in Marcuse's thought did not break through for the first time in the late 1960s. It was already apparent in 1955 in his critical appropriation of Freud's concept of Eros, a concept that still has broad theoretical significance and important implications for contemporary progressive political projects.[75] Following Freud's late metapsychology, Marcuse understood Eros as the source of the life instincts, as a force that can create ever-larger unities and decrease or inhibit the destructiveness of the death instincts, or Thanatos.[76] At the very end of his life, Marcuse defined a radical character structure as one in which Eros predominates over Thanatos.[77] Eros is also central to the stress Marcuse placed on the type of political coalition-building that avoids narrow and self-defeating sectarian formations and that would be necessary to create a movement for more liberated society.[78] As Angela Y. Davis points out in her contribution to the present volume, Marcuse's own activism, particularly his efforts to reach out to members of a wide variety of disenfranchised and oppressed groups as both an educator and a comrade, and his ability to overcome communicative barriers and forge new links of political solidarity, embodied this idea.[79] This idea, as well as Marcuse's conception of the Great Refusal, continues to have relevance today, as the sizable protests against the neo-liberal politics of globalization[80] in Seattle, Genoa, and other cities around the globe, as well as the development of an alternative World Social Forum in Porto Allegre, have made clear.[81]

Marcuse can also serve as an important historic and symbolic example of an actively engaged public intellectual who bravely spoke the truth to power and refused to be silenced by the controversies his thought provoked. From his earliest writings onward, Marcuse repeatedly stressed the essentially public nature of philosophy. Already in the late 1920s Marcuse had rejected vanguardism in both its right- and left-wing forms,[82] by arguing that the role of the critical intellectual is not to impose the truth upon the "ignorant masses," but to make the truth visible.[83] To illustrate this point, Marcuse describes, in an essay from 1929, Kierkegaard's passionate engagement in the public sphere at the end of his life:

> And so it necessarily came to pass that Kierkegaard, at the end of his career, recognized and grasped the public sphere, where contemporaneous Dasein existed in an active state, as the authentic sphere of activity even for a philosophizing entirely aligned with the eternal. He takes leave of his solitude; he, who had always addressed himself only to the "individual," and for whom the public impact of his books was completely unimportant, takes to the streets, in a truly Socratic act. He writes article after article for a daily newspaper, publishes pamphlets, and focuses his entire struggle on the central decision of the historical moment. And this struggle in the

public realm does not take the form of Kierkegaard abstractly opposing the truth of the eternal to concrete existence and addressing existence from the realm of the eternal. On the contrary, he directs his efforts with absolute precision toward a concrete movement of contemporaneous *Dasein*, toward a "real" transformation of its existence, and his attacks and demands are thus always directed at the concrete forms and tasks of this existence, keeping in sight the full range of possibilities for achievement available at that moment.[84]

Like Kierkegaard, Marcuse would also leap into the public sphere much later in his life in an attempt to aid various progressive political movements and to counteract what he saw as a dangerous "closing of the universe of discourse."[85] While Marcuse's awareness of the way in which the public sphere is dominated by powerful private interests in capitalist societies[86] occasionally led him to flirt with the idea of counter-censorship or even a Rousseauian educational dictatorship, this tendency never gained the upper hand in his thought. For example, in *Eros and Civilization* he writes:

The question remains: how can civilization freely generate freedom, when unfreedom has become part and parcel of the mental apparatus?...From Plato to Rousseau, the only honest answer is the idea of an educational dictatorship, exercised by those who are supposed to have acquired knowledge of the real Good. The answer has since become obsolete: knowledge of the available means for creating a humane existence for all is no longer confined to a privileged elite. The facts are too open, and the individual consciousness would safely arrive at them if it were not methodically arrested and diverted. The distinction between rational and irrational authority, between repression and surplus repression can be made and verified by the individuals themselves.[87]

A final testament to Marcuse's commitment to the open and public nature of philosophy was his fierce rejection of anti-intellectualism, not only in its vulgar form, but also in the masochistic behavior of some students in the late 1960s who called for the destruction of the universities, or demanded that intellectuals and artists not work with, but subordinate themselves to, the "workers" or the "people."[88]

History of Philosophy

Marcuse's work can also still contribute to scholarship in the history of philosophy and critical theory as well. Marcuse's first book on Hegel, which he wrote as a *Habilitationsschrift* for Heidegger, is now available in an excellent English translation by Seyla Benhabib.[89] Ostensibly conceived as an attempt to trace the origins of Dilthey's concept of life – which was crucial for Heidegger's concept of historicity – *Hegel's Ontology and the Theory of Historicity* was in reality an attempt to trace the development and decline of the dialectical method in Hegel's thought. Marcuse's study offers a detailed and penetrating critique of Hegel's *Logic*, as well as a fascinating exposition of the development of dialectical method in his early work through to the *Phenomenology of Spirit*. The philosophical essays Marcuse wrote during his collaboration with the Institute for Social Research in the 1930s address topics that are still discussed today, such as the relationship of philosophy to critical social theory, or the possibility of developing a historical concept of essence. As Jürgen Habermas has recently reminded us, *Reason and Revolution* is still one of the best surveys of nineteenth-century philosophy and social theory.[90] And as Carl E. Schorske recently pointed out,[91] *Reason and Revolution* also has the virtue of restoring dialectical thought to its rightful place in the Enlightenment tradition – as a logical development of eighteenth-century Anglo-American and French philosophy, rather than as a fundamental break with it, as it has often been seen in England and the US. *One-Dimensional Man* may have sold over 300,000 copies worldwide, but its political impact has often overshadowed its complex philosophical arguments. Marcuse's critique of analytic philosophy, for example, or his analysis of the formalization of logic and the operationalization of language, identified dominant intellectual tendencies that have persisted in different forms to the present day.

Technology

Marcuse's interest in technology can be traced back to the essay entitled "On Hedonism," which he published in the 1930s.[92] From this time onward, technology remained an important category in almost all of Marcuse's theoretical work. However, Marcuse did not establish himself as one of the major contemporary theorists of technology until the publication of *One-Dimensional Man* in 1964. *One-Dimensional Man* offers a trenchant and uncompromising critique of technological domination, but contrary to many superficial representations of his ideas, Marcuse was *not* a technophobe. Fortunately, the complexity of Marcuse's theory of contemporary technology has been recognized by scholars specializing in the philosophy of technology.[93] Instead of a rejection of technology per se, Marcuse developed a powerful critique of a historically and socially particular type of technocratic domination, namely that found in advanced industrial society. Instead of an atavistic, simplistic rejection of technology, Marcuse thinks that technology has created the prerequisites for a more humane civilization and that new forms of liberatory science and technology can and should be developed to help humanity realize its latent possibilities. These emancipatory aims

Aesthetics

Herbert Marcuse has been seen primarily as a political philosopher and social critic. This is perhaps another reason why his work was largely overlooked in the predominantly aesthetic reception of the Frankfurt School in the 1980s and 1990s, which focused primarily on Walter Benjamin and Theodor Adorno.[95] While justified to a certain extent, insofar as Benjamin and Adorno developed more substantial and nuanced aesthetic theories, it should not be overlooked that aesthetics were also central to Marcuse's critical theory, and that we can still learn much from his arguments. Like Adorno, Marcuse defended the truth value of art against Hegel's proclamation that only philosophical concepts could capture the contradictions of modern society and express the deepest needs of its members.[96] The centrality of the aesthetic dimension in Marcuse's work reflects his turn away from the "objective spirit" and the "iron laws of history" toward the subjective dimensions of social change. Taking his cue from Friedrich Schiller's reflections on the French Revolutionary terror, Marcuse argued that political change must be accompanied by a transformed sensibility in order truly to break with the historical continuum of domination and to prevent the recrudescence of past barbarism. In Marcuse's view, art's commitment to beauty and its appeal to the senses gives it the potential to create new subjective needs, which point beyond antagonistic social relations. Like Horkheimer and Adorno, Marcuse distinguishes sharply between the products of the culture industry, which reinforce repressive needs and standardized perceptions, and autonomous works of art, whose commitment to aesthetic form lets the bad immediacy of the status quo appear in an entirely different light.

Thus Marcuse's aesthetics provide an alternative to the postmodern leveling of the difference between any and all kinds of "culture," and not only because of his defense of autonomous art. Marcuse, like Horkheimer and Adorno, never conflated the culture industry with genuine popular art.[97] But Marcuse's greater stress in his aesthetics on subjective sensibility[98] made him more optimistic about the emancipatory potential of certain types of popular art[99] than Adorno, whose aesthetics were based in the objective truth content of hermetic works of art. Several recent commentators have picked up on this strand in Marcuse's aesthetics.[100] In the end, however, Marcuse returned to his commitment to aesthetic form as the placeholder of art's claim to transcendent truth. Although Marcuse never entirely forgot the "affirmative" character of art, later in his life he repeatedly defended art against attacks from several different quarters. He rejected all attempts explicitly to politicize art, by orthodox Marxists, epigones of the historical avant-garde, and anti-artists of various stripes. Thus Marcuse's aesthetics offer an alternative to the historical avant-garde, in their overly hasty attempts to merge art and life, and to orthodox Marxists, who viewed art merely as the expression of certain class interests. Marcuse's defense of the truth content of art also differentiates his position from functionalist interpretations, such as that of Pierre Bourdieu, who theorizes art primarily as a representation of social distinction or "cultural capital." Marcuse insisted that art has not only an important cognitive function[101] in sharpening people's critical understanding of society, but that it also has the potential to change people's needs and thus their conduct. These arguments, as well as his insistence upon the importance of aesthetics for developing non-instrumental forms of relating to nature, which could also be materialized in new forms of technology,[102] also sets Marcuse apart from Jürgen Habermas, who downplays the cognitive or practical function of art and views it instead primarily in terms of subjective expression, and as a placeholder for the residues of emancipatory desires for the "good life" which do not properly belong in the qualitatively different value spheres of science and morality.[103]

Psychoanalysis

Marcuse did not integrate Freud into his work until relatively late in his career. By the time he published *Eros and Civilization* in 1955, the struggle for the legacy of psychoanalysis was already well underway. Nearly a half century later, these debates have not declined in frequency or intensity. While psychoanalytic research has progressed greatly since the 1950s, and discussions have become more complex, many of the issues Marcuse addressed in *Eros and Civilization* are still central to contemporary debates. One of the most important trends that has developed in the past few decades has been the attempt to reinterpret psychoanalysis in terms of the "linguistic turn." The possibilities and limitations of a linguistic reconceptualization of psychoanalysis have often turned on the status of Freud's drive theory. Marcuse's nuanced discussion of Freud's drive theory, which succumbs neither to ahistorical essentialism nor to a disembodied linguistic or cultural determinism, could still contribute significantly to these debates.[104] Critical appropriations of psychoanalysis continue to play a crucial role in feminist and gender studies. Marcuse was one of the first to brush Freud's theory against the grain in order to develop a theory and critique of patriarchy. As John O'Neill's contribution to this volume demonstrates, Marcuse's critical reinterpretation of Freud can still serve as an important reference point for debates in feminist theory and gender studies.[105] Finally, Marcuse was one of the few to preserve the critical political and speculative cultural dimensions of psychoanalysis, which were so important in the early development of the psychoanalytic movement, against the conformist integration of psychoanalysis in the post-war period, particularly in the US.[106] Marcuse's recourse to Freud continued his long-standing interest in theorizing the subjective dimensions of social domination and potential resistance, which Marx – at least in his mature writings – had not adequately addressed.

Ecology

A significant portion of Marcuse's critical theoretical work dealt either explicitly or implicitly with nature and the relationship(s) between humans and their environment. However, there are two texts, in particular, in which Marcuse focused directly on nature and the necessary role for ecology in any movement that might radically, and progressively, transform society. Marcuse's first sustained discussion of these topics was in *Counter-Revolution and Revolt*, in which he stated: "The radical transformation of nature becomes an integral part of the radical transformation of society."[107] For Marcuse, nature was both a subject and an object of history. Consequently, liberating nature "cannot mean returning to a pre-technological stage, but advancing to the use of the achievements of technological civilization for freeing man and nature from the destructive abuse of science and technology in the service of exploitaion."[108] The passage is important because it reveals Marcuse's powerful critical conclusions concerning the abusive contemporary relationship of science and technology to nature, while making clear that – contrary to the claims of some of Marcuse's critics – Marcuse is not advocating a return to a prelapsarian golden age or to noble savagery.

What Marcuse does advocate in the essay is a liberation of nature that promotes nature's life-enhancing forces. Marcuse's proposal relies heavily on Marx's early *Economic and Philosophic Manuscripts of 1844*. Marcuse had been one of the first thinkers to recognize the importance of Marx's early text.[109] Marcuse's analysis concurs with Marx's emphasis on the vital importance of the multidimensional development of the sensuous aesthetic qualities presently blocked and/or blunted by alienation, hyper-competitive capitalism, and technological destruction and exploitation. Thus, for both Marx and Marcuse a new sensibility is necessary to produce and sustain radical change. Marcuse writes: "the construction of a free society *presupposes* a break with the familiar experience of the world: with the muted sensibility. Conditioned and 'contained' by the rationality of the established system, sense experience tends to 'immunize' man against the very unfamiliar experiences of the possibilities of human freedom."[110] Once the human senses were emancipated, Marcuse argues, nature would appear not as some utilitarian "stuff" but as a "life force in its own right, as subject-object."[111] Marcuse traces this notion back to Kant's *Critique of Judgment* and the crucial concept of "purposiveness without purpose," which pertains to the aesthetic experience of nature as well as art.[112] Finally, while Marcuse does draw heavily on Marx, he is also critical of the vestiges of *hubris* lingering in Marx's conception of the human appropriation of nature.[113]

Deficit in Democratic Theory

While Marcuse's critical theory still has the potential to contribute to contemporary discussions in all the ways mentioned above, it is not without its problems. Perhaps the most serious deficit in Marcuse's theory was his failure to make any significant contributions to democratic theory. At times Marcuse did not adequately appreciate the abstract political principles of liberal democracy as a historical achievement, which could and must serve as the foundation for further political critique. Marcuse's highly problematic appeal for the curtailment of the civil rights of those on the political Right in his essay "Repressive Tolerance," for example, demonstrated a willingness to prematurely dismiss a political tradition whose potential to serve as a basis for progressive social change was illustrated by some of the legal gains realized in the complex dialectic of the civil rights movement. Marcuse's hard-hitting criticisms of what he referred to as *bourgeois* democracy have to be understood against both the background of the failure of the Weimar Republic to prevent the rise of National Socialism, as well as the Western democracies' willingness to support fascist and authoritarian regimes during the Cold War. It was precisely this refusal to accept the Western democracies' ideological self-understanding that made Marcuse's criticisms so appealing to those who refused to accept its real contradictions and brutality. At a time when self-satisfied liberal-democratic ideology has returned with a vengeance, Marcuse's intransigence can serve as a model for the difficult task of forming critical concepts, which are needed more than ever. But Marcuse's tendency to see only the ideological aspects of liberal-democratic theory placed his critique in danger of devolving into merely abstract rather than determinate negation. As even Marx pointed out, Enlightenment political ideals ushered into the world by bourgeois revolutions were the necessary if by no means sufficient conditions for a just society.[114]

Summary of Papers

Many of the papers collected in this volume were originally given at the international conference "The Legacy of Herbert Marcuse," which was held at the University of California at Berkeley in November 1998 to commemorate Marcuse's 100th birthday. The conference was divided into several different sections, which are reflected in the differing nature of the papers presented here. Angela Y. Davis delivered the keynote address for the conference. While not intended to be an academic paper, Davis's talk on "Marcuse's Legacies" offered a thoughtful assessment of Marcuse's historical importance and his contemporary relevance. Davis stresses the importance of

INTRODUCTION

obstinacy in holding onto emancipatory possibilities, as her mentor Marcuse had encouraged, as well as the continuing importance of his aesthetics. Davis also cites Marcuse's ability to speak across barriers and divides and to engage in diverse conversations – something which is needed now more than ever in the attempt to forge a new political vocabulary and build new coalitions. Davis concludes by suggesting that Marcuse nostalgia must be overcome if his plural legacies are to benefit contemporary critical theory and social movements.

The next group of papers at the conference were delivered by veteran scholars of Marcuse and the Frankfurt School. In his paper, Detlev Claussen examines the ways in which Marcuse and his colleagues at the Institute for Social Research sought to understand the country to which they had been exiled: the US. He shows how their experiences in America reinforced their belief, which had already crystallized during the 1920s, that the social categories of the nineteenth century – liberal bourgeois society opposed by an organized proletariat – were no longer adequate to grasp the qualitatively new social forms that were developing in the twentieth century. Since the US was at the forefront of this process of universal development, it became a paradigmatic model for Marcuse and his Institute colleagues. Claussen shows how their understanding of the US decisively shaped their conception of critical theory as a whole.

In his essay, Andrew Feenberg attempts to clarify Marcuse's relationship to his former philosophical mentor, Martin Heidegger, by exploring the similarities and differences in their theories of technology. Feenberg argues that the important differences between Marcuse and Heidegger lie not in their diagnoses of the problems concerned with modern technology, but rather in the means proposed to overcome them. Both philosophers relied upon a distinction between ancient *techne* and modern technology – a distinction which Feenberg himself problematizes, based on his own extensive work in the philosophy of technology – but Heidegger pessimistically refrained from proposing any alternatives, while Marcuse turned to Hegel and Freud to develop an active, historical concept of essence that was materially grounded in Eros, or the life instincts. In contrast to Heidegger's anti-rationalist fatalism, Marcuse's critique of the hypertrophy of technological rationality in modern capitalist societies maintained an important place for critical, transcendent reason and active, political engagement with the world. In fact, Marcuse insisted that a "reinvention of technology" could only be possible by incorporating not only ethical but also – and even more importantly – aesthetic values within its material base. Feenberg concludes by exploring the reasons why Marcuse accorded such importance to the contentious "aesthetic dimension" for such a project of renewal.

Douglas Kellner's essay, "Marcuse and the Quest for Radical Subjectivity," maintains that Marcuse's conception of the subject is a valuable resource for attempts to reconstruct subjectivity in the wake of post-structuralist and postmodern critiques. Kellner's arguments are based on a re-reading of *Eros and Civilization* and Marcuse's essay, "Marxism and Feminism." Kellner proposes that Marcuse offers an embodied subjectivity that moves beyond the false opposition between reason and the senses. Kellner also discusses the importance of Rudolf Bahro's notion of "surplus consciousness" for Marcuse, and the desirability of drawing on Habermas and Marcuse in complementary ways in theorizing subjectivity.

While Marcuse was quick to embrace the burgeoning feminist movement in the 1970s, feminists were sometimes hesitant to accept Marcuse's theoretical overtures. Some claimed Marcuse had an essentialist concept of gender, because he maintained that women have not internalized the aggressive and repressive character structures produced by modern capitalism to the same degree as men, due to their relative exclusion from the sphere of production. In his essay, John O'Neill also argues that Marcuse's attempt to defend a "libidinal maternal ethic" as an alternative to capitalist patriarchy remains unconvincing because he does not adequately address the social, historical, and institutional factors that have prevented and continue to prevent its realization. But rather than simply rejecting Marcuse's argument out of hand, O'Neill revisits the studies of matriarchy of Robert Briffault and Johann Jacob Bachofen, to show how Marcuse's model could be placed on a more solid theoretical ground. O'Neill draws attention in particular to the social and historical factors that have transformed family law and family psychology, which he sees as the primary sites of contestation for the concrete realization of Marcuse's desirable, but overly abstract, maternal ethic.

In his essay, Gérard Raulet focuses on Marcuse's shifting conceptualizations of the imagination in order to outline a provocative reinterpretation of his work as a whole. Drawing on the Kantian distinction between *cognitive* and *aesthetic* imagination, he argues that the former concept – which Marcuse first articulated in the essays he wrote while studying with Heidegger and to which he returned in *One-Dimensional Man* – forms the core of his philosophical project and could serve as the basis for a badly needed theory of historical imagination today. Raulet maintains that the latter concept – which Marcuse developed most explicitly in *Eros and Civilization* and *The Aesthetic Dimension* – was ultimately a dead end, insofar as it rested upon a problematic separation of art and reality. In other words, his attempt to rescue the critical potential of imagination by anchoring it in the pleasure principle or the aesthetic dimension failed insofar as both of these spheres could not, as Marcuse would have it, truly be severed from the reality of late capitalism. When Marcuse, on the other hand, recognized the *cognitive* dimension of imagination, and the fact that reality and aesthetics have become inextricably fused, he was, according to Raulet, on the way to developing a critical theory capable of demystifying the real fictions that determine people's lives in contemporary societies.

INTRODUCTION

At a conference or in a publication dedicated to exploring the legacy of Herbert Marcuse, it seems only appropriate to examine the state of the discussion of his work among young people. Due to limitations of space we could not, unfortunately, publish all of the papers given by younger scholars at the conference, but we would like to present at least a few of them, to document Marcuse's reception among the next generation of critical theorists. In his essay, Samir Gandesha examines the critique of Marcuse's conception of technology that Jürgen Habermas set forth in an essay written in honor of Marcuse's 70th birthday. What comes to light in this early critique are some of the basic contours of Habermas's mature theoretical statement. Gandesha argues that Habermas's engagement with Marcuse misfires because it fails to recognize the extent to which Marcuse, following the phenomenological tradition, regards technology as a mode through which the world is disclosed. By revisiting this critique, suggests Gandesha, it is possible to identify some of the shortcomings of Habermas's own theory of modernity.

The debates about Martin Heidegger's involvement with National Socialism and the relationship between his philosophy and politics, which smoldered for several decades in the post-war period before bursting into flames with the publication of Victor Farias's and Hugo Ott's critical biographies in the late 1980s and early 1990s,[115] continue to attract passionate interventions, as a series of new books on the topic demonstrate.[116] But for many people it will probably still come as a surprise to hear that Herbert Marcuse, the idiosyncratic Hegelian-Marxist and long-time friend and colleague of some of Heidegger's most outspoken critics, Max Horkheimer and Theodor Adorno, studied with Heidegger for five years in Freiburg, immediately prior to Heidegger's engagement with the Nazis in 1933. In his piece, John Abromeit attempts to provide some preliminary answers to the many questions raised by Marcuse's involvement with Heidegger at this time. Why was a young critical Marxist like Marcuse attracted to Heidegger in the first place? How did Marcuse appropriate Heidegger's philosophy? Did his appropriation of Heidegger's philosophy bring with it problematic political implications for his own work? How did Marcuse reassess Heidegger's philosophy and his own work after Heidegger's political debacle in 1933?

Marcuse has often been criticized for linking his critical theory to a utopian second dimension which lies outside of history. This pertains not only to his recourse to art and the aesthetic dimension, but also to his invocation of human nature as an Archimedean standpoint for social critique. Was Marcuse's critical theory based upon a philosophical anthropology, in the sense of a static understanding of human nature? Stephan Bundschuh outlines a nuanced answer to this question in his paper, by distinguishing between two anthropological dimensions in Marcuse's work. The first, he argues, corresponds to what Max Horkheimer described as the anthropology of the bourgeois era – those human traits which have become second nature under modern capitalism. The second anthropological dimension in Marcuse's theory corresponds to what Immanuel Kant described as anthropology from a pragmatic point of view – "what man can, or should make of himself as a freely acting being."[117] Bundschuh uses this Kantian concept to explicate the utopian second dimension of Marcuse's anthropology while at the same time stressing the important differences between the two philosophers' positions. Marcuse's strong anthropological concepts – such as the notion of species being that he borrows from Marx in his early writings, or the Feuerbachian notion of new sensibility as a "biological" foundation for socialism in his late writings – serve the purpose of Kantian regulative ideas: norms of critique, not detailed blueprints for a better society. But in contrast to Kant, Marcuse denies the ahistorical validity of these regulative ideas. He ultimately subordinates philosophical anthropology to critical social theory and thereby makes the validity of the norms dependent upon historical conditions.

Marcuse's emergence in the 1960s as an extremely controversial and world-renowned critic of contemporary capitalism generated numerous attacks on his theoretical work. W. Mark Cobb's essay, "Diatribes and Distortions: Marcuse's Academic Reception," provides a consideration of three critiques of Marcuse's critical theory and historical relevance. Cobb assesses critiques of Marcuse offered by Alaisdair MacIntyre, Michel Foucault, and Richard Rorty. These three critiques were chosen because of the important influence all three theorists have had on the theoretical agenda of the academy over the past few decades. Cobb argues that the critiques fail to seriously challenge the major contentions of Marcuse's critical theory.

In the late 1960s and early 1970s Marcuse returned to Marx's *Grundrisse* in an attempt to understand the new forms of subjectivity that seemed to point beyond the grim picture of total integration he had depicted in *One-Dimensional Man*. Drawing on two lengthy manuscripts Marcuse wrote in the early 1970s,[118] Michael Werz argues that Marcuse's renewed interest in the *Grundrisse* was linked not just to the protest and new social movements of the 1960s and 1970s, but also to his experience of exile and the loss of tradition which necessarily accompanies it. In the late 1960s and early 1970s Marcuse returned to Marx's discussion of the concrete universal individual in the *Grundrisse*, and to Feuerbach's anthropological materialism, in order to recover those elements of subjectivity – critical reflection and sensuousness – which set the individual apart from all forms of abstract collectivity and which defined the limits of capitalist reification. Werz also demonstrates how Marcuse's critical and materialist theory of subjectivity is particularly well suited to critique the virulent forms of ethnic, religious, and nationalist identity that have returned with a vengeance since the end of the Cold War.

The next group of papers were originally given at a roundtable discussion on the topic of the relevance of Marcuse's work to contemporary discussions on ecological theory. Andrew Light, Tim Luke, and Steven Vogel gave presentations and responded to questions from the scholars and activists in attendance. Light, in his presentation entitled "Marcuse's Deep-social Ecology and the Future of Utopian Environmentalism," argued that Marcuse's richly pluralist political ecology could serve as a bridge linking theoretically warring ecological camps. Light concluded with a discussion of some of the problems with approaches such as Marcuse's. Luke's discussion, entitled "Marcuse's Ecological Critique and the American Environmental Movement," emphasized the various ways in which Marcuse's ecological thought continues to be valuable to present environmental concerns. Luke highlighted the complexity and subtlety of Marcuse's approach and drew particular attention to its psychosocial aspects. While Marcuse began to focus explicitly on ecological concerns in the 1970s, Luke reminds us that much of Marcuse's theoretical work was concerned with nature, technology, and values. Vogel's presentation, "Marcuse and the 'New Science,'" also suggested that Marcuse's critical social theory has considerable value for environmental theory. Vogel responds to Habermas's critique of Marcuse's notions of a new science and sensibility. He also addresses a possible problem arising out of a seeming ambiguity in Marcuse's claim that nature is both a historical category and that it also has an inherent character, which Vogel suggests implies a problematic essentialism.

The final section of the book contains two papers given at the conference in the context of a recollections panel, which was dedicated to Marcuse's person rather than his critical theory. Peter Marcuse provided an informative look back on his father's life in his discussion of "Herbert Marcuse's 'Identity.'" Marcuse considers his father's personal and political relationships to Germany and the US both before and after the Second World War. Marcuse also reflects on his father's decision to remain in the US after the war and provides a more general consideration of his "Americanization." Carl E. Schorske met Herbert Marcuse for the first time in 1943, when he joined him and several other eminent émigré intellectuals at the Office of Strategic Services (OSS) in Washington to conduct research on the political, social, and cultural developments in Nazi Germany, and to develop policy recommendations for the post-war period. Schorske reflects on his impressions of Marcuse during this period at the OSS, as well as Marcuse's lasting influence on his courses in intellectual history at Wesleyan in the 1950s. Schorske also describes his encounters with Marcuse and Norman O. Brown in the 1960s and 1970s.

Notes

1 English translation by Edith Fourier.
2 Eric Hobsbawm, *The Age of Extremes: A History of the World, 1914–1991*, New York: Vintage, 1996, p. 446.

3 *Ibid.*, p. 443. Hobsbawm is referring to George Katsiaficas, *The Imagination of the New Left: A Global Analysis of 1968*, Boston: Beacon, 1987.
4 Douglas Kellner, *Herbert Marcuse and the Crisis of Marxism*, Berkeley: University of California Press, 1984, p. 1.
5 Davis made this comment in a speech given on C-SPAN included in Paul Alexander Juutilainen's documentary, *Herbert's Hippopotamus: Marcuse and Revolution in Paradise* (1996). Davis studied with Marcuse at Brandeis and the University of California at San Diego. Marcuse supported her steadfastly throughout her political trials in the early 1970s, although he was critical of her joining the US Communist Party.
6 The question of the role that critical social theory played in the various social movements around the globe in the 1960s is of course extremely complex. But even in countries such as Germany, France, and Italy, in which social theory played an important role in the formation of critical consciousness, voluntarist tendencies often gained the upper hand in the end. While the emphasis on praxis, actions, events, or the creation of situations helped expand the movements and served as an emancipatory and unifying antidote against the reified "theories" of sectarian groups, it often spawned voluntarist and anti-intellectual tendencies which contributed to the weakening, cooptation, and disintegration of the movements. For an insightful examination of these issues in a context in which critical social theory played a particularly important role, namely in the German SDS, see Detlev Claussen, "Der kurze Sommer der Theorie," *Hannoversche Schriften 3, Aspekte der Alltagsreligion: Ideologie unter veränderten gesellschaftlichen Verhältnissen*, Frankfurt: Neue Kritik, 2000, pp. 154–63.
7 John Bokina, "Marcuse Revisited: An Introduction," in John Bokina and Timothy J. Lukes (eds) *Marcuse: From the New Left to the Next Left*, Lawrence, KA: University Press of Kansas, 1994, p. 1.
8 Mike Davis, *City of Quartz: Excavating the Future in Los Angeles*, New York: Vintage Books, 1992, p. 54.
9 See Paul Alexander Juutilainen's documentary, *Herbert's Hippopotamus: Marcuse and Revolution in Paradise*, for an exploration of the attacks on Marcuse during this period.
10 Allan Bloom, *The Closing of the American Mind: How Higher Education Has Failed Democracy and Impoverished the Souls of Today's Students*, New York: Simon & Schuster, 1987, p. 226.
11 Roger Kimball, *Tenured Radicals: How Politics Has Corrupted Our Higher Education*, New York: Harper & Row, 1990, p. 65.
12 *Ibid.*, p. 67.
13 The political Right in the US continues to assail Marcuse and groups such as Accuracy in Academia continue to perpetuate shoddy arguments similar to those offered by Bloom and Kimball.
14 There have also been a number of quality studies or translations of Marcuse's work in other languages, such as German, French, Italian, Spanish, Portuguese, Russian, Serbo-Croatian, Japanese, Korean, Hebrew, Persian, and Arabic. But we have decided to limit ourselves to English literature here. For an overview of the secondary literature on Marcuse in German, French, Italian, and Spanish through to 1992, see René Görtzen, "Kommentierte Bibliographie der Schriften über Herbert Marcuse," in Institut für Sozialforschung (ed.) *Kritik und Utopie im Werk von Herbert Marcuse*, Frankfurt: Suhrkamp, 1992.
15 These unpublished works are currently being published in both Germany and the US. In Germany a five-volume edition of Marcuse's *Nachgelassene Schriften* is being published by zu Klampen Verlag under the editorship of Peter-Erwin Jansen. In the US, a six-volume edition of Marcuse's *Collected Papers* is being

INTRODUCTION

published by Routledge, under the editorship of Douglas Kellner. See the brief discussion of Volume 1 below. For a review of the first volumes of both series, see John Abromeit, "Reconsidering Marcuse," *Constellations* vol. 8, no. 1 (March 2001), pp. 148–55.

16 Herbert Marcuse, *Technology, War and Fascism: Collected Papers of Herbert Marcuse*, vol. 1, ed. Douglas Kellner, London and New York: Routledge, 1998.
17 The second volume of Marcuse's *Collected Writings* is now available as well: *Towards a Critical Theory of Society: Collected Papers of Herbert Marcuse*, vol. 2, ed. Douglas Kellner, London and New York: Routledge, 2001.
18 Charles Reitz, *Art, Alienation and the Humanities: A Critical Engagement with Herbert Marcuse*, New York: State University of New York Press, 2000.
19 "The Foundation of Historical Materialism," trans. Joris de Bres, *Studies in Critical Philosophy*, London: NLB, 1972.
20 Reitz, *Art, Alienation and the Humanities*, pp. 195–6.
21 *Ibid.*, pp. 176–7.
22 *Ibid.*, p. 180.
23 *Ibid.*, p. 99. For an insightful examination of the concept of ontology in Marcuse's early work, see Robert Pippin, "Marcuse on Hegel and Historicity," in R. Pippin, A. Feenberg, and C.P. Webel (eds) *Marcuse: Critical Theory and the Promise of Utopia*, South Hadley, MA: Bergin & Garvey, pp. 66–94.
24 Reitz, p. 234. For a differing view on this issue, see Stephan Bundschuh's contribution to this volume.
25 For more detailed discussions of Marcuse's dissertation on the German artist-novel, see Barry Katz, *Herbert Marcuse and the Art of Liberation*, London: Verso, 1982, pp. 40–53, and Gérard Raulet, "Die 'Gemeinschaft' beim Jungen Marcuse," *Intelluelendiskurse in der Weimarer Republik: Zur Politischen Kultur einer Gemengelage*, Frankfurt: Campus, 1994, p. 97.
26 "The novel is the epic of an age in which the extensive totality of life is no longer directly given, in which the immanence of meaning in life has become a problem yet which still thinks in terms of totality" (Lukács, *Theory of the Novel*, trans. Anna Bostock, Cambridge, MA: MIT Press, 1971, p. 56).
27 A second dissertation that one had to write in order to become a professor in the German university system.
28 For Marcuse's essays from this period, see John Abromeit and Richard Wolin (eds), *Herbert Marcuse: Heideggerian Marxism* trans. John Abromeit, Matt Erlin, Eric Oberle, and Richard Wolin (forthcoming in 2004 from the University of Nebraska Press). On Marcuse's relationship to Heidegger, see also the essays by Andrew Feenberg and John Abromeit in this volume.
29 For Marcuse's essays from this period, see *Negations: Essays in Critical Theory*, ed. and trans. Jeremy J. Shapiro, Boston: Beacon, 1968.
30 In 1934 Marcuse wrote, for example: "It is often asserted today that Descartes, by beginning with ego cogito, committed the original sin of modern philosophy, that he placed a completely abstract concept of the individual at the basis of theory. But his abstract concept of the individual is animated by concern with human freedom: measuring the truth of all conditions of life against the standard of rational thought" (*ibid.*, p. 50). On this point, see also Stephan Bundschuh's contribution to this volume.
31 Marcuse started out working for the Office of War Information, but in 1943 he was reassigned to the Office of Strategic Services, which had been founded as part of Roosevelt's far-reaching reorganization of intelligence operations during the war. For a discussion of the role Marcuse and other left-wing emigrés played in US intelligence operations during and shortly after the war, see Barry Katz, *Foreign Intelligence*, Cambridge, MA: Harvard University Press, 1989.

32 See Marcuse, *Technology, War and Fascism*.
33 "Some Remarks on Aragon: Art and Politics in the Totalitarian Era," in Marcuse, *Technology, War and Fascism*, pp. 199–214; "Existentialism: Remarks on Jean-Paul Sartre's *L'Etre et le Néant*," *Journal of Philosophy and Phenomenological Research*, vol. VIII (March 1948), pp. 309–36.
34 For a more detailed examination of the strengths and weaknesses of the concept of performative contradiction in the context of the debate between Habermas and the post-structuralists, see Martin Jay, "The Debate over Performative Contradiction: Habermas Versus the Poststructuralists," *Force Fields*, New York and London: Routledge, 1993, pp. 25–37.
35 He states, for example: "The power to restrain and guide instinctual drives, to make biological necessities into individual needs and desires, increases rather than reduces gratification: the 'mediatization' of nature, the breaking of its compulsion, is the human form of the pleasure principle" (*Eros and Civilization*, Boston: Beacon, 1955, p. 35).
36 For a post-1989 review of Marcuse's work on real-existing socialism, see Peter Marcuse, "Marcuse on Real Existing Socialism: A Hindsight Look at Soviet Marxism," in Bokina and Lukes (eds) *Marcuse: From the New Left to the Next Left*, pp. 57–72, and Zarko Puhovski, "Marcuses Entdeckung des 'realen Sozialismus', " in Institut für Sozialforschung (ed.) *Kritik und Utopie im Werk von Herbert Marcuse*, Frankfurt: Suhrkamp, 1992, pp. 101–9.
37 For more on the protest movements, see James Miller's *"Democracy is in the Streets": From Port Huron to the Siege of Chicago*, New York: Simon & Schuster, 1987; Kirkpatrick Sale, *SDS*, New York: Random House, 1973; Todd Gitlin, *The Sixties: Days of Hope, Years of Rage*, New York: Bantam Books, 1987; and Katsiaficas, *The Imagination of the New Left*.
38 Herbert Marcuse, *One-Dimensional Man: Studies in the Ideology of Advanced Industrial Society*, Boston: Beacon, 1964, p. xlix.
39 For an insightful examination and analysis of the shift in several different academic disciplines in the US during the post-war period from historical to mathematically or scientifically based – putatively more "rigorous" – methodologies, see Carl Schorske, "The New Rigorism in the Human Sciences, 1940–1960," *Daedalus*, vol. 126, no. 1 (Winter 1997).
40 Marcuse, *One-Dimensional Man*, p. xlvii.
41 *Ibid.*, p. 98. See also Martin Jay's insightful investigation of memory in Marcuse's work, "Anamnestic Totalization: Memory in the Thought of Herbert Marcuse," *Marxism and Totality*, Berkeley and Los Angeles: University of California Press, 1984, pp. 220–40.
42 Herbert Marcuse, Barrington Moore, Robert Paul Wolff, *A Critique of Pure Tolerance*, Boston: Beacon, 1965.
43 Hobsbawm, *The Age of Extremes*, pp. 433–43.
44 In *One-Dimensional Man*, Marcuse had already introduced the two most important of these criteria: "1. the judgment that human life is worth living, or rather can and ought to be made worth living....2. the judgment that, in a given society, specific possibilities exist for the amelioration of human life and specific ways and means of realizing these possibilities....How can these resources be used for the optimal development and satisfaction of individual needs and faculties with a minimum of toil and misery?" (see pp. xlii-xliii).
45 See, for example, "Marxism and Feminism," a lecture Marcuse gave at Stanford University in March 1974, which was published in *Women's Studies*, Old Westbury, NY: The Feminist Press, 1974, pp. 279–88, and "Ecology and the Critique of Modern Society," a talk Marcuse gave at the University of Santa Cruz

in 1979, which was published in *Capitalism, Nature, Socialism: A Journal of Socialist Ecology*, vol. 3, no. 11 (September 1992), pp. 29–38.
46 Herbert Marcuse, *An Essay on Liberation*, Boston: Beacon, 1969, p. 8.
47 A particularly astute and informative recent source on this subject is Frances Stonor Saunders' *The Cultural Cold War: The CIA and the World of Arts and Letters*, New York: The New Press, 1999.
48 Marcuse, *An Essay on Liberation*, p. 1.
49 *Ibid*.
50 Marcuse also criticized the sectarian violence of the Red Army Faction in Germany and the Red Brigades in Italy in the late 1970s. See "Mord darf keine Waffe der Politik sein," *Die Zeit*, no. 39, 23 September 1977, pp. 41–2; an English translation of this article also appeared in *New German Critique*, no. 12 (Fall 1977), pp. 7–8.
51 Marcuse, *An Essay on Liberation*, p. 134.
52 *The Aesthetic Dimension*, Boston: Beacon, 1978, pp. ix, xii–xiii.
53 Marcuse writes, for example:

> Marxist literary criticism often displays scorn for "inwardness" [*Innerlichkeit*]...But this attitude is not too remote from the scorn of the capitalists for an unprofitable dimension of life. If subjectivity is an "achievement" of the bourgeois era, it is at least an antagonistic force in capitalist society....I have pointed out that the same applies to the critique of the individualism of bourgeois literature offered by Marxist aesthetics. To be sure, the concept of the bourgeois individual has become the ideological counterpoint to the competitive economic subject and the authoritarian head of the family. To be sure, the concept of the individual as developing freely in solidarity with others can become a reality only in a socialist society. But the fascist period and monopoly capitalism have decisively changed the political value of the these concepts....Today, the rejection of the individual as a "bourgeois" concept recalls and presages fascist undertakings.
>
> (*The Aesthetic Dimension*, pp. 37–8)

54 See Marcuse's essay, "Protosocialism and Late Capitalism: Toward a Theoretical Synthesis Based on Bahro's Analysis," in Ulf Wolter (ed.) *Rudolf Bahro: Critical Responses*, White Plains, NY: M.E. Scharpe, 1980, pp. 25–48.
55 Katz, *Herbert Marcuse and the Art of Liberation*, p. 217.
56 See, for example, Marcuse's review of John Dewey's *Theory of Valuation*, in *Studies in Philosophy and Social Science*, vol. 9, no. 1, New York: Institute for Social Research, 1941, pp. 144–8, or Horkheimer's critique of pragmatism in *Eclipse of Reason*, New York: Oxford University Press, 1947, pp. 41–57.
57 See, for example, James Bohman, "Two Versions of the Linguistic Turn: Habermas and Poststructuralism," in M. Passerin d'Entrèves and S. Benhabib (eds) *Habermas and the Unfinished Project of Modernity*, Cambridge, UK: Polity, 1996.
58 See, for example, "Individuierung durch Vergesellschaftung. Zu George Herbert Mead's Theorie der Subjektivität," *Nachmetaphysisches Denken*, Frankfurt: Suhrkamp, 1988, pp. 187–241. See also Douglas Kellner's essay in this volume.
59 For an insightful critique of Habermas's social theory, see Moishe Postone, *Time, Labor and Social Domination: A Reinterpretation of Marx's Critical Theory*, Cambridge, UK: Cambridge University Press, 1993, pp. 226–60. For a critique of Habermas's more recent efforts to elaborate the foundations of a critical

theory of contemporary democracy, see William E. Scheuerman, "Between Radicalism and Resignation: Democratic Theory in Habermas's *Between Facts and Norms*," in Peter Dews (ed.) *Habermas: A Critical Reader*, Oxford, UK, and Malden, MA: Blackwell, 1999, pp. 153–77.

60 Marcuse described the political climate of advanced industrial societies in this way in the early 1960s. See *One-Dimensional Man*, pp. 19ff.

61 Even the "smart" bombs proved that military intelligence still remains an oxymoron in many cases. This was demonstrated, for example, by the repeated and unsuccessful attempts to assassinate Jalaludin Haqqani, one of the most important figures in the Taliban regime. Between 12 and 19 November 2001, three houses, a school, a mosque, and a large building were destroyed by "smart" bombs. The result: 43 civilians, among them at least 25 children, were killed. Haqqani himself remained untouched. See "Der 'präziseste Krieg' der Geschichte," *Die Zeit* (the German weekly), no. 12, 14 March 2002, p. 3.

62 This introduction was written before the most recent war in Iraq.

63 See, for example, Marcuse's critique of the German Red Army Faction in the late 1970s: "Mord darf keine Waffe der Politik sein," *Die Zeit*, no. 39, 23 September 1977, pp. 41–2; an English translation appeared in *New German Critique*, no. 12 (Fall 1977), pp. 7–8.

64 See, for example, *An Essay on Liberation*, p. 27.

65 The fact that the largest and most influential neo-Nazi party in Germany, the *Nationaldemokratische Partei* (NPD), immediately condoned the attacks after they happened gives the lie to any attempt to justify them in the name of an assault on the "symbols" of "American imperialism." For a leftist critique of neo-liberal globalization, which attempts to move beyond the outdated concept of "imperialism" as well as ideological forms of "anti-Americanism," see Michael Hardt and Antonio Negri, *Empire*, Cambridge, MA: Harvard University Press, 2000.

66 See the film *Falling Down*, starring Michael Douglas, for a disturbing portrayal of one down-and-out member of the lower-middle class living out his xenophobic and authoritarian fantasies in the name of "American" values.

67 Marcuse, *One-Dimensional Man*, p. 1.

68 For example, the US has, on average, seven times as many prisoners per capita as the countries of the European Union. The ongoing legacy of racism in the US is blatantly obvious when one considers the composition of the prison population in the US. The ratio of incarceration for Blacks is, for example, seven times as high as that for Whites. For more details on the American prison-industrial complex, see Loïc Wacquant, *Les Prisons de la Misère*, Paris: Raisons d'Agir, 1999, pp. 73 and 87 respectively, and Angela Y. Davis, "Race and Criminalization: Black Americans and the Punishment Industry" and "Racialized Punishment and Prison Abolition," in Joy James (ed.) *The Angela Y. Davis Reader*, Malden, MA: Blackwell, 1998, pp. 61–73 and 96–107 respectively.

69 See, for example, his son Peter's contribution to this volume.

70 Marcuse, *Towards a Critical Theory of Society*, pp. 163–86. In the same volume, see also Marcuse's essay on Watergate, which was published – in an edited form – in the *New York Times* on 27 June 1973: "Watergate: When Law and Morality Stand in the Way," *ibid.*, pp. 189–92.

71 The bombing campaign in Vietnam that began soon after Nixon's re-election – the so-called "Christmas bombing" – was the most intense of the entire war. In less than two weeks, approximately 100,000 bombs were dropped, mainly on North Vietnam's two largest cities, Hanoi and Haiphong.

72 On the concept of "critical pessimism" in critical theory, see Gérard Raulet, "Kritik der Vernunft und kritischer Gebrauch des Pessimismus," in Alfred Schmidt and Norbert Altwicker (eds) *Max Horkheimer Heute: Werk und Wirkung*,

Frankfurt: Fischer, 1986, pp. 31–51, and Michael Löwy, *Walter Benjamin: Avertissement d'incendie. Une Lecture des Thèses "Sur le Concept d'histoire"*, Paris: Presses Universitaires de France, 2001, pp. 10ff.

73 As Douglas Kellner points out in *Towards a Critical Theory of Society* (p. 108), this the was the title that Marcuse had originally intended for *An Essay on Liberation*. In 1968 Marcuse also gave a talk bearing this title, which has recently been published for the first time: "Beyond One-Dimensional Man," in Marcuse, *Towards a Critical Theory of Society*, pp. 111–20.

74 To borrow Ernst Bloch's term. He distinguishes between warm and cold currents in the Marxist tradition. Marcuse, Bloch himself, Walter Benjamin, and the young Marx, for example, would be representatives of the former, while Horkheimer, the later Lukács, and the later Marx would be representatives of the latter. See *Das Prinzip Hoffnung*, vol. 1, Frankfurt: Suhrkamp, 1977, pp. 235ff.

75 For an explication of Marcuse's appropriation of Freud's term, and the distinction he makes between Eros and sexuality, see Chapter 10 of *Eros and Civilization*, "The Transformation of Sexuality into Eros," pp. 180–202.

76 See, in particular, Chapter 4 of *Eros and Civilization*, "The Dialectic of Civilization," pp. 71–95.

77 See "Ecology and the Critique of Modern Society."

78 The implications that Marcuse's concept of Eros might have for political coalition-building do not include a libidinization of abstract collectivities, such as the nation or ethnic group, or even a class. Marcuse explicitly criticized the irrational naturalization of imagined communities and the demand that the individual heroically sacrifice herself in their name. See "The Struggle Against Liberalism in the Totalitarian View of the State" and "On Hedonism," in Marcuse, *Negations: Essays in Critical Theory*, pp. 3–42 and 159–200 respectively.

79 In this sense, Freud's concept of Eros, as forming larger unities, parallels what many philosophers, from antiquity to the present, have seen as one of the defining characteristics of reason, namely its ability to unify through the give and take of dialogue and the persuasiveness of arguments. As Jürgen Habermas put it in a recent reconsideration of the relationship between theory and praxis:

> A philosophy that corresponded completely to the sharply defined conception of operations based on the division of labor would be robbed of the best, namely the anarchistic part, of its heritage: its quality as non-restricted thinking....Here we encounter the peculiar multilingual character of philosophy, which enables it to preserve unity among the differentiated moments of reason without leveling their different claims to validity. Philosophy is able to maintain this formal unity of a pluralist reason not based on the determinate content of a concept of being as a whole or the general good, but rather due to its hermeneutical ability to transcend linguistic and discursive boundaries…
>
> ("Noch einmal: Zum Verhältnis von Theorie und Praxis," *Wahrheit und Rechtfertigung*, Frankfurt: Suhrkamp, 1999, pp. 327–8; my translation)

One could also understand Marcuse's concept of "erotic reason" from this perspective.

80 "Politics of globalization" because "globalization" alone would imply that the neo-liberal methods of globalization are "natural" and inevitable. See Pierre Bourdieu, "Pour un savoir engagé," *Le Monde Diplomatique*, no. 575 (February 2002), p. 3.

81 Before these protests, many Left social theorists had cynically and erroneously declared that the age of protest was over, as the age of lowered expectations had rendered it irrelevant. One theorist who did not fall prey to such delusions was Martin J. Beck Matustik, whose *Specters of Liberation: Great Refusals in the New World Order* (Albany: State University of New York Press, 1998), revived a concept of Marcuse's Great Refusal informed by Frantz Fanon and a wide variety of contemporary social theorists. Matustik argues that Marcuse's Great Refusal remains a vital form of dissent against the horrors of the New World Order.

82 Marcuse was critical of Lukács' notion of class consciousness, which was to be imposed upon the working class from without: see "Zum Problem der Dialektik 1," *Schriften*, vol. 1, p. 421. Heidegger had an extremely negative view of the public sphere, which he believed reproduced inauthentic, "fallen" modes of existence. The Platonic model of politics to which he adhered at this time is expressed by the following passages from Count Yorck that he quotes approvingly near the end of *Being and Time*: "the communis opinio is nowhere in the truth...To dissolve elemental public opinion, and as far as possible, to make possible the moulding of individuality in seeing and looking, would be a pedagogical task for the state. Then, instead of a so-called public conscience...individual consciences – would again become powerful" (trans. John Macquarrie and Edward Robinson, San Francisco: Harper & Row, 1962, pp. 454–5).

83 "Über konkrete Philosophie," *Schriften*, vol. 1. Marcuse writes: "The meaning of philosophizing can be designated provisionally as the making visible of truth" (p. 385). Marcuse also writes in this essay: "Concrete philosophy will exist in the public realm, because only by so doing can it truly approach existence. Only when, in full public view, it grabs hold of existence in its daily being, in the sphere in which it actually exists, can it effect a movement of this existence toward its truth. Otherwise, only an absolute authority, which is believed unconditionally to be in possession of revealed truth, can call forth such a movement" (p. 401; trans. Matt Erlin).

84 *Ibid.*, pp. 401–2; trans. Matt Erlin.

85 See *One-Dimensional Man*, pp. 84–120.

86 Jürgen Habermas, *The Structural Transformation of the Public Sphere*, Cambridge, MA: MIT Press, 1991; Noam Chomsky and Edward Hermann, *Manufacturing Consent*, New York: Pantheon Books, 1988.

87 *Eros and Civilization*, p. 206. For another example of Marcuse's explicit rejection of the educational dictatorship model, see *One-Dimensional Man*, pp. 6 and 40–1.

88 See, for example, *The Aesthetic Dimension*, where Marcuse writes: "To work for the radicalization of consciousness means to make explicit and conscious the material and ideological discrepancy between the writer and the 'people' rather than to obscure and camouflage it. Revolutionary art may well become 'The Enemy of the People'" (p. 35).

89 *Hegel's Ontology and the Theory of Historicity*, Cambridge, MA: MIT Press, 1987.

90 Jürgen Habermas, "Die Verschiedenen Rhythmen von Philosophie und Politik: Herbert Marcuse zum 100. Geburtstag," *Die Postnationale Konstellation: Politische Essays*, Frankfurt: Suhrkamp, 1998, p. 234.

91 In his talk at "The Legacy of Herbert Marcuse" conference, held in Berkeley in November 1998.

92 See Kellner, *Herbert Marcuse and the Crisis of Marxism*, pp. 120–1, and Marcuse, *Negations*, p. 184.

93 See, for instance, Frederick Ferré's *Philosophy of Technology* (Englewood Cliffs, NJ: Prentice Hall, 1988), in which, in his discussion of "Technology and Modern Existence," Ferré analyzes the global assessments of four particularly influential

INTRODUCTION

theorists. Ferré discusses Marx, Buckminster Fuller, Heidegger, and Marcuse, and suggests that Marcuse's conception of technology combines elements from the thought of all three thinkers (p. 70). Whether Marcuse's critique of technology implies a global assessment of the concept is debatable, however.

94 Since Marcuse's death in 1979, there has been a great deal of critical theoretical work focusing on technology. While Marcuse generally, until very recently, seemed to have disappeared from the contemporary intellectual agenda, a considerable amount of contemporary critical studies concerned with technology have dealt with obvious Marcusean themes. One thinks of Neil Postman's *Amusing Ourselves to Death: Public Discourse in the Age of Show Business* (New York: Penguin, 1986), and Postman's later work, such as *Conscientious Objections: Stirring Up Trouble About Language, Technology, and Education* (New York: Knopf, 1988) and *Technopoly: The Surrender of Culture to Technology* (New York: Knopf, 1992). In these texts, particularly the later two, Postman argues that America has become a "totalitarian technocracy" that he labels a technopoly. Much of French theorist Jean Baudrillard's analysis of contemporary technology also draws on Marcusean insights. A recent work, Reg Whitaker's *The End of Privacy: How Total Surveillance is Becoming a Reality* (New York: New Press, 1999), draws heavily on Foucault's discussion of the panopticon and is animated by Marcusean concerns with the invasiveness of contemporary technology and the myriad ways in which technology erodes privacy. One notable theorist of technology, Andrew Feenberg, has continued to deal with Marcuse's critique of technocratic domination and Marcuse's hopes for a radically transformed science and technology in a direct and very thoughtful way. See his contribution to the present volume, as well as *Critical Theory of Technology*, New York: Oxford University Press, 1991; *Alternative Modernity: The Technical Turn in Philosophy and Social Theory*, Berkeley: University of California Press, 1995; and *Questioning Technology*, London and New York: Routledge, 1999.

95 See Russell Jacoby, "Das Veralten der Frankfurter Schule," in Detlev Claussen, Oskar Negt and Michael Werz (eds) *Hannoversche Schriften*, vol. 1, *Keine Kritische Theorie ohne Amerika*, Frankfurt: Neue Kritik, 1999, pp. 134ff.

96 See the introduction to *Hegel's Aesthetics: Lectures on Fine Art*, trans. T.M. Knox, Oxford and New York: Oxford University Press, 1998.

97 See Russell Berman, "Consumer Society: The Legacy of the Avant-Garde and the False Sublation of Aesthetic Autonomy," *Modern Culture and Critical Theory: Art, Politics and the Legacy of the Frankfurt School*, Madison, WI: University of Wisconsin Press, 1989, pp. 49–50.

98 See Shierry Weber-Nicholsen, "The Persistence of Passionate Subjectivity: Eros and Other in Marcuse, by Way of Adorno," in Bokina and Lukes (eds) *Marcuse: From the New Left to the Next Left*, pp. 149–69.

99 See, for example, "The New Sensibility," *Essay on Liberation*, pp. 31–54.

100 Angela Y. Davis's *Blues Legacies and Black Feminism: Gertrude "Ma" Rainey, Bessie Smith, and Billie Holiday* (New York: Pantheon Books, 1998) offers a radical reinterpretation of the contributions of these blues/jazz artists that critically appropriates Marcuse's aesthetics. In *Music and Social Movements: Mobilizing Traditions in the Twentieth Century* (Cambridge, UK: Cambridge University Press, 1998), Ron Eyerman and Andrew Jamison draw heavily on Marcuse's writings on aesthetics in the 1960s to analyze the important links between popular music and emancipatory social movements.

101 See Gérard Raulet's contribution to this volume.

102 See Andrew Feenberg's contribution to this volume.

103 For Habermas's views on art, see, for example, his early essay on Walter Benjamin, "Consciousness-Raising or Redemptive Criticism: The Contemporaneity of Walter Benjamin," *New German Critique*, no. 17 (Spring 1979). For an overview of his views on the modern differentiation of the aesthetic-expressive rationality from its cognitive-instrumental and moral-practical counterparts, see his famous, and highly controversial, essay, "Modernity vs. Postmodernity," *New German Critique*, no. 22 (Winter 1981). On Habermas's views on aesthetics, see also Martin Jay, "Habermas and Modernism," *Fin de Siècle Socialism*, New York: Routledge, 1988, pp. 123–36.

104 Some recent commentators have addressed Marcuse's work in this context, but very few do justice to the complexity of his position. Joel Whitebook, for example, in his otherwise excellent study entitled *Perversion and Utopia* (Cambridge, MA: MIT Press, 1995), casts Marcuse in the all-too-familiar role of the naïve romantic in search of an "uncorrupted first nature." But Whitebook fails to see that Marcuse did not advocate a return to a prelapsarian first nature. As Marcuse puts it in *Eros and Civilization*: "The power to restrain and guide instinctual drives, to make biological necessities into individual needs and desires, increases rather than reduces gratification: the 'mediation' of nature, the breaking of its compulsion, is the human form of the pleasure principle" (p. 35). Also, Whitebook recognizes the need to develop a new theory of sublimation, but he makes no reference to Marcuse's path-breaking efforts in this direction. For a discussion of Marcuse's theory of non-repressive sublimation, see Bernard Görlich, "Sublimierung als kulturelles Triebschicksal. Drei Brennpunkte der Sublimierungsfrage im Marcuse-Freud-Vergleich," and Gvozden Flego, "Erotisieren statt Sublimieren," in Institut für Sozialforschung (ed.) *Kritik und Utopie im Werk von Herbert Marcuse*, pp. 171–86 and 187–200, respectively.

105 Marcuse anticipated certain key issues of recent debates in feminist psychoanalytic theory, such as Jessica Benjamin's critique of a notion of autonomy that develops through identification with the dominant father and a concomitant rejection of "feminine" character traits: see Jessica Benjamin, *The Bonds of Love: Psychoanalysis, Feminism, and the Problem of Domination*, New York: Pantheon Books, 1988, pp. 133–82. For Benjamin's views on *Eros and Civilization*, see "Opposition and reconciliation: reason and nature, reality and pleasure," in Institut für Sozialforschung (ed.) *Kritik und Utopie im Werk von Herbert Marcuse*, pp. 124–41. For a discussion of Benjamin's reading of Marcuse, see Gad Horowitz, "Psychoanalytic Feminism in the Wake of Marcuse," in Bokina and Lukes (eds) *Marcuse: From the New Left to the Next Left*, pp. 118–30. Marcuse also developed a critique of Freud's notion of mature, genitally centered sexuality, which anticipates current discussions in queer theory: see Judith Butler, "The Lesbian Phallus and the Morphological Imaginary," *Bodies That Matter*, New York: Routledge, 1993, pp. 57–92. Marcuse differs from Butler and other critical reinterprations of psychoanalysis informed by post-structuralism in his grounding of the potential for a mature, non-destructive reactivation of polymorphous perversity in a materialist theory of subjectivity, and in his linking of the prevention of this potential to the capitalist system of production, which reduces the body to an instrument of labor.

106 See Russell Jacoby, *The Repression of Psychoanalysis: Otto Fenichel and the Political Freudians*, New York: Basic Books, 1983.

107 Herbert Marcuse, *Counter-Revolution and Revolt*, Boston: Beacon, 1972, p. 59.

108 *Ibid.*, p. 60.

109 See Marcuse's important essay, "The Foundations of Historical Materialism," in *Studies in Critical Philosophy*, pp. 1–48.

110 *Counter-Revolution and Revolt*, p. 62.
111 *Ibid.*, p. 65.
112 *Ibid.*, pp. 66–7. For an insightful discussion of the relationship between Marcuse's aesthetics and contemporary ecological issues, see Weber-Nicholsen, "The Persistence of Passionate Subjectivity: Eros and Other in Marcuse, by Way of Adorno."
113 *Counter-Revolution and Revolt*, pp. 68–9
114 See, for example, "On the Jewish Question," in Robert Tucker (ed.) *The Marx-Engels Reader*, New York: Norton, 1978, pp. 35–46. For an insightful analysis and contextualization of Marx's essay, see also Detlev Claussen, *Grenzen der Aufklärung: Die Gesellschaftliche Genese des modernen Antisemitismus*, Frankfurt: Fischer, 1987, pp. 85–108.
115 Victor Farias, *Heidegger and Nazism*, trans. Paul Burrell and Gabriel R. Ricci, Philadelphia: Temple University Press, 1989; Hugo Ott, *Martin Heidegger: A Political Life*, trans. Allan Blunden, New York: Basic Books, 1993.
116 To name just a few: Rudiger Safranski, *Martin Heidegger: Between Good and Evil*, trans. Ewald Osers, Cambridge, MA: Harvard University Press, 1998; A. Milchman and A. Rosenberg (eds), *Martin Heidegger and the Holocaust*, Atlantic Heights, NJ: Humanities Press International, 1996; Berel Lang, *Heidegger's Silence*, Ithaca, NY: Cornell University Press, 1997; Johannes Fritsche, *Historical Destiny and National Socialism in Heidegger's Being and Time*, Berkeley: University of California Press, 1999; and Richard Wolin, *Heidegger's Children: Hannah Arendt, Karl Löwith, Hans Jonas and Herbert Marcuse*, Princeton: Princeton Universtiy Press, 2001.
117 Immanuel Kant, *Anthropology from a Pragmatic Point of View*, trans. Victor Lyle Dowdell, Carbondale and Edwardsville: Southern Illinois Press, 1978, p. 3.
118 These manuscripts have been published recently: see "Cultural Revolution" and "The Historical Fate of Bourgeois Democracy," in Marcuse, *Towards a Critical Theory of Society*, pp. 121–86.

Part I

VETERAN SCHOLARS' REFLECTIONS ON MARCUSE'S THEORETICAL LEGACY

1

MARCUSE'S LEGACIES

Angela Y. Davis[1]

Any attempt to identify the plural legacies of Herbert Marcuse's life and work must seriously engage the political contexts of his writings as well as the discourse that has entombed his theoretical contributions within the history of radical activism during the 1960s. Academics and activists alike find it difficult to disassociate Marcuse from the era of the late 1960s and early 1970s. His persona and his work are often evoked as a marker of a radical era, our primary relationship to which tends to be defined by nostalgia. Consequently, the mention of the name Herbert Marcuse elicits a sigh; many of my generation and older tend to treat him as a sign of our youth – wonderful, exciting, revolutionary, but meaningful only within the context of our reminiscences. As those of us who came of age during the 1960s and early 1970s grow older and older, there seems to be a tendency to spatialize "the sixties." Recently I have noticed that many people of my generation like to introduce themselves by saying "I come from the sixties" – the 1960s being viewed as a point of origin, an originary place, rather than a historical moment. It is a place that we evoke with wonder and joy, but one that is forever beyond our reach. Ironically, the very era during which we were encouraged by Herbert Marcuse to think about the radical potential of utopian thought has itself survived in our historical memory as utopia – as a place that is no place.

It is no less ironic that the most well-known and most widely read thinker associated with the Frankfurt School thirty years ago became the least studied in the 1980s and 1990s, while Theodor Adorno, Max Horkheimer, and Walter Benjamin are extensively studied in the contemporary era. As Marcuse himself acknowledged, his celebrity had both productive and counter-productive aspects. But we can say that the historical conjuncture that linked his own intellectual development with the search for a new political vocabulary during the late 1960s allowed many of us to understand the extent to which he took seriously the charge of critical theory to develop interdisciplinary approaches, anchored in the emancipatory promise of the philosophical tradition within which he worked, that would signal the possibility and need for transformative interventions in the real, social world. And many of Marcuse's ideas during that period evolved in conversation with the contemporaneous social and cultural movements. When he addressed gatherings of young people from California to Paris to Berlin, he spoke as a philosopher who was perennially struggling with the challenges of critical theory to engage directly with contemporary social issues. He was received as a philosopher who urged participants in radical social movements to think more philosophically and more critically about the implications of their activism.

Despite my chronic critiques of nostalgia as an inadequate substitute for historical memory, I want to ask you to permit me to engage in what I would like to think of as a bit of productive nostalgia. Because I do long for the days of interminable philosophical discussions about such subjects as the historical agents of revolution, when the participants in such discussions might be students and professors, as well as organic intellectuals who were workers and organizers. Marcuse's interventions as a public intellectual helped to stimulate such discussions. Did the working class still have a revolutionary potential? What role could students play? I imagine that I am nostalgic today because so few people seem to believe that anybody has any revolutionary potential left .

The thinkers associated with the Frankfurt School were motivated in many of their intellectual endeavors by the desire to develop oppositional – which at that time meant anti-fascist – theoretical work. Herbert Marcuse and Franz Neumann (whose work should also be more seriously read today) were more interested in exploring more immediate oppositional possibilities than their colleagues Adorno and Horkheimer. The first volume of Herbert Marcuse's collected papers, edited by Doug Kellner, contains a prospectus, written in the late 1930s or early 1940s, for a study on which they apparently planned to collaborate – "A History of the Doctrine of Social Change."[2] While this study was not actualized as a result of the outbreak of the Second World War, both Neuman and Marcuse were active in the denazification program after the war – Neuman in the prosecution of Nazis, Marcuse in his work with the State Department helping to develop the US denazification policy. I urge you to read the recently published posthumous work,[3] especially because of the mystery surrounding Marcuse's involvement with the State Department – including the absurd rumors that he was a CIA agent. The first volume of the unpublished papers Kellner has made available allows us to see the important work he did on the cultural impact of Nazism.

Perhaps Marcuse's willingness to engage so directly in this anti-fascist project in the aftermath of the Second World War led him to later broaden his anti-fascist theoretical approach, drawing US society into the frame of his analysis. In other words, precisely because he was so immediately involved in opposing German fascism, he was also able and willing to identify fascist tendencies in the US. Because Adorno's and Horkheimer's anti-fascism expressed itself on a more formal theoretical register, it remained anchored in German history and tradition. When Marcuse wrote "The Struggle Against Liberalism in the Totalitarian View of the State,"[4] arguing that fascism and liberalism were not political opposites – that, indeed, they were closely linked ideologically – he had already established the foundation for his later analysis of US society. When Horkheimer and Adorno returned to Frankfurt and refused to permit the publication of *Dialectic of Enlightenment*, Marcuse's critical theory would explore the one-dimensional society in the US and would later identify the prominent role of racism, encouraging students like myself to attempt to further develop the emancipatory promise of the German philosophical tradition.

One of the most salient and persistent aspects of Marcuse's work is his concern with the possibilities of utopia. This powerful philosophical concept (which meant that he had to contest the orthodox equation of Marxist notions of socialism with the "scientific" as opposed to a "utopian" socialism à la Fourier) was at the core of his ideas. In his important 1937 essay, "Philosophy and Critical Theory," he wrote:

> Like philosophy, [critical theory] opposes making reality into a criterion in the manner of complacent positivism. But unlike philosophy, it always derives its goals from present tendencies of the social process. Therefore it has no fear of the utopia that the new order is denounced as being. When truth cannot be realized within the established social order, it always appears to the latter as mere utopia. This transcendence speaks not against, but for, its truth. The utopian element was long the only progressive element in philosophy, as in the constructions of the best state and the highest pleasure, of perfect happiness and perpetual peace. The obstinacy that comes from adhering to truth against all appearances has given way in contemporary philosophy to whimsy and uninhibited opportunism. Critical theory preserves obstinacy as a genuine quality of philosophical thought.[5]

This obstinacy is most productive, I believe, when it travels from one generation to the next, when new ways of identifying those promises and new oppositional discourses and practices are proposed. In this context, I want to acknowledge the important intergenerational character of this conference.[6] In a passage from the introduction to an *Essay on Liberation* that many of you – old as well as new Marcuse scholars – have probably committed to memory, Marcuse writes that

> what is denounced as "utopian" is no longer that which has "no place" and cannot have any place in the historical universe, but rather that which is blocked from coming about by the power of the

established societies. Utopian possibilities are inherent in the technical and technological forces of advanced capitalism and socialism: the rational utilization of these forces on a global scale would terminate poverty and scarcity within a very foreseeable future.[7]

Marcuse's life-long insistence on the radical potential of art is linked to this obstinate insistence on the utopian dimension. On the one hand, art criticizes and negates the existing social order by the power of its form, which in turn creates another universe, thus hinting at the possibility of building a new social order. But this relationship is highly mediated, as Marcuse continually emphasized – from "The Affirmative Character of Culture" (1937), to the recently published "Some Remarks on Aragon: Art and Politics in the Totalitarian Era" (1945), to the ninth chapter of *Eros and Civilization* (1955), to the last book he published before his death, entitled, like the ninth chapter of *Eros and Civilization*, *The Aesthetic Dimension*.[8] I cite a passage from his essay on Aragon:

> Art does not and cannot present the fascist reality (nor any other forms of the totality of monopolistic oppression). But any human activity which does not contain the terror of this era is by this very token inhuman, irrelevant, incidental, untrue. In art, however, the untruth may become the life element of the truth. The incompatibility of the artistic form with the real form of life may be used as a lever for throwing upon the reality the light which the latter cannot absorb, the light which may eventually dissolve this reality (although such dissolution is no longer the function of art). The untruth of art may become the precondition for the artistic contradiction and negation. Art may promote the alienation, the total estrangement of man from his world. And this alienation may provide the artificial basis for the remembrance of freedom in the totality of oppression.[9]

On the other hand, emancipatory possibilities reside in the very forces that are responsible for the obscene expansion of an increasingly exploitative and repressive order. It seems to me that the overarching themes of Marcuse's thought are as relevant today on the cusp of the twenty-first century as they were when his scholarship and political interventions were most widely celebrated.

At this point in my remarks I would like to make some comments about my own development. I have often publicly expressed my gratitude to Herbert Marcuse for teaching me that I did not have to choose between a career as an academic and a political vocation that entailed making interventions around concrete social issues. In Frankfurt, when I was studying with Adorno, he discouraged me from seeking to discover ways of linking my seemingly discrepant interests in philosophy and social activism. After the founding of the Black Panther Party in 1966, I felt very much drawn back to this country (the US). During one of my last meetings with him (students were extremely fortunate if we managed to get one meeting over the course of our studies with a professor like Adorno), he suggested that my desire to work directly in the radical movements of that period was akin to a media studies scholar deciding to become a radio technician.

In the summer of 1967, I was present when Herbert Marcuse delivered one of the major addresses during the Congress of the Dialectics of Liberation convened in London and organized by four British psychiatrists (including David Cooper and R.D. Laing) associated with the anti-psychiatry movement. Other presenters included Paul Sweezy, Lucien Goldmann, and Stokeley Carmichael. Having spent the two previous years studying at the University in Frankfurt with Marcuse's colleagues, scholars affiliated with the Frankfurt School, I attended this heterogenous gathering of radical scholars, students, activist leaders and organizers from black communities in the United States and Britain on my way back to the United States. The congress took place at the Roundhouse in Chalk Farm, which, originally a locomotive turntable, served as an overarching metaphor for the gathering's collective ambitions – to turn the motive power of radical intellectuals and activists in the direction of social revolution, or what Marcuse called "qualitative change."

Many of the young participants in the two-week conference decided to set up camp in the building, turning the congress into a brief utopian experiment in collaborative theorizing buttressed by cooperative living arrangements. In this sense it reproduced, in abridged format, the radical experiments in communal living that characterized the era of the hippies. Marcuse opened his own address by acknowledging the numerous flowers people had brought into the Roundhouse. But, he said, "flowers, by themselves, have no power whatsoever, other than the power of men and women who protect them and take care of them against aggression and destruction."[10] Later, he spoke pointedly about the hippies, identifying the more politically radical formations among them – the Diggers and the Provos – as uniting sexual, moral, and political rebellion, as encouraging new sensibilities, as exhibiting "a non-aggressive form of life: a demonstration of an aggressive non-aggressiveness which achieves, at least potentially, the demonstration of qualitatively different values, a transvaluation of values."[11]

I evoke this Congress on the Dialectics of Liberation because it took place during a historical moment of immense promise. The presence at this gathering of such diverse figures as economist Paul Sweezy, philosopher Jules Henry, anthropologist Gregory Bateson and activist Stokeley Carmichael, accentuated the gathering's mandate to explore contradictions for their productive, dialectical and transformative potential. Marcuse himself pointed out that liberation is necessarily dialectical and dialectics is necessarily liberatory. Precisely because of the absence of homogeneity and unity among the participants, their political strategies, their ideas, their lifestyles, the congress was animated by palpable imaginings of the possibility of forging alliances across these diverse and contradictory intellectual and activist oppositions precisely for the purpose of changing the direction of history. David Cooper's introduction to the conference proceedings, *To Free a Generation: The Dialectics of Liberation*, concluded with this observation: "Hope has to have another appointment. Not now and not then, but some other time, its own time – which is our time. We have to take over time and own it."[12]

Entitled "Liberation from the Affluent Society," the tone of Marcuse's lecture was in keeping with the overarching optimism of the conference. In his enthusiastically received remarks, he made reference to Walter Benjamin's allusion to the fact that during the Paris Commune:

> In all corners of the city of Paris there were people shooting at the clocks on the towers of the churches, palaces and so on, thereby consciously or half-consciously expressing the need that somehow time has to be arrested, and that a new time has to begin – a very strong emphasis on the qualitative difference and on the totality of the rupture between the new society and the old.[13]

Anyone familiar with Marcuse's life and work would not expect him to embrace a simple and untheorized assumption that the world – or at least some aspects of it – was on the cusp of radical transformation, as many of us believed at that time. However, he spoke encouraging words to those who took seriously the project of liberation:

> Our role as intellectuals is a limited role. On no account should we succumb to any illusions. But even worse than this is to succumb to the wide-spread defeatism which we witness. The preparatory role today is an indispensable role. I believe I am not being too optimistic – I have not in general the reputation of being too optimistic – when I say that we can already see the signs, nor only that They are getting frightened and worried but that there are far more concrete, far more tangible manifestations of the essential weakness of the system. Therefore, let us continue with whatever we can – no illusions, but even more, no defeatism.[14]

Marcuse's political interventions were always tempered with warnings about the limits of their own efficacy, but he was never one to chose silence and inaction. He insisted on possibility and hope, the power of negation, even there – or precisely there – where human possibility was obscured by exploitation and oppression, there where hope seemed nowhere to be found.

Marcuse played an important role during the late 1960s and early 1970s in encouraging intellectuals to speak out against racism, against the Vietnam War, for student rights. He emphasized the important role of intellectuals within oppositional movements, which, I believe, led more intellectuals to frame their work in relation to these movements than would otherwise have done so. And Marcuse's thought revealed how deeply he himself was influenced by the movements of his time and how his engagement with those movements revitalized his thought.

Today, it seems inconceivable that crowds of people at a political rally would be willing to enthusiastically applaud a philosopher trained in the classical tradition, who might just as easily evoke Kant and Hegel as Marx, Fanon, or Dutschke. It seems inconceivable that people did not complain when this philosopher compelled them to think deeply – and even philosophically – in order to engage with ideas he proposed in the context of a public rally. The lesson I draw from these reminiscences is that we need to recapture the ability to communicate across divides that are designed to keep people apart. At the same time we need to substitute a nostalgic attitude toward Marcuse with one that takes seriously his work as a philosopher and as a public intellectual.

One of the great challenges of any social movement is to develop new vocabularies. As we attempt to develop these vocabularies today, we can find inspiration and direction in Marcuse's attempts to theorize the politics of language. In *An Essay on Liberation* he wrote:

> Political linguistics: armor of the Establishment. If the radical opposition develops its own language, it protests spontaneously, subconsciously, against one of the most effective "secret weapons" of domination and defamation. The language of the prevailing Law and Order, validated by the courts and by the police, is not only the voice but also the deed of suppression. This language not only defines and condemns the Enemy, it also *creates* him…This linguistic universe, which incorporates the Enemy (as *Untermensch*) into the routine of everyday speech can be transcended only in action.[15]

While Marcuse was specifically referring to the way Nixon's law-and-order rhetoric conflated criminals, radicals, and communists in the former Soviet Union and freedom fighters in Vietnam and defenders of the revolution in Cuba, the challenge he presents is very much a contemporary one, particularly with respect to the need to create a "rupture with the linguistic universe of the Establishment" and its representation of crime and criminals, which has helped to imprison almost two million people – which has facilitated the horrifying pattern of the prison as the major institution toward which young Black men, and increasingly Black women, are headed.

While this is another topic entirely – and this is what I usually speak and write about, so I must restrain myself from beginning another talk – I do want to conclude by suggesting how important it is for us to consider the contemporary relevance of Marcuse's ideas within this context. How do we draw upon Marcuse's critical theory in our attempt to develop new vocabularies of resistance today, vocabularies that effect a rupture with the equation of affirmative action and "reverse racism," vocabularies that reflect a utopian vision of a society without prisons, at least without the monstrous, corporatized system that we call the prison-industrial complex?

I am not suggesting that Marcuse should be revived as the pre-eminent theorist of the twenty-first century. He, more than anyone, insisted on the deeply historical character of theory. It would certainly militate against the spirit of his ideas to argue that his work contains the solution to the many dilemmas facing us as scholars, organizers, advocates, artists, and, I would add, as marginalized communities, whose members are increasingly treated as detritus and relegated to prisons, which, in turn, generate astronomical profits for a growing global prison industry. An uncritical and nostalgic version of Marcuse, which, for example, fails to acknowledge the limits of an aesthetic theory that maintains a rigid distinction between high and low art, one that is not willing to engage seriously with popular culture and all its contradictions, would not be helpful to those who are seeking to forge radical political vocabularies today. But if we abandon our Marcuse nostalgia and attempt to incorporate his ideas into a historical memory that draws upon the useful aspects of the past in order to put them to work in the present, we will be able to hold on to Marcuse's legacies as we explore terrain that he himself could never have imagined.

Notes

1 This is a lightly revised transcript of the talk given by Angela Y. Davis at the "Legacy of Herbert Marcuse" conference at the University of Berkeley, CA, 1998.
2 Herbert Marcuse and Franz Neumann, "A History of the Doctrine of Social Change," in Herbert Marcuse, *Technology, War and Fascism: Collected Papers of Herbert Marcuse*, vol. 1, ed. Douglas Kellner, London and New York: Routledge, 1998, pp. 93–104.
3 Marcuse, *Technology, War and Fascism*.
4 Herbert Marcuse, "The Struggle Against Liberalism in the Totalitarian View of the State," in *Negations: Essays in Critical Theory*, trans. Jeremy J. Shapiro, Boston: Beacon, 1968, pp. 3–42.
5 Herbert Marcuse, "Philosophy and Critical Theory," in *Negations*, p. 143.
6 This paper was originally given at the conference "The Legacy of Herbert Marcuse," held at the University of California, Berkeley, in November 1998 [editors].
7 Herbert Marcuse, *Essay on Liberation*, Middlesex, UK: Penguin, 1969, p. 13.
8 Herbert Marcuse, "The Affirmative Character of Culture," in *Negations*, pp. 88–133; "Some Remarks on Aragon: Art and Politics in the Totalitarian Era," in *Technology, War and Fascism*, pp. 199–214; "The Aesthetic Dimension," in *Eros and Civilization*, New York: Vintage, 1962, pp. 157–79; *The Aesthetic Dimension: Toward a Critique of Marxist Aesthetics*, Boston: Beacon, 1978.
9 *Technology, War and Fascism*, p. 214.
10 David Cooper, ed. *To Free A Generation: The Dialectics of Liberation* (New York: Collier Books, 1969), p. 175.
11 Cooper, p. 190.
12 Cooper, p. 11.
13 Cooper, p. 177.
14 p. 191-2.
15 *Essay on Liberation*, pp. 76ff.

2

THE AMERICAN EXPERIENCE OF THE CRITICAL THEORISTS

Detlev Claussen

Without the United States, there would be no critical theory. This simple fact is often forgotten in discussions of critical theory. Not only did Horkheimer, Pollock, Adorno, Marcuse, and Löwenthal all spend the years of the Nazi regime in the US, Marcuse and Löwenthal stayed in America for the rest of their lives. In 1945, Horkheimer moved heaven and earth in order to be able to keep his American citizenship. Later, when the Vietnam War provoked massive demonstrations and fierce discussions in Germany as well as in the US, Horkheimer defended the American position with great vigor, if not with the most convincing arguments. And when it became clear to him that he would not be able to convince his own students of this position – *his students*, with whom, of course, he enjoyed a considerable intellectual authority – he could only smile and offer the memorable explanation, "You will, of course, allow me a certain, irrational moment of gratitude." For the rest of his life Horkheimer remained aware that neither the critical theorists nor critical theory could have survived in Europe under National Socialism or Stalinism. Columbia University's offer to let the Institute for Social Research relocate to New York made it possible for the refugees from Frankfurt to continue their work under a scientific (*szientifische*) guise in the distrustful, but democratic, United States of Franklin Delano Roosevelt. Those who have not learned how to think dialectically will find Horkheimer's way of capturing historical experience in theory wholly alien. To try to think about critical theory without thinking about the experience of American exile is to run the risk of misunderstanding the concept of critical theory.

It was only in the US that the critical theory of society became critical theory. To be sure, many of the crucial aspects of the theory received their first articulation during the Weimar years, but it was only in the US that they were crystallized into a concept. Only after coming to the US, that is, did Horkheimer come to reinterpret the experience of the "missing revolution"[1] as that of the impossibility of revolution within the relations of fully developed capitalism. The theoretical works that Marcuse and Horkheimer published in the *Zeitschrift für Sozialforschung*, culminating in the programmatic essay, "Traditional and Critical Theory," all attempt to understand the significance of this structural shift. And indeed, Marcuse's life work revolves around the attempt to better understand this foreclosure of possibility. *One-Dimensional Man* closes by examining this paradox, and all of Marcuse's major works (as well as many of his shorter pieces) revolve around it. The question of a hermetically sealed world impervious to change returns again and again in the language of the student protest movements, and in the conflicts the protest movements sparked between Horkheimer, Adorno, and Marcuse. Only by posing this question in terms of the common historical experience of all the critical theorists can its significance begin to be understood. The prominent position that Adorno gave to his pronouncement of the "missed moment" of philosophy's realization in *Negative Dialectics* is, in this sense, an answer to the grim riddle he had already posed, at the end of the second World War, in *Minima Moralia*: where is the proletariat?[2]

Anyone who is interested in the critical theory of the 1940s must confront certain questions – questions which seem more contemporary now than they did ten years ago. At first glance, Adorno's "riddle" seems rather far away from us; at the second glance it touches upon categorical problems long obscured in the social sciences by nominalistic hot air. In the 1940s, the critical theorists were interested in the historical dynamics of the class society, and in the way the identity between the key concepts of "bourgeois society" and "class society" was beginning to break down. The familiar image of nineteenth-century bourgeois society was that of a dominant liberalism challenged by the active opposition of organized socialism. Though the emerging society could not, of course, deny its roots in the old familiar bourgeois forms, it was experienced by the critical theorists in the US after the New Deal as the origin of an *affluent society* with neither opposition nor alternative. They described this new society as the sublation of class society through the intensification and generalization of the principles of class society. Just as bourgeois society disappeared into the "middle class," so too the proletariat disappeared under the pressure of big business and big labor. The melting pot, now criticized by many sociologists of culture as an ideological fiction, was in fact quite real: within it, all the traditional differences were melted down, making necessary the articulation and invention of new "imagined communities."

The social-historical gap between bourgeois society and advanced capitalist society coalesced, after 1945, into a geographic difference, one between Europe and America. In the Cold War era that followed, it became common to refer to differences between forms of social organization in terms of geography: it was simply natural to speak of the East–West conflict. Only with the end of the Cold War did the West accept the name "capitalism" to refer to itself – and then it took the word almost as an honorary title, lent to it by its defeated foe. Of course, this acceptance of "capitalism" as a self-description was not undertaken with any serious intent, since significant differences between nations and peoples had in the meantime come to be described much more in terms of ethnicity and culture than in terms of state-economic forms. The somewhat lazy acceptance and assumption of this world-historical category suggests, rather, the fundamental conceptual weakness characteristic of a contemporary society to which there seem to be no alternatives. Yet even such terminological disarray is expressive of a massive social change: in the era of bourgeois society, the bourgeois class was constantly busy with the articulation of its own consciousness, to which its culture left behind testaments in paper and in stone. In the contemporary public sphere, by contrast, the concept of culture has become vastly more flexible. The culture concept may now be applied to anything, and for this reason it has lost the dignity of a concept that arbitrates between what is and what is not the case. Words old and new have been emptied of their content, and have simply become labels which can be stuck to any observed phenomenon. Bourgeois society still produced a consistent ideology, within which thought and everyday life seemed to come together, but the old ideology has disappeared – and so irrevocably that many now speak of the end of the age of ideology.

From the very beginning of their time in America, the critical theorists investigated the character of the new. At first, in the 1930s, they concentrated their attention on the events in Europe. Until 1939, the major essays in the *Zeitschrift für Sozialforschung* were published in German. It was only with the beginning of the war that a transformation occurred. Herbert Marcuse's "Some Social Implications of Modern Technology" built upon material connections between the European and the American experience. Implicitly, this article was concerned with the question of the new – a question which did not, however, first arise in America, but rather was carried over from Europe by the critical theorists. The tendency of the life of the mind to drift toward the culture industry was evident not only in America, but in Europe as well. The concentration of media, both in film and print, was a phenomenon they knew well enough from the Weimar Republic; the problem of the new in products of the culture industry was not one they first asked themselves after their encounters with Radio City and Hollywood. Adorno had initially formulated this question in regard to music, and he took the question up again in his critique of Veblen. "How is the new possible?" he asked at the end of an essay which he wrote in 1941 and unreservedly published, like a kind of visiting card from the returning émigré, on his return to Germany in the mid-1950s. In *Prisms*, the path-breaking volume of essays which appeared in Germany in 1955, he allowed the Veblen essay to be directly followed by his text on Aldous Huxley and utopia, which he had similarly taken up in the early 1940s. In 1942 the Institute for Social Research had held a conference on Aldous Huxley in Los Angeles, at which Herbert Marcuse gave a paper on Huxley's *Brave New World* and Horkheimer and Adorno each presented their respective "Theses on Need."

The 1942 conference shed an especially clear light upon the uniqueness of critical theory's particular way of distinguishing itself from rationalistic Marxism, not least because Bertolt Brecht and Hans Eisler, both invited conference participants, were happy to play the role of the devil's advocate. Their version of Marxism was oriented toward a form of social-historical abstraction that possessed an unchanging essence. For these artists, theory was something useful – an instrument to be wielded in the fray. By contrast, the theorists Horkheimer, Adorno, and Marcuse were occupied by the question of the relationship of the old to the new. The moment of historical transformation, a moment which was not to be suppressed, constituted as well a new essence of society and its theory. The critical theorists found it extraordinarily difficult to arrive at a satisfactory concept of totality, since the new form of totality bore many resemblances to the old. At first they tried the expression "late capitalism," which implied the simultaneity of fascism with an authoritarian state socialism. There was – quite rightly – considerable disagreement within the group, particularly between Pollock and Franz Neumann, concerning the appropriateness of the term "state capitalism." The tendency toward state interventionism, which could no longer be ignored after the New Deal, played a role in the expression the "administered world," which Horkheimer and Adorno used in the 1950s to describe the American model of social relations. In 1967, when Herbert Marcuse spoke in Berlin to an expectant generation of student protesters, he emphasized from the very beginning the point that there was nothing "outside" of the capitalist system. Since he was speaking only a few kilometers from the Wall, this statement could not help but irritate Cold Warriors on both sides.

One can easily become disoriented. Did such chaos reign in the heads of the critical theorists in 1941, that even after thirty years they were unable to bring it under control? After the end of the Cold War and the opening of the archives, the answer is obvious: critical theory would never have been formulated without the critical theorists' experience in America. But what should we understand by "American experience?" A tentative, general answer might be formulated as a historical reflection: once there was a bourgeois society, but it does not exist any longer. This is no matter of mere speculation. Thomas Mann, Adorno's California neighbor (to put the matter poetically), expressed the situation with a crystalline clarity after his return to Europe. In a long-unknown 1951 letter to Walter Ulbricht, a top government advisor in the former East Germany, Thomas Mann thus argued that

> [a] world which still calls itself bourgeois seems not to want to know how far it has moved away from the lifestyle of the classical bourgeois world, how much it too finds itself in the middle of the general revolution, and how un-bourgeois it has already become, in every sense – spiritual, economic, moral, political.[3]

The critical theorists described this same experience; though, of course, their use of the concept of revolution was decidedly different than that of the staunchly bourgeois novelist. Developed capitalism, their thesis argued, seems to make revolution impossible by ensnaring all people and things in the network of "socialization." It was, in Adorno's words, a matter of "the prevention of revolution by means of the total society."

This experience forced the critical theorists to define the concept of capitalism more broadly than the concept of bourgeois society. It is only against this background that Marcuse's comment, that there is nothing outside of capitalism, makes sense. The European experience of failed revolution – first the German, then the Russian – was a constitutional prerequisite for critical theory. When the German émigrés came to America, they had already directed considerable attention toward the question of why revolution had become impossible even though the objective conditions for it seemed so opportune. On the daily agendas for internal debates within the Institute, from the late 1930s and early 1940s, there stood, along with discussions about Germany, shared reflections on the categories by which the social subject is constituted. Time and again, at the center of the discussion was the problem of how to understand the subjective side of these (objective) social categories – how to understand phenomena which are now called "social constructions" by the forgetful social sciences.

In Adorno's writings there is a text from 1942 with the heading "Reflections on a Theory of Class." Adorno translates historical experiences into theory – which he differentiates, in passing, from science. Science itself is subject to the drive to forget; for, in the division of labor of the science industry, science must, under the pressure to prove its own usefulness, constantly approach and present its respective objects as "the new." In thinking of the difficulties Adorno experienced with the Princeton Radio Research Project immediately after his arrival, it is tempting to contrast the German tradition of speculative thought with the American notion of applied social science. Yet the abstract opposition between European theory and American social science is itself a product of forgetting, a result of a post-festum construction. At the time, Adorno had no experience whatsoever as a sociologist; it was as a composer and musician that he got involved in what was, for the time, a fairly routine bit of research under contract.

At the same time, one should not simply identify American sociology with positivism and empiricism so as to flatter European prejudices. Social science in America has, in fact, a complex tradition, which cannot be separated absolutely from the European tradition. For the first and second generations of professional American sociologists in particular, the European academy was no *terra incognita*. The concrete experiences of European migration were constitutive for the famous Chicago School, in which intellectual concepts like that of the "other" – concepts which had themselves originally been brought from Europe and modified – formed the basis of much excellent scholarly work. Paul Lazarsfeld, Adorno's discussion partner in the Princeton Radio Research Project, had developed his notion of empirical social research in the context of the Austromarxist Workers' Movement. Even late in his life, this doyen of American social research described himself as a "Marxist on vacation" – one who, however, jokingly added that he had never come back from vacation.

Thus, when Adorno took up his "Reflections on a Theory of Class" in 1942, he had every reason to believe that he would be understood. The conflict was not one between German theory in exile and American science. In reality, the issue was one concerning the difference between theory and science. Theory claims to be able to recognize truth. On immanent grounds, theory must rely upon theory's other – on something outside of theory. Over and over again, the critical theorists reflected upon the intersection between materialism and idealism under changed historical conditions – but they did so with the awareness that the conflict between materialism and idealism must itself be dialectically transformed (*aufgehoben*) in a historical consciousness. At precisely this moment in time, the period in which the critical theorists were reflecting over class and needs, the sociology of knowledge was beginning to enjoy great success, particularly in the sociology of science. The discoveries produced by this form of study have since made their way, albeit with great distortion, into everyday language. In contemporary discussions of "paradigm shifts," this term already suggests distinctions of "in" and "out." Thomas Kuhn, who introduced the notion of "paradigm shifts," fought tooth and nail against the misuse of this category; but he was unable to prevent the spread of the belief that the phrase "paradigm shift" described conventions among scientists, independent of the object of investigation. In this way, things have come to a paradoxical situation: an academically expanded knowledge of historical occurrences can go hand in glove with a socially prescribed ahistoricality.

These changes may be explained with the help of the concept of class. The concept of class presumes a historical understanding of social being; it acquires its defining characteristics out of the process of social formation, which itself is a product of modern class society. The concept of class contains the moment of universal socialization, something that was already reflected in Hegel's philosophy. It was not just that Hegel developed a philosophy of history based on the self-realization of spirit; he also developed a concept of civil or bourgeois society as a "system of needs." Hegel had also given serious thought to America as "the land of the future."[4] America, of course, could only be compared with Europe when "civil society is forced to fall back upon itself."[5]

Hegel recognized in America a "community which had developed out of the atoms of individuals, such that the state was only an external development for the protection of property." Hegel used his reflections on America in the "Philosophy of History" as an occasion to work out the distinction between history and philosophy. History is concerned with the genesis of the present out of the past, he argued, "but philosophy concerns itself with that which has neither existed nor ever will exist."[6] The theoretical tradition in which the critical theorists saw themselves possessed precisely these qualities. Social classes are seen as a real component of a material society – components which, however, themselves contain a moment of not (yet)-ness, of mutability. Classes are constituted out of individuals, yet individuals in a class-based society are themselves prevented *by* that society from becoming individuals. Under the sign of the immutability of the class society, classes recede in the same way that individuals do – and the socialized society breaks into atoms.

Coming from Europe, the critical theorists experienced America as a "radically bourgeois" country – as Adorno put it in "On Tradition," one of his last essays.[7] Today this statement seems opaque unless it is interpreted against the concrete background of critical theory: America seemed to the European refugees to be free from *false* traditions. Whenever they experienced difference and alterity vis-à-vis their own conceptions of society, they had no choice but to interpret such experiences on purely social terms, rather than ascribing them to differences in national – much less cultural – mentality. America was understood by them in terms of the unfettered logic of the "system of needs." Here their knowledge of the difference between Western European and American society was useful for understanding this logic. The disappearance of historical genesis promoted the spread of social amnesia. Critical theory, which, in contrast to traditional theory, saw itself as capable of effecting social transformation, was thus forced by the objective relations to draw its power from anamnesis. It was the social-historical difference between Europe and America that became a source of their ability to remember. In the America of the 1930s, however, a different order of things began to establish itself, one which lasted until the end of what Eric Hobsbawm has called the "Golden Age" of the short twentieth century.[8] The immediate and reflected experiences of the critical theorists are thus no longer self-explanatory, but are, rather, in need of interpretation.

In his essay, "Scientific Experiences of a European Scholar in America," Adorno attempted to interpret the social-historical background of his own scientific biography. He did not, by any means, indulge in a simplified explanatory model based on a fixed and absolute distinction between Europe and America. Thirty years after his arrival in America, it was clear to him that America, too, had undergone fundamental changes. America, of course, was no longer thought of as the land of unlimited opportunity, although shortly before his death, Adorno did remark that in America "one still has the feeling that anything would be possible."[9] Adorno is often taken to task by critics for his hermetic pessimism; but this emphatic and quite pointed passage seems not to fit in with the standard image of Adorno. Perhaps it might shed light on the continued relevance of critical theory. There is a certain utopian content even in the late writings of the critical theorists, a utopianism implicit in the categories of thought which the theory had inherited. Indeed, in order to find this concept of theory at all palatable, however, one must recognize it in terms of a European inheritance – as the detritus of a European origin. Since the days of the English and French Enlightenment, the idea of a changed world had been connected with the human capacity for thought and knowledge (*Erkenntnis*). America is caught up with this notion in the most intimate and contradictory ways. In the American Dream – contrary to old-European prejudices – this utopian content proved for a very long time to have a noticeable mass appeal. Well into the Golden Age of the Short Century, the utopian stars of the American Dream seemed within reach. Martin Luther King and Herbert Marcuse lived, after all, in the same world.

From the very beginning of the exile – which is to say, already in the early 1930s – the critical theorists had the experience that social categories were losing their utopian power, not only in political propaganda, but also in the sciences organized and driven by the division of labor. Their notion – so strange to our contemporary ears – of America as a "radically bourgeois society" preserves the trace of this historical logic. In no other land have bourgeois society and liberalism been tied together so strongly as in America; but their unfettered logic, which recreates everything in its own image, has the effect of an unfettered universal upon the individual. Increasingly, class-based society made the force of this evident to individuals not in terms of the realities of class, but rather as a tendency to expose the individual immediately to the pressure of the entire system. With the disappearance of "class," the category of the "individual" also loses its substance. The family thus appears as the last, protective institution above the individual, becoming the defender of tradition in a traditionless present. If society hardly makes sense any more, the family becomes the last site of the production of meaning – the last place in which the pursuit of happiness becomes possible. It is precisely under the intensified conditions of a society that has been made "more flexible" that the family, the smallest unit above the individual, gains a new ideological function. The absolute pragmatism of a society that rejects all forms of tradition thus recoils into an anthropomorphically conceived image of reality, an image which the alien world presents as something intimate and trusted to subjects who have become the objects of anonymous processes. Accounts of family ancestry function as the ideological replacements for the absent image of a feudal past.

The concrete American experience of the critical theorists could perhaps be described as follows: in America, they met up with the regimented world of a bourgeois society without alternatives, a society which frustrated their legitimate need for life-historical continuity. This experience of contradiction, perceived at an individual level, served as the experiential kernel for a critical theory of contemporary society. What, in the American society of the

1930s and 1940s, admitted to being brought under a concept? It was just at that time that the social, economic, and cultural preconditions for Hobsbawm's Golden Age were being formed. For a short moment at the end of the war, there appeared a vision of "one world," – of a unified world, which seemed quite plausibly grounded in the social realities of advanced industrial society. The Cold War then quite quickly abandoned this notion of "One World" amid the front lines of confrontation among the various blocs. But this vision of "One World" as something more than ideology is preserved in critical theory in the form in which it was formulated by Horkheimer and his colleagues in America. Marcuse's formulation, that there was "no longer anything outside of capitalism," makes sense against this background. It is in this state of affairs as well that the relevance of critical theory *after* the end of the Cold War finds its grounding. It was thus taken for granted from the outset in critical theory that there were no alternatives to advanced Western social forms. The fascist and "real socialist" opponents to capitalism can be recognized simply as distorted forms of this general social development. The Cold War delayed the arrival of the "One World" for forty years: now it is here.

The new seems, in the present, inextricably bound up with the old. One can achieve surprising successes these days by reading long quotations from the 150-year-old Communist Manifesto to audiences without naming the authors, and passing the reading off as a clever contribution to "globalization" debates. There are good reasons for this effect. In their early years, when Marx and Engels formulated the Communist Manifesto, they took for granted the idea of an inexorable, worldwide trend toward the development of bourgeois society. According to its own logic, bourgeois society buries all historical traditions beneath itself without founding new ones; for Marx and Engels explained this society in terms of its transitory character. As such, the logic of bourgeois society gives primacy to the economic, a primacy recognized today by many more than just the disciples of neo-liberalism. If critical social theory since Marx has seen itself as tearing the ideological veil off of society, that veil is now torn. Today, indeed, the ideological veil has been torn to rags by reality itself. The end of ideology, a phenomenon which well-known American sociologists have been proclaiming for decades, has now become a journalistic commonplace for the entire world.

It is in this state of affairs, however, that the crucial difference between the contemporary world and past epochs becomes evident. Even in their lifetimes, Marx and Engels were forced to realize that bourgeois society does not exist in the real world in the same state of conceptual purity with which it was presented in the Communist Manifesto. Almost a hundred years later, the critical theorists in exile recognized that American society came surprisingly close to the concept of a bourgeois society without feudal vestiges. It was not just in Horkheimer's circle that intellectual immigrants, faced with this realization, considered writing new versions of the Manifesto – Brecht, for example, even did it in verse. The outlook, however, changed quickly. Around 1940, Adorno began to take up the problem not only of European but also of American ideology. He brought the essays on Veblen and Huxley back with him to Europe, and had them published after his return in the *Prisms* volume. Marcuse, Neumann, and Löwenthal went to work in the intelligence branch of the American government in order to join the fight against National Socialist Germany. And, last but not least, they all received American citizenship. Lack of alternative seems indeed to be a kind of key with which decisions made in personal life histories can be understood in conjunction with the recognition of larger, social transformation.

The writings of the critical theorists of this period are shot through with a certain sense of the ontological – an illusion which long made possible the unexpected effectiveness of their work, its message-in-a-bottle effect. Horkheimer had severed the connection between critical theory and the traditional notion that such theory must have an addressee. This served as a means of re-separating thought from a practice concerned with the seizure of political power, and differentiated critical theory from all traditional forms of Marxism. The "peculiarly ironic character of the Marxian categories" (as Horkheimer put it) thus reappeared almost a hundred years after it had been forgotten. (One might add that this "peculiarly ironic character" has so far escaped the notice of at least 95 per cent of all Marxists.) Yet the price that critical theory paid for this was high. The social system's systematicity reappears in the categories that should describe it – but precisely as a sense, or semblance, of the ontological. The world which should have been described in terms of mutability and transformability appears, instead, in the writings from the end of the war, in terms of immutability and inflexibility. A historical experience is sedimented in this contradictory situation as well: the liberation from National Socialism did not produce a break in historical continuity and open society up to a qualitative change; rather, the continuum closed itself up again – a fact that Herbert Marcuse told any later generation that was interested in hearing it. The idea of "salvation through revolution" disappeared after the confrontation with Nazism resulted in the installation of a new, and – in the eyes of the critical theorists – administered world. The vague concept of the "administered world," which was supposed to pinpoint a substantial transformation in society, stood for the American experience of the critical theorists.

In the course of the emigration, the critical theorists' sense of biographical continuity had been interrupted by the experience of the social and historical differences between European and American society. The need of the individual to maintain continuity runs up against a social structure that relentlessly demands an adjustment, an adaptation to the new social life-process. America's social structure as a developed industrial society, a structure which found a newly stable form in the New Deal at the time of the arrival of the critical theorists, immediately developed an appearance of ontological immutability which bore totalitarian traits. Critical theory – and this is often overlooked – implicitly contained a *sui generis* theory of totalitarianism. In critical theory, terrorism is interpreted not as an infringement of foreign ideology and terror into the good old bourgeois world, but rather as the consequence of the liquidation of history by social forces. America's advanced industrial society is not separated by an ocean from the development of European society toward fascism; rather, it is a matter of *one* world, which hangs together by virtue of its social divisions. It was this experience of the "One World" effect that created the semblance of the ontological within critical theory.

It is precisely in those passages in *Dialectic of Enlightenment* which sound most timelessly ahistorical to subsequent readers that historical experience is expressed in the most uncompromising ways. Anyone who does not believe this can look at the correspondence among the critical theorists, into which Martin Jay already, twenty-five years ago, provided us with important insights,[10] and which are now generally accessible. On 2 October 1946, Horkheimer wrote to Löwenthal as part of a discussion about the "Elements of Anti-Semitism":

> Deserving as it may be to point out the horrors of German and Russian despotism, the effort of conceptual thinkers has, in my opinion, still to be concerned with the social development in industrial society as a whole. To conceive the horror is as impossible as it is to see the night. The horror in the human world should be understood as a verdict against specific forms of social self-preservation. Today the world has become too much a totality as to justify the isolation of one power block so as to oppose it to the rest of civilization as good or bad, or better or worse. Such a procedure is justified in practical respects but not when it comes to theoretical thinking. Here, I must say, the principle of the lesser evil is even more dangerous than in politics.[11]

Horkheimer did not wish to deny the specific differences among the three forms of state-social organization. He seeks, rather, to grasp the ungraspable nature of the horror in terms of its connection to normality. Horkheimer understands critical theory's theory of totalitarianism as a social-critical form of knowledge, which should not serve as an instrument in the Cold War, but rather make it possible to grasp the totalitarian horror as a constituent aspect of the Cold War.

The productive possibilities of this thought would become more visible again after the end of the Cold War. It was precisely in the social sciences that an uncritical conformism revealed a self-destructive power. In the social sciences, which have been subject to a heightened pressure to prove their legitimacy after the end of the Cold War, lack of history and the invention of tradition have gone hand in hand. In a societal situation in which the ability to achieve a conscious structuring of social relationships may very well decide the fate of mankind as a whole, the social sciences have bent over backwards to purge the categories of "consciousness" and "subject" from social analysis. Though it was critical theory that took notice of the disintegration of the social content of these categories over fifty years ago, anyone who tries to build upon critical theory today, anyone who reflects upon the logic of disintegration that has been at work in these categories, is viewed as an antiquated fool. Yet the decay of these categories cannot be understood if the theorist has no concept of what it is that is decaying. The destruction of the categories goes along with an immediate naïvety, according to which disastrous social developments are explained as the product of "false thinking." The destructive aspects of public debates – for which Germany has started to become famous – usually go unrecognized: the *Historikerstreit*, the Goldhagen debates, and now as well the discussion about the "Black Book of Communism" – in the course of which, however, appearances of public exhaustion are beginning to be evident. Anti-Semitism, communism, and totalitarianism congeal, in these debates, into artifacts, which remain just as inscrutable as were the old "opaque items" of social research. What is definitely necessary in order to be able to imagine the torn contexts of these debates – memory – has become a kind intellectual fashion phenomenon, losing its power any time public funds for educational institutions and museums dry up.

The more self-destructively scientists deal with intellectual traditions in their academic fields, the more superficially public debates are carried out. This fact can easily be confirmed by a look at the career of the concept of "identity." When one realizes that it has already become impossible to invoke any living memories of the concept of identity within the tradition of classical German philosophy, then it becomes clear that the ideas of identity presently in general circulation in the social sciences and humanities are little more than a loose pastiche of psychoanalytical and social psychological forms. It is not just in idealist philosophy, but also in terms of biographical significance, that identity, like the old concepts of the individual, the class, or the nation, has taken on a transitory character. In people's daily lives, these categories take on new accents and coloring because they are interpreted by individual people in individual life-contexts independently of academic fashions. At the level of everyday life, the concept of consciousness – long ago dismantled by science – is making a comeback. Virtually everyone would go to the barricades to defend the character of the subject, for the denial of the subject signifies, for most people, not only the denial of agency, but also of the possibility of social interaction. In the form of what might be called "everyday religion,"[12] contemporary self-consciousness integrates and equates everyday experience, the need for meaning, and possibilities of communication. The perception of reality and its distortion thus fuse together to form a flexible ideology that enables the individual to act socially and to understand their action as meaningful under almost any set of conditions.

Critical theory can engage with this imagined world of everyday life by taking up the tools of critical self-reflection. Adorno himself developed his concept of "American experience" in the retrospective text of 1968. Looking back at the year of his arrival in the US – 1938 – he noted in himself a certain "naiveté regarding the American situation." Adorno himself admitted that he had not understood the problem of a "manipulated appearance" of spontaneity – of a "second-hand," manufactured spontaneity. The idea that Adorno formulates in a very sketchy, almost preconceptual way in this passage nonetheless marks a decisive step in his understanding: the critic of society who takes social reality à la lettre lags behind the experiences of individual people, even when these experiences are formulated in conventions and stereotypes. The theorist-emigrant thus had a personal experience which cast light on reified relations and on the self-understanding of the social atom. The emigrant had brought with him a need for biographical continuity – a traditional understanding of the self which, however, found little sustenance in the society into which the emigrant arrived. The American society in the age of the melting pot, at the high-point of developed industrial capitalism, proved to be radically anti-traditional. The new arrival could prove himself only by being productive. A fully developed system of commodity production becomes, in this respect, an avenue for the individual to become a recognized member of society, so long as he is willing to adapt to the system and life of the production processes.

In *Minima Moralia*, Adorno formulated the critical potential of this experience – the experience, that is, of being able to imagine a "better condition" in which "one can be different without fear."[13] This understanding of the non-identical was gained only through an understanding of the deep contradiction immanent within the ideology of the melting pot. This contradiction may only be articulated when one has a sense of how transitory a society can be, and how such a society will nonetheless appear to the individual as if it were eternal. Since the 1940s, critical theory has confronted the immediacy of the social whole by means of ideology critique. The semblance of the ontological that characterizes contemporary society is understood by them – however paradoxical it may sound – as a *real appearance*, a real illusion that is anchored in the structure of human social relations. This appearance clings as well to the categories by which this society is understood: class, individual, nation. One could call them *real fictions*. Despite all of the fashions of the social sciences, realities of consciousness must also be understood and perceived as constituent parts of reality. Precisely because critical theory took the ideology of bourgeois society seriously, its insights and observations become relevant and contemporary *after* the downfall of that society.

It was in America that the disappearance of bourgeois society could be studied for the first time within a class society. Ever since then, America has been correctly viewed as the "most progressive position of observation" – as Adorno formulated it in 1968. Many of the statements from *One-Dimensional Man*, statements which made Marcuse seem to be a kind of social prophet in the Western Europe of the 1960s, are indebted to this position of observation. But the critical theorists did not just observe the most advanced country with the eyes of new arrivals; they also looked back at Europe with a newly Americanized gaze. Many of the categories which Marcuse applied to that most advanced of countries in *One-Dimensional Man* are already to be seen in the recently published analyses of Germany that he prepared during the war for the American secret service.[14] It is not simply a matter of the effacement of historical differences, but rather a question of the social interconnection of the modern world. Nazism and Stalinist communism are not understood by them in terms of "teutonic" or "asiatic" inheritances, but rather as barbaric forms of modernization contemporaneous with the New Deal. America, too, was radically modernized as a consequence of the war.

For it is only in terms of comparisons between societies that the historical dynamic becomes clear: liberalism and socialism appear, from the perspective of the critical theorists, as past forms of bourgeois society; and fascism and communism are the products of their decay. Hobsbawm's Short Century could also be described as an age of dissolution. After the disappearance of fascism and communism, their surviving parents appear like ghosts – ghosts which do not seem any livelier when they are re-baptized as neo-liberalism or New Labour. Contemporary society appears on the stage in ill-fitting historical costumes that barely veil the naked facts of their lack of tradition. This new society is not only incapable of developing a theory of itself – it cannot even develop a consistent ideology. That which remained outside the system could not simply be passed over in silence. It produces a horror vacuum, one which is filled full of hot air and covered over with new labels. The ruined city of spirit gives the impression, in its current, so-called postmodern phase, of being nothing more than a badly organized flea market.

Horkheimer and Adorno returned from the New World as vehement critics of science. In a letter of 1946 to Löwenthal, Horkheimer had already complained bitterly about *social science* as a form of activity:

> I think that the continual pressure to keep this machinery functioning – a machinery whose only function is that of creating the impression that it has a function – eventually ruins one's character, or rather is a challenge that attracts and is sufferable by a very particular type of character.[15]

Social theory and life experience are tied up with each other in this statement. In the Institute, Horkheimer had, with Pollock, found a unique organizational form, one which gave them the possibility to develop the collective project of "critical theory" outside of the spheres of political dependencies and the duties of academic careers. One can only admire the talent and energy with which this intellectual Noah's Ark was steered through the Short Century. From her decks, outsiders gained a free view of the public triumphal parade of the social sciences, which, after the triumph of American armaments, also touched ground in the universities of Western Europe and in considerable portions of the Third World.

The "Dialectic of Enlightenment" cannot be understood without taking this experience into account. It could be called an "American experience," which also reappeared in Adorno's late essay on his scientific experiences in America. It is deeply rooted in the American situation at the beginning of the 1940s, a time in which science gained a significance and meaning it had never had in the old, bourgeois society. Intellectuals were becoming so deeply implicated in the scientific domination of mankind that science, as the heir of the Enlightenment, was losing its emancipatory *raison d'être*. The triumph of science left spirit behind, a hollow skull. The critical theorists attempted to remain aware of the distinction between scientific success and the impotence of spirit, even as they tried to avoid either worshipping that success or heroizing that impotence. They then carried this contradictory experience back to Europe and communicated it to their students. New and fresh insights can be articulated when the later-born do not deny the historical experiences of the critical theorists.

The old insights can remain productive only when one preserves an awareness of the historical gap. The Cold War staved off the development of a global society, a development which was already noticeable at the end of the Second World War. The inner dynamic of the Western societies allows this development to be seen not as the realization of a radically bourgeois society, but rather as a universal collate, the result of enormous systems geared toward overproduction – and not only in the material, but also in the intellectual sphere. The paradoxical culture-industry procedure of "second-hand" or recycled spontaneity, of which Adorno once spoke, has long lost its specifically American character (if it ever had that) and has become a cultural universal principle of a *syncretic world society*, whose most advanced form is nonetheless still that of the United States. The new, conceptless society in which we all live raises the question of tradition in a new way. Beneath the ruins of shattered ideologies, under which the experiences and hopes of past generations lie buried, fragments of truth are also to be found, elements of a truth which can no longer be found in any positive form. To develop the capacity of subjects to perceive the false – that, at least, does not exceed our power.

Notes

This chapter has been translated from German by Eric Oberle

1 Herbert Marcuse to Max Horkheimer, 6 April 1946. Max Horkheimer, *Gesammelte Schriften*, vol. 17, Frankfurt: Fischer, 1996, p. 721.
2 Theodor Adorno, *Minima Moralia, Gesammelte Schriften*, vol. 4, Frankfurt: Suhrkamp, 1997, p. 221.
3 Thomas Mann in a letter to Walter Ulbricht, 1951, published in *Neue Rundschau*, vol. 2, no. 101, 1990, p. 7.
4 G.W.F. Hegel, *Vorlesungen über die Philosophie der Geschichte: Werke 12*, Frankfurt: Suhrkamp, 1970, p. 114.
5 *Ibid.*, p. 112.
6 *Ibid.*, p. 114.
7 Theodor Adorno, "Über Tradition," *Gesammelte Schriften*, vol. 10.1, Frankfurt: Suhrkamp, 1977, p. 310.
8 Eric Hobsbawm, *The Age of Extremes: A History of the World, 1914–1991*, New York: Vintage, 1994, pp. 225ff.
9 Theodor Adorno, "Scientific Experiences of a European Scholar in America," trans. Donald Fleming, in Donald Fleming and Bernard Bailyn (eds) *The Intellectual Migration: Europe and America, 1930–1960*, Cambridge, MA: Harvard University Press, 1969, p. 368.
10 Martin Jay, *The Dialectical Imagination: A History of the Frankfurt School and the Institute of Social Research 1923–1950*, Boston: Little, Brown and Co., 1973, p. 278.
11 Max Horkheimer to Leo Löwenthal, 2 October 1946. Horkheimer, *Gesammelte Schriften*, p. 761.
12 For an explication of the concept of "everyday religion" using the example of the mass cultural transformation of Auschwitz into the "artifact Holocaust," see Detlev Claussen, *Grenzen der Aufklärung: Die gesellschaftliche Genese des modernen Antisemitismus*, Frankfurt: Fischer, 1994, pp. 20ff.
13 Theodor Adorno, *Minima Moralia*, p. 116.
14 See Herbert Marcuse, *Feindanalysen: Studien Über die Deutschen*, ed. Peter-Erwin Jansen, Lüneberg: Zu Klampen, 1998.
15 Max Horkheimer to Leo Löwenthal, 24 September 1946. Horkheimer, *Gesammelte Schriften*, p. 759.

3

HEIDEGGER AND MARCUSE
The Catastrophe and Redemption of Technology

Andrew Feenberg

> The fully enlightened earth radiates disaster triumphant.
> Max Horkheimer and Theodor Adorno, *Dialectic of Enlightenment*

We are several hundred years into the project of Enlightenment, initiated in the eighteenth century by thinkers who believed in progress. We are the heirs of that project, which freed science and technology for the adventure of modernity. This has made all the difference. No doubt human nature remains the same as always, but the means at our disposal are now much more powerful than in the past. Quantity has changed into quality as innovations alter the basic parameters of human action. New dilemmas emerge in a society reconstructed around these new technical means.

Two philosophers have reflected most deeply on this situation. Martin Heidegger invites us to study technology as the core phenomenon of modern life. Where most philosophers either celebrate technical progress or worry about its unintended consequences, he identifies the culture of modernity with the spirit of technology. The limits and aporia of technology give rise to general catastrophe. Heidegger's student, Herbert Marcuse, reformulated the philosophy of technology in the framework of a radical social theory and projected solutions to the problems Heidegger identified. For Marcuse, technology is still in evolution; it is not a fixed destiny as it is for Heidegger. The promise of technology remains to be fulfilled in a future stage of that evolution.

Together, these two philosophers offer the deepest insight into the catastrophe of Enlightenment and the possibilities of redemption. This is a paper about their thought and its continuing relevance. However, I should explain at the outset that my interest is not primarily historical but philosophical. I hope to show how the thought of Heidegger and Marcuse can serve in contemporary debates about technology and modernity.

The argument of this paper is framed by the distinction between the Greek notion of *techne* and the modern idea of technology.[1] *Techne* describes the traditional value-charged craft practice of all pre-modern societies. Craftsmen serve functional needs while also conforming to the broader ethical and aesthetic values of their society. By contrast, modern technology has freed itself in large measure from the valuative commitments of its society. Where the craftsman of the past built his society in making the product of his craft, modern technology destroys its social world to the extent of its technological success. The modern world is a place of total mobilization for ends that remain obscure. It is the apparent "value freedom" or "neutrality" of technology which Heidegger and Marcuse identify as the source of the uniqueness and the tragedy of modernity.

Heidegger's approach is based on a specific interpretation of this contrast between ancient *techne* and modern technology. In ancient Greece, craft served to bring out the supposedly objective meanings, or "forms," of its products and the materials with which it worked. The Greeks lived in a world of self-sustaining things confronting human beings with a rich variety of useful potentialities awaiting realization through skillful manipulation. Artistic practice resembles craft and belongs to this Greek *techne* as well. By contrast, modern technology dominates nature and extracts and stores its powers for later use. Technology organizes vast systems of mutually dependent components in which human beings serve alongside devices. Nothing any longer has intrinsic qualities that can provide the basis of technical or artistic creation. Everything has become a raw material in a process that transcends it.

Heidegger's philosophy of technology is a puzzling combination of romantic nostalgia for this idealized image of antiquity and deep insight into modernity.[2] His originality lies in treating technique not merely as a functional means, but as a mode of "revealing" through which a "world" is shaped. "World" in Heidegger refers not to the sum of existent things but to an ordered and meaningful structure of experience. Such structures depend on basic practices characterizing societies and whole historical eras. These constitute an "opening" in which "Being" is revealed, that is to say, in which experience takes place. The "world" in this sense is neither an independent reality nor a human construction. Rather, human being and Being interact in a mysterious dialectic of activity and receptivity which occupies the place in Heidegger's thought usually filled by notions such as consciousness, perception, or culture. It is in this context that we are to understand Heidegger's claim that different technical practices reflect different "worlds."

Heidegger's essay, "The Question Concerning Technology," is one of the founding texts of philosophy of technology. It is as difficult as it is important. Some of the difficulty is due to Heidegger's innovative terminology. He believes that modern languages have been colonized by the technological mindset. To avoid prejudging the answer to the "question," he therefore introduces a meta-language freed from the tell-tale marks of modernity. This is supposed to make possible an unprejudiced analysis and comparison of different eras in the history of technical making.

Other difficulties arise from Heidegger's treatment of the concept of essence, which plays three related roles in the essay.[3] First, Heidegger assures us that "the essence of technology is by no means anything technological," a puzzling statement on the face of it.[4] Secondly, pre-modern craft is said to actualize the essence (*eidos*) of its objects.[5] Thirdly, the "saving power" of technology, discussed at the end of the essay, is somehow related to the loss of essence in modern times.[6] Unraveling these difficulties suggests an original interpretation of Heidegger's philosophy of technology.

Why does Heidegger deny that the essence of technology is technological? With this provocative statement he distinguishes an instrumental account of technology from an ontological account. The former concerns the function of technology in fulfilling human desires, while the latter focuses on the role of the technological spirit in structuring a world shaped through and through by the exigencies of planning and control. The instrumental account is not wrong, but it is internal to modernity and cannot explain why its promise has gone awry. Only an ontological account illuminates the nature of modernity and its catastrophic outcome.

The ontological account of technology is not really about technology in the usual sense of the term, that is to say, devices and their uses. Rather, it is a chapter in the history of Being. In pre-modern times, the world consisted in independent things, Aristotelian substances, each with a unique essence. These are the things that enter the process of craft production as form and material for human actions that actualize slumbering potentials objectively present in the things themselves. But the modern technological "revealing" sweeps all this away and leaves only a collection of fungible stuff available for human ordering in arbitrary patterns. The danger of technology is not so much its threat to human survival as the incorporation of human beings themselves into this "enframing" as mere raw materials alongside things. Lost in this leveling is not just human dignity, but also awareness of the unique role of the human being as the site of experience, the locus of world-shaping encounters with Being.

Despite Heidegger's apparent nostalgia for the pre-modern past, he never suggests a return to a naïve acceptance of objective essences.[7] Instead, he looks forward to a new era in which new gods will enable human beings to reclaim their place in a world no longer shrouded in a technological order. This advance he attributes in part to technology itself, which is supposed to harbor a "saving power" that may someday serve as the catalyst for a new revealing.

In what does this saving power consist? Again, the text is obscure. I conjecture that it is the very deconstruction of essences that promises deliverance from technology. The concept of essence, Heidegger argues, refers to what is permanent and enduring. But just insofar as essences are dissolved in the acid of modernity, the role of the human being in "revealing" the world comes to the fore. It is not nature alone, *physis*, which reveals Being; human being too is involved. The belongingness of human being and Being in the making of worlds is the only constant that remains, and recognition of this fact is finally possible in modern times. Indeed, while shrouding Being in the technological enframing, modernity also contains the "other possibility...that [man] might experience as his essence his needed belonging to revealing."[8] Heidegger's own philosophy is this recognition. Thus the outlines of another modernity take shape, a modernity based on a new concept of essence as coming into being, the revelation of what is.

Unfortunately, the nature of this new era remains completely obscure. Heidegger neither describes it nor prescribes a path to reach it. This abstention has been interpreted by some readers as a sign of Heidegger's profundity, while others have dismissed his blurry vision as a dangerous mystification. I would like to try a different approach, a kind of immanent critique and synthesis of Heidegger's reflections on technique. He would no doubt have rejected my interpretation, but it bridges the gap between his thought and that of his student, Marcuse, who also entertained an apocalyptic vision of a post-technological era but went beyond his teacher in sketching a hopeful future. The point of this exercise is to show that implicit in Heidegger's own theory are the elements of a more concrete critique of technology and projection of its promise than he himself developed. Freely interpreted, Heidegger thus remains an interesting source for contemporary philosophy of technology.

Let me begin this (no doubt blasphemous) reconstruction of Heidegger's position by abstracting from the explicit historical narrative in which he situates technique in order to unfold an implicit narrative that unifies his text. From that angle, his story looks like this. The ancients understood the importance of Being as the source of meaning, and the moderns the role of human being in its essential activity. But each age misunderstood its own deepest principle. The ancients confounded Being with the essences of particular beings. The moderns confused the essential role of humanity in the process of revealing with technical command of nature. Stripped of these misunderstandings and adequately comprehended, this previous history opens us to what Heidegger claims is "a more original revealing, and hence...the call of a more primal truth."[9] "The question concerning technology" thus culminates in a kind of post-historical totality, a synthesis of ancient and modern through self-consciousness.

But this is a familiar figure of thought that goes back to Hegel: the "end of history" as history aware of itself. The young Marx repeats this figure in the notion of communism as a "dream" from which the world need only awaken to possess its reality. The implicit structuring of Heidegger's essay around the figure of self-consciousness suggests a way of reading Heidegger against the grain of his own self-understanding.

Most readers who are not confirmed Heideggerians are bothered by the arbitrariness of his version of history and the thinness of his response to the challenge of technology. At most, Heidegger's historical examples, such as the Greek chalice or the dam on the Rhine, are symbols of his ontological points. But this fact raises questions about the ontology: If it cannot be defended on historical grounds, is it believable at all? And furthermore, what are we to make of Heidegger's apparent indifference to the very real threat of actual technology once the ontological danger is faced by a salutary change in attitude?

In fact the sharp division between ontological eras Heidegger describes is not accurately reflected in an equally sharp division between historical eras. Delineated most abstractly, his contrast between ancient craft and modern technology rests on a difference in emphasis between receptivity and activity in technical practice. Ancient craft receives and welcomes the self-manifesting product. The chalice brings itself into being according to its time-honored form through the mediation of the craftsman. Modern technology actively levels down and orders its raw materials in systems. Plans and projects devised by the technologist are imposed on the world, as the Rhine is dammed to generate electricity.

However, this difference is only one of emphasis: all technical practice involves both receptive and active moments. Craft actively "gathers" the idea and material of its product, and technology receives its call to order the world from Being. These are the subordinate moments in the dialectic of receptivity and activity. These subordinate moments recognize the creative dimension of craft, which requires skill and effort to realize an ideal form the craftsman does not himself invent in a material he has not made. Similarly, the modern technologist willfully dominates his projects and materials far more thoroughly than the craftsman ever did. But he does not dominate his own commitment to domination, which is his way of being in the world and thus a function of Being rather than of will.[10] So far Heidegger.

Once again the historically informed reader is likely to be dissatisfied with this analysis. Notice the sketchiness of Heidegger's description of the subordinate moment in each era. It is hardly plausible to confine the active dimension of craft to gathering and the receptive dimension of technology to the call of Being. In fact many technical activities in ancient times, such as mining, look a lot like modern technology, if on a smaller scale. And the creative moment of modern technology looks a lot like craft activity, if in such thoroughly modern contexts as the Internet.

This fairly obvious point suggests a less obvious one. Rather than separating the attributes of pre-modern craft and modern technology as Heidegger does, let us combine them in a richer description of technical action. This description would locate the attributes he identifies with craft alongside the attributes of modern technology as two complementary dimensions of technique in all historical eras. Emphases among these dimensions may shift, accounting for epochal changes in technology from one era to another, but only a theory taking all aspects of technical practice into account can make sense of the actual history. And only such a theory can explain how a more self-conscious relation to technology can result in beneficial changes in technology itself and not merely in the subjective attitude toward it.

I have developed such an account in what I call the "instrumentalization theory" of technology.[11] This theory is anticipated by the overall structure of Heidegger's essay, if not by his actual argument. Let me offer one example of the kind of transformation that can be operated on Heidegger's discourse with fruitful results.

Heidegger describes modern technology as decontextualizing and reducing its objects to raw materials and system components. In this it supposedly differs from the *techne* of the ancient craftsman. The craftsman is described as gathering the ethical and aesthetic considerations which grant the craft object a meaning and integrate it into society. But in the real world of technical practice, these attributes of technique are complementary rather than characterizing different eras. Heidegger does not tell us how the materials with which the craftsman works are supplied, but surely that involves processes of decontextualization and reduction such as are involved in mining the silver for the chalice he offers as an example. Similarly, he does not seem to be aware that the decontextualized and reduced materials of modern technology are reconstructed in accordance with ethical and aesthetic norms to conform to social requirements, but this too is surely an essential part of technical making in every era, including our own. Combining the two descriptions, we conclude that decontextualizing and reducing on the one hand, and ethical and aesthetic mediation on the other, characterize all technical making. On this basis we can achieve a more adequate understanding of both craft and modern technology.

But this is not just an analytic problem in technology studies. The modern "constitution," as Latour calls it, conforms with Heidegger's truncated vision of technology in treating valuative mediations as extrinsic to a purified objectivity, more or less equivalent to the technical sphere.[12] This is what it means to claim that technology is value-free. Although we can show that this supposed value-freedom is at least partially illusory, it continues to have real significance in the world. As Heidegger and Marcuse argue, modern technology is in fact "free" with respect to many traditional values and humane considerations, but it is not therefore merely instrumental. Or rather, insofar as through it instrumentality characterizes the general relation to reality, it carries a particular world in itself, a world in which control and domination are the highest values. Where it differs most fundamentally from ancient *techne* is in its ignorance of its own value-ladenness. A different self-understanding would open up possibilities of radical technological reform.

The attitude toward this prospect is the most important point on which Heidegger's position contrasts with that of his student, Herbert Marcuse. There is a clear similarity between their critiques of modern technology, but not in their politics. After Heidegger's Nazi phase, he seems to have withdrawn completely and awaited a spiritual renewal. Marcuse was a Marxist of sorts, even while studying with Heidegger, and for him politics was a means of radical civilizational transformation. Given this fundamental difference between them, just how profoundly was Marcuse influenced by Heidegger? This is a difficult question because political antagonism led to the suppression of references to Heidegger in Marcuse's later work, with the exception of some very critical remarks in interviews and a single quotation in *One-Dimensional Man*.[13] Nevertheless, I will argue that there is a deep connection between these two thinkers. While he is not a crypto-Heideggerian, Marcuse is indeed addressing questions posed by Heidegger and offering an alternative solution. That solution involves the transformation of modern technology into a new *techne*. The modern *techne* would once again incorporate ethics and aesthetics in its structure and reveal a meaningful world rather than a heap of raw materials.

Marcuse's career as a philosopher begins with articles that attempt a synthesis of Heidegger and a Marxism strongly influenced by Lukács' early writings. But Marcuse is already discontent with what he perceives as the abstractness and ahistoricism of *Being and Time*.[14] For Marcuse, political positions are not mere opinions that philosophy can ignore, but modes of being in the world. Authenticity is not the Heideggerian return of the individual to himself from a state of alienation in the crowd, but must reflect the social character of existence, the fact that the world is a shared creation. Marcuse's early existential Marxism thus culminates in a call for a philosophy that unifies theory and practice in a critical encounter with its time and the issues of the day.[15]

This existential politics once adopted remains integral to Marcuse's thought for the remainder of his long career. The structure of the world, in something close to Heidegger's sense, is at stake in all serious political struggle. But Heidegger's terminology – categories such as existence, *Dasein*, authenticity – quickly drop by the wayside. Instead of developing an existential analytic of political engagement along Heideggerian lines as he first proposed, Marcuse turns to Marx and Freud. Under the influence of the Frankfurt School, which he joins between the wars, Marcuse develops the notions of technological rationality, one-dimensionality, and a historicized version of instinct theory that offer sociological and psychological alternatives to Heidegger, who disappears as a reference. But as we will see, vestiges of Heidegger's ontology persist in the background.

The most important of these vestiges shows up in Marcuse's theory of the two "dimensions" of society. Although his presentation of this concept in *One-Dimensional Man* references many sources other than Heidegger, on examination it reveals a remarkable resemblance to the argument of "The Question Concerning Technology." In fact Marcuse describes a sort of "history of Being" that parallels Heidegger's account in his famous essay.

Marcuse notes that for the Greeks truth was not merely propositional, but involved the disclosure of being. Truth and falsehood thus apply in the first instance to things before applying to statements. A "true" thing is one that manifests its own essence. But since essence is never fully realized, it actually negates every contingent realization in the imperfect objects of experience. The "is" always contains an implicit reference to an "ought" it has failed to some degree to achieve. This "ought" is its potential, which is intrinsic to it and not merely projected by human wishes or desires.[16]

The similarity between this description of the Greek concept of truth and Heidegger's interpretation of ancient craft is obvious. However, in contrast to Heidegger, Marcuse appears to have generalized the implicit normative structure of craft to being as a whole. Of course, neither Heidegger nor Marcuse suggest a return to the objective essences of the Greeks. But they do regard Greece as an emblem of the lost totality they project into the future in one form or another. For Heidegger, the importance of Greek essentialism lies in the recognition of Being as a source of meaning beyond human will. Marcuse draws a related conclusion with very different political implications. Whatever the ultimate validity of ancient metaphysics, it maintains the tension between the two dimensions of being – essence and existence, the ideal and the real. It thereby preserves the truth of critical reason, the notion that what is is fraught with tension between its empirical reality and its potentialities.

By contrast, Marcuse argues, modern technological rationality liquidates all reference to essence and potentiality. The empirically observed thing is the only reality. And just because it is wholly defined by its empirical appearance, the thing can be analytically dissected into various qualities and quantities and absorbed into a technical system that submits it to alien ends. Things no longer have intrinsic potentialities transcending their given form, but are simply there, unresistingly available for human use.[17] Means and ends, realities and norms, belong to separate realms, the one objective, the other subjective.

Nineteenth-century positivism glorified the one, while romanticism exalted the other. But in the twentieth century the subjective world no longer escapes operationalization. It too is brought under control through mass communications, management techniques, and psychological manipulation. Human beings are incorporated into the system as just one more item among the fungible stuff that makes up the social apparatus. A one-dimensional world emerges in which critical reason is easily dismissed as unmotivated neurotic discontent. Indeed, a few marginal critics may even be functional for the system, proving the full extent of its liberalism by their ineffective complaints.

So far, Marcuse's theory recapitulates Heidegger's contrast of ancient *techne*, based on the realization of essential potentialities, and modern technology, which "enframes" nature and society in a rationality of calculation and control. It is in their solutions that the difference between them appears. For Heidegger, philosophy can only reflect on the catastrophe of modernity, but Marcuse goes beyond earnest contemplation of the present to project a concrete utopia that can redeem Enlightenment. Despite the enframing, critical reason is still capable of formulating transcending demands for a better society.

But Marcuse has accepted enough of Heidegger to make this positive turn extremely problematic. A redeemed technology would respect the potentialities of things and recognize the creative human role in the shaping of worlds. These claims correspond roughly to Heidegger's notion of a new era in which Being and human being stand in a self-conscious balance. But for Marcuse, respect for things requires more than a change in attitude; it would also have to transform the bad technological practices of modernity.[18] Marcuse's new *techne* would enhance life rather than inventing new means of destruction. It would be environmentally aware and treat nature with respect.[19] Recognition of humanity's place in the order of revealing requires valorizing the sensibility and imagination through which the potentialities of things are manifested. A receptive – Marcuse calls it a "feminist" – subjectivity would animate the new *techne*, replacing the aggressive subject of technological rationality.[20] Can we make sense of these hopeful projections?

The core of the problem is once again the concept of essence. Like Heidegger, Marcuse dismisses any return to Greek metaphysics. But unlike Heidegger, he refuses to reduce all essential thinking to the contemplation of the process of revealing. Instead, he seeks to reconstruct the concept of essence historically. This involves him in astonishing encounters with Hegel, Freud, and the artistic avant-garde of the early twentieth century.

Hegel's dialectic is in fact an attempt to achieve the very reconstruction of essence Marcuse requires. Hegel's *Logic* dissolves the traditional distinction between essence and appearance in the dynamics of their relation. Things do not have fixed essences separate from their manifestations because things are not themselves stable and fixed. Rather, they belong to a field of interactions which establishes their inner coherence and their boundaries. These interactions are a source of tensions which drive things forward toward their developmental potentialities. For Hegel, potentialities are inscribed in things but do not constitute them as independent substances, as Aristotle believed. Instead, something in the constellation of their present connections gives a direction to their development. But what is this something? Why is "development" development rather than mere random change?

This question, so far as it concerns Hegel, is usually answered by reference to the "Absolute," which is supposed to be the end toward which all things tend. This is a theological interpretation of Hegel of no conceivable use to Marcuse. Once again I see a connection to Heidegger in Marcuse's innovative appropriation of Hegel for a radically future-oriented ontology. Heidegger's *Being and Time* describes *Dasein*, human being, as fundamentally engaged with the question of its own being. This question cannot be answered by reference to objective facts or metaphysical notions of human nature, but must be resolved through choices and actions in the world. Heidegger's existential account of the human substitutes time and movement for the atemporal essences that haunted philosophical speculation from Plato onward, hence the title of his book.

Marcuse's first book on Hegel was written as a doctoral dissertation for Heidegger.[21] In it, Marcuse refers to Hegel's concept of life, obscured in the *Logic* by the emphasis on the Absolute. Life in Hegel's early work is a process of movement, negating and accommodating an environment. The choice of life as a fundamental ontological theme makes sense of the emphasis on interconnectedness and process in the dialectics of development. The life process has a direction: life seeks to preserve and further itself. Yet it is not confined by a predetermined end but invents its future as it moves. This is of course eminently true of the life process of modern human beings and their society. In Marcuse's reading, Hegelian life, like Heideggerian *Dasein*, discovers its meaning ahead of itself as a conditioned choice, not behind as a determining cause. It is negative, not positive.

The concept of life advances Marcuse toward his goal of reconstructing the concept of essence, but like Heidegger's conception of Dasein, it remains too abstract to specify a politics. The gap is filled later, after he joins the Frankfurt School, by a radically historicized version of the Freudian instinct theory. The link between Marcuse's early Hegel and later Freud interpretations appears implicitly in *Eros and Civilization*.[22] The emphasis on life in both is not without significance. Marcuse appears to recast the Hegelian idea of life in terms of Freud's metapsychology. With Freud, Marcuse describes the affirmation of life in peace and reconciliation as rooted in a libidinal attachment to the world, a sort of generalized erotics. The death instinct is mobilized in the struggle for survival and takes exaggerated forms in competition, violence, and aggression. The balance between the instincts is historically relative. The great wealth of modern societies could tip that balance in favor of life if obsolete institutions and the associated character structures were transformed.

Marcuse is enough of a Marxist to believe that the affirmation of life cannot remain an attitude but must be incorporated into the material base, and that base is now technological. But modern scientific-technical rationality no longer makes any distinction between essential potentialities and accidental or destructive dimensions of objects. How can we revive this distinction today without regressing to the metaphysical notion of atemporal essences?

Marcuse does not hesitate to turn to an unscientific source for an answer to this question. That source is the aesthetic sensibility and imagination overflowing the boundaries of conventional art in accordance with the most ambitious manifestoes of the artistic avant-garde of the early twentieth century. Under the sign of aesthetic discrimination, the affirmation of life guides technical practice toward the choice of peace and harmony in the order of nature and human affairs.[23] There is a receptive aspect to this process: the imagination does not merely create its objects *ex nihilo* but responds to the demands of nature, of what lies at the limit of human power.[24] Specific possibilities which contribute to the affirmation of life constitute the modern equivalent of the essential, and call forth the technologies appropriate to their realization.[25] The submission of technology to these "essences" gradually reshapes it into an instrument of liberation, suited to a free society. Technology comes to resemble *techne*, but in a modern context where judgments are based not on metaphysical assumptions but on human experience.

Marcuse projects a possible evolution of modern technology by which it would internalize the ethical and aesthetic dimensions it has increasingly ignored in modern times. This projection presupposes the inherent compatibility of technical practice and ethical and aesthetic practice. As we have seen, Heidegger's sharp distinction of ancient craft from modern technology excludes such a reconciliation of the realms of practice. But the free reformulation of his position sketched previously opens the door to a solution such as Marcuse's and can be applied to concretizing it further. And, in fact, we can find evidence of the viability of such a solution in various fields of technical endeavor such as medicine and architecture, which have never been completely "modernized" on the "value-free" pattern both Heidegger and Marcuse deplore.

As Marcuse sees it, the demystification and critique of this supposed "value-freedom" is the theoretical preliminary to the reinvention of technology. Technology must appear as a civilizational project, and not as an expression of pure rationality, in order to be brought under the aegis of humane values. Implicitly in Heidegger, explicitly in Marcuse, liberation is a function of the self-consciousness of the technical subject, that is to say, we moderns. Once the question of technology is posed on these terms, it is possible to answer it in a constructive manner.

Marcuse's political resolution of the Heideggerian crisis of modernity is open to many kinds of objections. Perhaps the most damaging is the claim that reliance on aesthetics introduces rather than resolves conflict given the wide divergence of taste in modern society. Why, it may be asked, look to aesthetics, as contentious a realm of opinion as one can imagine, when a rationally grounded ethics offers a better chance of achieving consensus? Furthermore, ethics seems more directly relevant to the problems of modernity which have less to do with ugliness than with cruelty and indifference to human needs.

The implicit Heideggerian background of Marcuse's thought helps us to understand his peculiar emphasis on an aesthetic alternative to modernity as we know it. In that Heideggerian context, ethics cannot redeem modernity because the problems are not due to personal or even social decisions an ethic could inform. Rather, as the critique of technology argues, they result from the systematic ordering of individuals, nature, and society in a framework of planning and control. That framework, indifferent to intrinsic potentialities and meanings, devastates the earth and the human essence along with it. Heidegger proposes no ethical alternative. Perhaps he felt that ethics can only intervene a posteriori with warnings and limitations, but the harm lies in the most basic practices founding our way of life. To formulate the problem in terms of "values" that might be entertained by the enframed subject would simply reproduce the technological attitude. Changing those practices requires existential change in what it is to be a human being in this society, not better judgments about right and wrong. Heidegger argues that until modern times, art had the power to inspire or channel such change. At the end of "The Question Concerning Technology" he hints that it may someday recover that power.[26]

This reconstruction of the Heideggerian position strangely resembles Marx's critique of the all-encompassing market and the challenge it poses to ethical reform.[27] But Marx's confidence in a revolutionary alternative was of course not predicated on art but on the notion that the workers' pursuit of economic self-interest would transform them into individuals capable of appropriating and acting on the scientific critique of capitalism. What happens when that confidence is lost, when economic self-interest is no longer allied with critique but with conformism instead? At that point the revolutionary can turn to irrational sources of change such as nationalism or "new gods," as does Heidegger, or revise the concept of self-interest to enlarge its range beyond the economic sense it has in Marx. Marcuse exemplifies the latter alternative, which he pursues by restoring the claims of the imagination to a share in the rational comprehension of reality. This is where aesthetics comes in.

We can approach Marcuse's aesthetics from two different angles. Aesthetic radicalism has philosophical roots in Kant, Schiller, and the early Hegel. Marcuse attempts to concretize the implications of this tradition for contemporary society by relating it to such familiar concepts as "quality of life," invoked by thoughtful critics of consumerism and the protest movements of the 1960s and 1970s. There is an extraordinary tension between these two aspects of the Marcusean aesthetic. His willingness to work with that tension may appear either heroic or foolish from a contemporary perspective. I prefer to think of it as a promissory note for a renewal of radical critique, a premature response to the dilemmas of technological advance.

The category of aesthetics refers us at one and the same time to beauty and to the sensibility, the "aesthetic" in something close to Kant's sense of the term. But for Marcuse, unlike for Kant, the aesthetic is historical, reflecting the specific qualities of perception that can be actualized at a given stage in human development. What people "feel" in their encounter with the real is conditioned by what they "are" in their historical moment. This is not a matter of opinion or taste in the usual sense, but a deeper connection to forces in reality that resonate in the human psyche and pattern experience in one or another coherent form. The shape our world takes, what is foregrounded as significant and what backgrounded as unimportant, is an aesthetic matter in this historically informed sense.

In the present, the aesthetic critique is contentious, to be sure, and this is often considered an essential consequence of the freedom and diversity accompanying modernity. If that were true, one would have to seek consensus at the level of pure procedure, a level so abstract as to be largely irrelevant to the design of technology. Marcuse is after something much more concrete, not a vision of pure right but a substantive alternative to the existing society. He charges that the principal source of dissensus is the intense struggle of the established system to contain tendencies toward radical change evoked by its very success in "delivering the goods." Reducing the level of competition, aggression, and social misery is now an objective possibility, but one which contradicts the basic requirements of the system. Marcuse is nevertheless convinced that despite the lack of consensus, there is a definite measure of progress reflecting the conditions for enhancing life. His writings aim to transform our sensibility in accordance with this vision, to foster a pattern of perception in which the absurdities and inhumanities of our society are sharply focused rather than relegated to the background and ignored. These writings are, in short, aesthetic interventions with political intent.

Marcuse's faith in the significance of philosophical discussion is not to be confused with optimism about the ultimate triumph of life over death. The courage to affirm one's own individuality and ideas against received opinion is not a prediction of the future. In the last analysis, the difference between Heidegger and Marcuse lies in their understanding of the nature of this authentic self-affirmation. While Heidegger conceived individuality as a response to inevitable death, Marcuse followed a radical tradition in which self-affirmation is the individual's share in the affirmation of life itself. We can only hope that it is Marcuse's faith rather than Heidegger's despair that is vindicated by history.

Notes

1 For a fuller development of this distinction, see Andrew Feenberg, "*Marcuse and the Aestheticization of Technology*," in W. Wilkerson and J. Paris (eds) *New Critical Theory: Essays on Liberation*, Paris: Rowman & Littlefield, 2001.
2 For an account of Heidegger's philosophy of technology, see Michael E. Zimmerman, *Heidegger's Confrontation with Modernity: Technology, Politics and Art*, Bloomington, IN: Indiana University Press, 1990.

3 For an interesting account of the relation between Heidegger's notion of essence and technology, see Richard Polt, "Potentiality, Power and Sway: From Aristotelian to modern Heideggerian physics?" in *Proceedings of the 35th Annual Heidegger Conference*, Forham University, 2001.
4 Heidegger, *The Question Concerning Technology and Other Essays*, New York: Harper, 1977, p. 4.
5 *Ibid.*, pp. 7, 160–1.
6 *Ibid.*, pp. 30–2.
7 *Ibid.*, p. 30.
8 *Ibid.*, p. 26; see also pp. 28–9, 40–1.
9 *Ibid.*, p. 28.
10 *Ibid.*, p. 19.
11 See Chapter 9 of Andrew Feenberg, *Questioning Technology*, London and New York: Routledge, 1999.
12 Heidegger, *The Question Concerning Technology*, p. 142.
13 See Frederick Olafson, "Heidegger's Politics: An Interview with Herbert Marcuse," in R. Pippin, A. Feenberg and C. Webel (eds) *Marcuse: Critical Theory and the Promise of Utopia*, New York: Bergin and Garvey, 1988, and Herbert Marcuse, *One-Dimensional Man*, Boston: Beacon, 1964, pp. 153–4.
14 For accounts of Marcuse's early work and his relation to Heidegger, see Douglas Kellner, *Herbert Marcuse and the Crisis of Marxism*, Berkeley and Los Angeles: University of California, 1984; Barry Katz, *Herbert Marcuse and the Art of Liberation*, London: Verso, 1982; and Charles Reitz, *Art, Alienation, and the Humanities: A Critical Engagement with Herbert Marcuse*, Albany, NY: SUNY University Press, 2000.
15 Herbert Marcuse *Schriften*, vol. 1, Frankfurt: Suhrkamp, 1978, pp. 398ff.
16 Marcuse, *One-Dimensional Man*, pp. 124–5, 133–4.
17 *Ibid.*, pp. 146–8.
18 *Ibid.*, p. 231.
19 Herbert Marcuse, "Ecology and the Critique of Modern Society," *Capitalism, Nature, Socialism*, vol. 3, no. 11, 1992.
20 Herbert Marcuse, "Marxism and Feminism," *Women's Studies* vol. 2, no. 3, 1974.
21 Herbert Marcuse, *Hegel's Ontology and the Theory of Historicity*, trans. Seyla Benhabib, Cambridge, MA: MIT Press, 1987.
22 See Chapter 5 of Herbert Marcuse, *Eros and Civilization*, Boston: Beacon, 1966.
23 Herbert Marcuse, *An Essay on Liberation,* Boston: Beacon, 1969, p. 24.
24 Herbert Marcuse, *Counter-Revolution and Revolt*, Boston: Beacon, 1972, pp. 67–9.
25 Marcuse, *One-Dimensional Man*, pp. 239–40.
26 Heidegger, *The Question Concerning Technology*, pp. 34–5.
27 Gianni Vattimo, *The End of Modernity,* trans. J.R. Snyder, Baltimore: Johns Hopkins, 1985, pp. 25–7.

4

MARCUSE AND THE QUEST FOR RADICAL SUBJECTIVITY

Douglas Kellner

The past decades have witnessed a relentless philosophical assault on the concept of the subject, once the alpha and omega of modern philosophy. Materialists have decried the idealist and essentialist dimensions of the traditional concept of the subject in its various Cartesian, Kantian, and other philosophical forms. More recently, post-structuralist and postmodern theorists have attacked the universalizing pretensions of subject discourse, its positing of a (false) unity, its assuming a centered and grounded status as a linchpin for philosophical systems or knowledge-claims, and its transparent self-certainty from Descartes' *cogito* to Husserl's phenomenology. Following Nietzsche, post-structuralists have seen the subject as an effect of language, constructed in accord with the forms of grammar (i.e. subject/predicate) and existing linguistic systems, or, with Deleuze, have privileged the flux and flow of bodily experience over more idealist conceptions of consciousness and the self.

For traditional philosophy, the subject was unitary, ideal, universal, self-grounded, asexual, and the foundation for knowledge and philosophy, while for the post-structuralist and postmodern critique the human being is corporeal, gendered, social, fractured, and historical, with subjectivity radically decentered as an effect of language, society, culture, and history. Yet if the construction of the subject in language, the social, and nature is the key mark of a post-structuralist or postmodern conception of subjectivity, then the Frankfurt School analyses are not antithetical to such conceptions. The entire tradition of critical theory – which draws on Hegel, Marx, Nietzsche, Freud, and Weber – posits the historical and social construction of the individual, and members of this tradition can be read as providing aspects of theorizing the social construction of subjectivity in language, social interaction, and culture in specific historical contexts. Habermas in particular has followed this motif and has attacked the philosophy of the subject, while proposing replacing its subject/object model with an ego-alter model that is based upon the ideal of communicative reason.[1]

In this paper, however, I want to pursue Herbert Marcuse's sharp critiques of the rationalist subject of modern philosophy to which he counterposes notions of libidinal rationality, eros, and the aesthetic-erotic dimensions of an embodied subjectivity. Marcuse is part of a historicist tradition of critical theory which rejects essentialism and sees subjectivity developing in history, in interaction with specific socio-political conditions. Following Adorno and Horkheimer and the earlier Frankfurt School tradition, Marcuse also sees dominant forms of subjectivity as oppressive and constraining, while challenging us to reconstruct subjectivity and to develop a new sensibility, qualitatively different from the normalized subjectivity of contemporary advanced industrial societies. In particular, Marcuse was engaged in a lifelong search for a revolutionary subjectivity, for a sensibility that would revolt against the existing society and attempt to create a new one.

Hence, I will argue that Marcuse and the Frankfurt School contribute important perspectives for criticizing the traditional concept of the subject and for rethinking and reconceptualizing subjectivity to develop conceptions potent enough to meet post-structuralist, postmodern, materialist, feminist, and other forms of critique. Crucially, the assault on the subject has had serious consequences, for without a robust notion of subjectivity and agency there is no refuge for individual freedom and liberation, no locus of struggle and opposition, and no agency for progressive political transformation. For these reasons, theorists from diverse camps, including feminists, multiculturalists, and post-structuralists who have had second thoughts about the all-too-hasty dissolution of the subject, have attempted to rehabilitate constructive notions of subjectivity and agency, in the light of contemporary critique.

My argument is that Marcuse anticipates the post-structuralist critique of the subject, that these critiques suggest that the traditional concept of the subject contains too much philosophical and political baggage, and that we need a reconstructed notion of subjectivity, which Marcuse and the Frankfurt School helped initiate and enabled us to further develop. In drawing on Nietzsche, Freud, and aesthetic modernism, Marcuse posits a bodily, erotic, gendered, social, and aestheticized subjectivity that overcomes mind–body dualism, avoids idealist and rationalist essentialism, and is constructed in a specific social milieu. Moreover, Marcusean subjectivity is challenged to reconstruct itself and emancipate itself from limited and oppressive forms and to pursue the project of cultivating a new sensibility. In delineating Marcuse's reconstruction of subjectivity, I will first offer a re-reading of *Eros and Civilization*[2] to demonstrate how it anticipates the post-structuralist critique of the subject and offers an alternative conception of subjectivity. Then I pursue some of the contributions to rethinking subjectivity in Marcuse's later writings, focusing on his notion of the new sensibility and aesthetic education. At stake is developing a reconstructed Marcusean theory of subjectivity which emphasizes the need for a transformation of the affective dimension, sensibility, and our very notion of subjectivity to help create new conceptions of subjectivity and to provide conceptions of the subjective conditions for radical social change and of agency in order to promote individual and social transformation.

Re-reading *Eros and Civilization*

In *Eros and Civilization*, Marcuse draws on Freud to depict the social construction of subjectivity in the dramatic clash between the pleasure principle and the reality principle. For Freud, the instincts are originally governed by the pleasure principle: they aim solely at "gaining pleasure; from any operation which might arouse unpleasantness ('pain') mental activity draws back."[3] From early on, however, the pleasure principle comes into conflict with a harsh environment, and after a series of disciplinary experiences, "the individual comes to the traumatic realization that full and painless gratification of his needs is impossible."[4] Under the tutelage of the reality principle, the person learns what is useful and approved behavior, and what is harmful and forbidden. In this way, one develops one's rational faculties, becoming "a conscious, thinking *subject*, geared to a rationality which is imposed on him from outside."[5]

For Marcuse, then, rationality is a social construct and subjectivity is a product of social experience. Thus, like Foucault, Marcuse sees subjectivity not as a natural and metaphysical substance, pre-existing its social gestation, but as a product of societal normalization, whereby the individual is subjected to rationalizing forms of thought and behavior. According to Marcuse's conception, the reality principle enforces the totality of society's requirements, norms, and prohibitions that are imposed upon the individual from "outside." This process constitutes for him a domination of the individual by society which shapes thought and behavior, desires and needs, language and consciousness. In Marcuse's words, "neither his desires nor his alteration of reality are henceforth his own: they are now 'organized' by his society. And this 'organization' represses and transsubstantiates his original instinctual needs."[6]

Marcuse employs Freud's theory to produce an account of how society comes to dominate the individual, how social control is internalized, and how conformity ensues. He concludes that "Freud's individual psychology is in its very essence social psychology,"[7] and he repeatedly emphasizes that Freud's psychological categories are historical and political in nature. Hence, Marcuse boldly fleshes out the "political and sociological substance of Freud's theory" to develop what I call a *critical theory of socialization*. Whereas most theories of socialization stress its humanizing aspects by claiming that socialization makes individuals more "human" – and thus legitimate dominant social institutions and practices – Freud exposes the repressive content of Western civilization and the heavy price paid for its "progress." Although industrialization has resulted in material progress, Freud's analysis of the instinctual renunciations and unhappiness it has produced raises the question of whether our form of civilization is worth the suffering and misery.[8] In Marcuse's view, Freud's account of civilization and its discontents puts in question the whole ideology of progress, productivity, and the work ethic, as well as religion and morality, by "showing up the repressive content of the highest values and achievements of culture."[9]

Thus, Marcuse, like Foucault, stresses the social construction of subjectivity and the ways that subjectification (i.e. the ways of producing a socially submissive subject) are involved in a process of domination. But whereas Foucault and many post-structuralists call for resistance to domination, they often have no theoretical resources to construct a notion of agency that would efficaciously resist repression and domination.[10] For Marcuse, however, there is a "hidden trend in psychoanalysis" which discloses those aspects of human nature that oppose the dominant ethic of labor and renunciation, while upholding "the tabooed aspirations of humanity": the demands of the pleasure principle for gratification and absence of restraint.[11] He argues that Freud's instinct theory contains a "depth dimension" which suggests that our instincts strive for a condition in which freedom and happiness converge, in which we fulfill our needs and strive to overcome repression and domination. For Marcuse, *memory* contains images of gratification and can play a cognitive and therapeutic role in mental life: "Its truth value lies in the specific function of memory to preserve promises and potentialities which are betrayed and even outlawed by the mature, civilized individual, but which had once been fulfilled in the dim past and which are never entirely forgotten."[12]

Marcuse subtly reformulates the therapeutic role of memory stressed in psychoanalysis. In Freud's theory, the suppression of memory takes place through the repression of unpleasant or traumatic experiences, which are usually concerned with sexuality or aggression; the task of psychoanalysis is to free the patient from the burden of repressed, traumatic memories – whose repression often produces neurosis – by providing understanding and insight that would enable the individual to work through painful experiences of the past and to dissolve neurotic behavior. Although Marcuse preserves the psychoanalytic linkage between forgetting and repression, he stresses the liberating potentialities of memory and recollection of pleasurable or euphoric experiences, as well as the unpleasant or traumatic experiences stressed by Freud.

In his reconstruction of Freud, Marcuse suggests that remembrance of past experiences of freedom and happiness could put into question the painful performances of alienated labor and manifold oppressions of everyday life. These memories are embedded in individual experiences of a happier past and historical conditions that offered more and better freedom, gratification, and happiness. Marcuse will link these emancipatory dimensions of memory with phantasy and will argue that both human beings and their cultural tradition contain resources that can be mobilized against suffering and oppression in the present.

Memory for Marcuse thus re-members – reconstructs – experience, going to the past to construct future images of freedom and happiness. Whereas romanticism is past-oriented, remembering the joys of nature and the past in the face of the onslaught of industrialization, Marcuse is future-oriented, looking to the past to construct a better future.[13] Marcuse's analysis implies that society trains the individual for the systematic repression of those emancipatory memories, and devalues experiences guided solely by the pleasure principle. Following Nietzsche in *On the Genealogy of Morals*,[14] Marcuse criticizes "the one-sidedness of memory-training in civilization: the faculty was chiefly directed towards remembering duties rather than pleasures; memory was linked with bad conscience, guilt and sin. Unhappiness and the threat of punishment, not happiness and the promise of freedom, linger in the memory."[15]

Marcuse claims that for Freud, "phantasy" is a crucial mode of "thought-activity" that is split off from the reality principle.[16] For Freud, phantasy "was kept free from reality-testing and remained subordinated to the pleasure principle alone. This is the act of *phantasy-making* [*das Phantasieren*], which begins already with the games of children, and later, continued as *day-dreaming*, abandons its dependence on real objects."[17] Building on this conception, Marcuse suggests that "phantasy" – in day-dreaming, dreams at night, play, and its embodiments in art – can project images of integral gratification, pleasure, and reconciliation, often denied in everyday life.

Hence, along with memory, Marcuse argues that phantasy can imagine another world and generate images of a better life by speaking the language of the pleasure principle and its demands for gratification. He stresses the importance of great art for liberation because it refuses "to accept as final the limitations imposed upon freedom and happiness by the reality principle."[18] Art for Marcuse practices the "Great Refusal," incarnating the emancipatory contents of memory, phantasy, and the imagination through producing images of happiness and a life without anxiety. In Marcuse's view, phantasies and hopes embody the eruption of desires for increased freedom and gratification. The unconscious on this account contains the memory of integral gratification experienced in the womb, in childhood, and in peak experiences during one's life. Marcuse holds that the "psychoanalytic liberation of memory" and "restoration of phantasy" provide access to experiences of happiness and freedom which are subversive of the present life. He suggests that Freud's theory of human nature, far from refuting the possibility of a non-repressive civilization, indicates that there are aspects of human nature that are striving for happiness and freedom.

In defending the claims of the pleasure principle, Marcuse believes that he is remaining true to a materialism which takes seriously material needs and their satisfaction, and the biological "depth dimension" of human nature. In his view, defense of the validity of the claims of the pleasure principle has critical-revolutionary import, in that Freud's analysis implies that the human being can only tolerate so much repression and unhappiness, and when this point is passed the individual will rebel against the conditions of repression. Freud's theory thus contains elements of an *anthropology of liberation* which analyses those aspects of human nature that furnish the potential for radical opposition to the prevailing society.

Marcuse concludes that Freud's theory contains implications that have been covered over, or neglected, and which he wishes to restore in their most provocative form. He argues that this requires a restoration of Freud's instinct theory, preserving his claims for the importance of sexuality and acknowledgment of its vital and explosive claims. Neo-Freudians who deny the primacy of sexuality have, in Marcuse's view, repressed Freud's deep insights into human sexual being by relegating sexual instincts to a secondary place in their theory.[19] Marcuse believes that Freud's theory discloses the depth and power of instinctual energies which contain untapped emancipatory potential. He describes these instinctual energies which seek pleasure and gratification as "Eros." A liberated Eros, Marcuse claims, would release energies that would not only seek sexual gratification, but would flow over into expanded human relations and more abundant creativity. The released Eros would desire, he suggests, a pleasurable aesthetic-erotic environment requiring a total restructuring of human life and the material conditions of existence.

In addition, Marcuse also accepts Freud's concept of Thanatos, the death instinct, as well as the Freudian notion of "the political economy of the instincts," in which strengthening the life instincts enables Eros to control and master Thanatos, and so to increase freedom and happiness, while diminishing aggression and destruction. Thus, surprisingly, Marcuse adopts a rather mechanistic concept of the instincts, building on Freud's biologistic energy-instinct model – which has been sharply criticized and rejected both within various circles of psychoanalytic theory as well as within critical theory (Habermas and his students) and post-structuralism. I believe, however, that one can construct a Marcusean theory of subjectivity without deploying the problematic aspects of Freud's instinct theory.

The key to Marcuse's reconstruction of the concept of subjectivity, I would suggest, is the "Philosophical Interlude" in *Eros and Civilization*, in which he develops a critical analysis of the presuppositions of Western rationality and its concept of the philosophical subject. Marcuse claims that the prevalent reality principle of Western civilization presupposes an antagonism between subject and object, mind and body, reason and the passions, and the individual and society. Nature is experienced on this basis as raw material to be mastered, as an object of domination, as provocation or resistance to be overpowered.[20] The ego in Western thought is thus conceptualized as an aggressive, offensive subject, fighting and striving to conquer the resistant world. Through labor, the subject seeks continually to extend its power and control over nature. The Logos of this reality principle is, Marcuse argues, a logic of domination that finds its culmination in the reality principle of advanced industrial society, the performance principle. The performance principle is hostile to the senses and receptive faculties that strive for gratification and fulfillment. It contains a concept of repressive reason which seeks to tame instinctual drives for pleasure and enjoyment. Its values, which are the governing norms of modern societies, include:

> profitable productivity, assertiveness, efficiency, competitiveness; in other words, the Performance Principle, the rule of functional rationality discriminating against emotions, a dual morality, the "work ethic," which means for the vast majority of the population condemnation to alienated and inhuman labor, and the will to power, the display of strength, virility.[21]

This hegemonic version of the reality principle has been challenged, Marcuse argues, from the beginning of Western philosophy. Against the antagonistic struggle between subject and object, an opposing ideal of reconciliation and harmony has been formulated, in which the individual strives for fulfillment and gratification. This "Logos of gratification," Marcuse suggests, is found in Aristotle's notion of the *nous theos* and Hegel's ideal of spirit coming to rest and fruition in absolute knowledge.[22] In these philosophical conceptions, the human being is to attain a condition of reconciliation after a process of struggle, suffering, and labor, in which alienation and oppression are finally overcome. Schopenhauer advocates a similar idea of the restless, ever-striving "will" seeking peaceful Nirvana. In addition, Marcuse finds a logic of gratification and different conception of subjectivity in Nietzsche's emphasis on the body, the passions, joy, and liberation from time and guilt.[23] The values affirmed in this reality principle would be the antithesis of the repressive performance principle and its dominating subject, and would affirm

> receptivity, sensitivity, non-violence, tenderness, and so on. These characteristics appear indeed as opposites of domination and exploitation. On the primary psychological level, they would pertain to the domain of Eros, they would express the energy of the life instincts against the death instinct and destructive energy.[24]

This alternative reality principle and conception of subjectivity also finds expression in Freud's notion of the Nirvana principle, which holds that all instincts aim at rest, quiescence, and the absence of pain.[25] In addition, Marcuse draws on Schiller's conception of aesthetic education and play, arguing that in aesthetic and erotic experience, play, and fantasy, the conflict between reason and the senses would be overcome so that "reason is sensuous and sensuousness rational."[26] Operating through the play impulse, the aesthetic function would "abolish compulsion, and place man, both morally and physically in freedom." It would harmonize the feelings and affections with the ideas of reason, deprive the "laws of reason of their moral compulsion" and "reconciles them with the interest of the senses."[27]

In the language of post-structuralism, Marcuse thus envisages an embodied subjectivity in which the opposition between reason and the senses, central to the modern philosophical concept of the subject, is deconstructed. For Schiller and Marcuse, the play impulse is connected with the aesthetic function, which would mediate between the passive, receptive "sensuous impulse" and the active, creative "form impulse," thus reconciling reason and the senses. The play impulse aspires to a condition of freedom from restraint and anxiety, involving "freedom from the established reality: man is free when the 'reality loses its seriousness' and when its necessity 'becomes light.' "[28] This "freedom to play" and to create an "aesthetic reality" requires liberation of the senses and, as both Schiller and Marcuse called for, "a total revolution in the mode of perception and feeling."[29]

The resultant conception of an aestheticized and eroticized subjectivity preserves the connotation of *Sinnlichkeit* as pertaining to sensuality, receptiveness, art, and Eros, thus redeeming the body and the senses against the tyranny of repressive reason and affirming the importance of aesthetics, play, and erotic activity in human life. Hence, against the rational and domineering subject of mastery, Marcuse advances a notion of subjectivity as mediating reason and the senses, as seeking harmony and gratification. Thus, he affirms an intersubjective ideal of a libidinal subjectivity in harmonious and gratifying relations with others and, one might add, with nature itself. Instead of controlling and dominating objects, Marcusean subjectivity seeks gratifying and peaceful relations with others and with the external world.

Moreover, Marcuse proposes a new concept of reason which he describes as "libidinal rationality."[30] In this conception reason is not repressive of the senses, but acts in harmony with them, helping to find objects of gratification and to cultivate and enhance sensuality. Marcuse rejects the dominant philosophical paradigm, which sees reason as the distinctly human faculty and the senses as disorderly, animalic, and inferior. The concept of reason operative in this model, Marcuse suggests, is repressive and totalitarian and does not adequately allow for aesthetic-erotic gratification and development,[31] due to its embrace of the mind–body split. Marcuse's ideal is a form of human life in which reason becomes sensuous, protecting and enriching the life instincts, and whereby the unity of reason and the senses helps create a "sensuous order."[32] He assumes that as more restrictions are taken away from the instincts and as they freely evolve, they will seek *"lasting* gratification" and will help generate social relations that will make continual gratification possible. In this way, "Eros redefines reason in its own terms. Reasonable is what sustains the order of gratification."[33] This could make possible freer, more fulfilling human relations and could create a social order and community based on freedom, gratification, cooperation, and rational authority. Then, "repressive reason gives way to a new *rationality of gratification* in which reason and happiness converge."[34]

The New Sensibility, Emancipation, and Revolution: the Late Marcuse

Hence, against the notion of the rational, domineering subject of modern theory, Marcuse posits a subjectivity that is libidinal and embodied, evolving and developing, while striving for happiness, gratification, and harmony. Such subjectivity is always in process, is never fixed or static, and is thus a creation and goal to be achieved, and is not posited as an absolute metaphysical entity. Marcusean subjectivity is thus corporeal, gendered, oppositional, and struggles against domination, repression, and oppression, and for freedom and happiness. There is thus nothing essentialist, idealist, or metaphysical here. Instead, Marcuse's conception of subjectivity is both materialist and socially mediated, while active in cultivating the aesthetic and erotic dimensions of experience as it strives for gratification and harmonious relations with others, nature, and itself. Marcuse's radical subjectivity is also political, refusing domination and oppression, struggling against conditions which block freedom and happiness and for a freer and better world.

There is widespread agreement today that we need the discourse of subjectivity and agency for ethics, for politics, and for the positive reconstruction of self and society. Within this context, I have argued that Marcuse's perspectives on subjectivity stand up to at least some aspects of the post-structuralist and other critiques of the subject, as well as providing resources for reconstructing the concept of subjectivity in the contemporary era. It is important to note that for Marcuse, the reconstruction of subjectivity, the creation of eroticized rationality, and the development of a free creative self can only take place through practice and the transformation of social relations and activity. Marcuse argued that the existing society is organized precisely to prevent such a reconstruction of subjectivity and new social relations, prescribing instead a regime of domination, authority, repression, manipulative desublimation, and submission. Especially in *One-Dimensional Man*,[35] but throughout his work, Marcuse presents a critique of hegemonic forms of subjectivity and domination and a challenge to overcome the one-dimensional, conformist, and normalized subjectivity of the advanced technological society.

Throughout his later writings, Marcuse was vitally concerned to discover and theorize a "new sensibility," with needs, values, and aspirations that would be qualitatively different from subjectivity in one-dimensional society. To create a new subjectivity, there must be "the emergence and education of a new type of human being free from the aggressive and repressive needs and aspirations and attitudes of class society, human beings created, in solidarity and on their own initiative, their own environment, their own *Lebenswelt*, their own 'property.'"[36] Such a revolution in needs and values would help overcome a central dilemma in Marcuse's theory – sharply formulated in *One-Dimensional Man* – that continued to haunt him: "How can the administered individuals – who have made their mutilation into their own liberties and satisfactions ... liberate themselves from themselves as well as from their masters? How is it even thinkable that the vicious circle be broken?"[37]

In order to break through this vicious circle, individuals must transform their present needs, sensibility, consciousness, values, and behavior while developing a new radical subjectivity, so as to create the necessary conditions for social transformation.[38] Radical subjectivity for Marcuse practices the Great Refusal, valorized in both *Eros and Civilization* and *One-Dimensional Man*. In *Eros and Civilization*, the "Great Refusal is the protest against unnecessary repression, the struggle for the ultimate form of freedom – 'to live without anxiety.'"[39] In *One-Dimensional Man*, however, the Great Refusal is fundamentally political, a refusal of repression and injustice, a saying no, an elemental oppositional to a system of oppression, a noncompliance with the rules of a rigged game, a form of radical resistance and struggle.[40] In both cases, the Great Refusal is based on a subjectivity that is not able to tolerate injustice and that engages in resistance and opposition to all forms of domination, instinctual and political.

In the late 1960s, Marcuse argued that emancipatory needs and a "new sensibility" were developing within contemporary society. He believed that in the New Left and counter-culture there was the beginnings of "a political practice of methodical disengagement and the refusal of the Establishment aiming at a radical transvaluation of values" that was generating a new type of human being and subject.[41] The new sensibility "expresses the ascent of the life instincts over aggressiveness and guilt"[42] and contains a "negation of the needs that sustain the present system of domination and the negation of the values on which they are based."[43] Underlying the theory of the new sensibility is a concept of the active role of the senses in the constitution of experience, which rejects the Kantian and other philosophical devaluation of the senses as passive, merely receptive. For Marcuse, our senses are shaped and molded by society, yet constitute in turn our primary experience of the world and provide both imagination and reason with its material. He believes that the senses are currently socially constrained and mutilated and argues that only an emancipation of the senses and a new sensibility can produce liberating social change.[44]

Instead of the need for repressive performance and competition, the new sensibility posits the need for meaningful work, gratification, and community; instead of the need for aggression and destructive productivity, it affirms love and the preservation of the environment; and against the demands of industrialization, it asserts the need for beauty, sensuousness, and play, affirming the aesthetic and erotic components of experience. The "new sensibility" translates these values and needs into "a practice that involves a break with the familiar, the routine ways of seeing, hearing, feeling, understanding things so that the organism may become receptive to the potential forms of a non-aggressive, non-exploitative world."[45] This total refusal of the dominant societal needs, values, and institutions represents a radical break with the entirety of the society's institutions, culture, and lifestyle, and supplies prefigurations of a new culture and society.

The new sensibility would be developed, Marcuse claimed, by an aesthetic education that would cultivate imagination, fantasy, the senses, and memory. The new sensibility would combine the senses and reason, producing a "new rationality" in which reason would be bodily, erotic, and political. Far from being an irrationalist, Marcuse always argued that the senses and reason need to be mediated, that reason should be reconstructed, and that critical and dialectical thinking are an important core of the new sensibility. Marcuse maintained that aesthetic education constituted a cultivation of the senses and that theory and education were essential components of transformative social change.[46]

In his writings of the late 1960s, Marcuse believed that the new sensibility was embodied in the liberation movements of the day, the counter-culture, and the New Left (see, especially, *An Essay on Liberation*). Of course, he was disappointed that the new sensibility did not become the agent of revolutionary change that he envisaged; he was also dismayed that the New Left and counter-culture fell prey to the seductions of the consumer society, or were repressed and fragmented (see *Counterrevolution and Revolt* for a poignant account of Marcuse's failing hopes and continued attempts to theorize emancipation and radical social change). In the 1970s, however, he sought precisely the same values and subjectivity in new social movements, in particular feminism, the environmental movement, the peace movement, and various forms of grass-roots activism which came to be described as "new social movements."

In the 1974 lecture entitled "Marxism and Feminism," Marcuse notes for the first time the constitutive role of gender, while theorizing the differences between men and women in terms of his categories in *Eros and Civilization*. It is notable that his conception of the feminine is associated with the traits he ascribes to the new sensibility, while the masculine is associated with the features of the Western ego and rationality of domination that Marcuse long criticized, thus anticipating "difference feminism," which would also valorize the feminine and maternal against the masculine.[47] In this lecture, which generated significant debate, Marcuse argues that "feminine" values and qualities represent a determinate negation of the values of capitalism, patriarchy, and the performance principle. In his view, "socialism, as a qualitatively different society, must embody the antithesis, the definite negation of aggressive and repressive needs and values of capitalism as a form of male-dominated culture."[48] Furthermore,

> Formulated as the antithesis of the dominating masculine qualities, such feminine qualities would be receptivity, sensitivity, non-violence, tenderness and so on. These characteristics appear indeed as opposite of domination and exploitation. On the primary psychological level, they would pertain to the domain of Eros, they would express the energy of the life instincts, against the death instinct and destructive energy.[49]

Marcuse was, however, criticized by women within the feminist movement and others for essentializing gender difference, although he insisted the distinction was a historical product of Western society and not an essential gender difference. Women, he argued, possess a "feminine" nature qualitatively different from men because they have been frequently freed from repression in the workplace, brutality in the military, and competition in the public sphere. Hence, they developed characteristics which for Marcuse are the marks of an emancipated humanity. He summarizes the difference between aggressive masculine and capitalist values as against feminist values as the contrast between "repressive productivity" and "creative receptivity," suggesting that "increased emancipation of feminine qualities in the established society" will subvert the dominant masculine values and the capitalist performance principle.

During the same decade, Marcuse also worked with Rudolf Bahro's conception of "surplus consciousness." He argued that just as Bahro claimed that in the socialist countries a new consciousness was developing which could see the discrepancy between "what is" and "what could be" and was not satisfied with its way of life, so too was such an oppositional consciousness developing in the advanced capitalist countries.[50] "Surplus consciousness," in the Bahro–Marcuse conception, is a product of expanding education, scientific and technical development, and refinement of the forces of production and the labor process. On this account, contemporary societies are producing a higher form of consciousness and create needs that cannot be satisfied in the labor process or everyday life, producing resentment and the potential for revolt. In effect, Bahro and Marcuse are arguing that critical consciousness is produced by the very social processes of the technological society and that this subjectivity comes into conflict with existing hierarchy, waste, repression, and domination, generating the need for social change. This position maintains that existing social processes themselves are helping produce a subjectivity that demands participation and fulfillment in the labor process and socio-political life, as well as increased freedom, equality, and opportunities for advancement and development. If these needs are not satisfied, Bahro and Marcuse suggest, rebellion and social transformation will be generated.

Curiously, precisely this process happened in the socialist world in which rebellion against irrational and repressive bureaucratic social forms led to an overthrow of what Bahro termed "actually existing socialism."[51] The critiques of Marxism in the 1970s and 1980s in the increasingly hegemonic discourses of post-structuralism and postmodern theory among the radical intelligentsia, connected, I believe, with the collapse of "actually existing socialism," helped produce a rejection of Marxism, while defaming revolution as utopian and, in many cases, deconstructing concepts of oppositional subjectivity and politics. Such extreme versions of post-structuralism and postmodernism,[52] however, vitiate the project of emancipation and social reconstruction and undermine efforts to develop oppositional politics and alternative conceptions of society, culture, and subjectivity – alternatives found in the work of Herbert Marcuse, who I believe continues to provide important resources for theory and politics in the contemporary era.

The postmodern/post-structuralist conception of subjectivity, which stresses decentering, fragmentation, and flexibility, reproduces aspects of the crisis of contemporary subjectivity overwhelmed by big corporations, new technologies, seductive media culture, and the complex and contradictory forces of globalization. Many postmodern critiques of traditional notions of the subject or subjectivity thus end with fragmentation, crisis, decentering, and dispersal, which they either cynically affirm without hope of reconstruction, or valorize positively as conditions of the possibility of more flexible subjects that can in turn be rejected, reconstructed, and recreated at one's will and whim. Another possibility, however, is to call for a reconstructive concept of subjectivity and agency in the face of theoretical critique and practical fragmentation and dissipation. This is the position of Marcuse and much of critical theory, which begins by recognizing theoretical flaws in the modern concept of the (rational, unitary, ideal) subject, as well as the crisis of subjectivity in contemporary society.

Critical theory is dialectical, resisting the claims of both structure and agency to primacy, thus overcoming both determinism and idealism. Marcuse problematizes subjectivity and agency, recognizes the force of domination, and yet militates for liberation and transformation. Opposing mechanistic theories of history without agency and subjectivity, as well as idealist notions that see history as the development of humanity or subjectivity (i.e. the subject, spirituality, God, etc.), critical theory seeks to overcome unproductive dichotomies and to produce more sophisticated and transformative perspectives.

This problematization of subject and history discloses an intersection between critical theory and postmodern theory and significant differences between some of the versions. Both unveil the abstractness and mythological constitution of the subject; both reject a universal subject and the equation of the subject with metaphysical rationality. On the whole, critical theory is more reconstructive, with theorists like Adorno, Marcuse, Fromm, and Habermas offering quite different perspectives on the reconstruction of subjectivity and agency, while many postmodern theorists revel in difference and heterogeneity (Lyotard), cynically reject any possibility of reconstruction and transformation (Baudrillard), or assume neutral and/or micrological perspectives that eschew ambitious theoretical or political reconstruction (followers of Foucault, Rorty in some moods, and postmodern camp followers who don't yet see its transformative potential); other postmodern theorists, however, urge reconstruction of subjectivity and agency à la feminism and critical theory, and thus present supplementary positive reconstructive positions to critical theory.

Hence, some versions of postmodern theory reproduce liberal reformism and pluralism in their emphasis on difference, reform, and rejection of broader perspectives of social transformation. There is also a tendency for fragmentary, aleatory, and nomadic postmodern subjectivity to replicate the self-centered, competitive, yet interactive subjectivity of contemporary capitalism.[53] Yet in view of the complex and contradictory development of contemporary capitalist culture and subjectivity, the sort of critical and oppositional perspectives offered by Marcuse are needed more than ever. As in Marcuse's day, the ambivalent unity of the positive and negative, of production and destruction, continues to operate in the global restructuring of capitalism, with its technological revolution and seductions, growing discrepancies between the haves and the have-nots, and increasingly the powerful forces of domination and destruction. Now, much more than ever, critical consciousness and oppositional subjectivity are needed to counter the forces of domination, which appear more in the guise of the seductions of AOL Time Warner, the machinations of Microsoft, and the global maneuvering of near-invisible forces such as the WTO, IMF, and World Bank than in the boots and repression of Big Brother.[54]

Some Concluding Comments

In retrospect, the critique of the subject launched by the Frankfurt School, feminism, post-structuralism, postmodern theory, and others have enriched our thinking on subjectivity by challenging us to rethink the problematics of the subject and agency, and have helped us think through and conceptualize various dimensions of experience and action neglected in traditional accounts, as well as envisage alternative possibilities for thought, action, and everyday life. While traditional and modern conceptions of the subject were excessively rationalist, essentialist, idealist, and metaphysical, I have argued that the contemporary critiques of the subject provide the impetus and occasion to develop more critical and creative conceptions of post-metaphysical subjectivity.

But discussions of the "crisis of the subject" often conflate contemporary critique and rejection of the concept of a metaphysical unitary subject with the fragmentation, decline, or dispersal of subjectivity and agency under the sway of powerful social forces such as the compulsion to work and consume, the seduction of the media, or disciplinary agencies. I would argue that while critiques of problematic theoretical concepts of the subject are generally salutary, critical theory needs to respond reconstructively to evocations of the decline of agency, the will to resist and struggle, and the eclipse of politics in the present era. Marcuse always attempted to ground his conception of radical subjectivity in existing struggles, movements, and tendencies. He was aware that oppositional subjectivity, and the movements and revolts in which it was grounded, were fragile, subject to dispersion and defeat, or absorption and cooptation. Moreover, Marcuse was aware of the contradictions of oppositional subjectivities and movements that reproduced tendencies of the existing capitalist societies on the one hand, while opposing other aspects and seeking alternatives on the other.

Hence, subjectivity for Marcuse – whether the dominated subject of advanced capitalism or oppositional subjectivity which he sought first in the New Left and counter-culture and then in new social movements – was historical, and was always full of contradictions and ambiguities. Marcuse was more aware than most in the Marxian tradition of the need for a robust theory of subjectivity to generate the subjective conditions for change, and he was deeply interested in theory, culture, and social experience which would help create a new subjectivity. Hence, his attempts to reconstruct subjectivity are grounded in his political desire for radical social change and preservation of the individual.

In his sometimes tortured attempts to generate new perspectives on subjectivity, and an alternative society and politics, during his last decade of work in the 1970s, Marcuse privileged cultural revolution and the cultivation of a new sensibility as crucial catalysts for social change, as he (unsuccessfully) sought new social movements to embody his oppositional subjectivity and politics.[55] While this work provides important theoretical impulses to rethink radical politics, subjectivity, and culture in the contemporary era, we must move beyond Marcuse in a new historical situation, drawing on the best resources of the most advanced critical theories of our time.

Hence, in conclusion, I would like to make some comments contrasting Habermasian perspectives on subjectivity with Marcusean ones to indicate the specific contributions and strengths, and limitations, of Marcuse's position. I have suggested that Marcuse offers a notion of a corporeal subjectivity with an emphasis on its aesthetic and erotic dimensions, while Habermas's communicative reason lacks a body, grounding in nature and materiality, and the aesthetic and erotic components. That is to say, while Habermas's conception of subjectivity contains a grounding in sociality and ego-alter relations, he does not offer a notion of aesthetic, erotic, and embodied and sensual subjectivity as in Marcuse's conception. There is also not as strong a critique of the tendencies toward conformity and normalization as in Marcuse's conception, nor is there as forceful a notion of transformation and emancipation. Nor does Habermas offer a notion of revolutionary subjectivity.

There are, on the other hand, problems with Marcuse's conceptions of subjectivity. I have downplayed the extent of Marcuse's dependence on questionable aspects of Freud's instinct theory because I believe that a Marcusean conception of subjectivity can be produced without dependence on Freud's conception of the political economy of the instincts, the death instinct, and the somewhat biologistic notion of Eros that Marcuse draws from Freud. Yet while Marcuse's focus on the corporeal, aesthetic, erotic, and political dimensions of subjectivity constitutes a positive legacy, there are omissions and deficiencies in his account. Crucially, he underemphasizes the ethical and, arguably, concerning the political, does not adequately develop notions of justice and democracy. Since notions of ethical, just, and democratic subjectivity are not cultivated in Marcuse's writings, Habermas's analyses provide a necessary complement. Habermas's primary focus on the ego-alter relation and his subsequent treatises on morals and moral development, democracy and law, and the social obligations and constraints on subjectivity offer an important correction to Marcuse's analyses. Hence, both perspectives on subjectivity by themselves are one-sided and require supplementation by the other.

While I have been primarily concerned in this paper to interrogate Marcuse's resources for the rethinking and reconstruction of subjectivity, I would argue that no one thinker has *the* answer to the question and that we would thus be well advised to draw upon a wealth of thinkers to rehabilitate and reconstruct subjectivity in the contemporary moment. Within the Frankfurt School, Adorno, Benjamin, Fromm, Habermas, Marcuse, and others make important contributions, and outside of the tradition many feminist theorists, post-structuralists, and others also advance the project.[56] Marcuse and other critical theorists provide many important contributions to our understanding of subjectivity and agency, while challenging us to further rethink the problematics of subjectivity in relation to the socioeconomic developments and political struggles of our own turbulent period. In this way, the contemporary critiques of the subject challenge us to come up with better conceptions and to develop new resources for critical theory and practice.

Notes

1 See, in particular, Jürgen Habermas, *Theory of Communicative Action*, vols. 1 and 2, Boston: Beacon Press, 1984 and 1987.
2 Herbert Marcuse, *Eros and Civilization*, Boston: Beacon, 1955; new edition, London and New York: Routledge, 1997.
3 *Ibid.*, p. 13.
4 *Ibid.*
5 *Ibid.*, p. 14.
6 *Ibid.*, pp. 14–15.
7 *Ibid.*, p. 16.
8 *Ibid.*, pp. 3ff.
9 *Ibid.*, p. 17.
10 This is true of the Foucault of texts such as *Discipline and Punishment*, (trans. Alan Sheridan, New York: Pantheon Books, 1977), and *The History of Sexuality*, (trans. Robert Hurley, New York: Vintage, 1990); the late Foucault, however, like Marcuse, was engaged in a search for a stronger conception of agency, but I would argue that Marcuse offers a more robust account of resistance and agency than Foucault. On Foucault's later quests to develop a theory of subjectivity and resistance and its limitations, see Steven Best and Douglas Kellner, *Postmodern Theory: Critical Interrogations*, London and New York: Macmillan and Guilford Press, 1991, and Couze Venn, "Beyond Enlightenment? After the Subject of Foucault, Who Comes?," *Theory, Culture and Society*, vol. 14, no. 3 (August 1997), pp. 1–28.
11 *Eros and Civilization*, p. 18.
12 *Ibid.*, pp. 18–19.
13 This conception might be contrasted with Walter Benjamin, who in his "Theses on the Philosophy of History" claims that "images of enslaved ancestors rather than that of liberated grandchildren" drive the oppressed to struggle against their oppressors: see Walter Benjamin, *Illuminations*, trans. Harry Zohn, ed. Hannah Arendt, New York: Schocken, 1969, p. 260. Benjamin's conception is similar to Freud's, who holds that past traumas enslave individuals and who argues, in a different register than Benjamin, that working through the source of trauma can free the individual from past blockages and suffering. A dialectical conception of memory merging Marcuse and Benjamin might argue that both remembrances of past joys and suffering, happiness, and oppression can motivate construction of a better future if oriented toward changing rather than just remembering the world.
14 Friedrich Nietzsche, *On the Genealogy of Morals*, trans. Walter Kaufmann, New York: Vintage, 1969.
15 *Eros and Civilization*, p. 232.
16 *Ibid.*, pp. 14 and 140ff.
17 *Ibid.*, p. 140.
18 *Ibid.*, p. 149.
19 *Ibid.*, pp. 238ff.
20 *Ibid.*, p. 110.
21 Herbert Marcuse, "Marxism and Feminism," *Women's Studies*, Old Westbury, NY: The Feminist Press, 1974, p. 282. I am quoting from Marcuse's 1974 lecture on "Marxism and Feminism" here to suggest that he continued to hold to many key ideas in *Eros and Civilization* through his later work and that his strong adherence to feminism was deeply rooted in some of his fundamental ideas; I take up "Marxism and Feminism" later in this study.
22 *Eros and Civilization*, pp. 112ff.

23 *Ibid.*, pp. 119ff.
24 "Marxism and Feminism," p. 284.
25 *Eros and Civilization*, pp. 5ff. and 124ff.
26 *Ibid.*, p. 180.
27 *Ibid.*, p. 182.
28 *Ibid.*, p. 187.
29 *Ibid.*, p. 189.
30 *Ibid.*, pp. 223ff.
31 *Ibid.*, pp. 119ff.
32 *Ibid.*, pp. 223ff.
33 *Ibid.*, p. 224.
34 *Ibid.*
35 Herbert Marcuse, *One-Dimensional Man: Studies in the Ideology of Advanced Industrial Society*, Boston: Beacon, 1964; new edition, 1991.
36 Herbert Marcuse, "The Realm of Freedom and the Realm of Necessity: a Reconsideration," *Praxis*, International Edition, no. 1, 1969, p. 24.
37 *One-Dimensional Man*, pp. 250–1.
38 Herbert Marcuse, *An Essay on Liberation*, Boston: Beacon, 1969, p. 67.
39 *Eros and Civilization*, pp. 149ff.
40 *One-Dimensional Man*, pp. 256ff.
41 *An Essay on Liberation*, p. 6.
42 *Ibid.*, p. 23.
43 *Ibid.*, p. 67.
44 *Ibid.*, pp. 24ff. See also *Counter-Revolution and Revolt*, Boston: Beacon Press, 1972, pp. 63ff., where Marcuse connects his notion of the new sensibility with the analysis of the early Marx on the liberation of the senses; his conception is also influenced by Schiller's conception of aesthetic education.
45 *An Essay on Liberation*, p. 6.
46 For a systematic study of Marcuse's perspectives on art and education, see Charles Reitz, *Art, Alienation, and the Humanities: A Critical Engagement with Herbert Marcuse*, Albany, NY: SUNY University Press, 2000.
47 For an argument parallel to mine developed through an engagement with French feminism and post-structuralism, see Kelly Oliver, *Subjectivity Without Subjects*, New Jersey: Rowman and Littlefield, 1998. Oliver provides an extended argument that we can talk about subjectivity (and agency) without presupposing or needing a subject, claiming that subjectivity does not necessarily imply a "subject" and that we are better off without such a concept. She develops notions of subjectivity as relational and intersubjective at the "center," and contrasts varying discourses and forms of masculine and feminine subjectivity. This project is parallel, I suggest, to Marcuse and the Frankfurt School, disclosing a provocative affinity between critical theory, French feminism, and post-structuralism.
48 "Marxism and Feminism," p. 285.
49 *Ibid.*, pp. 285–6.
50 Herbert Marcuse, "The Reification of the Proletariat," *Canadian Journal of Philosophy and Social Theory*, vol. 3, no. 1 (Winter 1979), p. 21. See also Marcuse's reflections on Bahro in "Protosocialism and Late Capitalism: Toward a Theoretical Synthesis Based on Bahro's Analysis," in Ulf Wolter (ed.) *Rudolf Bahro: Critical Responses*, White Plains, NY: M.E. Sharpe, 1980, pp. 24–8.
51 One could, of course, argue that the Marxist–Leninist–Stalinist systems overthrown in the late 1980s were not really Marxist or socialist at all, but constituted a bureaucratic deformation of Marxian socialism. This is indeed Bahro's and Marcuse's position that continues to have force in explaining the

collapse of Soviet-style communism. See my analysis in "The Obsolescence of Marxism?" in *Whither Marxism?*, ed. Bernd Magnus and Stephen Cullenberg, London and New York: Routledge, 1995, pp. 3–30.

52 For fuller summaries of the varieties of postmodern theory, similarities and differences with critical theory, and reflections on productive and problematic versions of postmodern politics, see Steven Best and Douglas Kellner, *Postmodern Theory: Critical Interrogations*, London and New York: Macmillan and Guilford Press, 1991; *The Postmodern Turn*, London and New York: Routledge and Guilford Press, 1997; and *The Postmodern Adventure*, New York: Guilford Press, 2001.

53 Such a conception of postmodern subjectivity is found in a highly developed form in Sherry Turkle, *Life on the Screen. Identity in the Age of the Internet*, New York: Simon & Schuster, 1995.

54 For an argument that Huxley's *Brave New World* and Marcuse's *One-Dimensional Man* provide more salient perspectives on contemporary global capitalism than Orwell's *1984*, see Douglas Kellner, "From *1984* to *One-Dimensional Man*: Reflections on Orwell and Marcuse," *Current Perspectives in Social Theory*, Greenwich, CN: JAI Press, 1990, pp. 223–52. For my perspectives on globalization, see Douglas Kellner and Ann Cvetkovich (eds) *Articulating the Global and the Local. Globalization and Cultural Studies*, Boulder, CO: Westview, 1996, and Douglas Kellner, "Globalization and the Postmodern Turn," in Roland Axtmann (ed.) *Globalization and Europe*, London: Cassell, 1998, pp. 23–42.

55 See, in particular, his previously unpublished studies, "Beyond One-dimensional Man," "Cultural Revolution," and "The Historical Fate of Bourgeois Democracy," which have been published recently in Herbert Marcuse, *Towards a Critical Theory of Society* (2001), the second volume of *The Collected Papers of Herbert Marcuse* that I am editing for Routledge.

56 This paper was first presented in a panel at SPEP (Denver, 1998) in which my colleagues David Sherman and Pierre Lamarche presented the contributions of Adorno and Benjamin in rethinking subjectivity. See, in addition, Oliver's account of the contributions to refiguring subjectivity in post-structuralism and feminism, mentioned above.

5

MARCUSE'S MATERNAL ETHIC

John O'Neill

Does the civilizing process merely deepen repression, and in collusion with the economic and political forces of oppression make any notion of future emancipation an idle daydream? In short, how could Freud possibly be recruited into Marx's utopian project of an end to the double scarcity operative in nature and society? The point of the question, of course, is that such a merger runs the risk of psychologizing history and social structure, or else of watering down general psychology into the sociology of the day.[1]

Marcuse's *Eros and Civilization* goes to the heart of utopian theory.[2] It is in the unconscious that we have preserved a time when freedom and happiness were not yet separated by the civilizing demands of repressive sublimation. Thus the future does not erase the past; or else we should have no ground for it. Rather, both our future and our past are structured by our memory, which functions on the two levels of knowledge and morals to provide a critical standard of institutional freedom and happiness:

> If memory moves into the center of psychoanalysis as a decisive mode of *cognition*, this is far more than a therapeutic device; the therapeutic role of memory derives from the *truth value* of memory. Its truth value lies in the specific function of memory to preserve promises and potentialities which are betrayed and even outlawed by the mature, civilized individual, but which had once been fulfilled in his dim past and are never entirely forgotten. The reality principle restrains the cognitive function of memory – its commitment to the past experience of happiness, which spurns the desire for its conscious recreation. The psychoanalytic liberation of memory explodes the rationality of the repressed individual. As cognition gives way to re-cognition, the forbidden images and impulses of childhood begin to tell the truth that reason denies. Regression assumes a progressive function. The rediscovered past yields critical standards which are tabooed by the present. Moreover, the restoration of memory is accompanied by the restoration of the cognitive content of phantasy. Psychoanalytic theory

removes these mental faculties from the noncommittal sphere of daydreaming and fiction and recaptures their strict truths. The weight of these discoveries must eventually shatter the framework in which they were made and confined. The liberation of the past does not end in its reconciliation with the present. Against the self-imposed restraint of the discoverer, the orientation on the past tends toward an orientation on the future. The *recherche du temps perdu* becomes the vehicle of future liberation.[3]

Marcuse's return to Freud specifically revises Freud's essay, "On the Two Principles of Mental Functioning," where the psychic apparatus is described as follows:

> Just as the pleasure-ego can do nothing but *wish* work for a yield of pleasure, and avoid unpleasure, so the reality-ego need do nothing but strive for what is *useful* and guard itself against damage. Actually the substitution of the reality principle for the pleasure principle implies no deposing of the pleasure principle, but only a safeguarding of it...the endopsychic impression made by this substitution has been so powerful that it is reflected in a special religion myth. The doctrine of reward in the after-life for the – voluntary or enforced – renunciation of early pleasure is nothing other than a mythical projection of this revolution in the mind.[4]

Here we can see Freud's reduction of utopia to a postmodern paradise. In effect, religion undermines political revolt because its impulse is infantile and reinforces authoritarianism. At the same time, religion postpones political hope to the next life. Whereas Freud had set off the imagination from reason, like a "reservation" or a "nature reserve,"[5] Marcuse argued that reason's colonization of the imagination is never complete, anymore than the *ego* ever entirely controls the *id*. The imagination remains a collective, universal force, always opposed to rationalized individuation and defamilization. Freud's reconciliation of Eros and Thanatos in *Beyond the Pleasure Principle* is entertained only at the mythical interface of philosophy and science.[6] Here Freud envisages a non-selfish gene as something akin to an unconscious but mortal drive toward solidarity. Marcuse insists that, *pace* Freud, the imagination is neither a regressive nor an irrational force except from the standpoint of rationalized history, which it resists. Imagination is a progressive mode of knowledge grounded in the refusal of the oppressed to forget a past happiness which may be projected into the future to furnish a critical standard for present institutions: "In and against the world of the antagonistic *principium individuationis*, imagination sustains the claim of the whole individual, in union with the genus and with the 'archaic' past."[7] Utopia is neither a "nobody" enterprise nor a "nowhere" place, as civilized but repressive reason would have it. Nor is imagination to be set off from the everyday world as the inspiration for merely childish, artistic or mythical stories that distract us from the world but do not change it. To vary Marx slightly, *phantasy and mythology are good to think and to change the world*. Even so, one needs to be careful with the texts, as we shall see.

The argument I am introducing has had several previous runs. Martin Jay has told the story of the Frankfurt School's critical assimilation of psychoanalysis in order to understand the failure of revolution in the face of the politics of authoritarianism.[8] In that round, I want to draw attention only to Erich Fromm's focus upon *maternal theory* in Bachofen[9] and Briffault[10] as a critical alternative to Freud's paternity theory of institutions and failed revolutions.[11] I do so for the reason that it provides the missing institutional background to Marcuse's utopian appeal for a *libidinal morality*. There are second and third rounds in this story, which explodes in the 1960s with the American debate between Marcuse and Norman O. Brown over *love's body*.[12] The body in question shifts its ground in the 1970s from its embrace of Greek male narcissism to the rejection of corporate America's sponsorship of narcissistic consumerism ruled by momism and absentee popism.[13] In the same arena, Lash held that the politics of narcissism played into the hands of the welfare state to undermine the family,[14] while Sennett held that narcissism results in a *politics of intimacy* that undermines the public realm.[15] Here I would observe that, as Habermas then argued,[16] the two processes of the decline of the public and the rise of civic privatism work together to underwrite the *political economy of narcissism*.[17] Finally, the debate shifted into the feminist appropriation of psychoanalysis and Marxism, raising once again the critical functions of female narcissism and maternal bonding/bondage.[18] At first sight, this is as much of a paradox as is the original critical Marxist move toward psychoanalysis. Yet this is not entirely so, if we recall Engels' concern with the status of women under the patriarchal property system.[19]

Whereas Engels drew upon Bachofen, as did Freud, there is no reference by Marcuse to the theory of maternal right (*Mutterrecht*). The result – to anticipate the argument – is that Marcuse completely psychologizes the historical location of matriarchal values as the source of critical utopianism, whereas Freud represses the maternal as the always-regressive origin. Marcuse's own critical struggle with Freud concedes too much to the Freudian family and projects into a utopian future changes that had occurred in pre-capitalist society:

> *Historically*, the reduction of Eros to procreative monogamic sexuality (which completes the subjection of the pleasure principle to the reality principle) is consummated only when the individual has become a subject-object of labor in the apparatus of his society: whereas, *ontogenetically*, the primary suppression of infantile sexuality remains the precondition for this accomplishment.[20]

Admittedly, Marcuse reworks the myths of Orpheus and Narcissus (adopted from Rilke, Gide, Valéry, and Baudelaire) to emphasize the Orphic rather than Promethean world-building character of narcissism, though this is a forced distinction.[21] But his reinterpretation of Freud's drive theory obstinately presupposes his late-capitalist historicization of Freud's family psychology. Marcuse's project – or what I call Orphic Marxism[22] – needs to be grounded in an historical and sociological theory of family law as well as family psychology.

It turns out, if one reads Détienne,[23] that Marcuse, Valéry, Mallarmé, and Freud ignore the larger context of the Orpheus/Narcissus myth, in favour of the lover's tale given in Ovid's *Metamorphoses* (Book III). But in Virgil's *Georgics* (Book IV), the death of Eurydice occurs in flight from violent pursuit by Aristaeus, the beekeeper. Although Persephone tells Orpheus how to recover his beloved Eurydice, his backward glance lost her forever and he was torn to pieces for his carelessness by the maenads. What is the significance of the beekeeper and why should the maenads be so angry? Plutarch in his *Conjugalia Praecepta* (44, 144d) says that the beekeeper must handle the bee (Melissa), itself scrupulously clean and allergic to aromas, with the same care as a faithful husband accords his wife, i.e. without any odor of infidelity. Thus Aristaeus was punished with the loss of his bees for attempting to seduce Eurydice, imperiling his own and Orpheus' marriage. But in another myth, it was a nymph, Melissa or Bee-Woman, who discovered honey and prepared the food which brought man out of the wilderness. Now Demeter had entrusted to the daughters of King Melisseus the secret of the ceremonies of lawful marriage (*Thesmophoria*), which effect the shift in status from *nymph* (a young girl ready for marriage) to *Thesmophoros* (a lawful wife). But nymphs themselves are not in any wild state. They are females whose age-status lies between that of *koré*, i.e. an immature girl, unmarried (*agamos*), and the status of *métér*, i.e. a woman who has given birth. However, once a nymph marries, and before becoming a *thesmophoros* (a ritual bee), a young bride leads a life of love with its sweet smells, foods, and pleasure (*numphion bios*). It is in this state of "honeymoon" that Eurydice and Orpheus are destroyed by Aristaeus' attempted seduction and the fury of the nymphs is aroused by the couple's failure to cool the honeymoon and settle into marriage! Now we can explain the rage of the nymphs with both Orpheus and Narcissus whom they tear apart for *undervaluing* married woman and *overvaluing* (self) love, thereby collapsing the civilized distance between (wo)man and nature.

To ground the political imagination, Marcuse risked both the reduction of social categories to psychological categories and his own seduction by the regressive appeal of the category of male narcissism that overlooks woman's fate.[24] The missing figure in Marcuse's account of Orpheus and Narcissus is *woman*. As Bachofen shows, Eurydice and Echo are bodies lost by the male imagination, which privileges male parthenogenesis over kinship a state in subordinating sexual reproduction to patriarchal lineage:

> Though Athens itself has its roots in the Pelasgian culture, it wholly subordinated the Demetrian to the Appollonian principle in the course of its development. The Athenians revered Theseus as a second woman-hating Heracles; in the person of Athene they set *motherless paternity* in the place of *fatherless maternity*; and even in their legislation they endowed the universal principle of paternity with a character of inviolability which the old law of the Erinyes imputed only to motherhood. The virgin goddess is well disposed to the masculine, helpful to the heroes of the paternal solar law; in her, the warlike Amazonism of the old day reappears in spiritual form. Her city is hostile to the women who moor their ships on the coasts of Attica in search of help in defending the rights of their sex. Here the opposition between the Apollonian and the Demetrian principle stands out sharply. This city, whose earliest history disclosed traces of matriarchal conditions, carried paternity to its highest development; and in one-sided exaggeration it condemned woman to a status of inferiority particularly surprising in its contrast to the foundations of the Eleusinian mysteries.[25]

Here we should consider the story of Heracles rather than the proto-Marxist myth of Prometheus. The Twelve Labors of Heracles make him the very figure of the cultural hero. He was, however, the plaything of his tormenting mother, Hera, who imposes his labors upon him. Heracles' strength was overwhelmed by deadly threats and incredible sufferings, which pursued him from his mother's womb, drove him to kill his own children, and enslaved and womanized him as the servant of Queen Omphale. Hera and Hera(cles) are locked into a struggle over the boundaries of identity, sexuality, love, and hatred. The struggle between Hera and her son (the Glory of Hera) is a struggle between the gods, but it is not yet divine, just as the labors of Heracles are a civilizing force but not yet civilized.[26] This is because the story of Heracles belongs to the period between the *heteraic* and matriarchal stages of family formation, reflected in the ambivalent breasts of Hera that poisoned her son, who in turn wounded Hera's right breast with his arrows.[27] Thus Heracles' narcissism is that of an unstable character, at times bumptious and mostly self-defeating. Yet only he, through suffering and renunciation, becomes a god.

The metamorphoses and sexual transgressions characteristic of the heroic myth are only intelligible in terms of its retrospective exaggeration of the *heteraic* period of sexuality outside of marriage and matriarchy that is in turn remembered wildly once matriarchy has moved under patriarchy.[28] Thus Bachofen locates Orphic homosexuality and lesbianism as a reaction to *heteraic* rather than matriarchal/patriarchal sexuality.[29] Both are attempts to recombine physical and spiritual love, as in Sappho's poetry. In other words, there is a historical structure of love, kinship, and marriage. This is narrated, at first, in fables of sexual struggle and the transgression of human–animal, human–divine boundaries. But later, these become stories of the violation of religious and property laws. It is, then, the historical vicissitudes of sexuality and law, which structure utopian imagination. The imaginary does not arise in any state of nature except as the latter is itself a retrospective fiction of civilized anxiety. Marcuse, however, succumbs to Freud's psycho-sexualization of the conflict between patrilineage and matrilineage revealed by Bachofen's historico-structural analysis of the archaic myths.

So, rather than follow Marcuse's philosophical appeal to Aristotle, Hegel, and Nietzsche, in which he seeks to transvalue the return of the past as the fulfillment of the future,[30] I want to tease out further the matriarchal history that is the institutional basis for the civilizing function of utopian phantasy. I refer the reader to Jay's meticulous account of the critical issues behind Marcuse's attempt to eroticize Hegel,[31] as well as to Lenhardt[32] and O'Neill[33] on the politics of memory. We should then consider the historicist perspective of Bachofen, as well as Marx and Engels on family law, to gain a historical understanding of the contemporary politics of *gynesis*.[34] We cannot explore the larger nineteenth-century paradigm of Greek family history and politics at work here.[35] It should be noted, however, that Bachofen's *Mother Right* and Morgan's *Ancient Society*[36] were contested by Fustel de Coulanges' *The Ancient City*[37] and by Henry Maine's *Ancient Law*,[38] which reversed the historical priority of matriarchy and patriarchy. Engels' *Origin of the Family, Private Property and the State* belonged to the matriarchal school of Bachhofen and Morgan, which was taken up in contemporary feminism as a source of woman's "vision of power"[39] and the end of the "traffic in women."[40]

The broad picture of matriarchy may be derived from the comparative analysis of historical and mythological texts, which were already puzzling to the patriarchal mind and might be dismissed out of hand as mere myth or legend by modern minds. But we have known at least since Vico's *The New Science*[41] that we are entirely historical beings whose more contemporary practices are unthinkable except as developments of early forms of language, perception, and conduct.[42] Thus we cannot start from a radical hiatus between myth and history because the later form of knowledge presupposes the earlier one. Here Vico is a surer guide than Freud's *Totem and Taboo*[43] in lifting the veils of my *critical theory* "to enter into the fathers (*interpatrari*)" through the creative force of interpretation (*interpretari*), evinced in *The New Science* itself.[44] What interpretation reveals is the missing marriage of mother and child:

> The guarding of the institutions began in divine times from jealousy (the jealousy of Juno, the goddess of solemn matrimony) with

a view to *the certainty of the families* as against the nefarious promiscuity of women. Such vigilance is a natural property of the aristocratic commonwealths desirous of keeping family relationships, successions, and consequently wealth and through it power, within the order of the nobles.[45]

Vico's comment is remarkable for its resolution of both the psycho-sexual and the socio-political conflicts that underlie the legal fiction or *fantasia* of patrilineage (*patria potestas*). Patriarchy hangs by a genealogical thread (*filo genealogico*) to a powerful fiction of the origin of religion and law[46] that Freud reduces to an intra-familial phantasy. The Roman patriarchal system — in particular its severity — presupposes an earlier system of matriarchy which it had usurped but whose seduction it continued to repress, especially its rival values of universality and fraternity. It is the inviolability of the Sabine women that accounted for their military and political roles and not their ferocious feminism. The paradox here is removed once we set aside the patriarchal assumption that strength is physical and male rather than spiritual and female. The religious and civil primacy of pre-Hellenic womanhood was rooted in woman's function as *priestess* and *hierophant*, through which she mediated the material and spiritual worlds:

> If we acknowledge the primordial character of mother right and its connection with an older cultural stage, we must say the same of the mystery, for the two phenomena are merely different aspects of the same cultural form; they are inseparable twins. And this is all the more certain when we consider that *the religious aspect of matriarchy is at the root of its social manifestations*. The cultic conceptions are the source, the social forms are their consequence and expression. Kore's bond with Demeter was the source of the primacy of mother over father, of daughter over son, and was not abstracted from the social relationship. Or, in ancient terms: the cultic-religious meaning of the maternal ΚΤΕΙΣ (weaver's shuttle, comb, weaving woman) is primary and dominant; while the social, juridical sense *pudenda* (shame) is derivative. The feminine *sporium* (womb) is seen primarily as a representation of the Demetrian mystery, both in its lower physical sense and in its higher transcendent implication, and only by derivation becomes an expression of the social matriarchy, as in the Lycian myth of Sarpedon.[47]

Bachofen does not unearth the lost institution of matriarchy in order to set it beyond the vicissitudes of its own history. He was not a Romantic utopian. This would mean idealizing the middle or Demetrian period, which had itself overthrown an earlier stage of *hetaerism* before matriarchy yielded to patriarchy:

Although the struggle of matriarchy against other forms is revealed by diverse phenomena, the underlying principle of development is clear. *Matriarchy is followed by patriarchy and preceded by unregulated hetaerism.* The Demetrian ordered matriarchy thus assumes a middle position, representing the transition of mankind from the lowest stage of existence to the highest. With the former it shares the material-maternal standpoint, with the second, the exclusivity of marriage; it is distinguished from the early stage by the Demetrian regulation of motherhood, through which it rises above hetaerism, and from the later stage by primacy it accords to the generative womb, wherein it proves to be a lower form than the fully developed patriarchal system.[48]

To the surprise of later minds, not to mention our own, the Demetrian institution of marriage was an anti-religious restriction upon female sexuality that required a rite to propitiate the god whose law was transgressed by conjugal exclusivity. Thus the institution of the dowry served to emphasize that families exchanged woman's dignity and chastity rather than her sexuality or commodity value. The dowry removed woman's womb from nature (*iniussa ultronea creatio*) into (agri)culture (*laborata Ceres*). In the "civilizing process," children are removed from the exclusive power of woman's sexuality, which need not acknowledge fatherhood, into an intermediary stage of motherhood-in-marriage that presupposes an earlier stage of *hetaerism*, just as it is itself determined by a later stage of patriarchy. This development did not occur without struggle. Thus the Dionysian religion mobilized the *hetaeric* past, rejuvenating women's phallicism, raising Aphrodite over Demeter, putting wine rather than bread on the table! Yet, like Amazonism, Dionysianism also represented a stage in women's history toward the settlement of agriculturally based states organized around the patriarchal system in which the constitution overrides conception, just as the sky overlooks the earth (*flamma non urens*/flame without fire):

> Myth takes this view of the conflict between the old and the new principle in the matricide of Orestes and Alcmaeon, and links the great turning point of existence to the sublimation of religion. These traditions undoubtedly embody a memory of real experiences of the human race. If the historical character of matriarchy cannot be doubted, the events accompanying its downfall must also be more than a poetic fiction. In the adventures of Orestes we find a reflection of the upheavals and struggles leading to the triumph of paternity over the chthonian-maternal principle. Whatever influence we may impute to poetic fancy, there is historical truth in the struggle between the two principles as set forth by Aeschylus and Euripides. The old law is that of the Erinyes, according to which Orestes is

guilty and his mother's blood inexpiable; but Apollo and Athene usher in the victory as a new law; that of the higher paternity and of the heavenly light. *This is no dialectical opposition but a historical struggle, and the gods themselves decide its outcome.* The old era dies, and another, the Apollonian age, rises on its ruins. A new ethos is in preparation, diametrically opposed to the old one. The divinity of the mother gives way to that of the father, the night cedes its primacy to the day, the left side to the right, and it is only in their contrast that the character of the two stages stands out sharply.[49]

In the archaic period, the inalienable ancestral lands of the Greek family, based upon ancestor worship and worship of the Earth, were assigned a superior position to the vicissitudes of exchanging women and childbearing. The inalienability of ancestral land set off a retrospective patriarchal anxiety with regard to woman as both grounded land and mobile, as a wild card in the genre of property and exchange. The patriarchal principle demanded that consanguinity is inessential to patronymy. As such, woman is a Pandora figure, hiding all the power of parthenogenetic fertility, releasing all the troubles of heterosexual reproduction:

> Earth is thus seen, like the mother and the jar, as self-sufficient, self-generating, as giving or withholding; and the contradictory representation of Pandora as secondary, supplementary, fallen, is already an attempt to appropriate to the male the powers of cultivation, reproduction, thesaurization.[50]

In fact, males reversed the Fall by assigning autochthony to themselves as gods and by reinterpreting the pains of farming and ploughing woman as punishments due to the fall from divine grace. Once the aristocratic male order shifted from a pre-commercial agricultural base to a commercial economy and a relatively democratic polis, the place of women shifted so that citizen women became the reproductive guarantors of male lineages but also submitted to greater controls upon their sexuality. As the Demetrian rituals show, or the *Oresteia*, women were rendered archaic, sacral, and mythic actors, celebrated by the chorus in tragic conflict with the new political economy of the city launched by Pericles. The reduction of woman to the status of a male supplement is finally completed in the Platonic doctrine of androgynous love, in which woman is supplanted by the man/woman lover. In the *Phaedrus*, Socrates' love for his friend does not sow the seeds of family. But the words of philosophy employing the dialectic sew in the friend's mind the true fruits of philosophy. Socrates combines insemination and deliverance of the mind. As a midwife he, like the farmer, knows what seeds should go into a particular plot of ground or what words will take off in the soul feminized by the loving philosopher. With the aid of Diotima,

Socrates completes the journey of *male pregnancy*, ending the archaic struggle over parthenogenesis: "The male philosopher becomes the site of metaphorical reproduction, the subject of philosophical generation; the female, stripped of her metaphorical otherness becomes a defective male, defined by lack."[51] We cannot separate psychic process from historical social processes. Nor can we start from the modern family structure and its libidinal unconscious as the ground of utopian imagination.[52] In the archaic period, sexuality was, so to speak, *beyond* both women and men. It was a mysterious, cosmic force, animal, vegetable, and libidinal – not yet bound, not yet tied to kinship, and cultivated in marriage. Thus nature preceded both men and women. Woman preceded man once sexuality was brought under matriarchy. It was matriarchy and not patriarchy that first constituted the female unconscious.[53] Here woman symbolized the spiritual order of nature and cosmos, while man symbolized the instinctive and bestial (like woman before marriage). However, these remain contestatory statuses, unsettled because history is still unsettled.

Once patriarchy subordinated matriarchy, the eternal feminine (*ewige Weibe*) migrated into the male/female unconscious as a principle of imagination, creativity, and cosmic union. It is from there that Marcuse tried to retrieve it, but without any historical feminist consciousness. For the longest time, the male was at best an ancillary to the reproductive force of the self-birthing mother, recognized only as a baby-son but not as husband-father. It is the institution of property, which required woman's subjection to its owner who cannot stand to be "raped" through her by another male. Marriage only becomes a "sexual relation" once it derives from a juridical relation.[54] In the shift from matriarchy to patriarchy, woman shifted shape from being another species, approachable only as the mysterious other, to become the lower being in a hierarchical order of men (women, children, slaves, animals). There has never been a state of nature in which matriarchy prevailed, *pace* Pateman, because all institutions are postnatural, including "nature" itself.[55] Over a long history,[56] family law has been shaped by the Roman principle of *imperium*, which has lodged the family and the child in the juridical space between public and private life rather than in the primacy of paternal over maternal spirituality. This is not due to any cunning of reason, and far less of providence. It occurs because family law is reshaped by structural changes in the household economy, social democracy, and innovations in the bio-technologies of reproduction that are presupposed by current ideologies of sexual identity, maternity, kinship, and care.[57]

The discursive revision of gender and kin relationship has once again turned toward the myths and metaphors of ancient cosmology and sexology.[58] Current post-Freudian ideologies of gender and family relations often reverse the patriarchal order by opposing it with a vision of heteraic sexuality, forgetting that woman's oppression only became representable as a consequence of the shift into matriarchy and from there to patriarchy.

Patriarchy itself is grounded in a mystical act, which in turn grounds a class act. The alliance between the artist and maternity, therefore, is not immediately emancipatory for women until both patrician and plebeian women are released from the patrilineal myth of legitimacy. Nor is woman's assumption of authorial voice broadly emancipatory if it repeats the patriarchal disavowal of maternity in its espousal of Freud/Lacanian phantasies of self-birth. The myth of parthenogenesis cannot stand both *before* and *after* the Law that we are born of two and not one:

> Fatherhood, in the sense of conscious begetting, is unknown to man. It is a mystical estate, an apostolic succession, from only begetter to only begotten. On that mystery and not on the madonna which the cunning Italian intellect flung to the mobs of Europe the church is founded and founded irremovably because founded, like the world, macro- and microcosm, upon the void. Upon incertitude, upon unlikehood. *Amor matris*, subjective and objective genitive, may be the only true thing in life. *Paternity may be a legal fiction.* Who is the father of any son that any son should love him or he any son?[59]

In the process of reclaiming the imagination from capital culture by reopening its maternal sources, Marcuse risked restoring its critical task in male artists open to "their" femininity but not to imaginative women artists/critics. Thus there is a succession struggle at the heart of utopia that is repeated in later feminist criticism. The "gynema effect"[60] only emerges as an ethic of non-hierarchical male/female relationships in the wider society of citizenship rather than sexuality. Thus Marcuse's utopian invocation of a *maternal ethic* may be contested because it scrambles its own historical context, as I have tried to show by expanding Bachofen's historical account of maternal values. Had Marcuse derived his maternal ethic from the historicist account in Bachofen – or borrowed it from Engels' version – his revision of the Freudian family might have survived post-Freudian feminist criticism. As it stands, Marcuse's failure to connect family ethics, law, and politics remains an effect of his conviction that corporate capitalism sets the family agenda and reduces the welfare state to the warfare state. On this analysis, families lose both their private and their public constitution. But any such notion of revising intra-familial relations without addressing the constitution of the family and gender on the level of citizenship weakens the body politic, as I have argued elsewhere.[61]

Notes

1 See John O'Neill, "Psychoanalysis and Sociology: From Freudo-Marxism to Freudo-Feminism," in George Ritzer and Barry Smart (eds) *Handbook of Social Theory*, London: Sage Publications, 2001, pp. 112–24.

2 Herbert Marcuse, *Eros and Civilization: A Philosophical Inquiry into Freud*, New York: Vintage Books, 1962.
3 *Ibid.*, p. 18.
4 Sigmund Freud, "Formulations on the Two Principles of Mental Functioning," *The Standard Edition of The Complete Psychological Works of Sigmund Freud*, vol. 12, London: The Hogarth Press, 1911, p. 223 (my emphasis).
5 Freud, "General Theory of the Neuroses," *Standard Edition*, vol. 16, 1916/17, p. 372.
6 Freud, "Beyond the Pleasure Principle," *Standard Edition*, vol. 18, 1920.
7 Marcuse, *Eros and Civilization*, p. 130.
8 Martin Jay, *The Dialectical Imagination: A History of the Frankfurt School and the Institute of Social Research 1923–1950*, Boston: Little, Brown and Co., 1973.
9 J.J. Bachofen, *Myth, Religion and Mother Right*, trans. Ralph Manheim, Princeton: Princeton University Press, 1973.
10 Robert Briffault, *The Mothers: A Study of The Origins of Sentiments and Institutions*, London: George Allen & Unwin Ltd, 1927.
11 Erich Fromm, "The Theory of Mother Right and Its Relevance for Social Psychology," *The Crisis of Psychoanalysis: Essays on Freud, Marx and Social Psychology*, New York: Henry Holt and Co., 1970, pp. 109–36.
12 Norman O. Brown, *Life Against Death: The Psychoanalytical Meaning of History*, New York: Vintage Books, 1959.
13 See John O'Neill, *Sociology as a Skin Trade: Essays Towards a Reflexive Sociology*, London: Heinemann, 1972.
14 Christopher Lash, *The Culture of Narcissism: American Life in an Age of Diminishing Expectations*, New York: W.W. Norton and Co., 1979.
15 Richard Sennett, *The Fall of Public Man*, New York: Alfred A. Knopf, 1977.
16 Jürgen Habermas, *Legitimation Crisis*, Boston: Beacon Press, 1975.
17 See John O'Neill, "The Political Economy of Narcissism: Some Issues in the Loss of Family Eros," *Plato's Cave: Desire, Power and the Specular Function of the Media*, Norwood, NJ: Ablex Publishing Corp., 1991, pp. 59–78.
18 Rosalind Coward, *Patriarchal Precedents: Sexuality and Social Rrelations*, London: Routledge and Kegan Paul, 1983.
19 Frederick Engels, "The Origin of the Family, Private Property and the State," in Karl Marx and Frederick Engels, *Selected Works In Two Volumes*, Moscow: Foreign Languages Publishing House, 1956.
20 Marcuse, *Eros and Civilization*, p. 82 (my emphasis).
21 Jean-Pierre Vernant, "The Myth of Prometheus in Hesiod," in R.L. Gordon (ed.) *Myth, Religion and Society*, Cambridge: Cambridge University Press, 1981, pp. 43–56.
22 John O'Neill, "Orphic Marxism," in *The Poverty of Postmodernism*, London: Routledge, 1995, pp. 94–110.
23 Marcel Détienne, "The Myth of the 'Honeyed Orpheus,'" in Gordon (ed.) *Myth, Religion and Society*, pp. 95–110.
24 C. Fred Alford, *Narcissism: Socrates, the Frankfurt School, and Psychoanalytic Theory*, New Haven: Yale University Press, 1988.
25 Bachofen, *Myth, Religion and Mother Right*, p. 111 (my emphasis).
26 Philip E. Slater, *The Glory of Hera: Greek Mythology and the Greek Family*, Boston: Beacon: Beacon Press, 1968.
27 Homer, *Iliad*, V, 392–4.
28 Pierre Vidal-Nacquet, "Slavery and the Rule of Women in Tradition, Myth and Utopia," in Gordon (ed.) *Myth, Religion and Society*, pp. 187–200.
29 Bachofen, *Myth, Religion and Mother Right*, p. 204.

30 See Chapter 5, "Philosophical Interlude," of Marcuse, *Eros and Civilization*.
31 Martin Jay, *Marxism and Totality: The Adventure of a Concept from Lukács to Habermas*, Berkeley: University of California Press, 1984, pp. 220–40.
32 Christian Lenhardt, "Anamnestic Solidarity: the Proletariat and the Manes," *Telos*, no. 75 (Fall 1975), pp. 133–52.
33 John O'Neill, "Critique and Remembrance," in John O'Neill (ed.) *On Critical Theory*, New York: The Seabury Press Inc., 1977, pp. 1–11.
34 Alice A. Jardine, *Gynesis: Configurations of Woman and Modernity*, Ithaca: Cornell University Press, 1985.
35 Cynthia B. Patterson, *The Family in Greek History*, Cambridge, MA: Harvard University Press, 1998.
36 Lewis H. Morgan, *Ancient Society*, New York: Henry Host, 1877.
37 Fustel de Coulanges, *The Ancient City: A Study of the Religion, Law, and Institutions of Greece and Rome*, Boston: Northrop Lee and Shephard, 1901.
38 Henry Maine, *Ancient Law: Its Connection with the Early History of Society, and its Relation to Modern Ideas*, London: Dent, 1917.
39 Paula Webster, "Matriarchy: A Vision of Power," in Rayna R. Reiter (ed.) *Toward an Anthropology of Women*, New York: Monthly Review Press, 1975 p. 145.
40 Gayle Rubin, "The Traffic in Women: Notes on the Political Economy of Sex," in Reiter (ed.) *Toward an Anthropology of Women*, pp. 157–210.
41 Giambattista Vico, *The New Science of Giambattista Vico*, trans. Thomas Goddard Bergin and Max Harold Fisch, Ithaca: Cornell University Press, 1984.
42 See John O'Neill, "Vico and Myth," in Marcel Danesi and Marcel Nuessel (eds) *The Imaginative Basis of Thought and Culture: Contemporary Perspectives on Giambattista Vico*, Toronto: Canadian Scholar's Press Inc., 1994, pp. 99–112.
43 Sigmund Freud, *Totem and Taboo: Some Points of Agreement Between the Mental Lives of Savages and Neurotics*, London: Routledge and Kegan Paul, 1950.
44 Vico, *The New Science*, pp. 448 and 938.
45 *Ibid.*, p. 985 (my emphasis).
46 Gian Balsamo, *Pruning the Genealogical Tree: Procreation and Lineage in Literature, Law, and Religion*, Lewisburg: Bucknell University Press, 1999.
47 Bachofen, *Myth, Religion and Mother Right*, p. 88 (my emphasis).
48 *Ibid.*, p. 93.
49 *Ibid.*, p. 110 (my emphasis).
50 Page Du Bois, *Sowing the Body: Psychoanalysis and Ancient Representations of Women*, Chicago: University of Chicago Press, 1988, p. 57.
51 *Ibid.*, p. 50.
52 Erich Neumann, *The Great Mother: An Analysis of the Archetype*, Princeton: Princeton University Press, 1963, pp. 268–9.
53 Briffault, *The Mothers*.
54 *Ibid.*, vol. 11, p. 95.
55 Carole Pateman, *The Sexual Contract*, Oxford: Basil Blackwell, 1988.
56 Goran Therborn, "The Rights of Children Since the Constitution of Modern Childhood: A Comparative Study of Western Nation," in Louis Moreno (ed.) *Social Exchange and Welfare Development*, Madrid: CSIC, 1993, pp. 67–121.
57 See John O'Neill, "Cultural Capitalism and Child Formation," in Henay Cavanna (ed.) *The New Citizenship of the Family*, Aldershot: Ashgate, 2000, pp. 79–98.
58 Lisa C Bower, "Mother in Law: Conception of Mother and the Maternal in Feminism and Feminist Legal Theory," *Differences: A Journal of Feminist Cultural Studies*, vol. 3, no.1, 1991, pp. 8–37.

59 James Joyce, *Ulysses*, Harmondsworth: Penguin Books, 1971, p. 207.
60 Jardine, *Gynesis*, p. 25.
61 John O'Neill, *The Missing Child in Liberal Theory: Towards a Covenant Theory of Family, Community, Welfare and the Civic State*, Toronto: University of Toronto Press, 1994.

6

MARCUSE'S NEGATIVE DIALECTICS OF IMAGINATION

Gérard Raulet

Surrounded by the simulacra of what he termed advanced industrial society, Herbert Marcuse struggled, as tenaciously as Walter Benjamin, to preserve the utopia of an emancipated society. Indeed, Marcuse attempted to wrest it dialectically from these very simulacra. Over the years, he countered the protean manifestations of irrational rationalization with various philosophical interventions that attempt to re-dialecticize the rationality of domination from within, but that are nonetheless characterized from the beginning by the search for a "third way." Marcuse's goal was the negation of domination in domination itself. The way out, however – that is to say, the means for both realizing and maintaining this negation – was linked even in his earliest philosophical writings to a third dimension of rationality, a dimension that Marcuse, in the period spanning from *Eros and Civilization* to *The Aesthetic Dimension*, increasingly came to identify with the aesthetic. The crucial question in this context is whether this third dimension can in fact be equated with the Hegelian–Marxist negation of the negation, that is to say, whether it can be the sphere of mediation. In *The Aesthetic Dimension*, this strategy leads to a conceptual dead end. When the goal is a subversion of the prevailing rationality at its foundations, art proves inadequate. At best, it bears negative witness to an ill-fated rationalization, as Marcuse had already admitted much earlier:

> philosophy, in opposition to poetry, is dependent on the logical discourse which has been determinant in the history of thought. It is the logic of domination which, as theoretical and practical reason, lead the organization of the subjective and objective world. Everything that went beyond its concepts has always been considered as metaphysical and suspect, or tolerated as literature.[1]

I

Marcuse's original project addresses the question on a deeper level. In his early writings, he describes his search for an alternative reason as "concrete philosophy." Alfred Schmidt, in an essay entitled "Existential-Ontology and Historical Materialism in Herbert Marcuse," has called attention to the critical impulses Marcuse drew in this regard from his reading of *Being and Time*, in particular from the Heideggerian critique of the historical decline of occidental metaphysics.[2] Following Heidegger, Marcuse countered the understanding of history (*Geschichte*) as a mere succession of events (*Geschehen*), a false view to which Heidegger felt Hegel's ontology had also fallen victim, with the notion of "historicity" (*Geschichtlichkeit*) as a "fundamental structure of Dasein." This affirmation of Heideggerian historicity in the sense of "concrete philosophy" implied a theory of social and historical imagination that could base itself on the function attributed by Heidegger to the transcendental imagination in *Kant and the Problem of Metaphysics*. For Heidegger, it is in the temporality of the schemata that the openness of *Dasein* resides, that is to say, in its ability to comprehend Being (*Sein*).

Marcuse's 1930 essay, "Transcendental Marxism," moves decisively in this direction. Here he seeks in the temporality of the schemata the simultaneously transcendental and concrete dimension of a historical time which the transcendentalism of the *Critique of Pure Reason* had at once implied and eclipsed. In doing so, he is well aware that a similar approach could be applied to Heidegger's existential analysis. Through a "reciprocal revision of phenomenology and materialist dialectics,"[3] as Alfred Schmidt says, he attempts to demonstrate the "concrete material content"[4] of both in order to transform them into a theory of praxis. For, as Marcuse writes, "the ontological (*seinsmäßig*) interrelation of Dasein and world is no free-floating abstraction; rather, it constitutes itself in concrete, historical processes."[5]

Characteristic in this context is the fact that Marcuse, like Heidegger himself, was less interested in *aesthetic* imagination than he was in *transcendental* imagination, in which he discerned an a priori spatio-temporality that he felt was constitutive for the particularly human form of existence (*Daseinsweise*). Whereas the later interest in *aesthetic* imagination and Marcuse's inclination toward an ontology inspired by *Lebensphilosophie* – an inclination documented in *Eros and Civilization* and particularly apparent in the late works *An Essay on Liberation* and *The Aesthetic Dimension* – are obviously connected, the engagement with Heidegger's existential analytic is guided by an intention wholly opposed to such an approach. It is an attempt to "de-ontologize" historicity, which offers an early articulation of that "poetics of history," according to which the imaginary co-determines our knowledge of reality and in which, in my opinion, the nucleus of Marcuse's philosophical project is to be found. This project takes up a problem that Kant himself addressed and left open in the seventh paragraph of his introduction to the *Critique of Judgment*:

> If pleasure is connected with the mere apprehension (*apprehensio*) of the form of an object of intuition, apart from any reference it may have to a concept for the purpose of a definite cognition ... that apprehension of forms in the imagination can never take place without reflective judgment, even when it has no intention of so doing, comparing them at least with its faculty of referring intuitions to concepts.[6]

The formulation "even when it has no intention of so doing" points to the riddle of the transcendental imagination and to the originary synthesis of apperception, described by Kant in the *Critique of Pure Reason* as "an art concealed in the depths of the human soul".[7] It was this same riddle that occupied Max Horkheimer in these years; Horkheimer saw in it the enigma of "the activity of society" as a "transcendental power."[8]

In the end, all of Marcuse's later works can be assessed in terms of their view of the relationship between these two forms of imagination: whether the transcendental imagination – which is constitutive in cognitive judgments – and the aesthetic imagination are distinguished or conflated. Already in the works written between 1930 and 1932, two opposing approaches to this relationship begin competing with one another. Whereas "Transcendental Marxism" interprets the transcendental imagination as a structure of human existence and attempts to make it concrete by developing it into an organon of historical consciousness and historical praxis, the *Habilitationsschrift Hegel's Ontology and the Theory of Historicity* conceives the "unifying unity" as the "motility" of life. Even as early as in the dissertation "The German Artist-Novel,"[9] the metaphysics of life plays a role whose significance can hardly be exaggerated.

Thus, in the period between 1930 and 1932, Marcuse's thought stands at a crossroads: either it attributes synthetic capacities to life, or it uses the imagination unique to human existence to construct the organon of historical consciousness. Marcuse's turn to Hegel and his corresponding attempt to interpret Hegel's ontology as the "foundation of a theory of historicity" supplant this alternative in 1932, but they simultaneously eclipse the role of imagination. On the one hand, life is posited as the foundation of historicity; on the other, Marcuse, following Hegel, endeavors to rid the "life" concept of its metaphysical vitalism. He now understands life as the motility of being; it is this motility that functions as the unifying unity in knowledge and action. It reaches its completion, according to Hegel, in the concept. Of course, in emphasizing the primary role of human life, that is to say, the role of the cognizing subject, Marcuse gives his interpretation here an undeniably Young–Hegelian twist. Thus in *Hegel's Ontology* he writes: "Through the concept of truth (*phos*), the meaning of life comes to focus exclusively on *human* existence."[10] The unity of life is contained in the "significant relationship" between the "world" and human life; the world is "ontologically (*seinsmäßig*) that of the *anthropou photos*; indeed, in all its 'relations' and 'determinations,' it is 'the work of humans who develop themselves.'"[11]

Life nonetheless achieves fulfillment as *Geist*, and it is into this *Geist* that history, as the mode of being unique to human life, is also absorbed. The penultimate sentence of the book expresses this point in sibylline fashion: "It is precisely as something historical and through its historicity that life becomes *Geist*."[12] In his 1931 essay, "On the Problem of the Dialectic," Marcuse claims that it would be a "grave error to interpret Hegel's view of history primarily from the lectures on the philosophy of history or the philosophy of right."[13] In a similar vein, he writes that "Hegel's later lectures on the *Philosophy of Right* and the *Philosophy of History* ... no longer consider historicity as an ontological feature (*Seinsbestimmung*) of life. History is here viewed from the beginning ahistorically and from the standpoint of Absolute Knowledge."[14] In contrast, the *Phenomenology of Spirit* represents "Hegel's first and last attempt to unify both motifs as equally fundamental ... one can characterize this attempt by the prescription: to demonstrate how life, as something historical, carries in itself the possibility of becoming unhistorical, and to show how it realizes, as something historical, this possibility."[15] Returning now to the penultimate sentence of *Hegel's Ontology*, we find that Marcuse's attempt to build on Hegel's foundation results in a subjugation of all historical experience to *Geist*. The victim of this motility of human knowledge striving toward *Geist* is *imagination*. Thus, although he underestimates the significance of the Young–Hegelian moment in *Hegel's Ontology*, one can agree with Martin Jay's judgment of the book: "What set *Hegel's Ontology* apart from *Reason and Revolution* ... was its basic indifference to the critical elements in Hegelian philosophy. Marcuse's stress on unity and identity led to a kind of theodicy."[16]

II

A decade after *Eros and Civilization*, whose characterization in terms of the aforementioned standard of whether transcendental and aesthetic imagination are distinguished or conflated we will turn to later, *One Dimensional Man* (1964) takes up the theory of the historical imaginary that Marcuse had left unelaborated in the early 1930s. Here this theory achieves its full explosive force, for it is in the one-dimensional society, where the quest for totality realizes itself as false totality – indeed, as the totality of the false and as totalitarian falsity – that any distinction between true and false, reality and fiction becomes impossible, thus bringing the realm of the imaginary and the fictional into the foreground. When "the whole *appears* to be the very embodiment of reason,"[17] a context of delusion (*Verblendungszusammenhang*) comes into being that can only be unraveled through a radicalized engagement with fictionality. The insight that "the whole *appears* to be the expression of reason," such that a critique of ideology can no longer distinguish between illusion and reality, implies a *fictionalization* of any attempt to construct ontological or rational foundations. As Marcuse claims: "The advancing one-dimensional society alters the relation between the rational and the irrational ... The two antagonistic faculties (imagination and reason) become interdependent on common ground."[18] As a result, "The values alien to these requirements (of advancing one-dimensional society may perhaps have no other medium of communication than the abnormal one of fiction."[19]

Already in their 1937 contributions to the program of Critical Theory, Horkheimer and Marcuse had concluded that truth had become utopian: "When truth cannot be realized within the established social order, it always appears to the latter as mere utopia."[20] Yet, in this period, it was precisely this utopia that seemed to them the refuge of negative thought. For Horkheimer, this situation even privileges the function of imagination:

> One thing that this way of thinking has in common with imagination is that an image of the future which springs indeed from a deep understanding of the present determines men's thoughts and actions even in periods when the course of events seems to be leading far away from such a future and seems to justify every conclusion except belief in fulfillment. While this thinking does not possess the arbitrariness and supposed independence of imagination, it shares its obstinacy. Within the most advanced groups it is the theoretician who must summon up this obstinacy.[21]

For, as Marcuse emphasizes in his contribution, "Philosophy and Critical Theory":

> In order to retain in the present the not-yet-present as a goal, imagination is required ... Imagination does not relate to the other cognitive faculties as illusion to truth (which in fact, when it plumes itself on being the only truth, can perceive the truth of the future only as an illusion). Without imagination, all philosophical knowledge remains in the grip of the present or the past, severed from the future, which alone links philosophy to the real history of mankind.[22]

To be sure, Marcuse already admits here that "(the limits of imagination are prescribed by the level of technological development."[23] To the extent that this technological development gives rise to the "technological veil" that Horkheimer and Marcuse diagnosed in 1941,[24] the sense for the possible, to which the program of critical theory could still appeal in 1937, is enfeebled, even disappears. This is precisely the starting point of *One-Dimensional Man*:

> In this process, the "inner" dimension of the mind in which opposition to the status quo can take root is whittled down. The loss of this dimension, in which the power of negative thinking – the critical power of Reason – is at home, is the ideological counterpart to the very material process in which advanced industrial society silences and reconciles the opposition.[25]

If one wants to hold on to the possibility of a philosophy of history with practical intent, then the technological "context of delusion" (*Verblendungszusammenhang*) cannot be ignored; on the contrary, its figures must be examined hermeneutically, because the desired productive imagination, however distorted its expressions, is at work here and nowhere else.

This theory of the imagination proposed by *One-Dimensional Man*, however, can no longer even rely on the oppositional potential of art for support. The reason is that this potential itself is revealed as mediated and thereby contaminated. In the first place, it can only transcend alienated existence as "artistic alienation,"[26] as a "higher level" of alienation, so to speak; moreover, it is capable of this only insofar as it remains conscious of its own fictional status, that is to say, only insofar as it knows itself to be a fiction and *as illusion* denounces the illusory, fallacious "reality": "Fiction calls the facts by their name and their reign collapses."[27]

To the extent that "the developing technological reality undermines not only the traditional forms but the very basis of the artistic alienation,"[28] Marcuse's subsequent reflections on various techniques of alienation employed by avant-garde art (including Brecht's alienation effect) are of less interest than the insight that reification as deception gives rise to a "world of imagery"[29] that seizes control of the imagination: "Imagination is abdicating to this reality, which is catching up with and overtaking imagination."[30]

The argument of *One-Dimensional Man* thus culminates in what can be termed a "negative dialectics of imagination." It has too often been overlooked that the first chapter, "The conquest of unhappy consciousness: repressive desublimation," already addresses this negative dialectics. According to Marcuse, if the "means and ways by which the administered individuals might break their servitude and seize their own liberation"[31] are becoming increasingly inconceivable, this is because "imagination has not remained immune to the process of reification" and because "we are possessed by our images."[32] To give free reign to this contaminated imagination would mean falling victim to the deception: "However, 'to give to the imagination all the means of expression' would be regression."[33]

The emancipation of the imagination is in the end nothing more than the program of "repressive desublimation." If the sphere of the fictional, of the imaginary, is the realm in which the possibility of a different world finds expression, then this sphere is nonetheless always dependent upon the "system," particularly since imagination has been integrated into it and the system as a whole is itself only a fiction: that false totality that results from the indistinguishability of the real and the fictive as it is expressed in the "obscene merger of aesthetics and reality."[34]

This dialectic of an imprisoned imagination is the closest Marcuse comes to the insight that only an acceptance of the fictional status of all putatively "ontological" grounds can lead us beyond the crisis of foundations, an acceptance that would of course also require the translation of ontology into a theory of the fictionality of reason. With such a theory, perhaps – at least this is my working hypothesis here as it has been elsewhere – one could rescue the possibility of a practical philosophy through a hermeneutics of the apparently inscrutable *figures* in which the fiction of "reason" manifests itself.

Introductory steps toward such an approach can be found in *One-Dimensional Man*, steps which build, however implicitly, upon the "concrete philosophy" of 1929–30. Aesthetic experience, for example, appears here as the model of a mediation between the fictive and the real with a significance that points beyond its realization in art:

> In [its] vagueness and directness, beauty is experienced *in* the beautiful – that is, it is seen, heard, smelled, touched, felt, comprehended. It is experienced almost as a shock, perhaps due to the contrast-character of beauty, which breaks the circle of everyday experience and opens (for a short moment) another reality (of which fright may be an integral element).[35]

Beauty thus involves more than the purely subjective Kantian aesthetic judgment. It belongs to those "concrete universals," which, more than mere concepts or ideas, constitute real qualities of the world.[36] As such, these universals represent categories of historical experience:

> Now there is a large class of concepts – we dare say, the philosophically relevant concepts – where the quantitative relation between the universal and the particular assumes a qualitative aspect, where the abstract universal seems to designate potentialities in a concrete, historical sense. However "man," "nature," "justice," "beauty," or "freedom" may be defined, they synthesize experiential contents into ideas which transcend their particular realizations as something that is to be surpassed, overcome. Thus the concept of beauty comprehends all the beauty not *yet* realized; the concept of freedom all the liberty not *yet* attained.[37]

III

The philosophical contributions made by *Eros and Civilization* are beyond dispute. Not the least of these contributions was the book's willingness to grapple with Freud's late metaphysics and with the problem of the death drive, which had been largely ignored in psychoanalytic theory.[38] Nonetheless, I would argue that *Eros and Civilization* cleared the way and served as the basis for Marcuse's regression into an ontology of subjectivity. Habermas rightly points out that *Eros and Civilization* builds not only on the legacy of Freud's final theory of drives, but also on that of the anthropology and ontology of 1932,[39] with the result that the horizontal axis of history is exchanged for a "posthistorical ontology."[40]

It is true that the dialectics of liberation in *Eros and Civilization* unfolds as a dialectic between the "desublimation of reason" and the non-repressive "self-sublimation of sensuousness": "The desublimation of reason is just as essential a process in the emergence of a free culture as is the self-sublimation of sensuousness."[41] Precisely because the imaginary receives, in the development that leads to the differentiation between pleasure-ego and reality principle, the status of a "separate mental process,"[42] it appears to enjoy relative autonomy vis-à-vis the transformation of the psyche through the reality and then the performance principle. But the cost of this "recognition of phantasy"[43] is the unambiguous primacy of reason and the trivialization of imagination:

> The mental process formerly unified in the pleasure ego is now split: its main stream is channeled into the domain of the reality principle and brought into line with its requirements ... The other part of the mental apparatus remains free from the control of the reality principle – at the price of becoming powerless, inconsequential, unrealistic ... Phantasy as a separate mental process is born and at the same time left behind by the organization of the pleasure ego into the reality ego. Reason prevails: it becomes unpleasant but useful and correct; phantasy remains pleasant but becomes useless, untrue – a mere play, daydreaming.[44]

Rather than searching for an inextricable coupling of reality and phantasm in the prevailing "rationality" itself – as described by the dialectics of imagination in *One-Dimensional Man* – Marcuse turns the civilization-induced split of human capacities into the foundation for a theoretical dualism that becomes entangled in an alternative between art and metaphysics. *Either* "Phantasy (imagination) retains the structure and the tendencies of the psyche prior to its organization by the reality (principle)"[45] – in other words, it preserves the memory of a time when individual and species were still one,[46] of a prehistorical life prior to division, in which case the imaginary becomes the expression of a *Lebensphilosophie*-inspired metaphysics – *or* it limits itself to the realm of art as subjective achievement. The constitutive function of imagination for historical cognition and practice is abandoned in favor of a dualism of art and sensuousness, which Marcuse is only able to transcend to the extent that an autonomous art detached from concrete historical references safeguards the archetypal memories of an originary human nature prior to ontogenic or phylogenic deformation.[47]

Marcuse struggled to break free from this dualism in *An Essay on Liberation*. But despite the link suggested by the work's subtitle – *Beyond One-Dimensional Man* – the essay is in fact more of a continuation of *Eros and Civilization*, as becomes clear when Marcuse asserts that "the new sensibility has become a political factor."[48] Unreconciled subjectivity, so the argument goes, finds in the development of advanced industrial society an objective, socio-economic foundation; the advancement of productive forces makes possible the liberation of instinctive energies to such a degree that the "Great Refusal" no longer represents a mere utopia. Marcuse sees in the protest movements a concrete realization of this development: a political opposition that adopts as its own the fundamental demands of the aesthetic dimension[49] and does not conceive of these simply as the experience of the beautiful or the symbolic experience of life, but rather as the historical productivity and creativity of sensibility. This new state of affairs can be discerned, according to Marcuse, in the emergent "new language," the "methodical reversal of meaning" that one observes in the "most militant areas of protest."[50] Marcuse freely admits, however, that it is a Kantian form of aesthetic experience, restricted to purely subjective validity, which resurfaces in the artificial paradise of drug-induced "trips." As such, these paradises remain "subject to the law of this society."[51] Drug-induced experience places one above the opposition between reality and fiction, but it does it in such a way as to eliminate *not only* the prevailing rationality *but also* the reality of a practice that opposes this rationality on any level other than the merely subjective.[52]

Once again emancipation withdraws into illusion, and once again the interpreter cannot escape the conclusion that illusion – the indistinguishability of the real and the fictional – constitutes the central issue that any theory of liberation that hopes to move "beyond one-dimensional man" must confront. Once again Marcuse is faced with the alternative of either developing a theory of historical imagination adequate to this state of affairs or merely placing his hopes in sensibility, in the drives, in life.

An Essay on Liberation takes an important step in the former direction, insofar as it more closely connects illusion, domination, and art, which it conceives as a "beautiful illusion" that points beyond the limits of domination. As in *One-Dimensional Man*, the argument builds on the central insight that the impossibility of liberation depends to a large degree on the ability of advanced capitalist societies to manipulate the mechanisms of repressive sublimation as well as repressive desublimation.[53] For my line of interpretation it is significant that Marcuse refers back in this context to the distinction between the status of the imagination in the *Critique of Pure Reason* and its status in the *Critique of Judgment*,[54] albeit in order to conclude that the aesthetic imagination acquires its status in one-dimensional society at a double cost: as the capacity whose role it is to mediate between sensibility and reason, it ends up being exposed to both the manipulation of sensibility and the "technological veil."[55]

Precisely at this point one would have expected Marcuse to take up again the basic ideas of the 1930s, in order to demonstrate the validity of the transcendental imagination as the organon of historical consciousness. But instead he turns once again to art, viewing its capacity to become a productive force in its own right as the only possibility of resisting this double bind.[56] The strengths and weaknesses of this attempt are more closely intertwined here than in any of Marcuse's earlier works. On the one hand, the immediate consequence of this approach is that art's contribution to liberation runs up against practical limits: "Its realization has been stopped at the point at which it would have become incompatible with foundational institutions and social relationships."[57] At the same time, however, it should be noted that imagination appears here as the sphere in which the problem of emancipation first presents itself definitively: "A universe of human relationships no longer mediated by the market ... demands a sensitivity receptive to forms and modes of reality which thus far have been projected only by the aesthetic imagination."[58] The subjunctive mood that dominates the entire essay – the mood of possibility – corresponds in turn to the alternative that I want to make clear: on the one hand, flight into the "aesthetic dimension," on the other, the grounding of emancipation in the emergence of new needs that would demolish the integration of sensibility and would offer a new foundation for aesthetic illusion.

The Aesthetic Dimension – Marcuse's philosophical last will and testament – argues unequivocally that this hope remains alive only in and through art. Art constitutes a productive force qualitatively different from labor; it harnesses libidinal energy in a different manner and can thus become "a factor in the transformation of consciousness", but, as Marcuse adds, "the subversion of experience proper to art and the rebellion against the established reality principle contained in this subversion cannot be translated into political praxis."[59] This understanding leads to the concept of a "non-repressive desublimation," which Marcuse introduces in *The Aesthetic Dimension* and which is only possible to the extent that art is removed from reality.

Marcuse's offensive against "a certain Marxist aesthetics" thus becomes the pretense for a defensive strategy of withdrawal, one that succeeds in establishing the unique nature of the aesthetic only at the cost of renouncing its basis and effectiveness in reality. One can only approve of Marcuse's criticisms of a vulgar-Marxist position that reduces art to the collective consciousness of a particular moment in history. What is really needed here, however, is not only the acknowledgement of art's fictional as well as fictive essence, but also and above all a conjunction of this fictionality with the "reality" of a history that is itself largely played out as fiction. To recognize this "fictional" history was one of the accomplishments of *One-Dimensional Man*, albeit without being able to overcome the antinomies of the "negative dialectics of imagination."

Here the transcendence of art consists in its general plea for humanity, which would be a mere platitude if Marcuse did not mean by this, as he had already suggested in *Eros and Civilization*, that art preserves the memory of "the structure and strivings of the psyche as they existed prior to their organization through reality (the reality principle)."[60] By this measure, however, the subjective, not to mention the individualized character of art is not overcome through that concretization of existence which the essays of the 1930s required, but rather through a vitalistic ontology. In *The Aesthetic Dimension*, this ontology no longer limits itself to an appeal to the metaphysics of the late Freud; it even goes so far as to invoke Greek tragedy and its concept of fate:

> The convergence of fulfillment and death preserves its real power despite all romantic glorification and sociological explanation. The inexorable human entanglement in nature sustains its own dynamic in the given social relations and creates its metasocial dimension. Great literature knows a guiltless guilt which finds its first authentic expression in *Oedipus Rex*. Here is the domain of that which is changeable and that which is not. Obviously there are societies in which people no longer believe in oracles, and there may be societies in which there is no incest taboo, but it is difficult to imagine a society which has abolished what is called chance or fate.[61]

If, then, we were to distill out the essence of *The Aesthetic Dimension*, it could be summarized along the following lines: Art is at its root a mere "fiction" – this fact must be recorded in opposition to the vulgar-Marxist view. To be sure, this fiction is not meaningless, but its meaning consists in a general, pre- and transhistorical, indeed ontological message.

IV

Ultimately, what remains relevant in Marcuse's philosophy is not, or at least not primarily, the idea of a transformation of needs whose naturalism stands opposed to the conversion of needs into desires in late capitalism. This conversion has long since been completed. Rather, its contemporary significance lies in the diagnosis, found above all in *One-Dimensional Man*, of the displacement of forms of social interaction into the aesthetic sphere. Today, it is the development of expressivity – in the new technologies of communication as well as in newspaper and television journalism – that represents the contemporary form of the "new sensibility."[62] To the extent that it asserts itself as a parallel to performativity, it appears as an aspect of "repressive desublimation." We find ourselves – as Marcuse himself ascertained – in an age of the obscene, what Baudrillard has termed a "white obscenity": "The obscene exposures of the affluent society normally provoke neither shame nor a sense of guilt, although this society violates some of the most fundamental moral taboos of civilization."[63] These manifestations of "historical imagination" pose a double challenge to social philosophy. First, it must take seriously the fictionalization of reason, since historical imagination, which constitutes our knowledge of reality, is inseparable from this "aesthetic dimension." In addition, it must realize that there is no alternative to a serious engagement with the figures in which the thus-constituted "knowledge" leaves its traces. Social philosophy must transform itself, in other words, into a philosophy (or sociology) of symbolic forms that treats these "fictions" as creations of the productive imagination. Only on this condition will it be able to fulfill the task that Marcuse set for it: a theory of historical subject–object mediation.

Notes

1 Herbert Marcuse, "Zur Stellung des Denkens heute," in Max Horkheimer (ed.) *Zeugnisse. T.W. Adorno zum 60. Geburtstag*, Frankfurt/M: Europäische Verlagsanstalt, 1963, p. 46. All translations, unless noted otherwise, are by Matt Erlin.
2 Alfred Schmidt, "Existential-Ontologie und Historischer Materialismus bei Herbert Marcuse," in Jürgen Habermas (ed.) *Antworten auf Herbert Marcuse*, Frankfurt: Suhrkamp, 1968.
3 *Ibid.*, p. 42.
4 Herbert Marcuse, "Beiträge zu einer Phänomenologie des Historischen Materialismus," *Schriften*, vol. 1, Frankfurt: Suhrkamp, 1978, p. 369.
5 *Ibid.*, p. 374. On Marcuse's critique of the abstractness of the Heideggerian categories "Geschick," "Sorge," "Geworfenheit," etc., as well as of the political decisionism resulting therefrom, see Gérard Raulet, *Herbert Marcuse. Philosophie de l'émancipation*, Paris: Presses Universitaires de France, 1992, pp. 40–4, as well as "Die Gemeinschaft beim jungen Marcuse," in Manfred Gangl and Gérard Raulet (eds) *Intellektuellendiskurse in der Weimarer Republik*, Frankfurt: Campus, 1994, pp. 103–6.
6 Immanuel Kant, *Critique of Judgment*, trans. James Creed Meredith, Oxford: Clarendon Press, 1952, p. 30.
7 Immanuel Kant, *Critique of Pure Reason*, trans. Norman Kemp Smith, London: Macmillan, 1961, p. 183.
8 Max Horkheimer, "Traditional and Critical Theory," *Critical Theory. Selected Essays*, trans. Matthew J. O'Connell, New York: Herder and Herder, 1972, p. 203.
9 Herbert Marcuse, "Der deutsche Künstlerroman," *Schriften*, vol. 1, pp. 7–343.

10 Herbert Marcuse, *Hegel's Ontology and the Theory of Historicity*, trans. Seyla Benhabib, Cambridge, MA: MIT Press, 1987, p. 207.
11 *Ibid.*
12 *Ibid.*, p. 324.
13 Marcuse, *Schriften*, vol. I, p. 442.
14 Marcuse, *Hegel's Ontology*, p. 227.
15 *Ibid.*
16 Martin Jay, *The Dialectical Imagination*, Boston and Toronto: Little, Brown & Co., 1973, p. 74.
17 Herbert Marcuse, *One-Dimensional Man. Studies in the Ideology of Advanced Industrial Society*, London: Routledge and Kegan Paul, 1964, p. ix (my emphasis).
18 *Ibid.*, pp. 247 and 249.
19 *Ibid.*, p. 247.
20 Herbert Marcuse, "Philosophy and Critical Theory," *Negations. Essays in Critical Theory* ed. and trans. Jeremy J. Shapiro, Boston: Beacon Press, 1968, p. 143.
21 Horkheimer, "Traditional and Critical Theory," p. 220 (translation slightly amended).
22 Marcuse, "Philosophy and Critical Theory," pp. 154–5 (translation slightly amended).
23 *Ibid.*, p. 154.
24 See Max Horkheimer, "The End of Reason," in *Studies in Philosophy and Social Science*, vol. 9, New York: Institute for Social Research, 1941, pp. 366–88, and Herbert Marcuse, "Some Social Implications of Modern Technology," in *ibid.*, pp. 414–39.
25 Marcuse, *One-Dimensional Man*, pp. 10–11.
26 *Ibid.*, p. 60.
27 *Ibid.*, p. 62.
28 *Ibid.*
29 *Ibid.*, p. 72.
30 *Ibid.*, p. 247.
31 *Ibid.*, pp. 6–7.
32 *Ibid.*, p. 250.
33 *Ibid.*
34 *Ibid.*, p. 248.
35 *Ibid.*, p. 210.
36 "Universals are primary elements of experience – universals not as philosophic concepts but as the very qualities of the world," *ibid.*, p. 211.
37 *Ibid.*, pp. 231–2.
38 See Gérard Raulet, "La Mort aux Deux Visages," in Jacques Le Rider, Michel Plon, Gérard Raulet and Henry Rey-Flaud (eds) *Autour du "Malaise dans la culture" de Freud*, Paris: Presses Universitaires de France, 1998.
39 *Gespräche mit Herbert Marcuse*, Frankfurt: Suhrkamp, 1978, p. 27. The participants in the conversations were Jürgen Habermas, Tilman Spengler, Silvia Bovenschen, Marianne Schuller, Berthold Rotschild, Theo Pinkus, Erica Sherover, Heinz Lubasz, Alfred Schmidt, Ralf Dahrendorf, Karl Popper, Rudi Dutschke, and Hans Christoph.
40 See also Claus Offe, "Technik und Eindimensionalität. Eine Version der Technokratiethese?", in Habermas (ed.) *Antworten auf Herbert Marcuse*, p. 84.
41 Herbert Marcuse, *Eros and Civilization. A Philosophical Inquiry into Freud*, New York: Vintage Books, 1962, p. 178.
42 *Ibid.*, p. 129.
43 *Ibid.*, p. 128.

44 *Ibid.*, pp. 128–9.
45 *Ibid.*, p. 129.
46 *Ibid.* "Imagination preserves the 'memory' of the subhistorical past when the life of the individual was the life of the genus."
47 *Ibid.*, p. 133. "(T)he subhistorical past of the genus (and of the individual) prior to all civilization."
48 Herbert Marcuse, *An Essay on Liberation*, Boston: Beacon Press, 1969, p. 23.
49 See *ibid.*, p. 26.
50 *Ibid.*, pp. 33–4.
51 *Ibid.*, p. 37.
52 *Ibid.*
53 *Ibid.*, pp. 13 and 9.
54 See *ibid.*, p. 32.
55 *Ibid.*, pp. 29 and 13.
56 *Ibid.*, p. 33.
57 *Ibid.*, p. 38.
58 *Ibid.*, p. 27.
59 Herbert Marcuse, *The Aesthetic Dimension*, Boston: Beacon, 1978, p. 39.
60 Marcuse, *Eros and Civilization*, p. 129.
61 Marcuse, *The Aesthetic Dimension*, p. 24.
62 See Gérard Raulet, "Singuläre Geschichten und pluralishe Ratio," in Jacques Le Rider and Gérard Raulet (eds) *Verabschiedung der (Post-)Moderne?*, Tübingen: Narr, 1987, pp. 275–92, and "Leben wir im Zeitalter der Simulation?" in Peter Kemper (ed.) *"Postmoderne," oder, der Kampf um die Zukunft*, Frankfurt: Fischer, 1988, pp. 165–88.
63 Marcuse, *An Essay on Liberation*, p. 8.

Part II

NEW CRITICAL VOICES INTERPRET MARCUSE

7

HERBERT MARCUSE'S CRITICAL ENCOUNTER WITH MARTIN HEIDEGGER 1927–33

John Abromeit

Like many other intellectuals of his generation, the publication of *Being and Time* in 1927 had a tremendous impact on the 29-year-old Herbert Marcuse. Marcuse was so impressed by *Being and Time* that he decided to return to Freiburg to renew his academic studies, which he had broken off in 1922. Two years later Marcuse would describe *Being and Time* as a work that "seems to mark a turning point in the history of philosophy: the point where the internal tendencies of bourgeois philosophy lead to its own dissolution and clear the way for a new 'concrete' science."[1] At first glance it may seem puzzling why a young critical Marxist like Marcuse was attracted to a philosopher like Heidegger. Marcuse had, after all, actively participated in the workers' and soldiers' councils that formed in Berlin during the failed revolution of 1918,[2] whereas Heidegger's attempts to place the question of the meaning of being on the philosophical agenda once again, after nearly 2,500 years of neglect, seemed very far removed indeed from crisis-ridden Weimar Germany. But if one examines the philosophical climate of the time more closely, Marcuse's enthusiasm at the publication of *Being and Time* makes more sense.

The other major philosophical work of the 1920s that captured Marcuse's attention was George Lukács' *History and Class Consciousness*. On the surface, Lukács' work seems to have little in common with *Being and Time*, but if one looks beyond the important differences in language and strategic intent, it is clear that *History and Class Consciousness* addressed some of the same problems. Furthermore, if one recognizes the important similarities between *History and Class Consciousness* and *Being and Time*, Marcuse's enthusiasm for Heideggerian phenomenology becomes much less mysterious. According to Lucien Goldmann, who delivered a series of lectures at the Sorbonne in 1967–68 on the affinities between Lukács' and Heidegger's work in the 1920s, the most important similarity between *Being and Time* and *History and Class Consciousness* was the attempt by both to move beyond the positivist methodologies that – despite the increasing influence of

Lebensphilosophie and Husserl's phenomenology – still dominated the human sciences in German universities in the early 1920s.[3] With their indiscriminate rejection of idealism as empty "metaphysics," nineteenth-century positivists eliminated the "critical," self-reflexive, subjective moment in theory, which Kant had introduced as philosophy's "Copernican turn."[4] As a result, philosophy reassumed the dualistic form Descartes had given it in the seventeenth century. The subject was strictly separated from the objective world and reduced to passivity, in the form of either an ethereal spectator or a powerless object of "natural" laws. Lukács and Heidegger both tried in their own way to overcome this Manichean dualism and to recover the active subjective moment in philosophy. Lukács sought to overcome the "antinomies of bourgeois thought" through recourse to Hegel's dialectic and his concept of totality, which he believed formed the methodological foundation of Marx's revolutionary theory. Heidegger undertook an existential analysis of *Dasein*, which by its very definition was a being-*in*-the world, and which could not, in other words, be adequately understood as a discrete, present-at-hand entity separated from its environment or its own uniquely human modes of understanding and interacting with the world.[5] In short, at the heart of both *Being and Time* and *History and Class Consciousness* was an attempt to overcome the reduction of active human subjectivity to the status of an inert object: what Lukács called the *reification* and Heidegger *inauthenticity*.

Marcuse had read and was impressed by *History and Class Consciousness*,[6] but he thought that *Being and Time* addressed certain problems that Lukács had overlooked. He was critical of the implicit vanguardism of Lukács' concept of correct class consciousness imposed upon the proletariat from outside.[7] Although he never explicitly addressed the topic in his published writings from this time, Marcuse was probably also highly suspicious of Lukács' model of the proletariat as the identical subject-object of history; for one of his primary concerns during this period was to criticize the subordination of the individual to abstract collectivities or ideological constructs, such as Lukács' idealized notion of the proletariat.[8] One of the cornerstones of Marcuse's thought throughout his life, which was already clearly apparent in his early writings, was his emphasis on the concrete, universal individual as the subject of social and historical transformation.[9] For example, in a discussion of Kierkegaard in the essay "On Concrete Philosophy" from 1929, Marcuse writes:

> Although it is true that the purpose of philosophizing is not restricted to the "individual," it can only be fulfilled through each individual and it has its basis in the existence of each individual. The concreteness of philosophy in the existence of each individual can never be shifted onto an abstract they-subject [*Man-Subjekt*], the decisive responsibility shoved off onto this or that generality.[10]

The unmistakably Heideggerian terms of Marcuse's argument here demonstrate clearly one of the main reasons for his interest in *Being and Time*. Marcuse recognized in Heidegger's existential analysis of *Dasein* a path-breaking attempt to move beyond the abstract concepts of subjectivity that had dominated Western philosophy and to re-establish the concrete individual as the proper agent of history. In fact, a few years later, Marcuse would explain Heidegger's political engagement for National Socialism in terms of the subordination of non-conformist, authentic *Dasein* to the authoritarian community of destiny [*Schicksalsgemeinschaft*], a reversal in his position which could – all the more clearly in retrospect – be discerned already in the development of *Being and Time*.[11] In 1934 Marcuse would write:

> The meaning of philosophical existentialism lay in regaining the full concretion of the historical subject in opposition to the abstract "logical" subject of rational idealism, i.e. elimination of the domination, unshaken from Descartes through Husserl, of the *ego cogito*. Heidegger's position up through *Being and Time* was philosophy's furthest advance in this direction. Then came the reversal. This philosophy had good reasons for avoiding a closer examination of the material facticity of the historical situation of the subject it addressed. This is where its concreteness ended, this is where it remained content with talk of the "destiny" of the people [*Volk*], of the "inheritance" that every individual must assume, of the community of the "generation"[12]

In other words, prior to 1933, Marcuse still believed that Heidegger's existential analytic of *Dasein* and his attempt to grasp *Dasein* in its radically individuated totality, as a Being-toward-death, marked a decisive step beyond the abstract concepts of subjectivity that had characterized the rationalist and idealist traditions in particular.

Marcuse was convinced that the most influential interpretations of Marx at that time had all overlooked the centrality of the concrete individual as the active subject of historical change. This included Kautsky's "orthodoxy," which had emerged as the dominant position in the Second International, Bernstein's revisionism, which found a broad audience among Social Democrats in Germany, as well as the vanguardism of the Bolsheviks, which had, in 1920, also been established as the official position of the Third International and all its members, including the substantial German Communist Party. Marcuse suspected that even Marx himself, insofar as he had developed his own dialectical method through a critical appropriation of Hegel's thought, may have inherited this theoretical deficit from German idealism, which Heidegger had rightly criticized.[13] Since Marcuse came to Heidegger's philosophy as a committed, albeit critical Marxist, his primary concern was to address the weaknesses of Marxist theory in his day, which also included Lukács. This he thought he could do with Heideggerian phenomenology. In other words, Marcuse's interest in Heidegger's philosophy was more or less instrumental from the very beginning. As impressed as he was with *Being and Time*, he viewed it, from the beginning, as a way of revitalizing Marxist theory, not superseding it. This is why Marcuse never became an orthodox Heideggerian himself. On the other hand, he initially believed that without the corrective provided by Heidegger's phenomenology, the most influential interpretations of Marxist theory at the time ran the risk of unwittingly reproducing the domination of the concrete subjects they were intended to emancipate. Marcuse outlined his arguments for why Marxism needed to be supplemented with Heideggerian phenomenology in his first two published essays from 1928 and 1929, respectively "Contributions to a Phenomenology of Historical Materialism" and "On Concrete Philosophy."[14]

While Heidegger's existential analytic of *Dasein* appealed greatly to Marcuse, it was not the only aspect of *Being and Time* that interested him. Heidegger's theory of historicity was even more important for Marcuse's attempt to revitalize the Marxist theory of his time. It was particularly important for his critique of the scientistic economism and the evolutionist philosophy of history that had become so influential during the Second International and continued to determine the Social Democratic party line in Germany.[15] It was not a coincidence that these interpretations of Marx's theory – which downplayed the role of active subjectivity and stressed the importance of objective historical laws – were widely accepted at the same time that positivism established its virtually unquestioned dominance of the sciences on the European continent. As Lucien Goldmann points out, key figures in the Second International had been influenced by the spread of positivism in the late nineteenth century nearly as much as had German university philosophy:

> The evolution from Marx to Bernstein, Kautsky and Plekhanov is quite homologous to that which caused the German university philosophy of Hegel and the Neo-Hegelian to pass, via Schopenhauer and Haym, to Neo-Kantianism and university positivism. It was in relation to this positivism, both university and Marxist, that the beginning of the century was to produce a rather profound break.[16]

Marcuse sought to reinforce this break by arguing that Marxist theory needed to integrate certain aspects of Heidegger's theory of historicity in order to overcome the quietistic implications of Kautsky's and Bernstein's positions.[17] Marcuse objected to Kautsky's scientism in particular, not only because it had laid the groundwork for Lenin's vanguardist position,[18] but also because it subordinated the historical process to the deterministic "iron laws" of capitalism, over which humans actors had no control. As an alternative to Kautsky's model, which reduced individuals to passive spectators of an objective historical process, Marcuse defended Heidegger's theory of historicity, arguing that it represented the most advanced attempt to date to capture the full significance of history for human existence. While an adequate discussion of Heidegger's theory of historicity lies beyond the scope of this paper,[19] I would like point to those aspects of it that were most important for Marcuse's appropriation of Heidegger.

One of the prime symptoms diagnosed by Lukács as the reification of consciousness, and by Heidegger as inauthenticity, was a false understanding of temporality in modern Western philosophy. Both authors pointed to Descartes' philosophy as the quintessential example of the tendency in Western philosophy to subordinate historical time to abstract notions of quantitative space. It is true that Lukács and Heidegger ultimately traced the origins of this problem to different sources – the former to the domination of abstract, quantifiably measurable labor time brought about by the rise of modern capitalism and the proliferation of the commodity form,[20] the latter to Aristotle's projection of an abstract notion of "now-time" (*Jetzt-Zeit*),[21] derived from his physics, back onto the human subject.[22] Nonetheless, the two of them could not agree more that reification had reached unprecedented proportions at the beginning of the twentieth century. Heidegger's response to this problem in *Being and Time* was to attempt to recover the unique temporality of *Dasein* – what he called its historicity, happening (*Geschehen*) or motility. Building upon the philosophy of Wilhelm Dilthey, and in particular upon his efforts to develop a historical science of man that did not rely upon the methodologies of the natural sciences, Heidegger argued that the specific mode of *Dasein*'s historical being-in-the-world differed ontologically from that of all other things. *Dasein*'s motility (*Bewegtheit*) was distinguished from the mere movement (*Bewegung*) of other things due to *Dasein*'s consciousness of the past and the future. For Heidegger, to exist purely in the present, cut off from the truths of the past and the possibilities of the future, was to exist inauthentically, in the manner of a thing rather than a human being. Heidegger's definition of authentic existence, as awareness of one's own-most possibilities and the firm resolve to realize them in the future, is based directly on his understanding of the historicity of *Dasein*.

Marcuse believed that Heidegger's attempt to recapture the full ontological significance of history for *Dasein* was exactly what the reified Marxism of his day needed. He was attracted to Heidegger's theory of historicity not only because it restored active, dynamic elements of the historical process that had been obscured by the "scientific" Marxism of the Second International, but also because Heidegger insisted that reification could be overcome only through a collective effort to change the material world. In

Being and Time, Heidegger argued that *Dasein* could not exist authentically in isolation, nor could *Dasein* exist authentically without realizing its ownmost possibilities in the ontical-existentiell realm. Reading the first three-quarters of *Being and Time*, one could easily get the impression that authenticity was merely a problem of individual will, that is to say, a question of forcibly distancing oneself from the idle talk, curiosity, and the other fallen modes of being characteristic of the bad immediacy of "*das Man*." Furthermore, in several places in *Being and Time*, Heidegger implies that inauthenticity is rooted in the very ontological structure of *Dasein*.[23] But in the last two chapters of *Being and Time*, in his discussion of historicity, Heidegger demonstrates that both of these impressions are false. Departing from his earlier analysis of authenticity as Being-toward-death, which had focused on the extreme individuation brought about by existing in the full awareness of one's own mortality, Heidegger redefines authenticity as "destiny" and shows that it can be completely realized only collectively, within a larger context of Being-with others:

> But if fateful Dasein, as Being in the World, exists essentially in Being-with Others, its happening [*Geschehen*] is also a co-happening and is determinative for it as destiny [*Geschick*]. This is how we designate the happening of the community, of a people.... Only in communication and struggling does the power of destiny become free. Dasein's fateful destiny in and with its "generation" goes to make up the full authentic happening of Dasein.[24]

Furthermore, in his foregoing analysis of the "call of conscience," Heidegger had also shown that authenticity necessarily implies taking action to change the surrounding world. He writes:

> To hear the call [of conscience] authentically signifies bringing oneself into a factical taking action.... Anticipatory resoluteness is not a way of escape...; wanting-to-have-conscience [does not] signify a kind of seclusion in which one flees the world; rather, it brings one without illusions into the resoluteness of 'taking action'."[25]

Thus, far from relegating *Dasein* to a passive role, as the "shepherd of Being," as he would do in his later philosophy, in *Being and Time* Heidegger insisted that authenticity was not merely a way of interpreting the world, but that it necessarily entailed changing it through collective action.

This brief excursion into Heidegger's theory of historicity should have begun to show why *Being and Time* might have appealed to the young Marcuse. As removed as Heidegger's concerns may have seemed from the crises of Weimar Germany, *Being and Time* did lend itself fairly easily to a political reading, as Heidegger himself would prove in 1933. In fact, in a conversation with Karl Löwith in 1936, Heidegger averred that his concept of historicity was the philosophical basis for his political engagement.[26] But in view of the catastrophic consequences of National Socialist dictatorship – with which Heidegger believed, for several years at least, his own philosophy was fully compatible – Marcuse's appropriation of Heidegger's philosophy appears more problematic. The question arises, how did Marcuse's own theoretical approach differ from that of Heidegger? Was his appropriation of Heidegger's concept of historicity, and his emphasis on the "historical act,"[27] also susceptible to a decisionist or authoritarian interpretation?[28]

While there can be no doubt that Marcuse was deeply impressed with *Being and Time*, and that he felt that it had something substantial to contribute to the Marxist theory of his day, it must also be emphasized that he was critical of Heidegger's project from the very beginning. In the very first essay that Marcuse wrote in Freiburg, at a time when his enthusiasm for Heidegger was at its height, he leaves no doubt about his reservations:

> Phenomenology cannot stop with the demonstration of the historicity of its object, only to take it back into the sphere of abstraction once again. It must...constantly maintain the utmost concreteness of the object. That is, it must include in its analysis the concrete historical situation and the "material conditions." A phenomenology of human Dasein has insufficient fullness and clarity if, for example, it passes by the material conditions of historical Dasein. This is...the case with Heidegger.[29]

In other words, as much as Marcuse praises Heidegger's attempts to restore the full historicity of *Dasein*, he still argues that Heidegger does not go far enough in analyzing the concrete social and material conditions that are at the root of inauthentic forms of existence. This critique of Heidegger's insufficient concreteness, which Marcuse had already articulated in 1928, is one of the same arguments he would use later to explain Heidegger's political engagement for National Socialism. In an unpublished text on the history of contemporary German philosophy that Marcuse wrote in 1933, after taking a position at the Geneva branch of the Institute for Social Research, he spells out clearly the implications of Heidegger's pseudo-concreteness:

> Since the material sphere remains entirely outside of this philosophy and can in no case serve as a criteria for real existence, man, isolated within himself, becomes easy prey for any real power, that, by referring to the present situation as the true historical situation,

demands of man total submission to its domination. The characteristics of authentic existence, the disposition of resoluteness toward death, the decision, the risking of life, the acceptance of destiny are separated from any relationship to real misery and the real happiness of mankind and from all relations to the rational aims of humanity.[30]

In short, Marcuse was convinced from the very beginning that Heidegger's lack of concreteness was a serious limitation of his philosophy, a limitation which demonstrated that his phenomenology still needed the corrective of Marx, who had moved beyond philosophy to concrete social theory. In this crucial respect Marcuse never allowed his commitment to Marx's critical social theory to waver. It was not until 1933, however, that Marcuse was confronted with the disastrous consequences of Heidegger's attempt to draw concrete political conclusions based on the categories he had developed in *Being and Time*.[31]

Other important differences between Marcuse and Heidegger began to emerge in the early 1930s as well. Although the first two essays he wrote in Freiburg called for a phenomenological revision of Marxism, in which phenomenology was to play a role nearly as important as Marxism, Marcuse, beginning in 1930, began to search for a corrective to the reified Marxist theory of his day in the philosophical origins of Marx's own thought. In a lengthy two-part philosophical essay entitled "On the Problem of the Dialectic,"[32] Marcuse outlined the project that would occupy him for the next two years and would culminate in the publication of his *Habilitationsschrift*, *Hegel's Ontology and the Theory of Historicity*, in 1932. Following the lead of Lukács and Karl Korsch, Marcuse was determined to recover the origins of Marxist theory in the philosophy of Hegel.[33] Marcuse believed that the superficial understanding of Hegel prevalent at that time was to blame for the energetic efforts of reformists such as Eduard Bernstein to divorce Marx's theory completely from the philosophy of Hegel.[34] But it was precisely this jettisoning of the dialectical method which had led to the passivity of the orthodox and reformist positions of the Second International, according to Marcuse. Thus a revision of the widespread understanding of Hegel as a dogmatic metaphysician or conservative statist was far more than a mere academic exercise for Marcuse; it was an important step in restoring the dynamic, critical thrust of the Marxist theory of his day.

Marcuse believed that the widespread misunderstanding of Hegel's philosophy was due in large part to an over-reliance on Hegel's later writings, and a lack of familiarity with his earlier work. Marcuse writes:

> It is a serious mistake to interpret Hegel's attitude toward history primarily from the *Lectures on the Philosophy of History* or the

Philosophy of Right – a mistake which still conceals the intimate relationship between Hegel and Marx. Both works presuppose the *Phenomenology of Spirit* on the one hand, and the *Science of Logic* on the other hand, in the sense that they already represent a reduction of their original discoveries.[35]

Marcuse attempted to defend this claim in the 300 densely written and tightly argued pages of his *Habilitationsschrift*. It is true that *Hegel's Ontology and the Theory of Historicity* begins with a deferential gesture to Heidegger; in the introduction, Marcuse writes that "any contribution this work may make to the development and clarification of problems is indebted to the philosophical work of Martin Heidegger."[36] It is also true that *Hegel's Ontology* has the same point of departure as Heidegger's theory of historicity, namely the work of Wilhelm Dilthey, whose research, as Marcuse says, "forms the most advanced stage of these investigations, and even today...define the basis and the limits of this problem."[37] But Marcuse quickly departs from the path marked out by Heidegger. He maintains that Dilthey had borrowed his central category of "Life" from Hegel, and that therefore, in order properly to understand the presuppositions and limits of his theory of historicity, one needs to return to the original elaboration of the concept of "Life" in Hegel's work. Dilthey plays only a very marginal role and Heidegger is not mentioned at all in the rest of Marcuse's *Habilitationsschrift*, which is devoted to a careful exposition of the *Science of Logic* followed by a cursory, but nonetheless systematic re-examination of his early writings up to and including the *Phenomenology of Spirit*. While it would take us too far afield to explore the arguments of *Hegel's Ontology* in any detail here, his interpretation as a whole rests upon a distinction between a critical, immanent, action-oriented current in Hegel's early works, which culminates in the *Phenomenology of Spirit*, and an affirmative, transcendent, passive, epistemological current, which gains the upper hand in the *Logic* and dominates Hegel's late philosophy. It is not a coincidence that Marcuse locates the zenith of Hegel's philosophy in the *Phenomenology of Spirit*, the work that Marx considered "the true point of origin and the secret of the Hegelian philosophy."[38] For even though he does not mention Marx's name in the study, there is no doubt that Marcuse viewed his *Habilitationschrift* as a contribution to the restoration of the dialectical philosophical foundations of Marx's theory.[39]

For his part, Heidegger was also continuing his explorations into the foundations of historicity in the years after the publication of *Being and Time*, albeit in a different direction than Marcuse. In addition to continuing his investigations into the origins of contemporary "fallen" modes of being in ancient Greek philosophy, Heidegger also devoted considerable attention to German idealism during the late 1920s and early 1930s. In 1929 he published a major reinterpretation of Kant.[40] He believed that Kant too had recognized the necessity of moving beyond the subject–object dichotomies that formed the foundations of his own thought – between the noumenal and phenomenal realms, or understanding and sense impressions, for example. Heidegger argued that Kant's concept of transcendental imagination, as discussed in certain key passages in the first edition of the *Critique of Pure Reason*, pointed to a level of analysis that underlay and was more fundamental than these dichotomies.[41] But Kant never fully explored the far-reaching implications of his claim that transcendental imagination was the "primordial root" of knowledge and experience; according to Heidegger, he shied away from the radical insights he had expressed in the first edition of the *Critique of Pure Reason* by re-establishing the priority of understanding (*Verstand*) over transcendental imagination in the second edition of his path-breaking work.[42] In 1929 Heidegger also offered a seminar on German idealism that focused on Fichte, and in 1930 he offered a seminar on Hegel's *Phenomenology of Spirit*.[43] But Fichte and Hegel fared even worse in Heidegger's interpretations than had Kant. Whereas Kant had at least taken a first important step beyond Western metaphysics with his concept of transcendental imagination, Fichte and Hegel remained beholden to the abstract model of subjectivity initiated by Descartes' *ego cogito*.[44] Heidegger linked the metaphysical tendencies in the *Phenomenology* to Hegel's belief in the infinity of absolute spirit, which he believed was fundamentally at odds with the concrete being-in-the-world of finite *Dasein*.[45]

So while Heidegger was continuing the project he had begun in *Being and Time*, of looking for the ontological foundations of Dilthey's concept of historicity, by developing a radical reinterpretation of Kant's philosophy and continuing his explorations in ancient Greek metaphysics, Marcuse was looking for the foundations of Dilthey's concept of "Life" in Hegel's early thought. The two men's philosophical paths were clearly diverging in the late 1920s and early 1930s. While Marcuse did agree with certain aspects of Heidegger's critique of the abstract models of subjectivity found in German idealism, he also believed that a counter-trend existed, at least in Hegel's early thought. In the early 1930s Marcuse was interested in rescuing this moment in the early thought of Hegel and showing how Marx had developed it to its logical end. Marcuse's increasing disillusionment with Heidegger around 1929 is also apparent in his personal correspondence from this time. In a letter to a friend from May 1929, Marcuse describes Heidegger's legendary charismatic aura, but also leaves no doubt that he had not fallen under its sway to the same extent as had many of Heidegger's other students:

> It is hard to imagine a greater difference than between the shy and obstinate lecturer, who talked out of the window in a small lecture hall eight years ago, and the successor of Husserl, who lectures in an overflowing auditorium with at least six hundred listeners (mostly female) in brilliant lectures with unshakeable certainty, talking

with a pleasant tremor in his voice which so tickles the young women, dressed in a sports suit that almost looks like a chauffeur's uniform, darkly tanned, with the pathos of a teacher who feels himself completely to be an educator, a prophet, and a pathfinder and whom one indeed believes to be so. The ethical tendencies found in *Being and Time* – which aim at philosophy becoming practical – seem to have really broken through, although to be sure, in a way that is somewhat alienating. It's all too rhetorical, too preachy, too primitive.[46]

Although Marcuse was clearly disappointed by Heidegger's development in the years immediately following the publication of *Being and Time*, his doubts were not serious enough to make him change his plans to write a *Habilitationschrift* under Heidegger's direction. Marcuse continued his research on the origins of the dialectic and he continued to employ many of Heidegger's key concepts, such as historicity, happening, motility, and ontology.

The next decisive event in Marcuse's intellectual development during this period was the publication in 1932 of the first complete edition of Marx's *Economic and Philosophical Manuscripts of 1844*. These manuscripts provided a strong confirmation of the hypotheses Marcuse had recently been exploring in his project on the dialectic. Marcuse's discovery of the *Paris Manuscripts* also pushed him one step further out of Heidegger's orbit. As Marcuse put it in a later interview in 1932, "the *Economic and Philosophical Manuscripts* appeared. That was probably the turning point. This was, in a certain sense, a new practical and theoretical Marxism. After that Heidegger versus Marx was no longer a problem for me."[47] In the last two articles Marcuse wrote while he was in Freiburg, "The Foundations of Historical Materialism" and "On the Philosophical Foundation of the Concept of Labor in Economics,"[48] he explains why the *Manuscripts* "must become a crucial event in the history of Marxist studies."[49] The most important points brought to light by the *Manuscripts*, according to Marcuse, are precisely those which he had been at pains to demonstrate during the preceding few years, namely Marx's great theoretical debt to Hegel, and the central importance of a "quite particular, *philosophical* interpretation of human essence"[50] for Marxist theory. While Marcuse by no means neglected Marx's numerous criticisms of the idealist and metaphysical tendencies in Hegel's thought, he portrays the *Paris Manuscripts* as an attempt to develop the critical, humanist tendencies in Hegel's early work. He sees the most important link between Hegel and Marx as the concept of labor. He writes: "Marx takes up the Hegelian concept of labor with all its essential characteristics."[51] Far from fetishizing a repressive or purely instrumental concept of labor in Marx's work, as have many commentators,[52] Marcuse shows that Marx's concept of labor, as the "self-creating or self-objectifying action of man,"[53] must be understood in the broader, "ontological"[54] sense captured in Hegel's concept of "doing" (*Tun*).[55] Against the definition of labor as the polar opposite of free activity, which was prevalent in both bourgeois and socialist economics at the time, Marcuse invokes this philosophical conception of labor, which captures the unique ability of human beings to transform the outside world and themselves, not only based upon objective necessity, but also freely and consciously, in terms of aesthetic considerations or the well-being of the species as a whole.[56] In other words, the passage of the concept of labor from Hegel and Marx to the national economists of the late nineteenth and early twentieth century led to a transformation and impoverishment of its original meaning, which, according to Marcuse, can only be recovered by returning to the early work of Hegel and Marx.

With the recovery of the *Economic and Philosophical Manuscripts of 1844* it had become even clearer to Marcuse that the Marxist theory of his day did not necessarily need the corrective of Heideggerian phenomenology as much as a critical confrontation with its own philosophical roots. So while the publication of the *Manuscripts* deepened the rift between Marcuse's project and Heidegger's own concerns in the early 1930s, Marcuse's writing continued conspicuously to display Heideggerian concepts such as historicity and ontology, right through to the last essay he wrote in Freiburg in early 1933. But when Heidegger enthusiastically embraced the ascendant National Socialist Party in his inaugural address as the new president of Freiburg University on 27 May 1933, Marcuse was forced to re-evaluate his relationship to Heidegger. Marcuse, his wife Sophie, and their 5-year-old son Peter had already fled from Freiburg in mid-January, first to Zürich, then, six months later, to Geneva. During this time Marcuse had also established contact with Max Horkheimer and the Institute for Social Research in Frankfurt.[57] After a favorable interview with Leo Löwenthal in Freiburg, Horkheimer decided to offer Marcuse a position at the Geneva branch, until the headquarters of the Institute could be relocated to New York City. Marcuse and his family moved from Geneva to New York in July 1934. It was in the essays he wrote in the 1930s for the Institute journal, the *Zeitschrift für Sozialforschung*, that Marcuse would re-evaluate his relationship to Heidegger's philosophy.

After 1933, Marcuse re-evaluated Heidegger's philosophy and its influence on his own work in light of Heidegger's support of National Socialism.[58] Although we cannot discuss Marcuse's complex re-evaluation in any detail here, the main explanation Marcuse provides for Heidegger's ill-fated political engagement was, as we have seen, his pseudo-concreteness. The terms in which Heidegger analyzed *Dasein* – anxiety, care, inauthenticity, idle talk, Being-toward-death, resoluteness – seemed tangibly to address the concerns of crisis-ridden Weimar Germany, and this certainly helps explain the widespread appeal of his philosophy at the time. But from the critical

Marxist perspective of Herbert Marcuse, Heidegger did not go far enough in analyzing the concrete social, political, and economic forces that were at the root of the reified forms of human existence under contemporary monopoly capitalism. This is not to say that Marcuse completely abandoned the concerns that had drawn him to Heidegger's philosophy. Even after 1933 Marcuse continued to maintain that Heidegger's philosophy contained valid insights that were not disqualified by his political debacle.[59] He continued to praise *Being and Time* as the most advanced critique of abstract forms of subjectivity in Western philosophy. This problem remained central to Marcuse's work in the 1930s and beyond, although he turned away from Heidegger to other theorists, such as Freud, in order to address it. On the other hand, Marcuse also felt it necessary to re-evaluate his own work in view of the possible political consequences resulting from Heidegger's philosophy. Most important in Marcuse's self-criticism was a renewed appreciation of the rationalist tradition in Western philosophy.[60] This tendency would culminate in his 1941 study *Reason and Revolution*, which placed Hegel squarely within the rationalist tradition and criticized the perception – widespread in the Anglo-American world at the time – that Hegel's philosophy had been a precursor of the Nazi's authoritarian policies.[61]

In this paper, however, I have attempted to show that it did not take Heidegger's engagement for the Nazis to alert Marcuse to the shortcomings of his philosophy. In contrast to what commentators past and present have claimed, Marcuse was critical of Heidegger from the beginning and he became increasingly more so during the years he was in Freiburg.[62] At the risk of being overly schematic, one could say that Marcuse's relationship to Heidegger traversed three phases between 1927 and 1933. The first, articulated in the essays "Contribution to a Phenomenology of Historical Materialism" and "On Concrete Philosophy," marked the high point of Marcuse's enthusiasm for Heidegger. He called for a synthesis of phenomenology and Marxism in which the strengths of each were intended to cancel the weaknesses of the other. The second phase, which began with the essay "On the Problem of the Dialectic" and ended with the publication of *Hegel's Ontology*, was marked by a turn from Heideggerian phenomenology to Hegelian dialectics in an attempt to recover the philosophical origins of Marx's thought. The third phase was precipitated by the publication of Marx's *Economic and Philosophical Manuscripts of 1844* in 1932, whose theoretical importance Marcuse immediately recognized and emphatically defended in the articles "The Foundations of Historical Materialism" and "On the Philosophical Foundation of the Concept of Labor in Economics." Marcuse discovered in the *Paris Manuscripts* a strong confirmation of his project of demonstrating the importance of philosophy in general and Hegel's early work in particular for the development of Marx's theory. The *Manuscripts* made it clear to Marcuse that the best corrective for the reified Marxist theory of his day lay not so much in Heideggerian phenomenology as in the philosophical origins of Marx's own work. So even before Heidegger declared his allegiance to National Socialism in May 1933 – to the surprise of everyone – Marcuse's interest in his work had already waned considerably.

Notes

1. Herbert Marcuse, "Beiträge zu einer Phänomenologie des Historischen Materialismus," *Schriften*, vol. 1, p. 358 (all translations my own, unless noted otherwise).
2. On Marcuse's involvement in the revolutionary activities in Berlin in 1918, and their importance for his subsequent development, see Barry Katz, *Herbert Marcuse and the Art of Liberation*, London: Verso, 1982, pp. 29–31.
3. *Lukács and Heidegger: Towards a New Philosophy*, trans. William Q. Boelhower, London: Routledge and Kegan Paul, 1977, pp. 1–25.
4. On the rise of positivism and the concomitant loss of self-reflexivity in the sciences, see also Jürgen Habermas, *Erkenntnis und Interesse*, Frankfurt: Suhrkamp, 1968.
5. For example, in a letter to Husserl, Heidegger discusses the central problem of his forthcoming book, *Being and Time*, in the following way: "what is the manner of being of the being-in-the-world in which 'world' constitutes itself? That is the central problem of *Being and Time*....The point is to show that the manner of human being is completely different from all other beings, and that precisely it, as the one it is, contains the possibility of transcendental constitution" (quoted in Rainer Ansen, *Bewegtheit: Zur Genesis einer kinetischen Ontologie bei Heidegger*, Cuxhaven: Junhans, 1990, p. 15).
6. For example, in his essay from 1929, "On the Problem of the Dialectic," Marcuse defends *History and Class Consciousness* against "the primitive 'critique,' which believes it can dismiss Lukács' work as 'metaphysics' and which has been repeated most incessantly precisely by the communists" (*Schriften*, vol. 1, p. 421). Marcuse was also aware of Lukács' earlier aesthetic writings, *The Soul and the Forms* and *The Theory of the Novel*. Both played a significant role in his 1922 dissertation, "Der deutsche Künstlerroman." For a discussion of the dissertation and the theoretical importance of Lukács' early work for its conceptualization, see Katz, *Herbert Marcuse and the Art of Liberation*, pp. 46–7, and Gérard Raulet, "Die 'Gemeinschaft' beim Jungen Marcuse," *Intellektuellendiskurse in der Weimarer Republik: Zur Politischen Kultur einer Gemengelage*, Frankfurt: Campus, 1994, pp. 97ff.
7. In a discussion from 1929 of a new book on the dialectic by Siegfried Marck, Marcuse writes: "His [Marck's] critique pinpoints the weak point in Lukács' dialectic: the concept of 'correct class consciousness.' This notion is (as the conception of class consciousness has been on the whole) a violation of the dimension of historicity, a fixation 'outside' of what happens from which only an artificial and abstract connection with history can be reestablished" (*Schriften*, vol. 1, p. 421). The fact that Lukács had, by this time, accepted Zinoviev's censure, renounced his earlier works as "left-wing infantilism," and begun to toe the party line of the Bolshevik-dominated Third International probably increased Marcuse's sensitivity to the vanguardist implications of his work. Marcuse never expressed any interest in the state-socialism of the Soviet Union in his writings during this time. See, for example, note 6 above.
8. In his 1967 preface to the new edition of *History and Class Consciousness*, Lukács himself admitted that his concept of proletariat was an idealist "out-Hegeling of Hegel": "Thus the proletariat seen as the identical subject-object of the real

history of mankind is no materialist consummation that overcomes the constructions of idealism. It is rather an attempt to out-Hegel Hegel, it is an edifice boldly erected above every possible reality and thus attempts objectively to surpass the Master himself" (*History and Class Consciousness*, trans. Rodney Livingstone, Cambridge, MA: MIT Press, 1971, p. xxiii).

9 In one of the very last pieces he published, Marcuse reiterated the importance of the individual for his own "orthodox Marxist" critical theory: "This is orthodox Marxism: the 'universal individual' as the goal of socialism" ("Protosozialismus und Spätkapitalismus. Versuch einer revolutionstheoretischen Synthese von Bahros Ansatz," *Zeitschrift für Sozialdiskussion*, no. 19, 1978, p. 13.

10 Marcuse, *Schriften*, vol. 1, p. 403.

11 To put it roughly, Heidegger's discussion of resolutely authentic, non-conformist *Dasein* dominates the first ten chapters of *Being and Time*. It is not really until the final two chapters, in which he reveals the centrality of the concept of historicity, that *Dasein* is re-collectivized as a member of a "generation" and a "community of destiny." For a more recent examination of the links between *Being and Time* and Heidegger's Nazi politics, see Johannes Fritsche, *Historical Destiny and National Socialism in Heidegger's* Being and Time, Berkeley: University of California Press, 1999.

12 "The Struggle Against Liberalism in the Totalitarian View of the State," *Negations*, ed. and trans. Jeremy Shapiro, Boston: Beacon, 1968, p. 32 (translation modified).

13 This was, once again, a position that Marcuse maintained throughout his life, in his various attempts to explore the subjective dimensions of social change, which he believed Marx – at least in his mature writings on political economy – had not adequately addressed. In a recently published manuscript from 1971, for example, he writes the following about Marxism: "It seems that one decisive factor has not been conceptually incorporated into this theory, namely, the individual as the particular human being who, although the member of a class, still remains the 'natural' elementary agent of change, who, no matter how much he may be 'socialized' can never be 'dissolved' into an aliquot part of a class: his concreteness resists abstract generalization." See "Cultural Revolution," in *Towards a Critical Theory of Society: Collected Papers of Herbert Marcuse*, vol. 2, ed. Douglas Kellner, London and New York: Routledge, 2001, p. 127. On the other hand, Marcuse always remained sufficiently committed to Marxism to avoid falling into a merely abstract defense of the individual, as is characteristic, for example, of a liberal, humanist or existentialist position. As Barry Katz aptly puts it, "For Marcuse Marxism was rather a theory of the 'universal individual,' but one which surpasses simple humanism because it speaks both to the material forces which obstruct its realization, and to the existing emancipatory forces that may yet achieve it" (Katz, *Herbert Marcuse and the Art of Liberation*, p. 218). See also Marcuse's trenchant critique of Sartre's *Being and Nothingness*, "Sartre's Existentialism," in *Herbert Marcuse: Studies in Critical Philosophy*, Boston: Beacon, 1973.

14 For the German original of these texts, see Marcuse, *Schriften*, vol. 1, pp. 347–406. See also Alfred Schmidt (ed.), *Existentialistische Marx-Interpretation*, Frankfurt: Europäische Verlagsanstalt, 1973, which contains these two essays as well as two insightful essays by Alfred Schmidt on Marcuse's early Heideggerian Marxism. For an English translation of the texts, see John Abromeit and Richard Wolin (eds), *Herbert Marcuse: Heideggerian Marxism*, forthcoming in 2004 with the University of Nebraska Press.

15 Like Max Horkheimer and many other critical leftists of his generation, Marcuse was highly critical of the German Social Democrats and the role they had played

in dampening and ultimately destroying the critical, international, and revolutionary potential of the Second International. Most importantly, the German Social Democrats had voted in favor of war credits in 1914, an unforgivable concession to the nationalist hysteria of the day which would soon propel the entire continent into the prolonged, pointless, and unprecedented carnage of the "Great War." In Marcuse's and other leftists' eyes, the Social Democrats egregiously betrayed their principles once again at the end of the war, when they made a pact with key figures in the deposed imperial regime, which led to, among other things, the brutal repression of worker revolts and the murder of Karl Liebknecht and Rosa Luxemburg. For a good description of how these events affected Marcuse's own development at this time, see Richard Wolin, *Heidegger's Children: Hannah Arendt, Karl Löwith, Hans Jonas and Herbert Marcuse*, Princeton: Princeton University Press, 2001, pp. 135ff. For more general histories of the Second International and the role the German Social Democrats played in its development, see James Joll, *The Second International*, New York: Harper & Row, 1966, and Carl Schorske, *German Social Democracy 1905–1917: The Development of the Great Schism*, Cambridge, MA: Harvard University Press, 1955.

16 Goldmann, *Lukács and Heidegger*, p. 3.
17 By lumping him together with Kautsky and Plechanov under the rubric of positivism, Goldmann does not really do justice to Bernstein's revisionism, insofar as he rejected Kautsky's economicist interpretation of the "laws" of capitalist development and grounded his position instead in recourse to Kant's ethics. Nevertheless, his evolutionist philosophy had the same quietistic implications as Kautsky's positivist determinism.
18 Kautsky's stress on the scientific nature of Marxism meant that only those who were thoroughly schooled in this science could possess "correct" class consciousness. In his early days, Lenin was, in fact, influenced by Kautsky and his scientism was just a step away from Lenin's theory of the primacy of the vanguard party, whose duty it was to impose "revolutionary conscious" upon the masses, who would, allegedly, never progress beyond "trade-union consciousness" on their own. Lenin's theory was, of course, refuted by the spontaneous outbreak and escalation of the Russian Revolution in 1917, which took him completely by surprise. Once it had already begun though, he succeeded in harnessing the spontaneity of the masses to the Bolshevik project, much to the chagrin of many, including Rosa Luxemburg, whom Marcuse deeply respected. For the affinities between Kautsky's and Lenin's positions, see, for example, Iring Fetscher, *Karl Marx und der Marxismus: Von der Philosophie des Proletariats zur proletarischen Weltanschauung*, Munich: R. Piper & Co., 1967, p. 90.
19 For an insightful discussion of Heidegger's concept of historicity, see Ansen, *Bewegtheit*.
20 Lukács, *History and Class Consciousness*, pp. 89ff.
21 Not to be confused with Walter Benjamin's concept of the same name. For an insightful discussion of the important differences between Heidegger's and Benjamin's use of the concept, see Peter Osborne, *The Politics of Time*, London: Verso, 1995, p. 64.
22 Heidegger, *Being and Time*, pp. 472–84.
23 In Chapter 4 of the first division of *Being and Time*, he writes, for example: "*Authentic Being-one's-Self* does not rest upon an exceptional condition of the subject, a condition that has been detached from the 'they' [*das Man*]; *it is rather an existentiell modification of the 'they' – of the 'they' as an essential **existentiale**"* (p. 168, Heidegger's italics and emphasis).
24 Heidegger, *Being and Time*, p. 436.

25 *Ibid.*, pp. 357–8.
26 Löwith, "My Last Meeting with Heidegger in Rome, 1936," in Richard Wolin (ed.), *The Heidegger Controversy*, Cambridge, MA: MIT Press, 1993, p. 142.
27 Marcuse, *Schriften*, vol. 1, p. 347.
28 Some interpreters have argued that Marcuse's essays between 1928 and 1933 displayed structural similarities to the increasingly influential "conservative revolutionary" discourse of the time, to which Heidegger and others, such as the sociologist Hans Freyer, contributed. For example, in a brief discussion of Freyer's "existentialist" sociology, Jürgen Habermas writes that "[Freyer's existentialist sociology] appears to him as a project drawn from a conservative revolutionary guide for action. From a structural point of view, certain similarities even exist with the Heideggerian Marxism of the young Herbert Marcuse" (Habermas, "Soziologie in der Weimarer Republik," *Texte und Kontexte*, Frankfurt: Suhrkamp, 1991, p. 196. Gérard Raulet also argues that Marcuse's essays from this period rely on a concept of community that betrays his closeness to conservative revolutionary thinkers during this time: see Raulet, "Die 'Gemeinschaft' beim Jungen Marcuse," *Intellekteullendiskurse in der Weimarer Republik*. While Habermas and Raulet are correct to point to certain similarities of some of Marcuse's ideas from this time with those of conservative revolutionary thinkers – Marcuse even wrote an essay praising Freyer during this period – his basic categories and his overall approach differed in fundamental ways from theirs, such that one must conclude in Marcuse's case that *les extremes ne se touchent pas*, that is to say, that Marcuse would not have been susceptible to the lure of fascism, and not only because he was Jewish, as Adorno once claimed. Marcuse's involvement with the workers' and soldiers' councils in Germany after the war, his identification with Rosa Luxemburg, his interest in avant-garde art, his lack of interest in Bolshevism, and his critical Marxist theoretical stance, which was already firmly in place before he returned to Freiburg in 1927, all make it extremely unlikely that Marcuse would have been susceptible to fascism of any kind. Some of Marcuse's basic assumptions, that I highlight in this essay, such as his rejection of vanguardism, his defense of the concrete individual, and his defense of philosophy as a critical and public activity, illustrate that the basic differences at this time between Marcuse and the conservative revolutionaries were much greater than their similarities.
29 Marcuse, *Schriften*, vol. 1, pp. 368–9.
30 "La Philosophie Allemande entre 1871 et 1933," Herbert Marcuse Archive. This text will also be published in English translation in Abromeit and Wolin (eds), *Herbert Marcuse: Heideggerian Marxism*.
31 Heidegger's sudden and passionate engagement for National Socialism in 1933 came as a big surprise to Marcuse and just about everyone else who knew Heidegger. In an interview from 1947, Marcuse said: "Now, from personal experience I can tell you that neither in his lectures, nor in his seminars, nor personally, was there ever any hint of [Heidegger's] sympathies for Nazism....So his openly declared Nazism came as a complete surprise to us. From that point on, of course, we asked ourselves the question: did we overlook indications and anticipations in *Being and Time* and the related writings?" (Frederick Olafson, "Heidegger's Politics: An Interview," in R. Pippin, A. Feenberg and C. Webel (eds) *Herbert Marcuse, Critical Theory and the Promise of Utopia*, South Hadley, MA: Bergin & Garvey, 1988, p. 99). For a description of the general surprise among Heidegger's colleagues at Freiburg University, who had just elected him as their new Rector, when he announced in his inaugural address in May 1933 that he fully supported the National Socialist *Gleichschaltung* of the German university system, see Bernd Martin, "Universität im Umbruch: Das Rektorat Heidegger

1933/34," in Eckhard John (ed.) *Die Freiburger Universität in der Zeit des Nationalsozialismus*, Freiburg: Ploetz, 1991, p. 14.

32 Marcuse, *Schriften*, pp. 407–45. For an English translation of this essay, see Abromeit and Wolin (eds), *Herbert Marcuse: Heideggerian Marxism*.

33 In an article from 1931, Marcuse credits Korsch's book, *Marxism and Philosophy*, as the first in a long time to have recognized and treated the problem of the relationship of Marx to philosophy: see "Das Problem der geschichtlichen Wirklichkeit," *Marcuse*, Schriften, vol. 1, p. 469. In *History and Class Consciousness*, Lukács wrote the following passage which could very well serve as a summary of Marcuse's project between 1930 and 1932: "Hegel must not be treated as a 'dead dog,' but even so we must demolish the 'dead' architecture of the system in its historical form and release the extremely relevant and modern sides of his thought and help them once again to become a vital and effective force in the present" (p. xiv).

34 One of the other consequences of the rise of positivism in the nineteenth century was a widespread disregard of Hegel's philosophy, which was usually dismissed cursorily as a remnant of a pre-scientific, "metaphysical" era. With a few isolated exceptions, such as Wilhelm Dilthey, or Benedetto Croce in Italy, this superficial understanding of Hegel persisted into the twentieth century, even among outspoken critics of positivism, such as Husserl, who considered Hegel's philosophy a mere *Weltanschauug* that lacked the logical rigor demanded of true philosophy. This view of Hegel was by no means limited to "bourgeois" philosophers either. Social Democrats such as Bernstein and Kautsky tried to separate Marx's theory from Hegel, as did more orthodox Marxists, such as Carl Grünberg, the "father of Austro-Marxism" and the first director of the Institute for Social Research. This situation did not change substantially until the 1920s with the beginning a Hegel renaissance in both philosophy and Marxist theory. For a good account of the rise of positivism as a reaction to and an abstract negation of Hegel's philosophy, see Marcuse's 1941 study, *Reason and Revolution: Hegel and the Rise of Social Theory*, New York: Oxford University Press, 1941.

35 Marcuse, *Schriften*, vol. 1, p. 442.

36 *Hegel's Ontology and the Theory of Historicity*, trans. Seyla Benhabib, Cambridge, MA: MIT Press, 1987, p. 5. At the time at which Marcuse wrote *Hegel's Ontology* he was still planning on pursuing a career in the German university system, which depended in no small part upon the support of Heidegger. Thus strategic considerations may well have played a role in the content and structure of Marcuse's *Habilitationsschrift*. For a more detailed description of Marcuse's attempt to get Heidegger to accept *Hegel's Ontology* and his subsequent decision to publish it without Heidegger's seal of approval, see Seyla Benhabib's introduction to *Hegel's Ontology*, pp. ix–xi, as well as the introduction to Abromeit and Wolin (eds), *Herbert Marcuse: Heideggerian Marxism*.

37 Marcuse, *Hegel's Ontology and the Theory of Historicity*, p. 1. On the crucial relationship of his own research on historicity to Dilthey's work, Heidegger says: "In the following study, we shall content ourselves with indicating the ontological locus of the problem of historicity. The research of Dilthey was pioneering work, but today's generation has not yet made it its own. At base, the following analysis is concerned solely with doing its part to prepare the way for its reception" (Heidegger, *Being and Time*, p. 429, translation modified).

38 Robert Tucker (ed.), *Marx-Engels Reader*, New York: Norton, 1978, p. 109.

39 Once again, strategic considerations probably played a role in Marcuse's careful avoidance of Marx's name in *Hegel's Ontology*. Although Marcuse had already publicly proclaimed his commitment to some version of Marx's theory – in his

articles in the prominent Social Democratic journal, *Die Gesellschaft* – he also knew that Heidegger had no sympathy at all for Marx. See note 36 above.
40 *Kant und das Problem der Metaphysik*, Frankfurt: Klostermann, 1991. See also the English translation, *Kant and the Problem of Metaphysics*, trans. James S. Churchill, Bloomington, IN: Indiana University Press, 1965.
41 Heidegger, *Kant und das Problem der Metaphysik*, pp. 127–41.
42 *Ibid.*, pp. 160f. Heidegger does not address Kant's discussion of transcendental imagination in the *Critique of Judgment*.
43 A revised version of this seminar has been published as volume 32 of the *Gesamtausgabe* of Heidegger's works. An English translation in now available as well: *Hegel's Phenomenology of Spirit*, trans. Parvis Emad and Kenneth Maly, Bloomington, IN: Indiana University Press, 1988.
44 Heidegger, *Hegel's Phenomenology of Spirit*, pp. 78–80.
45 *Ibid.*, p. 74.
46 Letter to Maximillian Beck, 9 May 1929, located in the Herbert Marcuse Archive, Frankfurt, Germany. Another example of Marcuse's reservations about Heidegger's development at this time can be found in a letter he received from Siegfried Marck on 1 April 1930. Marcuse's letter to Marck has not been preserved, but Marck's response makes it clear that Marcuse had expressed some serious doubts about Heidegger: "I very much welcome the sentence in which you see Heidegger's current development and self-interpretation as heading not toward 'concrete,' 'anthropological,' 'realistic,' existentialism, but rather in the direction of the most intractable metaphysics. I have to openly admit that the 'worlding world' [*weltende Welt*] ("The Essence of Reasons") and the 'nothing-ing nothing' [*nichtende Nichts*] ("What is Metaphysics?") seem to lead to genuine and completely indigestible metaphysics."
47 Marcuse, "Theory and Politics: a Discussion," *Telos*, no. 58 (Winter 1978–79), p. 125.
48 Marcuse, *Schriften*, vol. 1, pp. 509–55, and 556–94, respectively. For English translations of these essays, see Abromeit and Wolin (eds), *Herbert Marcuse: Heideggerian Marxism*.
49 Marcuse, *Schriften*, vol. 1, p. 509.
50 *Ibid.*, p. 510 (my emphasis).
51 *Ibid.*, p. 561.
52 Jürgen Habermas, for example, criticizes Marx for "reducing the self-creating action of the human species to labor," which also implies a "reduction of reflection to the level of instrumental action" (*Erkenntnis und Interesse*, Frankfurt: Suhrkamp, 1968, pp. 58 and 60 respectively). Even Theodor Adorno once claimed, with his characteristic hyperbole, that Marx wanted to "turn the whole world into a giant workhouse" (Martin Jay, *The Dialectical Imagination: A History of the Frankfurt School and the Institute of Social Research, 1923–1950*, Boston: Little, Brown and Co., 1973, p. 57).
53 Quoted in Marcuse, *Schriften*, vol. 1, p. 561.
54 Marx speaks of the ontological necessity of "labor," in the widest sense of the term, as the mediator, or *Stoffwechsel*, between humans and nature, in the first book of *Das Kapital*. He writes: "Labor is, as the creator of use values, as useful labor, a condition of human existence independent from all specific societal forms, an eternal natural necessity, which mediates the material exchange between humans and nature, i.e. human life" (*Das Kapital*, vol. 1, Berlin: Dietz, 1962, p. 57, my translation). This does not, of course, prevent Marx from moving beyond this abstract-universal determination of labor and analyzing the specific form that labor takes in different historical periods, such as the form of exchange-value-producing, abstract wage-labor in capitalism. Marcuse is

completely aware of this as well in his defense of the "ontological" foundations of Marx's concept of labor. He stresses throughout the article that labor is thoroughly historical and can only be understood in terms of the role it plays and the way it is organized in a specific socio-historical context. Marcuse is interested in criticizing and moving beyond a society that is organized around the principle of wage-labor. Thus, despite his defense of an "ontological" concept of labor, he does not subscribe to a "trans-historical" concept of labor, which is "understood in terms of a goal-directed social activity that mediates between humans and nature, creating specific products in order to satisfy determinate human needs," in the sense recently criticized by Moishe Postone in *Time, Labor, and Social Domination: A Reinterpretation of Marx's Critical Theory* (Cambridge, UK: Cambridge University Press, 1993, pp. 7–8). Like Postone, Marcuse is interested in a critique of the form that labor has assumed in contemporary capitalist societies, not a critique of the way in which the fruits of that labor are distributed. But Marcuse tries to criticize the contemporary form of labor – which is reflected in the "scientific" understanding of labor in economics – from the standpoint of a much broader, "ontological" concept of labor he discovers in Hegel's philosophy. In this respect, Marcuse was still indebted to Heidegger's seemingly paradoxical attempt to develop a dynamic concept of ontology which had history, or historicity, as its very basis. For an insightful attempt to explain Marcuse's idiosyncratic concept of ontology at this time, see Robert Pippin, "Marcuse on Hegel and Historicity," *The Philosophical Forum*, vol. 16, no. 3, pp. 181–2.

55 Marcuse writes: "It is precisely the doing [*Tun*] of man as his mode of being-in-the-world, through which he first becomes 'for-himself' what he is, comes to his self, acquires the 'form' of his Da-sein, his 'permanence' and at the same time makes the world his own. Conceived in this way, labor is not determined by the nature of its objects, nor by its goal, content, result, etc., but by what happens to human Dasein itself in labor" (*Schriften*, vol. 1, p. 562).

56 Marcuse distinguishes between two types of labor, both of which are included in the Hegelian-Marxist "ontological" concept of labor he defends. On the one hand, there is labor as necessity, as a means to the reproduction of life. On the other hand, there is "labor" or "doing" beyond the realm of necessity, as an end in itself. Marcuse's intention, in other words, is by no means an apology of repressive "labor," in its contemporary capitalist form, of exchange-value-producing wage-labor, or any other form. Rather, he wants to allude to the possibility of the "labor" process – as interaction with the outside world and ultimately the self-creation of "man" – being conducted, at least to a large extent, under free and consciously chosen conditions. In this regard he is in agreement with Marx's formulation in the third volume of *Das Kapital* about the realms of necessity and freedom, which he explicitly cites. See Marcuse, *Schriften*, vol. 1, pp. 583ff.

57 For a brief description of this tumultuous period in Marcuse's life, see Katz, *Herbert Marcuse and the Art of Liberation*, pp. 84–9.

58 Marcuse's essays from the 1930s have been translated and edited by Jeremy J. Shapiro in *Negations*.

59 In his first published essay after his departure from Freiburg, "The Struggle Against Liberalism in the Totalitarian View of the State," which contains a detailed critique of Heidegger and other political existentialists such as Carl Schmitt, Marcuse maintains a distinction between Heidegger's philosophy and his politics. He writes, for example: "Existentialism collapses the moment its political theory is realized. The total-authoritarian state for which it longed gives the lie to all its truths.... In philosophy, existentialism begins as the antag-

onist in a great debate with Western rationalism and idealism, intending to save their conceptual content by injecting it into the historical concretion of individual existence. It ends by radically denying its own origin; the struggle against reason drives it blindly into the arms of the powers that be" (*Negations*, p. 32, translation modified).

60 In 1934 Marcuse mentions Descartes – Heidegger's favorite whipping boy – for the first time in a positive light. He writes: "It is often asserted today that Descartes, by beginning with *ego cogito*, committed the original sin of modern philosophy, that he placed a completely abstract concept of the individual at the basis of theory. But his abstract concept of the individual is animated by concern with human freedom: measuring the truth of all conditions of life against the standard of rational thought" (*ibid.*, p. 50).

61 Marcuse writes, for example: "No better witness to this fact exists than the one serious political theorist of National Socialism, Carl Schmitt....[H]e summarizes the entire process in the striking statement that on the day of Hitler's ascent to power 'Hegel, so to speak, died' " (*Reason and Revolution*, p. 419).

62 In his review of *Hegel's Ontology and the Theory of Historicity* in the first volume of the *Zeitschrift für Sozialforschung*, Adorno claimed that Marcuse had up to that point defended the Heideggerian line "with the stringency of a disciple." In his recent study, *Heidegger's Children*, Richard Wolin also overemphasizes Marcuse's indebtedness to Heidegger at this time, and later. Although Wolin recognizes that "Marcuse's interest in Heidegger's thought was always moderated by an enduring commitment to Marxism" (p. 135), he fails to see that Hegel and Marx were far more important for Marcuse than Heidegger, particular after the initial enthusiasm for *Being and Time*, which was expressed in Marcuse's first two published essays (see p. 138f above), had largely worn off – by 1930 at the latest. Wolin misleadingly claims, for example, that "the Heidegger-Marx synthesis that preoccupied Marcuse during this period remained [the]...unstated central theme in *Hegel's Ontology*" (p. 153), and that Marcuse's 1933 essay on the philosophical foundations of the concept of labor (see p. 141f above) was "resolutely Heideggerian" (p. 156). Furthermore, Wolin overemphasizes Heidegger's influence on Marcuse's later work, arguing that Marcuse "continued to idolize his fallen Master" (p. xiii) and that he essentially remained a "Left Heideggerian" for the rest of his life (pp. 167–72). An adequate discussion of these complex issues cannot obviously be undertaken here, but one should note that even in what might be considered Marcuse's most Heideggerian work after 1933, *One-Dimensional Man* – the only work in which he explicitly refers to Heidegger's philosophy – many other theorists play a more important role than Heidegger: not just Hegel and Marx, but also Horkheimer and Adorno. Even Marcuse's analysis of the hypertrophy of technical reason – the context in which he invokes Heidegger – was just as indebted to other theorists, such as the later Husserl, whose *Crisis of the European Sciences* Marcuse also cites several times. See *One-Dimensional Man*, Boston: Beacon, 1964, pp. 144–69.

8

THE THEORETICAL PLACE OF UTOPIA

Some Remarks on Herbert Marcuse's Dual Anthropology[1]

Stephan Bundschuh

It is well known that Herbert Marcuse studied philosophy with Martin Heidegger in Freiburg and tried to develop a concrete philosophy on an anthropological basis with the intention of making Heidegger's fundamental ontology more concrete. In this chapter I will argue that there are two anthropological dimensions which can be found throughout Marcuse's work, not just in his early essays. One must note that Marcuse's theory is not a philosophical anthropology in the strong sense, like the philosophical anthropology of Helmut Plessner or Max Scheler. The German conservative philosopher Odo Marquard defined anthropology in the following way: "'Anthropology' is {...} that philosophy of man which becomes possible with the 'turn to the life world' and becomes fundamental with the 'turn to nature'."[2] For this turn to the life world the philosophy of Ludwig Feuerbach is paradigmatic, because he criticized Hegel's privileging of logic and put sensuality in the center of his anthropological materialism. Marcuse develops a concrete philosophy – as he calls it in his early writings – in this philosophical tradition. But Marcuse did not elaborate the concept of nature until late in his life, in *An Essay on Liberation* and *Counterrevolution and Revolt*, in which he presents his case for a new anthropology. In his early writings Marcuse is not particularly interested in nature; on the contrary, he discusses Heidegger and Marx in terms of historicity and history as the ontological determination of human being. At this point Marcuse was not trying to develop an anthropological position, but rather – through the influence of Heidegger – an ontological foundation of social theory. However, in Marcuse's essays the difference between the anthropological and ontological foundations of man is complicated and not very clear. But one could say that Marcuse's concrete philosophy has an anthropological basis. He is not concerned with being in general like Heidegger, but with the concrete being of man. Man stands in the center of his philosophy as a species being, and is defined by the historical character and unique nature of his labor. These characteristics enable man to distance himself from the heteronomy of nature. This is a classical subject of the philosophy of history. Marquard calls such anthropological argumentations a moment in the philosophy of history,[3] and that is exactly the way Marcuse uses anthropology. In this way the concept of anthropology itself is transformed and historically relativized. It now has a strategic function in social science.

In Marcuse's philosophy one finds two different concepts of anthropology. I shall call the first the "anthropology of the bourgeois era" – in reference to Max Horkheimer's essay "Egoism and Freedom Movements," which bears the subtitle "On the Anthropology of the Bourgeois Era."[4] I will call the second "anthropology from a practical point of view" – in reference to Kant's *Anthropology from a Pragmatic Point of View*.[5] In this sense, anthropology has the status of a regulative idea.[6] The anthropology of the bourgeois era explains the basic characteristics of the second nature of man in modern society. The two-dimensionality of Marcuse's concept of anthropology sets him apart from Horkheimer and Theodor Adorno. Horkheimer and Adorno say that an anthropological conception is only possible if history comes to an end. But this would require a society that can successfully maintain the status quo and redirect the wish for social transformation. This would mean that the end of history had been reached in a negative way – Horkheimer and Adorno call this the totally administered society. If social development comes to an end, human behavior will no longer change either. Critical philosophy of history will be transformed into an anthropology because of the real cessation of development. The German sociologist Stefan Breuer also sees this transformation of a critical philosophy of history into anthropology in the work of Horkheimer and Adorno. He writes:

> Critical theory's early rejection of anthropology cannot be seen as their final position. ...[I]f the dialectic leads merely to the perpetuation of this society, and history culminates in post-history, anthropology becomes relevant once again ... in the sense of a "turn to second nature," that describes human beings and their interactions as petrified, as sediments of their completely ossified relations.[7]

Although Marcuse also tends toward this position in some parts of his later work, in his early works he clearly has a different, more positive understanding of anthropology. He attributes to the human species several patterns of being which underlie the historical process; they remain the foundation of human being through the passage of time. Historicity, work as the activity of the species, and sensuality are the anthropological foundations of every specific historical form of human life. They are the essence or the "nature" of man. Marcuse's anthropological conviction is apparent when he speaks about the latent consciousness of authenticity or the latent discontent of the individual in a repressive culture, which eventually leads to the rebellion of human nature. This nature possesses an emancipatory potential.

One finds a good example of Marcuse's dual anthropology in his book *Eros and Civilization*. The first part of the book deals with the reality principle and the concrete form it takes in advanced industrial society: the performance principle. Here Marcuse discusses the factors that have formed human beings during the bourgeois era. In the second part of the book, "Beyond the Reality Principle," Marcuse outlines a utopian reality principle in which Eros rules over Thanatos and the pleasure principle triumphs over aggression. He sketches in vague outlines the patterns of human behavior which could exist in the future. This model then serves as a normative idea in the present time, which manifests itself practically as a theoretical project in the social, cultural, and political opposition. One sees this in *An Essay on Liberation* where Marcuse writes: "[T]he theoretical projection seems to be fatally premature – were it not for the fact that the awareness of the transcendent possibilities of freedom must become a driving power in the consciousness and the imagination which prepare the soil for this revolution."[8] Theory changes reality through its influence on consciousness and imagination, the means by which man shapes reality. Let us now examine in more detail the two conceptions of anthropology in Marcuse's work.

The Anthropology of the Bourgeois Era

To explain the concept of the anthropology of the bourgeois era I will refer to Max Horkheimer's essay from 1936, "Egoism and Freedom Movements." Horkheimer's subtitle, "On the Anthropology of the Bourgeois Era," has a double meaning. On the one hand, Horkheimer analyzes and criticizes various philosophical anthropologies in modern philosophy, or, in other words, various attempts to define the essence of man. On the other hand, he analyzes specific human patterns of behavior that are determined by the development of the capitalist form of production. The fact that the male citizen is taken as the model for man in general in bourgeois anthropology makes it possible, according to Horkheimer, to make some important generalizations about the condition and structure of man in the modern era. Horkheimer's subtitle has a dual meaning in the same way as has the subtitle of Marx's *Capital*: *Critique of Political Economy*. It means that both classical economic theory and real capitalist social relations are the subject of the critique. In the same way, Horkheimer's title announces a discussion of both anthropological theories and real patterns of behavior. He also makes it clear that he stands in the tradition of Marxian ideology critique, according to which the intellectual products of an epoch contain the real social relations in a mystified form such that the critique of ideology leads to an understanding and a critique of reality itself.

It is important to keep in mind that Horkheimer wrote his essay with contemporary problems in mind. He was concerned with the transformation of bourgeois society in the 1930s into an authoritarian society of a new type. He wanted to explain the rise of fascism and National Socialism. He believed he had identified a recurring social-psychological structure that underlies periods of social transformation in the modern era. But the direction of the transformation depends on the specific conditions of the era: it can manifest itself in progressive or barbaric forms. Horkheimer argues that various modern social movements are identical in structure, but differ in their function. Those which had a progressive function in the seventeenth century could have a conservative function in the twentieth century and vice versa.

Horkheimer discusses the following historical-anthropological patterns of behavior, which are necessary for both the individual and society in the capitalist era: self-preservation, coldness, ruthlessness, and hardness. The early modern philosophers projected the principle of self-preservation into nature and then transferred it back onto society. The isolated individual, seen as "man himself," stands at the center of bourgeois anthropology.[9] But individual egoism and pleasure-seeking are criticized as anti-social impulses. This ideological denigration of egoistic impulses corresponds to the real repression of drives necessary in bourgeois society and prepares the turn from individualistic society to abstract collectivism which eliminates the individual as a self-conscious being. The history of the development of the individual is at the same time the history of rising psychological repression. The bourgeois era made possible the "formation and consolidation of representative character types."[10] The leaders of bourgeois revolts such as Rienzo, Savonarola, Luther, Calvin, and Robespierre are only "the magnified version[s]"[11] of the average bourgeois individual. They all condemn sexuality and leisure, practice an ascetic life, and preach performance. Egoism, which guides the reality of bourgeois society, is condemned in ideology; the drives are repressed and sublimated. Self-discipline and responsibility become much more important than they were in former times. These qualities characterize the individual under the "domination of the performance principle."[12]

Although Horkheimer makes use of a critical concept of anthropology, he sharply criticizes the academic discipline of philosophical anthropology. In his essay "Remarks on Philosophical Anthropology," he rejects the assumption "that a constant and unchanging human nature functions as the foundation for an epoch."[13] He emphasizes that history has no static or identical essence through time. Anthropology is possible only as negative anthropology: "A theory free from illusions can only conceive of human purpose negatively, and reveals the inherent contradiction between the conditions of existence and everything that the great philosophies have postulated as a purpose."[14] The images of ideal man play an important role in the fight for a better life, but they may not be hypostatized as archetypes of man. Their value and their limits lay in their historical specificity. In the *Dialectic of Enlightenment*, Horkheimer and Adorno did claim that they want to develop "a dialectical anthropology,"[15] but this does not mean that they were no longer critical of philosophical anthropology. Max Scheler, the founding father of philosophical anthropology, writes programmatically:

> The task of philosophical anthropology is precisely to show how all the specific monopolies, performances and works of humans emerge from the foundation of human being [*Menschsein*]: this would include language, conscience, tools, weapons, ideas of right and wrong, the state, leadership, the representative function of the arts, myth, religion, science, historicity and sociability.[16]

But Horkheimer gives voice to an opposing, very nominalistic view:

> Culture does not have its basis in human being, but rather in human beings, and the ways in which they change and influence each other through their similarities and differences. In the horribly fragmented world in which we live it is not possible to attribute the forms of social life to a more or less constant human essence.[17]

The only way anthropological studies can attain scientific status is to limit their field of inquiry to a specific historical era. Horkheimer writes:

> Anthropological studies...do not need to dispose of the concept of value; they can extend and refine the understanding of historical tendencies. They would then be concerned with historically determined human beings and groups of human beings instead of with man as such, and would seek to understand their existence and development not as isolated individuals but rather as integral parts of the life of society.[18]

To accomplish this task anthropology must become historical anthropology, because in every new era human characteristics and expressions change. Horkheimer says: "The period of transition to the monopolistic phase of economic systems is characterized by a change in human beings. The names remain the same, but the anthropological realities are altered."[19] Horkheimer defines the task of critical theory as observing "the special characteristics of modern man."[20] But he would not claim that these are characteristics of modern man as a whole, because there exists a "difference in human qualities between different social groups."[21] For Horkheimer, anthropology can only supplement critical theory. He leaves no doubt about his rejection of philosophical anthropology as a fundamental science:

> Regardless of how much the notions of change and progression are integrated into the idea of man, this way of stating the problem assumes a fixed, abstract hierarchy. It contradicts the dialectical character of historical events, in which the foundational structure of individual existence is interwoven with that of the group, and can lead, at best, to paradigms not unlike those of the natural sciences.[22]

In other words, philosophical anthropology necessarily eliminates the dynamic of society.

In most respects Marcuse agrees with Horkheimer's position on anthropology; he too subordinates anthropological propositions to concepts derived from social theory and the philosophy of history. The differences between Horkheimer's and Marcuse's positions are most apparent in the early works of Marcuse, in which he discusses an ontological basis of man which manifests itself historically in different forms. According to Marcuse, humans do have a timeless essence, although it suffices to define the concrete human being only abstractly. So even though he defends a concept of abstract human essence, he still insists that only the analysis of the concrete historical situation can produce a binding definition of man in his time. In his late work, *One-Dimensional Man*, he describes late-capitalist man as an instrument of technical power. Marcuse has two intentions in *One-Dimensional Man*. He wants to describe precisely the conditions of the people living in Western capitalist countries and at the same time he wants to show why this picture could become the dystopian future of mankind. If the tendencies he discusses in the book remain dominant, his depiction of Western society as it stands now will also point to an anthropology of damaged life to come.

Anthropology from a Practical Point of View

Marcuse's anthropology from a practical point of view stands in opposition to his description of mankind in the present. The word "practical" should make clear that the utopian dimension in Marcuse's theory has relevance for the actual behavior of individuals. It is not necessary that the utopian project exists or potentially exists in reality. Rather, its importance lies in its regulative and practical function. The individuals ought to act as if this utopian project was realistic, even though the pessimism of Marcuse's theory does not support the hope that the history of domination will come to an end. Marcuse strongly believes that his utopian project is scientific because it is not merely a fantastic wish, but derives its possibility from real social conditions. Utopia as a regulative idea is constructed as the next necessary step beyond the status quo. But Marcuse's later argument about the end of utopia – for example, at the end of *One-Dimensional Man* or in his essay "The End of Utopia"[23] – demonstrates against his own intentions the weakness, if not impossibility, of utopian conceptions at a time when their realization seems indefinitely suspended, even though the conditions necessary for their existence are present.

Marcuse does not claim that his theory contains a complete description of what man, as a free species being, would look like. Instead, he provides guiding ideas that help distinguish the man of the future from the man of the present. Future man is so only projected in contrast to the present reality; nothing precise can be said about the future development of man. The theoretical status of Marcuse's utopian construction – especially in his later work – has nothing to do with the possibility of its realization. It serves as a theoretical instrument to negate the present, that is to say, a theoretical medium of critique. This claim contradicts Marcuse's expressed intention to prepare the way for a new anthropology as a real form of existence. This anthropology provides the normative guidelines for his theory of action. At the same time – as is apparent already in the early essays – he postulates such an absolute and total transformation that its concrete realization seems impossible. Although his intention was to outline a concrete utopia, Marcuse develops, almost from the beginning, an abstract utopia, to borrow a term used by Helmut Fahrenbach in reference to Ernst Bloch. Fahrenbach argues that there is a transition from a concrete to an abstract concept of utopia in Marcuse's work:

> The utopian character of the "transcendent plans" of possible praxis (from "outside" and aiming at a qualitatively different society) were forced from the status of concrete utopia (mediated by reality and related to praxis) in the direction of a "more abstract" (transcendent) utopia.[24]

Marcuse casts his lot with a radical break, a departure from history, total revolution, because there are no immanent tendencies in society that support the rise of a new society. Fahrenbach writes: "In the dialectic of concrete and abstract utopia it seems as if only the path of abstract utopia (or even utopianism) is still open."[25] Marcuse explicitly develops his utopian anthropological concept in his earliest and latest works. In his early essays, Marcuse drew upon the *Economic and Philosophical Manuscripts of 1844* of Marx – which were published for the first time in 1932 – to develop a concept of the species being of man, which could serve as the basis of critique and define the goals to be attained. In the late essays, he develops the idea of a new anthropology as a normative principle to direct concrete historical actions.

One finds here the Kantian "as-if," which is used to characterize the regulative ideas in his epistemology, but which is transformed into practical-constitutive ideas in Kant's practical philosophy. The subtitle of this part of my chapter, "Anthropology from a *Practical* Point of View," is of course a reference to Kant's anthropology, but it is also intended to emphasize the critically transcendent nature of Marcuse's concept. Kant's anthropology serves as a guide for social and moral life in a given society. Pragmatic anthropology is not concerned with all dimensions of human being; it focuses on "what man can, or should make of himself as a freely acting being."[26] An explanation is pragmatic if it passes the test of practice, that is to say, if it serves as a guide for moral conduct. Pragmatic anthropology searches for rules of conduct and supports the "knowledge of man as *a* citizen of the world."[27] At this point philosophy moves beyond the realm of abstract theory. Kant distinguishes between metaphysics and anthropology. Metaphysics deals with the conditions of the possibility of a priori knowledge. Anthropology deals with the human sensual-intellectual experience. All propositions of Kant claim absolute validity with respect to the activities of the human senses and reason. Kant's description of human cognition in particular is based on general principles that are not affected by the passage of time. In Kant's philosophy temporal development has only a peripheral significance.

Marcuse takes the contrary position. He does not consider anthropology to be a separate discipline, distinguished from other spheres of philosophy. His historical-anthropological propositions are an integral part of his social-theoretical analyses, insofar as they cannot be presented separately as an anthropological doctrine. They are the point of reference for Marcuse's critique of the present. But in contrast to Kant, Marcuse denies the universal validity of this reference point; he makes it dependent on the historical conditions of the present. In his essay "On hedonism" from 1938, Marcuse stresses that the propositions of critical theory about the happiness of individuals are not propositions about nature but about the history of mankind:

> That the true interest of individuals is the interest of freedom, that true individual freedom can coexist with real general freedom and, indeed, is possible only in conjunction with it, that happiness ultimately consists in freedom – these are not propositions of philosophical anthropology about the nature of man but descriptions of a historical situation which humanity has achieved for itself in the struggle with nature.[28]

For Marcuse, philosophical anthropology is concerned with the nature of man, while critical theory is concerned with the history of mankind, which, in turn, is inextricable from natural history. Kant too distinguishes two sciences of man: the physiological, which investigates "what nature makes of man,"[29] and the pragmatic, which asks what man can make of himself. On this issue in particular Marcuse's utopian anthropology is closely related to Kant's pragmatic anthropology. Both are characterized by their freedom from nature. But while Kant founds human freedom in the realm of ideas and not in the material realm, Marcuse follows Hegel's turn to history, in which the freedom of man must be realized.

The main aims of Kant's anthropology are knowledge of man, self-cultivation, and intelligent and successful interaction with others. His anthropology accepts the established social framework of his time. Marcuse's anthropology demands the contrary. It criticizes the totality of present existence and insists on the necessity of a new project of man. In this way Marcuse emphatically links man and society, making impossible any separate discussion of their roles in his theory. From both its problematic points of departure — anthropology and the philosophy of history — Marcuse's theory develops eventually into social philosophy. Nonetheless, his early interest in anthropology and the philosophy of history continues to inform his later analyses of oppression and freedom. The barbarism of the present is readily apparent against the backdrop of Marcuse's utopian construct, which represents not merely a fantastic alternative to the present, but an objective possibility. These alternative patterns of human behavior are elaborated in *Eros and Civilization* and *An Essay on Liberation*. In the latter, Marcuse discusses a new anthropology based on a new sensual structure of man. This structure will reactivate regions of the pleasure principle, which are repressed in the society based on labor and the performance principle. Imagination will become a central category of knowledge. Art, as the repository of past hopes and suffering, also moves to the center of Marcuse's theory. His emphasis on its historical specificity notwithstanding, Marcuse anthropologizes art by attributing to it transhistorical qualities. Art preserves the main elements of Marcuse's utopian dimension: love, happiness, pain, and death. A classical formulation of a utopian form of human existence is a life free from fear. One can find this idea in the work of Adorno and Marcuse, and also in the compositions of Hanns Eisler. This sentence demonstrates clearly these men's distance from Heidegger, for whom fear is an existential of man. Whereas Heidegger reifies fear, Marcuse argues that the human existence has been dominated by fear throughout history, to the present day, but that this should be changed. Marcuse believes that Heidegger, at least in his early work, asks the right questions but gives the wrong answers. He accuses Heidegger of creating an ideology of death.

In Marcuse's work the utopian dimension is a precondition of theoretical critique. But does this imply that a transformation of the essence of man must also be a real possibility? On this point there is a difference between Marcuse's understanding of his own theory and the real theoretical position of his utopia. Marcuse thinks that his new anthropology is not only a theoretical project but also a real form of existence. This contradicts his own theoretical approach which argues that the realization of the utopian, for which the economical, technical, and social means are at hand, is prevented by the internal and external domination of technical reason over individuals. The effective prevention of concrete possibilities renders them abstract. The elimination of the desire for liberation makes the objective possibility of freedom unreal, such that the end of utopia is reached through its elimination, not its realization. Marcuse's "Great Refusal," first set forth as a determinate negation, lapses into an abstract refusal. Furthermore, a pacified mankind cannot undo the misdeeds and suffering of the past. Absolute claims for happiness cannot be realized because the recollection of the dead cannot bring them back to life. So the possibility of human happiness remains marred by the insurmountable obstacles of pain and death.

Notes

1 This essay is based on the first chapter of my book *"Und weil der Mensch ein Mensch ist..." Anthropologische Aspekte der Sozialphilosophie Herbert Marcuses*, Lüneberg: zu Klampen, 1998, pp. 14–23. It has been translated from German by John Abromeit.
2 Odo Marquard, "Zur Geschichte des philosophischen Begriffs 'Anthropologie' seit dem Ende des achtzehnten Jahrhunderts," *Schwierigkeiten mit der Geschichtsphilosophie*, Frankfurt: Suhrkamp, 1982, p. 125.
3 *Ibid.*, p. 140.
4 Max Horkheimer, "Egoism and Freedom Movements: On the Anthropology of the Bourgeois Era," in G. Frederick Hunter (ed. and trans.) *Max Horkheimer: Between Philosophy and Social Science*, Cambridge, MA: MIT Press, 1993, pp. 49–110.
5 Immanuel Kant, *Anthropologie in pragmatischer Hinsicht*, ed. Karl Vorländer, Hamburg: Meiner, 1980; *Anthropology from a Pragmatic Point of View*, trans. Victor Lyle Dowdell, Carbondale and Edwardsville: Southern Illinois University Press, 1978.
6 On the terms "regulative idea" and "utopia," see Helmut Fahrenbach, "Das Utopieproblem in Marcuses Kritischer Theorie und Sozialismuskonzeption," in Institut für Sozialforschung (ed.) *Kritik und Utopie im Werk von Herbert Marcuse*, Frankfurt: Suhrkamp, 1992, pp. 81–2.
7 Stefan Breuer, "Adornos Anthropologie," *Aspekte totaler Vergesellschaftung*, Freiburg: Ça Ira, 1985, p. 50.
8 Herbert Marcuse, *An Essay on Liberation*, Boston: Beacon, 1969, p. 31.
9 Max Horkheimer, "Egoism and Freedom Movements," pp. 50–1.
10 *Ibid.*, p. 58.
11 *Ibid.*, p. 93.
12 *Ibid.*, p. 85.
13 Max Horkheimer, "Remarks on Philosophical Anthropology," in Hunter (ed. and trans.) *Max Horkheimer: Between Philosophy and Social Science*, p. 151.
14 *Ibid.*, pp. 156–7.
15 Max Horkheimer and Theodor W. Adorno, *Dialectic of Enlightenment*, New York: Continuum, 1972, p. xvii.
16 Max Scheler, "Die Stellung des Menschen im Kosmos," *Gesammelte Werke*, vol. 9, Bern: Francke, 1976, p. 67.

17 Max Horkheimer, "Korreferat zu Rothackers Probleme und Methoden der Kulturanthropologie," *Max Horkheimer: Gesammelte Schriften*, vol. 13, Frankfurt: Fischer, 1989, p. 14.
18 Max Horkheimer, "Remarks on Philosophical Anthropology," p. 161.
19 *Ibid.*, p. 172.
20 Max Horkheimer, "English Abstract of 'Remarks on Philosophical Anthropology,'" *Zeitschrift für Sozialforschung*, vol. 4, Paris: Felix Alcan, 1935, p. 25.
21 *Ibid.*
22 Max Horkheimer, "Remarks on Philosophical Anthropology," p. 153.
23 "The End of Utopia," *Herbert Marcuse: Five Lectures*, trans. Jeremy J. Shapiro and Shierry Weber Nicholsen, Boston: Beacon, 1970, pp. 62–9.
24 Helmut Fahrenbach, "Das Utopieproblem in Marcuses Kritischer Theorie und Sozialismuskonzeption," p. 84.
25 *Ibid.*
26 Immanuel Kant, *Anthropology from a Pragmatic Point of View*, p. 3.
27 *Ibid.*, p. 4.
28 Herbert Marcuse, "On Hedonism," *Negations*, Boston: Beacon, 1969, p. 192.
29 Immanuel Kant, *Anthropology from a Pragmatic Point of View*, p. 3. This investigation found its place in Kant's *Physical Geography*.

9

DIATRIBES AND DISTORTIONS
Marcuse's Academic Reception

W. Mark Cobb

A Haunting Absence

The influence of the Frankfurt School on cultural studies, the humanities, and the social sciences would be difficult to overestimate. The past two decades have witnessed a proliferation of publications and studies of most of the major thinkers associated with the Frankfurt School. Scholarly work detailing the lives and dissecting the thought of Theodor Adorno, Walter Benjamin, and Jürgen Habermas line the shelves of university bookstores in the United States, while the texts these thinkers produced regularly show up on the syllabi of university courses in a wide variety of disciplines. The presence of these works is more than justified by the depth and range of the thought of all three theorists. However, this project will focus not on this presence but on an interesting absence or lacuna among studies of the Frankfurt School. The missing figure this paper will focus on is Herbert Marcuse, who, during the rediscovery of the Frankfurt School in the 1960s and 1970s, was the School's most influential and prominent member.

Marcuse's sudden rise to prominence during this period was one of the most unexpected developments in his long and distinguished life. At the age of almost 70, an age when other philosophers faced hemlock or the hopefully genteel poverty of the retired professor's pension, Marcuse became a worldwide intellectual phenomenon. Marcuse's critical theory was much discussed in both the mainstream and underground or alternative media. Photos of Marcuse's venerable visage often accompanied these articles that varied tremendously in both their openness to and comprehension of Marcuse's thought. That a philosophy professor teaching at an American university had become the subject of so much attention was quite unusual. Equally unusual was Marcuse's open identification with Marxism and willingness, as an engaged public intellectual, to raise and take on the most controversial issues of the time.

Not surprisingly, the mainstream American media, unschooled in dialectical thought, proved to be particularly inept in its attempt to make sense of Marcuse's critical theory. These attempts often combined a lack of comprehension with a seethingly vicious tone and the efforts to demonize Marcuse are, when read from the distance of several decades, disturbing and unintentionally amusing. However, the mainstream American media was far from alone in distorting or failing to comprehend Marcuse's critical theory. Joining the mainstream American media in demonizing Marcuse was an odd assortment of characters and forces who fiercely opposed both Marcuse and what they took or mistook for his message. Marcuse's opposition included the Pope, *Pravda*, California Governor Ronald Reagan, and Vice-President Spiro Agnew.[1] Such a motley collection of repressive bedfellows brings to mind Swift's remark that "When a true genius appears in the world you may know him by this sign, that the dunces are all in confederacy against him."[2]

The dunces, however, were not alone. Joining them in cause and spirit were scores of academics whose responses to Marcuse's thought ranged from bafflement to belligerence. Furthermore, while the mainstream media and most politicos eventually lost interest in Marcuse, academics have tended to continue criticizing Marcuse on the rare occasions when the opportunity arose. There have been exceptions to this tendency. Edward Said, in *Culture and Imperialism* (1993), mentioned Marcuse's continuing relevance,[3] and a small but thoughtful group of scholars continue to give Marcuse a prominent role in their thinking. However, Marcuse's general academic reception is best characterized as hostile. This hostility has been expressed in various ways. Some critics have responded with diatribes and distortions, while others have opted for a forced "forgetting," creating revisionary histories informed by highly selective memories. While Marcuse has been largely excluded from contemporary intellectual discussions, he has not quite been forgotten. Instead, the exclusion of Marcuse's thought from contemporary intellectual discussions has caused his theoretical corpus to take on a ghostly twilight existence in which Marcuse is absent from even those contemporary works that seem to show his influence and/or focus on explicitly Marcusean themes.

In my view, this exclusion is particularly unfortunate because Marcuse still has a great deal to offer. My strategy in this chapter will be to critically explore and partially explain Marcuse's peculiar contemporary position, namely Marcuse's haunting absence from, and his ghostly presence in, contemporary intellectual discussions. There are at least four key, and interrelated, reasons for Marcuse's current exclusion. One reason is that Marcuse's hostile academic reception has discouraged consideration of his thought. Other reasons include the current decline of the public intellectual, the demise of the New Left with which Marcuse is perhaps over-identified, and the emergence of the modernism/postmodernism distinction. The paper will deal with the first reason directly and the other reasons indirectly. In so doing, an attempt will be made to counter the critiques that have aimed at exorcizing Marcuse's thought from contemporary discussions, while remaining sensitive to extra-theoretical factors that may also be involved in dismissing his work. The discussion will focus on three thinkers who, like Marcuse, have received an unusual amount of public attention. All three thinkers have advocated rethinking the ways in which philosophy and theory are currently practiced. The three thinkers whose criticisms of Marcuse will be considered are Alasdair MacIntyre, Michel Foucault, and Richard Rorty.[4] The discussion of these thinkers' critiques of Marcuse will vary in length significantly, and in proportion to the length of the critiques offered. These three thinkers have been influential in setting the theoretical agenda in the academy since the 1980s and their critiques of Marcuse are particularly revealing. An important contention of the paper is that critically assessing these critiques may help illuminate Marcuse's impact on the academy. By closely inspecting these academics' representations of Marcuse we may be able to better understand what Marcuse represented to the academic world and why there has been a strong effort to repress rather than remember him.

MacIntyre's Tirade

In 1970 at the height of Marcuse's popularity, Alasdair MacIntyre's *Herbert Marcuse: An Exposition and Polemic* was published. MacIntyre, who would later gain a great deal of prominence himself with the publication of *After Virtue* (1981), produced the Marcuse study for Frank Kermode's *Modern Masters* series, which was/is intended to introduce philosophers and their theories to larger reading publics. At the time of the book's publication MacIntyre was teaching philosophy and the history of ideas at Brandeis University, where Marcuse had taught until 1964. One difficulty MacIntyre faced in writing the book was that at the time there was no published account of the Frankfurt School's origin and history. Martin Jay's impressive history of the Frankfurt School, *The Dialectical Imagination*, did not appear until 1973.[5] Consequently, it was probably difficult for MacIntyre to fully appreciate the rich historical context that Marcuse, as a member of the Frankfurt School, was a part of. As a result, MacIntyre had to rely exclusively, or almost exclusively, on Marcuse's texts in producing his exposition and polemic.

MacIntyre's subtitle for the book is a telling one, though the book contains much more polemic than exposition. The entire book, all 106 pocket-sized pages, includes only nineteen specific references to Marcuse's texts. However, MacIntyre's lack of textual attention does not keep him from drawing amazingly sweeping conclusions about Marcuse's critical theory. In the book's opening discussion MacIntyre states: "It will be my crucial contention in this book that almost all of Marcuse's key positions are false."[6] Given the complexity of Marcuse's thought, the task that MacIntyre sets before him is a Herculean one – particularly for such a tiny tome. While it may be conceivable that one might produce a critique of such elegant concision, MacIntyre's effort fails to suggest such a possibility. MacIntyre also states: "I am under an exceptional obligation to portray what Marcuse says faithfully."[7] The nature of the series that MacIntyre is writing for and his own hyperbolic conclusion suggest just such an obligation, but this is an obligation that MacIntyre fails to fulfill, faithfully or otherwise.

The first aspect of Marcuse's thought that MacIntyre calls into question is Marcuse's conception of philosophy, which began developing in the 1920s and 1930s. MacIntyre writes:

> When Marcuse wrote about the history of philosophy his perspective was a peculiarly German one. The Greeks and especially Aristotle received a lot of attention; the Middle Ages very little. Descartes was important and then Kant, who prepared the way for the philosophical climax achieved by Hegel. After Hegel, apart from Marx, attention was paid to Husserl and Heidegger. Positivism and empiricism appeared usually as very general and imprecise doctrines, of which the Vienna Circle was the main representative, only to be rejected. In all this Marcuse was at one with the mainstream of German philosophers. But in accepting that the great philosophers are Aristotle, Kant, and Hegel, Marcuse interpreted their greatness in a particular way of his own. The essential function of philosophy, he argued, was criticism of what exists.[8]

Unless one rejects any philosophy that is "peculiarly German" or rejects the right of philosophers to develop individual interpretations of the tradition, the criticism above falls flat. In his assessment of Marcuse's conception of philosophy MacIntyre accurately points out Marcuse's neglect of the Middle Ages, which must be hard for a Thomist to resist, but does not explain why such neglect is a problem.

MacIntyre emphasizes the importance Marcuse places on Aristotle, who later became the protagonist of MacIntyre's *After Virtue*. However, MacIntyre offers little explanation as to why Marcuse's discussions of Aristotle are problematic. A particularly interesting omission occurs in MacIntyre's first chapter, where, in discussing the importance for Marcuse of distinguishing between what things are at a given moment and what they could become, MacIntyre mentions Plato and Hegel, but not Aristotle. MacIntyre fails to mention Aristotle here even though he quotes Marcuse regarding human fulfillment and its relation to understanding humans in terms of their potentialities.[9] Had MacIntyre mentioned Aristotle in this context, it might have suggested a consideration of the philosophical complexity of not only Marcuse's thought, but also that of Hegel and Marx.

After stating that Marcuse rejected Husserl's Cartesian-inspired phenomenology because it had been detrimentally influenced by positivism[10] and neglecting to discuss the attention Marcuse paid to Heidegger, MacIntyre introduces his thesis. The thesis is that Marcuse is really a Hegelian, a Young Hegelian, rather than a Marxist. An inspection of the passage quoted above, where MacIntyre downplays Marcuse's almost (as of 1970) forty-year focus on Marx with the phrase "apart from Marx," gives an early indication of the shallow waters into which MacIntyre is headed. Early in his polemic MacIntyre asks: "how does Marcuse's view stand in relation to classical Marxism?"[11] MacIntyre overlooks the fact that what constitutes Marxism has long been a question of contention. MacIntyre does not offer a definition of "classical Marxism" and seems unwilling to consider the possibility that gaining more access to Marx's theorizing might help de-ossify hardened variations of Marxism. Nowhere does MacIntyre even mention Marcuse's ground-breaking 1932 essay "The Foundations of Historical Materialism," which, as one of the first studies of Marx's *Economic and Philosophical Manuscripts of 1844*, was enormously influential in helping theorists more fully appreciate Marx's project and break away from the scientistic version of Marxism owing more to the formulations of Engels than Marx. The importance of Marcuse's 1932 essay was immediately apparent in Germany and first introduced Marcuse's name to a wider public.[12] Marcuse's essay also aroused attention in the English-speaking philosophical community years before MacIntyre produced *Herbert Marcuse*. One reason for the importance of Marcuse's study was that it helped invalidate attempts to bisect Marx's theoretical corpus into early philosophical idealist and late social scientific periods. Marcuse's study illuminated the threads of continuity that ran through Marx's entire project.

Furthermore, among scholars who have carefully studied Marcuse, there has not been any shift in the view of either Marx's importance for Marcuse or the significance of Marcuse's early essay on Marx. Douglas Kellner, in his thoughtful study *Herbert Marcuse and the Crisis of Marxism* (1984), states that Marcuse "wrote one of the first and best reviews of the *Manuscripts* when they were first published in 1932, and henceforth would utilize the early Marx to secure the basic presuppositions of his theory, and would no longer rely on Heidegger's anthropology or phenomenology."[13] Kellner points out that Marcuse was one of the first to use Marx's *German Ideology* in his theoretical work.[14] More recently, Rolf Wiggershaus, addressing Marcuse's search for theoretical foundations, states in his monumental *The Frankfurt School: Its History, Theories, and Political Significance*: "it was only because he discovered other philosophers whose 'tremendous concretion' outdid Heidegger's: Dilthey and Hegel. But all of them were overshadowed for Marcuse by Marx when he discovered the *Economic and Philosophic Manuscripts of 1844*."[15] Wiggershaus adds: "Marcuse offers one of the pioneering interpretations of the Paris Manuscripts."[16] MacIntyre's ignoring such a significant essay seriously distorts his presentation of Marcuse's thought, and is a deception that helps him advance his problematic contention that Marcuse is an elderly Young Hegelian.

MacIntyre could have drawn on a variety of Marcuse's early texts from the 1930s that demonstrated commitment to a Marxist project. In 1968, *Negations: Essays in Critical Theory* was published in English by Beacon Press. *Negations* included many of the essays Marcuse produced between 1934 and 1938 when he was working with the Institute for Social Research. These essays contain a plethora of passages demonstrating Marcuse's Marxism. Particularly relevant in the context of MacIntyre's claims is the influential 1937 essay "Philosophy and Critical Theory." In this essay Marcuse writes:

> In the conviction of its founders the critical theory of society is essentially linked with materialism. This does not mean that it thereby sets itself up as a philosophical system in opposition to other philosophical systems. The theory of society is an economic, not a philosophical, system. There are two basic elements linking materialism to correct social theory: concern with human happiness, and the conviction that it can be attained only through a transformation of the material conditions of existence.[17]

Furthermore, in the same essay, Marcuse states:

> Critical theory is, last but not least, critical of itself and of the social forces that make up its own basis. The philosophical element in the theory is a form of protest against the new "Economism," which would isolate the economic struggle and separate the economic from the political sphere. At an early stage, this view was countered with the criticism that the determining factors are the given situation of the entire society, the interrelationships of the various social strata, and relations of political power. The transformation of the economic structure must so reshape the organization of the entire society that, with the abolition of economic antagonisms between groups and individuals, the political sphere becomes to a great extent independent and determines the development of society. With the disappearance of the state, political relations would then become, in a hitherto unknown sense, general human relations: the organization of the administration of social wealth in the interest of liberated mankind.[18]

Thus, in his early essays, Marcuse clearly expresses that critical theory is a continuation of the Marxian project. Interestingly, there is evidence in MacIntyre's first chapter, dubiously entitled "Marcuse's Early Doctrine," that he had read some of Marcuse's early essays. However, MacIntyre's "reading" and distorted representation of these texts appears to cause him to break his earlier promise of faithfulness to Marcuse. In short, MacIntyre's odd elision of Marcuse's 1932 essay on Marx, and his highly selective reading of Marcuse's other early essays, raises more questions about MacIntyre's methodology and purposes than about Marcuse's relation to Marx.

MacIntyre tries to distinguish Marcuse's conception of philosophy from Marx's conception by quoting Engels on the nature of philosophy.[19] MacIntyre quotes Engels circa 1888 – five years after Marx's death – and draws on some of the statements that eventually led to the ossification of Marxism, which thinkers such as Marcuse helped to eradicate by providing us with a better understanding of Marx's thought. One reason that Marcuse wrote *Reason and Revolution* (1941) was to attempt to rediscover and revive dialectic. Much of the Marxism of the 1930s had become doctrinaire and scientistic, and Marcuse wanted to reinvigorate Marxism by emphasizing the centrality of a more supple dialectical method that had its origins in Hegel. Thus, *contra* MacIntyre, Hegel is an extremely important thinker for Marcuse not because Marcuse is a pre-Marxist Young Hegelian, but because Marcuse helps recover Hegelian aspects of Marx that had been lost during Marxism's vulgarization.

Furthermore, while Hegel gave comprehensive and unprecedented attention to the history of philosophy, Marcuse agrees with Marx that the history of philosophy has been largely ideological. Turning again to one of the most important essays Marcuse authored in the 1930s, "Philosophy and Critical Theory," Marcuse writes:

> The utopian element was long the only progressive element in philosophy, as in the constructions of the best state and the highest pleasure, of perfect happiness and perpetual peace. The obstinacy that comes from adhering to truth against all appearances has given way in contemporary philosophy to whimsy and uninhibited opportunism. Critical theory preserves obstinacy as a genuine quality of philosophical thought.[20]

Thus, Marcuse thought that the entire history of philosophy, excepting the utopian elements, had been ideological. Critical theory developed as an attempt to preserve Marxian obstinacy in an age when fascist intimidation had spawned terror and obedience. MacIntyre, fighting a losing battle with the standard of internal consistency, cannot keep from contradicting himself as he tries to paint Marcuse as an overly abstract Hegelian, while admitting that "Marcuse praised Marxist materialism."[21]

The third chapter of *Herbert Marcuse*, entitled "Marcuse's Interpretation of Hegel and Marx," provides what should have been ample opportunity for MacIntyre to develop his Young Hegelian thesis. MacIntyre uses the chapter to discuss Marcuse's *Reason and Revolution* (1941), a thoughtful study of over four hundred pages, widely regarded as one of the more important twentieth-century works on Hegel and Marx. However, almost half of MacIntyre's twenty-one page chapter is spent producing a gloss on Hegel's philosophy. MacIntyre then offers a simplistic discussion of *Reason and Revolution*. At one point MacIntyre slips, in his attempt to label Marcuse as a Left/Young Hegelian, when he states that Marcuse, in opposition to Left Hegelianism, treats not only *The Phenomenology of Spirit* but also Hegel's "*Logic* with extreme seriousness."[22] While one might wish that some of this seriousness would rub off on MacIntyre, the more important point is that MacIntyre's casual contact with *Reason and Revolution* exposes further weaknesses in his thesis.

The most interesting aspect of the chapter is MacIntyre's contention, against Marcuse, that freedom and happiness are incompatible. Had MacIntyre developed this discussion his study might have become more provocative. For instance, such a discussion could have led into a consideration of alienation, a topic MacIntyre strangely downplays, and how the possible overcoming of alienation is related to freedom and happiness. Instead, we are left with MacIntyre's concluding claim that it is "strikingly clear that Marcuse's attitude to Hegel and Hegelian theory is not the attitude of Hegel himself nor is it that of Marx."[23] This statement presumes that MacIntyre somehow possesses privileged access to *the* attitudes of Hegel, Marx, and Marcuse, and also misses the enormous complexities and the fascinating ambiguities of their theorizing. Consequently, MacIntyre's "analysis" provides an object lesson in reification.

Another problem MacIntyre attempts to raise concerns Marcuse's style or mode of presentation. MacIntyre writes: "Marcuse's manner is both literary and academic; he is allusive and seems to presuppose not only a high level of general culture but a wide area of presumed agreement on academic matters."[24] Marcuse does offer the reader an aesthetic playful style that is simultaneously unusually serious, but where MacIntyre sees this style as a difficulty, different tastes might find it delightful. Certainly Marcuse's prose style is markedly different from the dreariness that most analytic philosophers were weaned on. However, though MacIntyre does not quite raise this paradoxical problem, accessibility is an issue for a thinker as concerned with broad social transformation as is Marcuse. The dilemma that Marcuse faces is that if his description of the dominance of one-dimensional thinking is accurate then he will need to produce creative, provocative, and seductive dialectical texts to have any chance of stimulating critical thinking in a populace numbed by conditioned intellectual responses and bombarded daily with cliché-ridden inanity. If, on the other hand, the populace is so effectively conditioned then how can Marcuse elicit any response with his challenging texts? Importantly, Marcuse's allusive, occasionally elliptical, literary style is inextricably connected to the importance he places on pleasure. In the concluding section of my discussion of MacIntyre's critique, some signs will be given that suggest MacIntyre found Marcuse's prose more pleasing than he lets on in *Herbert Marcuse*.

The critique MacIntyre offers of Marcuse's *Eros and Civilization* fares no better than earlier attempts. MacIntyre's major problem is that he misses or ignores the purpose of the book. In *Eros and Civilization* Marcuse imaginatively interrogates Freud's pessimistic and absolutist conclusion that civilization always requires a high degree of instinctual repression. In suggesting an alternative to Freud's conclusion, Marcuse is also at odds with a vast amount of conventional "political wisdom," from antiquity to the present. In his text, Marcuse engages in a philosophical exploration aimed at articulating an alternative possibility. Thus, Marcuse's proposal required imagining an emancipated and erotic alternative civilization grounded in present (1955) technological capacities and realities. Instead of critically engaging Marcuse's provocative proposal, MacIntyre obsesses over Marcuse's reluctance to back all of his ideas with facts. The nature of Marcuse's project makes such a demand absurd. MacIntyre is also unwilling to seriously entertain Freud's metapsychology, which Marcuse bases his project on, because of the difficulty in applying truth and falsity to this area.[25] MacIntyre seems to long for a return to simpler thinking, to the binary safety of Aristotelian logic. Does MacIntyre really think that political and social theorizing should be limited to empirically verifiable premises? Would MacIntyre accept the process of reasoning that led to Aristotle's conclusions regarding the necessity of a slave state? Would MacIntyre support Aristotle's rejection, based on a lack of empirical evidence in a state that discriminated cruelly against women, of Plato's view that women could effectively rule a state? If imagination is allowed no role in theory the likelihood of sacrificing innovation and progress will be increased.

Marcuse's important conceptions surplus repression and the performance principle are explicated by MacIntyre but without significant critique. Instead, ignoring Eros and focusing on the sexual, MacIntyre asks: "What will we do in this sexually liberated state?"[26] MacIntyre also expresses an interest in the facts about sexuality and a frustration in Marcuse's failure to supply them.[27] Thus, MacIntyre seems unable to grasp that *Eros and Civilization* is a philosophical enquiry and not a sexual survey or instructional manual.

After mentioning alienation for the first time (the topic was left out of his discussion of Hegel and Marx), MacIntyre states that Freudian and Marxian modes of explanation are incompatible, rendering Freudo-Marxism incoherent.[28] MacIntyre fails to consider the possibility that the two modes of explanation are compatible and offer us explanations focused on different levels of human experience. Marxian explanation focuses on the social and economic aspects of human experience, while Freudian explanation focuses on the individual psychic aspects of human experience. Additionally, both Marxian theory and Freudian theory are secular and humanistic forms of materialism. Thus, the two theories share important common ground that suggests a synthesis may have some plausibility.

Tellingly, MacIntyre concludes the chapter without any discussion of Eros or of the dynamic Eros–Thanatos relationship. One would think that the title of Marcuse's text would suggest to an intelligent reader the centrality of these concerns. Instead, MacIntyre wonders what assurance we have that the new needs Marcuse speaks of will not create new conflicts and forms of domination.[29] Marcuse's answer to such a question would require an understanding of the Eros–Thanatos relationship. Having failed to critique this relationship, MacIntyre states, in regard to his alleged "new conflicts and domination," that "On this Marcuse is silent, and perhaps he is silent because his account is in fact empty."[30] Perhaps not. Perhaps what is empty is MacIntyre's melodramatic and totally unsubstantiated claim(s). In summary, *Eros and Civilization*, which presents one of Marcuse's boldest proposals, is left unscathed by MacIntyre.

Early in the brief chapter on *Soviet Marxism* MacIntyre "reveals" his consistently held and inconsistently argued-for thesis that against all evidence, Marcuse is a Young Hegelian. MacIntyre tells us: "Marcuse explicitly disowns a Hegelian perspective, if that implies history is to be treated teleologically. But how much of Hegel does he disown in disowning this?"[31] Hegel's major innovation in Western philosophy was to introduce history into the subject, to make philosophy a historical endeavor understood historically, with a particular teleological philosophy of history. To reject this teleology, as Marcuse does in *Soviet Marxism*, is of major consequence. If one does not think Hegel's philosophy of history necessarily entails the progressive teleology Hegel committed to, then one is not a Hegelian in the full sense – Left or Right, Young or Old. MacIntyre admits as much when he complains of Marcuse reading Soviet history "in the light of his own Marxist generalization."[32] MacIntyre's conclusion to the chapter is that Marcuse is a Young, albeit senile, Hegelian.[33] But nowhere in his text does MacIntyre substantiate his claim that the elderly Marcuse is either a Young Hegelian or senile.

MacIntyre then proceeds to Marcuse's *One-Dimensional Man: Studies in the Ideology of Advanced Industrial Society* (1964). MacIntyre begins his discussion by stating that

> *One-Dimensional Man* marks a sharp break in Marcuse's thought, even though the substance of his thesis is already to be found in *Eros and Civilization*, and that about Soviet society in *Soviet Marxism*. What is new is twofold: his virtual relinquishing of any distinctively Marxist – as against Hegelian – categories, and his pessimism.[34]

Once more, MacIntyre offers us a typically inaccurate and inconsistent set of claims. While MacIntyre is correct in stating that the substance of the thesis of *One-Dimensional Man* can be found in the two texts that precede it, which does not suggest a sharp break, his claim that *One-Dimensional Man* relinquishes any distinctively Marxist categories is simply inaccurate. Interestingly, nowhere in MacIntyre's *Herbert Marcuse* does he mention the subtitle of *One-Dimensional Man*, which would wave a red flag suggesting that the text, as a study of ideology, may offer a Marxist perspective. As a reading of the text easily demonstrates, Marcuse is concerned with modern ideology connoting, in the Marxian sense, "false consciousness." MacIntyre's elision is also interesting because he attempts to conflate Marcuse's thesis, that the working class is not likely to catalyze revolutionary change, with Daniel Bell's "end of ideology" thesis.[35] However, Marcuse was highly critical of Bell's position and considered it ideological. Moreover, ideology is not the only Marxian category emphasized in Marcuse's text. Reification and alienation are also major themes in *One-Dimensional Man*, though Marcuse's conception of alienation is nuanced and subtle, conceived stipulatively to reflect the ways in which modern industrial capitalist society alienates by numbing the populace, squelching opposition, and manufacturing consent. Additionally, Marcuse maintains emancipatory desires in *One-Dimensional Man*, suggesting the possibility that the "Great Refusal" of the marginalized might be a catalyst for social change.

MacIntyre also objects to Marcuse's distinction between true and false needs, but rather than developing the issue, MacIntyre claims that the urgent question is "how has Marcuse acquired the right to say of others what their true needs are?"[36] MacIntyre wants to label Marcuse an elitist, albeit one concerned about rather than disdainful of everyone's needs, rather than address the issue. One wonders why any person would not have the right to theorize about human needs and why such a right must be acquired/bought. MacIntyre writes as if the right to free thought must be purchased, and perhaps unconsciously reflects his own ideological assumptions. Additionally, MacIntyre objects to Marcuse equating freedom with happiness but fails to account for Marcuse's important distinction between happiness and "happy consciousness."[37]

MacIntyre concludes his work by rejecting the bohemian values he says Marcuse champions. He also mentions and "critiques" Marcuse's controversial essay "Repressive Tolerance" without a single reference to this text, and then says that Marcuse is inviting us to repeat Stalinism.[38] MacIntyre then adds: "One cannot liberate from above; one cannot re-educate them at this fundamental level. As the young Marx saw, men must liberate themselves. The only education that liberates is self-education."[39] Thus begins the last paragraph of MacIntyre's tirade. MacIntyre's Marx – is this his classical Marxism? – seems to say: "Workers of the world split up and liberate yourselves individually." The passage also raises questions about MacIntyre's philosophy of education and one wonders if he considers all liberatory teaching elitist. No stranger to absurd hyberbole, MacIntyre ends the paragraph and the book with the following "conclusion": "Marcuse has produced a theory that, like so many of its predecessors, invokes the great names of freedom and reason while betraying their substance at every point."[40] At this point, it may be helpful to consider an early review of MacIntyre's *Herbert Marcuse* to see if MacIntyre's purpose for this bizarre "study" might be illuminated.

In a biting review of MacIntyre's *Herbert Marcuse* published in *Telos* in 1970, Robin Blackburn informs us that the editor of the *Modern Masters* series, Frank Kermode, said in an interview that MacIntyre's book was intended to be "the first, and last, book about Marcuse."[41] If this attribution is accurate, the book, contrary to its ostensible purpose, was meant to end rather than further discussion and reflection. Though Blackburn does not deal extensively with MacIntyre's text itself, he has a good deal to say pertinent to the context in which the book was written. Interestingly, Blackburn writes: "With this book MacIntyre is lining up with his old friends in Moscow as they continue their dirge of hate against Marcuse and all that is most vital in revolutionary thought."[42] Moreover, Blackburn writes that

> [MacIntyre's] threadbare political and intellectual clothing can no longer hide the nakedness of his opportunism. Superficially MacIntyre has occupied nearly every conceivable political and intellectual position but it would be truer to say he has never really understood any of them. In the past he has been a "Christian" without God, a "Trotskyist" without commitment to revolution, a "Marxist" patronized by the Central Intelligence Agency, an "anti-elitist" adornment of the world's most mediocre and servile bourgeois intelligentsia, a "socialist" avid for the approval of his social "superiors." Now he is a liberal who rattles the faces of law and order, a libertarian instrument of academic authoritarianism.[43]

It may be tempting to write Blackburn's comments off as symptomatic of the tensions of the time, but giving in to such a temptation would be a mistake. MacIntyre's opportunism is not irrelevant to Marcuse's critique of contemporary academic philosophy. Earlier in the discussion, attention was drawn to Marcuse's important 1937 essay "Philosophy and Critical Theory," where Marcuse was critical of the whimsy and uninhibited opportunism of contemporary philosophy. MacIntyre's *Herbert Marcuse* instantiates this opportunism, if not whimsy. Additionally, in *Essay on Liberation* (1969), Marcuse wrote of the obscenity of our "kept intellectuals."[44] MacIntyre's obscenity can be seen in his repeated use of straw arguments and suppressed evidence, and his only "virtue" seems to be the lack of cleverness involved in his deceptions. MacIntyre seems to be performing here as what Ishmael

Reed, in his novel *Japanese by Spring* (1993), calls an academic fireman. For Reed, an academic fireman is someone who, while claiming allegiance to or expertise in a movement or subject, actually attempts to dampen enthusiasm for the movement or subject.[45] Given the timeliness of MacIntyre's *Herbert Marcuse* (published in 1970 at the height of Marcuse's popularity), MacIntyre seems to be attempting to throw water on the enflamed desires for change that Marcuse helped arouse.

In 1981, MacIntyre's *After Virtue* was published. Considering aspects of this work can be interesting in connection with MacIntyre's attack on Marcuse's critical theory. In *After Virtue*, MacIntyre rejects the viability of analytic philosophy without any mention of Marcuse's earlier rejection of the approach, which MacIntyre found so problematic. MacIntyre devotes a major portion of *After Virtue* to an analysis of the shortcomings of Enlightenment rationality without any mention of Adorno and Horkheimer's *Dialectic of Enlightenment*, which addressed the issue so provocatively more than thirty years earlier. MacIntyre also calls for the necessity of interdisciplinary research in the humanities and social sciences. MacIntyre fails to mention that the Frankfurt School had been engaged in such a project since the 1920s, making his suggestion less than novel. One of the important moves Marcuse made in *One-Dimensional Man* was to point to the social margins as potential catalysts for social change. MacIntyre makes a similar call in *After Virtue*, and seems to be quietly copying moves Marcuse made (though the contents of these margins are extremely different) and taking part in the conservative attempt to re-appropriate the rebellious spirit of the 1960s. Marcuse's ghost seems to have haunted MacIntyre considerably.

Perhaps the most telling example of MacIntyre's larcenous borrowing occurs in his much ballyhooed conclusion to *After Virtue*, where, on the last page, he writes:

> we are not entirely without grounds for hope. This time however the barbarians are not waiting beyond the frontiers; they have already been governing us for some time. And it is our lack of consciousness that constitutes part of our predicament.[46]

Seventeen years earlier on the last page of *One-Dimensional Man*, Marcuse had written that

> the spectre is there again, inside and outside the frontiers of the advanced societies. The facile historical parallel with the barbarians threatening the empire of civilization prejudges the issue; the second period of barbarism may well be the continued empire of civilization itself.[47]

Marcuse then mentions the possibility that the most advanced consciousness of humanity might meet with humanity's most exploited force, before ending the text with a quote from Walter Benjamin about the importance of hope. The amazing similarity of the language in these two texts throws MacIntyre's complaints about the irritability of Marcuse's prose into question and adds a new resonance to MacIntyre's phrase "after virtue."

Foucault's Foray into Freudo-Marxism

Another particularly important example of Marcuse haunting a text is found in Michel Foucault's *The History of Sexuality, Volume One: An Introduction*,[48] where Marcusean ideas are critiqued and Marcusean language used without any mention of Marcuse. Marcuse's explicit absence from Foucault's text is interesting, and a comprehensive comparison of the critical projects of Foucault and Marcuse might prove to be helpful in making sense of this haunting, but such a discussion will not be possible here. A more complete discussion of the relationship between the projects of Foucault and Marcuse would involve a careful consideration of a number of texts and is beyond the scope of the present discussion. The present discussion is concerned with both Marcuse's curious absence from *The History of Sexuality, Volume One* and Foucault's treatment of some of Marcuse's ideas in this text. One contention of the discussion is that Foucault's provocative *History*, while never mentioning Marcuse, is a direct response to and criticism of several of Marcuse's important theoretical conceptions. A second contention is that Marcuse's version of the repressive hypothesis is rejected, but not refuted, by Foucault.

While Marcuse is not the only thinker being critiqued, others, such as Wilhelm Reich, are at least mentioned. Not mentioning Marcuse is odd from a scholarly point of view and makes it easier to deal with straw arguments instead of Marcuse's actual positions. As the present paper demonstrates, Foucault is certainly not alone in such mistreatments, and his influence as a theorist makes it interesting to consider the almost invisible intellectual collision that takes place when Foucault rejects ghostly Marcusean approaches and ideas.

Foucault's discussion of Freudo-Marxism in *The History of Sexuality* is a complicated, if not equivocal, one. While Foucault is ostensibly rejecting the repressive hypothesis, he says that Reich's political critique of sexual repression was important and its impact substantial,[49] and Foucault states that he is not arguing that sex has not been barred or prohibited during the pertinent epoch.[50] Furthermore, Foucault does not emphasize the possible effects such prohibitions may have had on individuals' psyches. To Foucault's credit, he does raise a possible objection to his position that would interpret his own data in favor of the repressive hypothesis.[51] Additionally, by arguing that the repressive hypothesis actually serves power by being an instance of, and perpetuation of, the incitement to sexual discourse, Foucault cleverly poisons the well against anyone wishing to refute his thesis in favor of the repressive hypothesis. Recognizing the fallaciousness of Foucault's appeal, the present discussion will delve into issues of repression and sexuality.

Reich and Marcuse were attempting, in related but distinctive ways, to understand why the European proletariat failed to create a progressive new society and, to a large extent, supported fascism. The question led Reich and later Marcuse into an investigation of individual, psychological factors that culminated in the development of the theory of the authoritarian personality and led to a deep critique of traditional family structures, patriarchy, and religion. Contrary to Foucault's characterization of repression, in the repressive hypothesis, being caused solely by bourgeois economics and capitalism,[52] Reich and especially Marcuse thought that the capitalist economic system was only one aspect of the problem. Furthermore, Foucault wants to argue that power relations are much more complex than a discussion of repression would suggest, but the problem with Foucault's critique is that his discussion of repression is one-dimensional. For instance, Foucault does not distinguish between the significantly different notions of repression and the necessity of repression articulated by Freud, Reich, and Marcuse. Consequently, Marcuse's important distinction between necessary and surplus repression is not discussed in the text. Nor does Foucault discuss Marcuse's contention that "women have been subjected to a specific kind of repression" in patriarchal civilizations.[53] These are serious omissions. However, at this point, it may be more useful to consider passages where Marcuse's ghost haunts Foucault's text and temporarily forgo any broader conclusions.

Foucault offers several characterizations of positions that are easily attributable to Marcuse, whom the mainstream press had labeled as (one of) the philosopher(s) of the sexual revolution. Foucault writes:

> Something that smacks of revolt, of promised freedom, of the coming of a different law, slips easily into the discourse on sexual repression. Some of the ancient functions of prophecy are reactivated therein. Tomorrow sex will be good again. Because this repression is affirmed, one can discreetly bring into coexistence concepts which the fear of ridicule or the bitterness of history prevents most of us from putting side by side: revolution and happiness; or revolution and a different body, one that is newer and more beautiful; or indeed, revolution and pleasure. What sustains our eagerness to speak of sex in terms of repression is doubtless this opportunity to speak out against the powers that be, to utter truths and promise bliss, to link together enlightenment, liberation, and manifold pleasures; to pronounce a discourse that combines the fervor of

knowledge, the determination to change the laws, and the longing for the garden of earthly delights.[54]

While this description might also apply to Wilhelm Reich, it is clearly a response to Marcuse's erotic utopianism. Foucault problematizes some issues that characterized Marcuse's project, namely the linkages between revolution, happiness, and pleasure. These difficult issues should be raised in considering Marcuse's proposals, and it is in regard to these issues that Marcuse's thought gets most interesting. Marcuse's most complete treatment of these issues is found in *Eros and Civilization* (1955) and continued in *An Essay on Liberation* (1969). But Foucault does not mention these texts, and his treatment of these issues is more mocking than thoughtfully critical. While the new body language does not sound Marcusean, other parts of Foucault's passage are. The phrase "smacks of revolt" is pertinent and seems a bit strange coming from Foucault, given his association with the Left. Freudo-Marxism is explicitly concerned with freedom and revolt. It is almost as if, in the French hangover from May 1968, nothing beyond resistance is allowed. While May 1968 may have sent Foucault and many of his fellow French theorists into despair, why should "the bitterness of history" quell the desires for social transformation of Marcuse, who survived victimization by fascism and Nazism with his hope intact? Marcuse was painfully aware of history's bitterness but refused to ontologize the past or present and succumb to the cynicism so often confused with maturity. One might argue that there is something life-affirming about Marcuse's hardiness, resilience, and vitality. One might also ask whether "the fear of ridicule" should really be a guiding motivation for a critical or social theorist? Would not such motivation tend to produce ambiguous, muddled, or, worse, spineless theory that inspired more perplexity than praxis? Furthermore, is it really fair or accurate to associate Marxists or Freudo-Marxists such as Marcuse (an atheist) with religious concepts or prophecies? Is Marcuse's view that a radically improved human future is a possibility any more prophetic than cynical proclamations about the inevitable failure of any revolutionary endeavor? Where does healthy skepticism end and "skeptical omniscience" begin?

Foucault goes further and discusses what he calls "preaching" and "a great sexual sermon" that led to dreams of a "New City" and brought to mind the Franciscans.[55] Allegedly, these were the guises and stratagems used by Freudo-Marxists to seduce and incite the populace into talking about sexuality and sexual repression. Foucault wisely covers himself by admitting:

> Let there be no misunderstanding: I do not claim that sex has not been prohibited or barred or masked or misapprehended since the classical age; nor do I even assert that it has suffered these things any less from that period on than before.[56]

Foucault wants to know why sexuality has been so widely discussed.[57] However, given the pleasure sex is capable of producing and its centrality, to this point in history, in the continuation of the species, what *would* call for more of an explanation would be any prolonged muteness on the issue. More pertinently, insofar as the repressive hypothesis is concerned, the nature of sexual discussions would seem to be crucial, and Foucault suggests that since the Age of Reason, sexual discourse has been coercive and regulated.[58] Such characterizations can be read to suggest that political power has a role in sexual repression.

However, the main concern here is Foucault's critique of Marcusean ideas, and Foucault may have fallen victim to the same temptation that the mass media did in their coverage of Marcuse. The mass media in the US focused on sexuality instead of Eros in discussing Marcuse's thought. Sexuality was an important issue for Marcuse, and Foucault does not hesitate to use descriptive Freudian phrases such as "polymorphous sexualities"[59] which Marcuse had advocated as human sexual ideals in *Eros and Civilization* in 1955. However, as the title of the work suggests, Eros was always the main subject for Marcuse, not sexuality. Sexuality was a part of Eros, the life instinct. Eros involved the preservation of life and promotion of creativity and was, consequently, a multidimensional concept. However, in a one-dimensional culture tiring of prudish Puritanism, it was probably not altogether surprising that the media fixated on a single aspect of Marcuse's rich conception. Does Marcuse's absence from Foucault's text allow Foucault to avoid dealing with Marcuse's more nuanced version of the repressive hypothesis and conception of Eros, while enabling a less specific wholesale rejection of a simpler version of the idea?

Reich's earlier version of the repressive hypothesis was the first to radically reject Freud's conservative view regarding the necessity of high levels of repression for civilization. Like Freud, Reich thought that only genital sexuality was mature sexuality, but for Reich the orgasm was the key to psychological health. Additionally, Reich is infamous for his intolerance of homosexuality. Foucault's position regarding the normalizing judgments of psychoanalysis is well known and certainly Reich's atavistic position on the subject of homosexuality should be rejected. Unfortunately, what gets left out of Foucault's repressive hypothesis discussion is Marcuse's advocacy of an erotic bisexuality and his open affirmation of homosexuality, in his discussion of Orpheus in *Eros and Civilization*, in the middle of the heterosexually normalized 1950s. In *Eros and Civilization*, Marcuse writes:

> The classical tradition associates Orpheus with the introduction of homosexuality. Like Narcissus, he rejects the normal Eros, not for an ascetic ideal, but for a fuller Eros. Like Narcissus, he protests against the repressive order of procreative sexuality.[60]

For Marcuse, this protest against repression is an important part of the "Great Refusal." While Foucault ignores this aspect of Marcuse's thought it does not escape the attention of Dennis Altman or Paul Robinson, who write glowingly of Marcuse's importance for the emerging gay liberation movements of the 1960s and 1970s. In his essay "Revisiting Marcuse with Foucault: *An Essay on Liberation* Meets *The History of Sexuality*," Paul Breines discusses the significance Marcuse had for both Altman and Robinson.[61] In their view, Marcuse was a progressive force in the struggle against sexual repression prior to Foucault's arrival.

Additionally, Marcuse's focus on Eros allowed him to offer a powerful critique of the "sexual revolution" of the 1960s that often banalized, commodified, and trivialized sexuality. Marcuse articulated a concept, repressive desublimation, to explain the way in which advanced capitalism handled the new sexual demands. For Marcuse, repressive desublimation involves the release of sexual desire from inhibitions stemming from sublimation; however, this release is a repression in that it limits pleasure to immediate gratification in consumption. An investigation of this concept along with Foucault's notion of docile bodies can help one begin to understand the ways in which Eros, the life instinct, is weakened.

Another passage in Foucault's *History* that is particularly relevant to this chapter's present concerns is the following one:

> Where there is power, there is resistance, and yet, or rather consequently, this resistance is never in a position of exteriority in relation to power. Should it be said that one is always "inside" power, there is no "escaping" it, there is no absolute outside where it is concerned, because one is subject to the law in any case? Or that, history being the ruse of reason, power is the ruse of history, always emerging the winner? This would be to misunderstand the strictly relational character of power relationships. Their existence depends on a multiplicity of points of resistance: these play the role of adversary, target, support, or handle in power relations. These points of resistance are present everywhere in the power network. Hence there is no single locus of great Refusal, no soul of revolt, source of all rebellions, or pure law of the revolutionary. Instead there is a plurality of resistances.[62]

In this passage, Foucault offers a critique of Marcuse's tactical conception, the Great Refusal. However, Foucault's critique either relies on confusion about Marcuse's position or it is a straw argument. This issue is complicated by the fact that Marcuse is alluded to rather than cited or mentioned. Had Foucault read Marcuse at this point? If not, why not? And if not, then why the critique? Marcuse was famous or infamous, depending on one's perspective, for breaking away from the view that a single locus of change or revolution, such as the proletariat, could be the agent of radical social transformation. Marcuse drew the ire of orthodox Marxists for precisely this reason. Instead, Marcuse looked to the margins and the marginalized as potential catalysts of revolutionary change. In *One-Dimensional Man* (1964), Marcuse states that traditional forms of protest and struggle have been rendered ineffective by the one-dimensional society.[63] For Marcuse, the proletariat or the masses, assimilated (in the early 1960s) into capitalist society, will not initiate a revolution. Furthermore, he writes:

> However, underneath the conservative popular base is the substratum of outcasts and outsiders, the exploited and persecuted of other races and other colors, the unemployed and the unemployable. They exist outside the democratic process; their life is the most immediate and the most real need for ending intolerable conditions and institutions. Thus their opposition is revolutionary even if their consciousness is not. Their opposition hits the system from without and is therefore not deflected by the system; it is an elementary force which violates the rules of the game and, in doing so, reveals it as a rigged game. When they get together and go out into the streets, without arms, without protection, in order to ask for the most primitive civil rights, they know that they face the dogs, stones, and bombs, jail, concentration camps, even death. Their force is behind every political demonstration for the victims of law and order. The fact that they start refusing to play the game may be the fact which marks the beginning of the end of a period.[64]

Marcuse also makes clear that the Great Refusal of the marginalized does not guarantee anything teleologically, but only represents a chance for change. He concludes *One-Dimensional Man* by stating that critical theory offers no easy solution, but that it "wants to remain loyal to those who, without hope, have given and give their life to the Great Refusal." Marcuse then ends the book by quoting a line Walter Benjamin wrote at the beginning of the fascist era:

Nur um der Hoffnungslosen willen ist uns die Hoffnung gegeben.

It is only for the sake of those without hope that hope is given to us.[65]

Thus, for Marcuse, the age of a single force of transformation seemed to be behind us; consequently, he focused his attention on plural forces, even unorganized forces, of opposition. So, contrary to Foucault's characterization of the Great Refusal, Marcuse is not talking about a single locus of change but rather multiple or plural forces of opposition. In so doing, Marcuse foreshadows the interest Foucault, and in a different way Derrida, later showed in margins and the marginalized, the social outcasts. However, unlike Foucault, Marcuse does this without claiming that the marginalized are power-holders within a network of power. While Foucault's observations about the complexities of power relationships are helpful in explaining some subjects, such as the power dynamics within an organized proletariat or vanguard Leninist group, Marcuse's view better explains the ways in which hopeless outcasts are outside the systems of power. Marcuse's view allows for the distinction between power and powerlessness. Particularly interesting is Foucault's claim that where there is power there is resistance. While Marcuse might not agree that this statement is necessarily true, he would probably find its hopeful optimism attractive. If Foucault is right about power entailing resistance, a bigger question would seem to be: why? Is there, and will there always be, a human spirit struggling for freedom? If this is what is implied in Foucault's statement, then Foucault begins to sound Hegelian or Marxian.

In his introduction to *Foucault: A Critical Reader*, David Hoy writes, "The life of the mind requires controversy,"[66] and certainly, in the last decades of their lives, neither Foucault nor Marcuse were strangers to controversy. Interestingly, in *The Lives of Michel Foucault* (1993), David Macey discusses the fact that in France some of the controversy surrounding Foucault involved attempts to place his work, however inaccurately, in the revolutionary wake of Marcuse.[67] Perhaps Marcuse's explicit absence from *The History of Sexuality* is partially due to Foucault's desire, as a Nietzschean individualist, to create his own controversies and avoid being associated with another controversial thinker (Marcuse), or groups of thinkers (the Freudo-Marxists). But while Foucault seemed to desire an individual and iconoclastic break with other thinkers and the past, one could argue that Foucault's theorizing in *The History of Sexuality* seems to be subtly informed by the shadow of Descartes. Both in Foucault's focus on the Christian confessional and the Catholic hierarchy which must be placated, whether by Descartes' obsequious dedication to the *Meditations* or a detailed narrative of sexual "transgressions," Foucault likewise replicates Descartes' mind/body split by focusing on the incitement to discourse at the expense of the Freudo-Marxian focus on the bodily desires for sex that call for satisfaction if psychological health is to be attained/maintained. Thus, Foucault's own discourse on sexuality, in the section of his text under discussion, is distantly abstracted from the sexual needs and acts felt and practiced in embodied human existence, and this distancing causes Foucault to downplay the importance of the psycho-sexual human well-being that Freudo-Marxism brought attention to. However, the preceding discussion is primarily intended to suggest that the particular controversy Foucault created in rejecting the repressive hypothesis is not the result of Foucault's refutation of Marcuse's influential version of Freudo-Marxism, and that Foucault's celebrated "critique" of the repressive hypothesis does not confront or refute but artfully dodges Marcuse's version.

Rorty's Dismissal

Another example of the treatment Marcuse has received from the academic community can be seen by considering some comments Richard Rorty made in an interview with Giovanna Borradori for her book *The American Philosopher* (1994). In the interview, Rorty claims that "American intellectuals forgot about philosophy until the sixties, when people like Habermas, Gadamer, Foucault, and Derrida reminded them."[68] Borradori seems surprised by Rorty's statement and she asks him why he mentioned those thinkers instead of Marcuse and Adorno, who had both immigrated to the US and taught there. Rorty responds:

> They were here and they weren't here. They were here in body, but not in spirit, since they never noticed America, and the things they used to say about America were just absurd. They lived here in exile without believing this was a real country. I think to get caught up on Adorno and Marcuse one has to take Marx more seriously than he has ever been taken in America. Derrida, Foucault, and Heidegger don't ask you to take Marx all that seriously. Before the sixties we had no Marxist tradition; in the United States people simply didn't read Marx, people still don't read Marx.[69]

Rorty's response says quite a bit, perhaps more than he had intended. Rorty, perhaps because of Borradori's question, does not distinguish between Adorno and Marcuse, and this is a problem. While Adorno emigrated to the US while the Nazis were in power in Germany, he returned to live in Germany after the Second World War. Marcuse, on the other hand, emigrated to the US, became a citizen, and never gave up his citizenship or his residence in the US. Additionally, Marcuse was much more open to and concerned with American culture than was Adorno.

Marcuse was a socialist and an internationalist who actively supported Third World liberation movements and avidly read authors such as Fanon. But this, fortunately, was true of many American socialists. Marcuse spent almost four decades in America (half of his life), worked in American intelligence against the Nazis, taught in American universities, voted, was engaged in political activism in the US, published a significant critique of the Soviets during the Cold War, and even fell in love with the beaches of San Diego! Why would Rorty say Marcuse never noticed America? Marcuse openly acknowledged that much of his later work focused on the US, and Marcuse certainly noticed when the then Vice-President Spiro Agnew and California Governor Ronald Reagan led the successful effort to force him out of the University of California system. Just how involved do you have to be in the US for Rorty to consider you a *real* American? What sense does it make to argue that one of America's most intellectually powerful social critiques was produced by someone who never noticed America?

In the interview, Rorty maintains that American intellectuals rediscovered philosophy in the 1960s because of an encounter with Habermas, Gadamer, Foucault, and Derrida.[70] However, Derrida, Foucault, and Habermas were not widely read by American intellectuals until the mid- to late 1970s. It would be stretching things quite a bit to say that Gadamer has ever been read as widely by American intellectuals as Derrida, Foucault, and Habermas have been. Marcuse and Adorno, on the other hand, were widely read by American intellectuals in the 1960s, particularly students, and these readings are part of the reason that Americans started or revived a Marxist tradition in the US in the 1960s and 1970s.

Borradori, seemingly bewildered by Rorty's responses, asks: "Marx has been of fundamental importance for all the French post-structuralist authors: Lyotard, Deleuze, Virilio, and also Foucault. Have you ever read Marx?" Rorty responds: "My parents' home was full of Marx. They read him, so I read him as a kid, but not as a philosopher. I still can't read him as a philosopher."[71] Later, Rorty says: "nobody cares whether you read Marx – not even Fredric Jameson."[72] Rorty's responses, unless intended as conservative revisionary intellectual history, are bizarre. Rorty is a self-professed admirer and adopter of French post-structuralism, but avoids Marx. One wonders what Rorty thinks of Derrida's *Spectres of Marx*, which was published in the same year as Borradori's interviews?

Perhaps it is unfair to hold Rorty to comments he made in an interview, but the harshness of his judgment, along with the inaccurate history he constructs, inspired this response. More importantly, Rorty's response to Marcuse is all too typical of the responses that have caused Marcuse's critical theory to be ignored. One would hope that Rorty, who, like MacIntyre and Foucault, broke with mainstream theoretical practices in the academy, might be more open to Marcuse's innovative theorizing. In the first half of the twentieth century, Marcuse was engaged in interdisciplinary philosophical activity that provocatively employed literature and psychoanalysis in a critical theory intensely concerned with embodied human existence. Furthermore, in *Eros and Civilization*, Marcuse began to seriously engage Nietzsche long before the Nietzsche revival in the US academy, and seven years before Deleuze's important *Nietzsche and Philosophy*. Additionally, Marcuse stressed the political and theoretical importance of art, the imagination, and literature at a time when much philosophical work was excessively dry, narrow, and disengaged. In these senses Marcuse was decades ahead of his time, if we have reached his time yet.

Conclusion

When reflecting upon these critiques of Marcuse's critical theory, one begins to wonder about some of the motives inspiring them. Determining motives can be difficult, but a passage from Richard Bernstein's *Philosophical Profiles* will be offered as a partial explanation for the hostile academic reception Marcuse often received. The passage is taken from a chapter on Marcuse in Bernstein's book. Bernstein writes:

> But he never gave up hope; he never submitted to the despair of thinking that the power of negativity could not assert itself. He searched – in what sometimes seems like a desperate manner – for the signs of those social movements and tendencies that were progressive and liberating. He was open to new possibilities and enthusiastically supported them in speech and deed. He never accepted the lament over the death of the New Left, and he claimed that the women's movement may yet turn out to be the most radical movement of our times. To the end he personified the demand for happiness and liberation. In all his activities he was "life affirming." I have been primarily focusing on Marcuse as a negative thinker, as one of the most persistent radical critics of our time, but what was so beautiful about Marcuse (and I am using "beautiful" in a way in which he would have used it) is that there was a deep harmony between Marcuse as a thinker and Marcuse as a man. Those who knew him even slightly were deeply affected by his charm, his humor, his playfulness, his sheer zest and delight in living, his own capacity for the pleasure of being alive. It is this quality that evoked such profound resonances among those who were inspired by him, and so much hostility and *resentment* among those who envied him.[73]

Bernstein's remarks provide some insight into Marcuse's rude academic reception.

For all the bombast and hostility of the critiques discussed in this paper, it is striking that Marcuse's devastating critique of contemporary capitalism is left untouched. Given the depth of Marcuse's social critique and his characterization of contemporary capitalism as totalitarian, this "oversight" is astounding. That Marcuse's challenging indictment has tended to raise personal attacks, hairsplitting, straw arguments, and faulty memories, speaks volumes about both the discomfort Marcuse has always caused and the serious social problems we still face.

Notes

1. See Paul Breines (ed.), *Critical Interruptions*, New York: Herder & Herder, 1970, p. ix, and see Paul Alexander Juutilainen's documentary film *Herbert's Hippopotamus* (1996).
2. Jonathan Swift, "Thoughts on Various Subjects," *Satires and Personal Writings*, New York and London: Oxford University Press, 1949, p. 407.
3. Edward Said, *Culture and Imperialism*, New York: Vintage, 1984, p. 292.
4. An extended version of this discussion can be found in my doctoral dissertation, which is entitled "Marcuse's Ghost."
5. Martin Jay, *The Dialectical Imagination*, Boston: Little, Brown, 1973.
6. Alasdair MacIntyre, *Herbert Marcuse: An Exposition and Polemic*, New York: Viking, 1970, p. 2.
7. *Ibid.*, p. 2.
8. *Ibid.*, pp. 4–5.
9. *Ibid.*, pp. 6–9.
10. *Ibid.*, p. 7.
11. *Ibid.*, p. 17.
12. Douglas Kellner, *Herbert Marcuse and the Crisis of Marxism*, Berkeley and Los Angeles: University of California Press, p. 400, endnote 48.
13. *Ibid.*, p. 395, endnote 78.
14. *Ibid.*, p. 394, endnote 73.
15. Rolf Wiggershaus, *The Frankfurt School: Its History, Theories, and Political Significance*, trans. Michael Robertson, Cambridge, MA: MIT Press, p. 102.
16. *Ibid.*, p. 102.
17. Herbert Marcuse, *Negations*, Boston: Beacon, 1968, p. 135.
18. *Ibid.*, pp. 156–7.
19. MacIntyre, *Herbert Marcuse*, p. 5.
20. Marcuse, *Negations*, p. 143.
21. MacIntyre, *Herbert Marcuse*, p. 8.
22. *Ibid.*, pp. 31–2.
23. *Ibid.*, p. 41.
24. *Ibid.*, p. 13.
25. *Ibid.*, p. 45.
26. *Ibid.*, p. 50.
27. *Ibid.*, p. 50.
28. *Ibid.*, p. 53.
29. *Ibid.*, pp. 57–8.
30. *Ibid.*, p. 58.
31. *Ibid.*, p. 59.
32. *Ibid.*, p. 63.
33. *Ibid.*, p. 67.
34. *Ibid.*, p. 69.
35. *Ibid.*, p. 75.
36. *Ibid.*, p. 73.
37. *Ibid.*, p. 73.
38. *Ibid.*, p. 105.
39. *Ibid.*, p. 105.
40. *Ibid.*, p. 106.
41. Robin Blackburn, in *Telos*, no. 6 (Fall 1970), p. 348.
42. *Ibid.*, p. 351.
43. *Ibid.*, p. 351.
44. Herbert Marcuse, *An Essay on Liberation*, Boston: Beacon, 1969, pp. 7–8.

45 Ishmael Reed, *Japanese by Spring*, New York: Penguin, 1996, p. 30.
46 Alasdair MacIntyre, *After Virtue*, Notre Dame: University of Notre Dame Press, 1984, p. 263.
47 Herbert Marcuse, *One-Dimensional Man: Studies in the Ideology of Advanced Industrial Society*, Boston: Beacon, 1964, p. 257.
48 The French edition was published in 1976 and the English edition in 1978.
49 Michel Foucault, *The History of Sexuality, Volume 1: An Introduction*, trans. by Robert Hurley, New York: Vintage, 1990, p. 131.
50 *Ibid.*, p. 12.
51 *Ibid.*, pp. 36–7.
52 *Ibid.*, pp. 3–4 and throughout the text.
53 Herbert Marcuse, "Marxism and Feminism," *Women's Studies*, vol. 2, no. 3 (1974), p. 280.
54 Foucault, *The History of Sexuality*, p. 7.
55 *Ibid.*, pp. 7–8.
56 *Ibid.*, p. 12.
57 *Ibid.*, p. 11.
58 *Ibid.*, p. 34.
59 *Ibid.*, p. 12.
60 Herbert Marcuse, *Eros and Civilization: A Philosophical Inquiry into Freud*, Boston: Beacon, 1955, p. 171.
61 Paul Beines, "Revisiting Marcuse with Foucault: *An Essay on Liberation* Meets *The History of Sexuality*," in John Bokina and Timothy J. Lukes (eds.) *Marcuse: From the New Left to the Next Left*, Topeka, KA: University of Kansas Press, 1994, pp. 49–51.
62 Foucault, *The History of Sexuality*, pp. 95–6.
63 Marcuse, *One-Dimensional Man*, p. 256.
64 *Ibid.*, pp. 256–7.
65 *Ibid.*, 257.
66 David Hoy (ed.), *Foucault: A Critical Reader*, Oxford: Blackwell, 1992, p. 1.
67 David Macey, *The Lives of Michel Foucault*, London: Vintage, 1994, p. 214.
68 Giovanna Borradori, *The American Philosopher: Conversations with Quine, Davidson, Putnam, Nozick, Danto, Rorty, Cavell, MacIntyre, and Kuhn*, trans. Rosanna Crocitto, Chicago and London: University of Chicago Press, 1994, pp. 110–11.
69 Rorty quoted in Borradori, *The American Philosopher*, p. 111.
70 *Ibid.*, pp. 110–11.
71 *Ibid.*, pp. 111–12.
72 *Ibid.*, p. 112.
73 Richard Bernstein, *Philosophical Profiles*, Philadelphia: University of Pennsylvania Press, 1986, p. 188.

10

MARCUSE, HABERMAS, AND THE CRITIQUE OF TECHNOLOGY[1]

Samir Gandesha

In an important essay published by Marcuse just as the Second World War was entering its second year, one finds an example of the kind of "existential judgment on society" that Horkheimer defines as constitutive of critical theory.[2] Such a judgment captures with particular insight the pervasiveness of technology in post-liberal capitalism:

> A man who travels by automobile to a distant place chooses his route from highway maps. Towns, lakes and mountains appear as obstacles to be bypassed. The country-side is shaped and organized by the highway. Numerous signs and posters tell the traveler what to do and think; they even request his attention to the beauties of nature and the hallmarks of history. Giant advertisements tell him to stop for the pause that refreshes. And all this is indeed for his benefit, safety and comfort; he receives what he wants. Business, technics, human needs and nature are welded together into one rational and expedient mechanism. He will fare best who follows its directions subordinating his spontaneity to the anonymous wisdom that ordered everything for him.[3]

Now, some sixty years later, consider a prime-time television advertisement for sports recreational vehicles. Aimed at the managerial class, and invoking a 1950s B-movie plot-line, the ad charts a young couple's "Escape from the City." Against a grim backdrop of grinding poverty, amid the ruins of a once-thriving metropolis, at every step of the way, our young couple is terrorized by menacing bicycle couriers and speeding eighteen-wheelers in their attempt to flee a history shot through with nature to their bunker-like, gated communities in the suburbs. The advertisement sells a postmodern dream of security, welded together in the "expedient mechanism" of what is perhaps the only kind of vehicle suited to traversing the increasingly dilapidated landscape of post-New Deal America.

What we see in the first image is an excellent example of the unity of the "essential" and the "historical," which, according to Barry Katz, characterizes the whole of Marcuse's work.[4] Clearly, in choosing the automobile as the exemplary instance of technology, Marcuse grounds his critique of technology in the historical practice of society. In as much as it presents the automobile as an example of technological reason, and all that it implied – from production techniques, patterns of consumption and distribution, down to city planning – the nature of this historical practice is Fordism. Thus, the automobile represents, in the form of a synecdoche, the displacement of critical by technological reason and, therewith, the increasing eclipse of the possibility of a qualitatively different set of social arrangements.

Now, however, half a century later, the automobile has given way to the ubiquitous sports utility vehicle, which, with its tank-like exterior, becomes the allegory not of freedom and social mobility, but of safety in a period marked by the catastrophic collapse of nature into history, the return of society to a condition of a "bellum omnium contra omnes."[5] While the menacing bicycle couriers signify the nihilism of increasing sections of society structurally unable to play anything but a marginal role within it, the speeding truck allegorizes the restiveness of organized labor whose demands, while certainly not revolutionary, are no longer functional; such demands can no longer be met within the system without evoking the dreaded specter of "stagflation." The general context of urban decay and squalor none-too-subtly suggests the multicultural and hence threatening nature of the city. While the automobile represented the "dream image" for the promise of material abundance,[6] the militarized sports utility vehicle represents, amid the return of the savage inequalities of globalization, the abrupt revocation of that promise: a sober recognition that perhaps capitalism cannot "deliver the goods" after all.[7]

It would not be too much of an exaggeration to suggest that the distance between these two images is indexed to the temporal distance between two distinct periods in late capitalism. The transformations in the period following the oil crisis and the ensuing slump have led social scientists to think in terms of a shift from "Fordism" to "Post-Fordism," or "organized" to "disorganized" capitalism. According to David Harvey, for example, while organized capitalism was based on the hegemony of technical-scientific rationality, the concentration of capital within relatively few industries and regions, and an emphasis on economies of scale, gained through increases in the size of fixed and variable capital, disorganized capitalism comes to be characterized by "cultural fragmentation and pluralism coupled with an undermining of traditional class or national identities, and the dispersal and diversification of the territorial-spatial division of labor."[8] The effect of this is to render problematic Pollock's conception of state capitalism, which, along with Neumann's reflections on the totalitarian state, serves as the basis for Marcuse's sociological reflections.[9] We could say, therefore, that the obsolescence of Marcuse's writings is at least a partial result of their direct empirical entanglements with the "historical practice of society."

Yet, at the same time, what is of enduring importance in Marcuse's critical theory is its conceptual grasp of technological reason. Notice that Marcuse's example of the automobile draws out the manner in which the driver's experience of nature is organized in advance. The automobile functions, therefore, in a manner not unlike Kant's "schematism of the pure understanding." However, in contrast to the Kantian conception, which presupposed an active contribution from the subject, technology has now appropriated the role of relating the sensible content of experience to concepts; that the subject subordinates his spontaneity to the "anonymous wisdom that ordered everything for him."[10] It is this latter aspect of Marcuse's critique of technology that will be what concerns me here. If "ideology" refers to the intertwining of power and validity, as in Marx's analysis of the universalization of particular interests, then Marcuse's critique of technology as ideology seeks to grasp the manner in which the preponderance of technological reason emerges as a particular and contingent historical project that nonetheless claims universality and necessity. The "historical" project of technology is inherently contradictory precisely because it forestalls reflection on these conditions of its own emergence, that is to say, it resists reflection *on its own history*. A form of reason that is defined as efficiency – like Wittgenstein's early conception of philosophy as rigorously confining itself to the "the totality of facts"[11] – relinquishes the ability to reflect upon itself. Like its positivist incarnation, such a conception of reason becomes self-revoking.

The aim of this essay is to examine Habermas's critique of Marcuse's conception of technology as set forth in an important essay dedicated to Marcuse on his 70th birthday, written over thirty years ago. Revisiting Habermas's critique of Marcuse, it is hoped, will contribute to identifying possible paths leading to the revitalization of the intentions of the first generation of critical theory without at the same time ignoring the importance of the insights generated by the so-called "linguistic turn." In particular, what I wish to suggest is that Habermas's critique of Marcuse reveals aspects of his own theory that are susceptible to criticism in light of its own understanding of modernity. I first briefly outline Marcuse's critique of technology by way of his engagement with Weber, after which I examine Habermas's alternative reading of the concept of rationalization and his critique of Marcuse. In the final section, I try to defend Marcuse against some of Habermas's charges by revealing the presuppositions of Habermas's critique.

Marcuse and the Critique of Technological Reason

As a way of coming to terms with the radical transformation of technology in the middle of the twentieth century from a revolutionary force that pointed beyond the social order to a conservative force that served to consolidate it, Marcuse undertakes a critique of technological reason via an engagement with Weber's account of rationalization in an important essay entitled "Industrialization and capitalism in Max Weber," published in the same year as *One-Dimensional Man*. The very abstract nature of Weber's account of rationalization reveals its concreteness and elucidates how, qua abstraction, it conceals substantive domination. This critique of Weber is of interest for three reasons: (1) it is an important example of Marcuse's ambivalence toward technology that results from the two, often strongly discordant, though not wholly unproductive, sources of his critique of technological reason: historical materialism and phenomenology; (2) it stands in sharp contrast to Habermas's own critique of Weber in the *Theory of Communicative Action*, to which we shall return below; and, therefore, (3) it enables us to identify what is at stake in the respective critiques of technological reason of Marcuse and Habermas.

The starting point of Marcuse's critique of Weber is the alleged "value-freedom" of social science, of which the concept of formal rationality is an exemplary instance. Marcuse challenges such a notion by situating Weber solidly within the political context of Wilhelmine Germany. The whole force of Marcuse's critique lies in showing how, in its insistence on value-freedom, Weber's concept of rationality reveals its undeniable *political determinations*. In contrast to Weber, Marcuse argues that neutrality is contingent upon self-reflection: "neutrality is *real* only when it has the power of resisting interference."[12] Conversely, the absence of such a self-reflection of reason, the abstracting of reason (as *formal* rationality) from every context, makes it available for use by value orientations that come to it from the outside; such orientations are by definition irrational. Marcuse outlines three elements of Weber's account of reason: (1) the progressive mathematization of experience, proceeding from the natural to the social sciences; (2) the insistence on the necessity of rational experiment and proofs in the organization of both science and life-conduct; and (3) the genesis and solidification of a technocracy.[13] It is in the transition from theoretical to practical reason that the allegedly neutral conception of formal rationality reveals itself to be limited by the conditions of its own historical emergence; in this particular case, genesis limits validity. More specifically, just as Marx had historicized classical political economy, Marcuse argues that Weber's concept of formal rationality is *inexorably* marked by its own historicity (*Geschichtlichkeit*). This consists of the "liberation" of labor from the means of production and its progressive control by private enterprise; in short, liberal capitalism. In the eclipse of liberal capitalism – which privileges the *rationality* of the individual entrepreneur – by monopoly capitalism, we see unfolding the inescapable *irrationality* of technical reason. "Inner worldly asceticism," the basis for the life-conduct of the bourgeoisie, becomes deeply irrational in a society ever driven by the satisfaction of false needs:

> In the unfolding of capitalist rationality, *irrationality* becomes *reason*: reason as frantic development of productivity, conquest of nature, enlargement of the mass of goods (and their accessibility for broad strata of the population); irrational because higher productivity, domination of nature, and social wealth, become destructive forces.[14]

While Weber's conceptual apparatus could not have accounted for such a development directly, it "is implied in his conceptual scheme – implied at such a deep level that it appears as inexorable, final, and thereby, in turn (in the bad sense), rational."[15] Here we have a provisional answer to the question posed at the beginning of this section, namely: how does it come to pass that what Marx called the "icy waters of egotistical calculation," which had played such a liberating role in the overturning of the *ancien regime*, now actually contribute to the freezing of social relations in a kind of eternalized present? In his understanding of industrialization as a logic of the "iron cage," Weber lays bare the material or substantive rationality that lies at the heart of his conception of formal reason: "he generalizes the blindness of a society which reproduces itself behind the back [*sic*] of the individuals, of a society in which the law of domination appears as an objective, technological law."[16] Weber's concept of rationalization elucidates how, in contrast to previous modes of production in which economic and political domination were fused, the specific nature of domination in capitalist society takes on an increasingly impersonal, necessary, and, therefore, fateful quality. However, that this fate has *become* a fate, that is to say, a historical rather than a natural phenomenon, implies the possibility of its negation. Indeed, any scientific analysis not pledged to such negation places itself in the service of "really existing" domination.

As a way of further elucidating what is at stake in his critique of Weber, it might be helpful to cast a glance at Marcuse's appropriation of the late Husserl for a teleologico-historical critique of science. For Husserl, modern Galilean science, that is to say, empirically grounded mathematical science, is the end of the Western idea of reason, in the doubled sense of termination point and realization (*telos*). Like Weber, Husserl seeks to chart the process of disenchantment through which reason becomes increasingly subjective. Husserl's evaluation of this process, however, differs markedly from Weber, insofar as he unfolds the manner in which science, having originated in the Greek idea of knowledge, culminates in a form of scientific rationality whose truth and validity conceal "illusion and repression." But what constitutes the Greek concept of reason? According to Marcuse's interpretation, it is the idea "of human being as self-determination and determination of its world by virtue of man's intellectual faculties." In other words, reason is the basis for human self-realization, yet such self-realization moves in a cosmos that is, itself, the embodiment of *logos*. There are three implications that follow from this "original" conception of reason: (1) the validity of reason is transcendent (its validity is time- and space-independent); (2) true being is ideational being – hence Platonism is the paradigm of knowledge; and (3) objectivity is correlated with subjectivity. This idea of knowledge culminates as a specific project in Galileo's idea of science. However, such a culmination is also a collapse, for the price it pays for success in the natural sciences is a relinquishing of the original idea of reason: the self-determination of human being. Marcuse reads this concept of "project" through Sartre as: "a specific way of experiencing, interpreting, organizing, and changing the world, a specific historical project among other possible ones, not the only necessary one."[17] As we shall see below, Habermas takes Marcuse to task for understanding science and technology as a project in this sense.

Because it relinquishes the ability to determine its own ends, reason becomes dependent upon authorities outside of itself, that is to say, it becomes heteronomous. At the same time, science becomes autonomized, the operations of which can be learned, without, however, necessitating a corresponding understanding of the principles on which it is based. Given its inability to reflect on itself, science reveals itself to move in a vicious circle: it simultaneously projects and intuits (*Voraussicht*) the contents of the pre-reflective, pre-given *Lebenswelt* that it mistakes for objectivity. In other words, "Science is *Aufhebung der Lebenswelt*."[18] In a way that reinforces his critique of Weber's concept of value-neutrality, Marcuse writes: "This is the famous neutrality of pure science which here reveals itself as an illusion, because neutrality disguises, in the mathematical-ideational forms, the essential relation to the pre-given empirical reality."[19] Science, in the final instance, is undermined not by virtue of its external dependence upon society, history, etc., that is to say, not by virtue of a sociological limitation, but rather by an intrinsically philosophical one.

Here Marcuse provides an ontological elaboration of the immanent, sociological critique he provides of Weber. The "provocative" thesis that Marcuse wants to draw out of his reading of Husserl is that scientific and technological reason are ideological precisely because of a forgetfulness of their own historicity.[20] Consequently, science and technology are only apparently dynamic; understood at an ontological level, they are grounded in a projection into the future of categories through which the present is grasped, thereby closing off other historical, as opposed to transcendental, possibilities. Nonetheless, Marcuse is deeply critical of Husserl's merely philosophical solution to the crisis, that is to say, the attempt, by way of a doubled *epokhē*, of the *Lebenswelt* and of the scientific concept of objectivity, to ground objectivity in transcendental subjectivity. Marcuse argues that

Husserl fails to provide an adequate solution to the problem precisely because he cannot grasp that the transcendental constitution of the object is not simply a question of theory, of intentionality, but is also a matter of action or praxis. We shall come back to the proposed solution to the crisis of the Western sciences in a moment.

It is possible to summarize Marcuse's critique of Weber in the following terms: Weber's account of the emptying out of a substantive conception of reason through its formalization, the progressive withdrawal of reason from every context, is itself marked by the substance of its own context. Yet Marcuse's identification of the limits of Weber's concept of reason implies, at the same time, a transcendence of those limits. In other words, Marcuse's critique is premised on the possibility of a historical alternative offering a path beyond the solidification of rationalization into an "iron cage." Such an alternative is necessary if the triumph and domination of formal rationality is not to be thought of as *inexorable*. It is here that Marcuse locates a path beyond the iron cage in a totalizing form of practical reason grounded in a conception of non-alienated labor: "For there is not a structure that has not been *posited* or *made* and is not as such dependent."[21] This stands in contrast to Lukács, who had also sought to locate a definitive answer to Weber, in the subject-object of History, and, who would later admit, made the fatal error of conflating "objectification" and "alienation."[22] With the newly discovered *Economic and Philosophical Manuscripts of 1844* at his disposal, Marcuse makes no such mistake and offers an "existential" and "ontological" interpretation of labor as the "foundation" of historical materialism. That is to say, labor is not simply an open-ended, material transformation of nature, but rather a fundamentally ontological activity inasmuch as it becomes the means through which humanity produces its own essence.[23]

> The *Phenomenology* presents the "self-creation of man," which means, after what has already been said, the process in which man (as an organic, living being) becomes what he is according to his essence – i.e. human essence. It thus gives the "genetic history" (p.173) of the human essence or man's essential history. Man's "act of creation" is an "act of self-genesis" (p.188), i.e. man gives his essence to himself: he must first make himself what he is, "posit" himself, and "produce" himself...This history which is given in man's own hands is grasped by Hegel as a "process" characterized by alienation and its supersession. The process as a whole stands under the title of "objectification."...It is this establishing of an objective world which Hegel treats merely as the alienation of "consciousness" or knowledge, or as a relation of abstract thought to "thinghood," while Marx grasps it as the "practical" realization of the whole man in historical and social labor.[24]

Against the backdrop of Marcuse's earlier reading of the young Marx's indebtedness to Hegel's *Phenomenology of Spirit*, Marcuse's proposed answer to a technological reason gone wild becomes clear. Technological reason is *aufgehoben* through a dialectic of "historical and social labor." Here, it would seem, we are confronted with an original presentation of the manner in which the truth content of Husserlian phenomenology is realized by way of historical materialism.[25] What the *epokhē* reveals is, in actuality, far from pure intentionality – or consciousness that is always consciousness *of* an object; rather, the objectivity of the Object is, in the final instance, objectified subjectivity. The dissolution of the crisis of the European sciences comes about by virtue of a continuous process through which the subject attains radical self-knowledge consummated as practical reason. Through practical reason, the calcified, static structures of the *Lebenswelt* are dynamized into pure actuality; they cease, therefore, to stand over and against humanity as a heteronomous order.

In his reading of Weber, what comes to the fore is Marcuse's ambivalent relation to technology, stemming, as I have already suggested, from the two sources of his critique: historical materialism and phenomenology. Thus, if my interpretation is correct, Marcuse wishes to appropriate the concept of the *Lebenswelt* as the always already given meaningful structures that exist prior to the individuals socialized into them *and* offer the possibility of their radical transformation as by way of practical reason now understood as "historical and social labor." Such a tension can be seen, moreover, in Marcuse's argument that Weber's identification of technological reason with bourgeois capitalist reason "prevents him from seeing that not 'pure', formal, technical reason but the reason of domination erects a shell of bondage...and that the consummation of technical reason can well become the instrument for the liberation of man."[26] Yet, on the very next page, Marcuse argues that (and it is worth quoting him here at length);

> The very concept of technical reason is perhaps ideological. Not only the application of technology but technology itself is domination (of nature and men) – methodical, scientific, calculated, calculating control. Specific purposes and interests of domination are not foisted upon technology subsequently and from the outside; they enter into the very construction of the technical apparatus. Technology is always a historical-social *project*: in it is projected what a society and its ruling interests intend to do with men and things.[27]

Here, then, the ideological nature of technology does not simply come from the outside – that is to say, in the specific uses to which technology is put – as Marcuse suggests earlier, but rather constitutes its innermost essence. What this means is that, as a project, technological reason is the principal means in and through which human beings and things are constituted; in short, it is the way in which the world is revealed and made available for domination. Thus, we find in this passage an ambivalent juxtaposition of technology as neutral instrumentality, fettered only by society's production relations, on the one hand, and technology as a world-disclosing *project* on the other.

This ambivalence in his conception of technology runs throughout Marcuse's post-war work, in particular *Eros and Civilization* (1955) and *One-Dimensional Man* (1964), but is also clearly in evidence in "Some Social Implications of Modern Technology" (1941). In the latter essay, Marcuse distinguishes between "technology" and "technics." While technology comprises the overall relations of a given society, technics is the "technical apparatus of industry, transportation and communication."[28] If by technology Marcuse means the mode of production, then technics is defined in terms of the productive forces. Technics by itself, therefore, "can promote authoritarianism as well as liberalism, the extension as well as the abolition of toil." Technology is defined by Marcuse not simply in terms of the structures of a given society, but also, in phenomenological terms, as "nothing technological." That is to say, technology is not something that can be grasped like a tool *in the world*, but rather that which *discloses the world* as meaningful in the first place.

The two phenomena, technology and technics, are exemplified in the example of the automobile, to which I have already referred. As we shall argue below, this relation – between technology and technics – is not as contradictory as it might first appear. Marcuse argues that the automobile exemplifies the *new* "matter-of-factness" of technological reason. While historically such matter-of-factness had *enlightening* effects, for example in ancient materialism and hedonism, modern physics, and the radical rationalism of the Enlightenment, now it *reproduces the existing order*.[29] This gets to the heart of Marcuse's analysis, which seeks to elucidate in concrete fashion the dialectic through which the normative ideals of bourgeois society, in particular the idea of reason as the actualization of individual autonomy in direct opposition to external authorities, are progressively reversed. With the increasing preponderance of technics – as both the cause and effect of the monopolistic tendencies of capital – reason comes to be increasingly understood as the ever efficient realization of ends that, themselves, lie beyond the reach of rational determination; reason, in other words, becomes unreason. In a way that looks forward to *One-Dimensional Man*, Marcuse argues that the pervasiveness of technological reason eclipses negativity and discharges in a thoroughgoing unidimensionality.

Unlike his later position, however, Marcuse retains the orthodox Marxian view of the productive forces as inherently dynamic and potentially explosive. If organized labor, and with it critical rationality, is at the point of being eclipsed by technological reason, technics still embodies contradictory tendencies which, in fact, result from its inherently dynamic nature; as such, it is able to "democratize functions" and, in the process, reveal the existing relations of production as increasingly arbitrary. At the same time, technics would appear to make possible, through the elimination of scarcity, the "individualization" of the sphere of human realization.[30] While, in and of itself, technics does not break through calcified social relations, it can clear the ground for a critique of the prevailing production relations as increasingly arbitrary and, therefore, as increasingly historically obsolete. How this actually comes about in a context marked by the decline of critical rationality, however, remains a question that goes unanswered in this particular essay. Nevertheless, what is crucial here is that Marcuse keeps open the possibility of a reciprocal relation between technology and technics. Let us now turn to Habermas's critique of Marcuse, which emphasizes the latter's treatment of technological reason with its inherent ambivalence.

Habermas's Critique of Marcuse

Taking as his point of departure an apparently insufficient differentiation of work and interaction in Marx, Habermas seeks quite early on in his career to differentiate these two forms of action: the productive forces are to be differentiated from the relations of production; and action oriented toward progressive mastery of nature is to be differentiated from action oriented toward understanding. Habermas therefore engages in an immanent critique of Weber's apparently one-sided account of societal rationalization. According to Habermas, while showing that the "innerworldly asceticism" of Protestantism was central to the process of rationalization as the spread of cognitive-instrumental rationality ("formal" as opposed to "substantive" rationality), Weber does not emphasize enough the transposition of the rationalization of world-views into societal rationalization. As religion comes to be rationalized, questions of the "true," the "beautiful," and the "good" become differentiated and eventually supplant the metaphysical systems that once bound them together. Moreover, as alluded to above, they become institutionalized within different value spheres, namely science, aesthetics, and morality. While Weber, in his Nietzschean diagnosis of nihilism as the war between contending "gods and demons," drew the pessimistic conclusion that reason has lost its unity and universality in the process of its differentiation into mutually exclusive spheres of value, Habermas proposes a more elaborate version of the allegedly vague conceptions of reason offered by Weber. The fragmented dynamic of cultural rationalization is unified by communicative rationality, guided by the regulative ideal of undistorted communication: "The unity of rationality in the multiplicity of value spheres rationalized according to their inner logics is secured precisely at the formal level of the argumentative redemption of validity claims."[31]

Habermas therefore seeks to show that communicative reason mediates the universal structure of action oriented toward understanding and the particular claims made within each quasi-autonomous sphere of value. Indeed, Weber's mistake lies precisely in failing to adequately distinguish "between the particular value *contents* of cultural traditions and those universal *standards* of value under which the cognitive, normative, and expressive components of culture became autonomous value spheres and developed complexes of rationality with their own logics."[32]

What immediately comes into view are the fundamental differences in Marcuse's and Habermas's respective assessments of Weber, which, in turn, provide insight into Habermas's critique of Marcuse. Especially worthy of mention are the differences in the normative grounding of their respective critiques. As we have already seen, Marcuse seeks to historicize Weber by way of a materialist translation of Husserlian "transcendental subjectivity" into the accomplishments of "historical and social labor." Thus, Marcuse criticizes Weber for the construal of rationalization that only gains its own sinister autonomy and works behind the backs of historical individuals precisely because, as a historical possibility, the mediation of subjective and objective forms of reason is closed off. For Habermas, by contrast, the shortcomings of Weber's account of modernity lie in the refusal to recognize that the extension of *Zweckrationalität* is accompanied by a simultaneous differentiation of value spheres no longer rooted in traditional or religious world-views, and the corresponding possibility of a "rationalization" of the *Lebenswelt*. Thus, Marcuse's and Habermas's critiques are almost exactly inverse images of each other. While Marcuse argues for an extension of the concept of labor as the crucial mediation of subject and object, Habermas argues for its foreshortening in an account of the rationalization of the symbolically mediated action of the *Lebenswelt* that is attendant upon the spread of "purposive-rationality."

Habermas therefore argues that Marcuse's ambivalence toward technology, to which we have already alluded, stems from his inability to untangle the concepts of "work" and "interaction." Work is defined as "purposive-rational action," which is itself further differentiated into instrumental action, rational choice (strategic action), or some combination thereof. Purposive action is action geared to realizing goals defined under given conditions guided by criteria of the effective control of reality (instrumental action) and correct evaluation of possible alternative choices (strategic action). Interaction, in contrast, is defined as communicative action or symbolic interaction and "is governed by binding *consensual norms*, which define reciprocal expectations about behavior and which must be understood and recognized by at least two acting subjects."[33] Crucial to Habermas's differentiation of work and interaction are its implications for the question of validity:

> While the validity of technical rules and strategies depends on that of empirically true or analytically correct propositions, the validity of social norms is grounded only in the intersubjectivity of mutual understanding of intentions and secured by the general recognition of obligations. Violation of a rule has different consequences according to type. *Incompetent* behavior, which violates valid technical rules or strategies, is condemned per se to failure through lack of success; the "punishment" is built, so to speak, into its rebuff by reality. *Deviant* behavior, which violates consensual norms, provokes sanctions that are connected with the rules only externally, that is by convention.[34]

According to Habermas, the central problem with Marcuse's critique of technology lies in its misguided attempt to cash out a philosophical critique of technological reason in sociological terms. Such a critique is articulated, as we have already seen, via Marcuse's assessment of what he takes to be Weber's questionable conflation of reason with *rationalization*, and hence domination. Habermas argues that it is possible, indeed, necessary, to separate Marcuse's sociological from his philosophical critique of technology. The philosophical dimension derives, as it does for the other members of the first generation of critical theory, from the problematic normative horizon of a "secret hope" of the redemption of a fallen nature, of restoring "nature's voice." Such a hope involves the elaboration of "a different scientific methodology in general – The viewpoint of possible technical control would be one of preserving, fostering and releasing the potentialities of nature."[35] Habermas attempts to free critical theory of the metaphysical presupposition, of the relation between subject and object understood in terms of labor. This is the presupposition under-girding the normative ideal of "releasing nature's potentiality" – the idea of communication between subject and object. It is precisely because Marcuse articulates his philosophical critique from within the limited confines of the "philosophy of consciousness" that his critique of technology becomes philosophically obsolete. If technology can be viewed as a "project" at all it could only be as a "generic" one, which has the human species as a whole as its subject, "not one that could be historically surpassed."[36] Marcuse thus makes the category mistake of attempting to apply concepts that are only applicable to relations between subjects to relations between subject and object.[37]

Habermas is much more receptive, however, to Marcuse's sociological critique of technology as the preponderant ideology of late capitalism. Here he agrees with Marcuse that, in contrast to the explosive configuration of the production relations and forces in liberal capitalism, identified by Marx and Engels, under conditions of post-liberal capitalism, the latter tend to legitimize the former; technological reason becomes the means by which the "productive forces...continually threaten the institutional framework *and at the same time* set the standard of legitimation for the production relations that restrict the potential."[38] In other words, this is an early articulation of the "colonization" thesis – that the fundamental "pathology" of late capitalist societies lies in the tendency of the steering mechanisms of the social subsystems, namely money and power, to colonize the symbolically mediated interaction of the *Lebenswelt*. Habermas seeks to build on Marcuse's critique of technological reason by providing it with firmer, post-metaphysical foundations. This is accomplished by arguing that the ideological nature of technology (and science) inheres not in its orientation toward controlling nature, but rather in the transgression of the boundary of its own sphere of value. In other words, because its legitimate orientation consists of controlling nature, technological or instrumental reason becomes ideological when it overflows the sphere of subject-object relations or the sphere of "work," and spills over into that of intersubjective relations or "interaction." This argument is built upon a theoretical edifice that only becomes clearer in Habermas's subsequent work, the foundation of which is a specific conception of language that privileges validity over meaning.

The Relation Between Technology and Technics, World Disclosure, and Validity

Crucial to Habermas's elaboration of the "paradigm shift" from philosophy and "consciousness" to that of communicative action is, of course, a particular interpretation of the nature of language. What interests us here is the relationship between such a theory of language and the critique of technological reason. In opposition to the tradition of language philosophy, which holds that what distinguishes human beings from other animals is the ability to represent states of affairs, Habermas argues that what is specifically human is the communicative function of propositionally differentiated language. The primacy of representation is decentered if linguistic analysis is shifted from the level of the sentence to that of speech acts more generally.[39] Viewed from the perspective of speech act theory, the "representational" (or propositional) form of language is combined with two other components, the "illocutionary" and the "expressive." The first enables one to represent objects in the world, the second to take up relations with other subjects, and the third to express one's intentions. Moreover, Habermas expands "truth-conditional semantics," the idea that the meaning of a sentence is reducible to its truth conditions, to extend beyond the realm of truth-claims themselves. This division of speech acts corresponds to three distinct claims to validity: truth, rightness, and truthfulness. Such a move necessitates, according to Habermas, a further ontological step; that is to say, the concept of world must be extended beyond the "logocentric" or objectivistic concept to include more than simply the "world" of a totality of objects or existing states of affairs. Rather, speakers take up relations not simply to an external world, but also to a shared social world and to their subjective worlds.

The relationship between this appropriation of speech act theory and rationality is articulated in terms of a formal conception of argumentation. Rationality, in general, refers "in the first instance to the disposition of speaking and acting subjects to acquire and use fallible knowledge."[40] Inasmuch as we presuppose that knowledge refers to the knowledge of states of affairs in the objective world, rationality is geared to "standards of truth and success that govern the relationships of knowing and purposively acting subjects to the world of possible objects or states of affairs."[41] However, by shifting the perspective from the relation between subject and object in the direction of intersubjectivity, rationality becomes grounded in the "argumentative procedures for directly or indirectly redeeming claims to propositional truth, normative rightness, subjective truthfulness and aesthetic harmony."[42] Thus, the dirempted spheres of validity, viz. science, morality, and art, are unified, not in the strong sense, as moments of Absolute Spirit, as in Hegel, but rather in terms of the communicative structures of the *Lebenswelt*.

Habermas's critique of Marcuse in particular, and, indeed, his project as a whole, is premised upon a marginalization of the world-disclosive conception of language. That is to say, with his emphasis on the argumentative redemption of differentiated claims to validity in the "objective," "social," and "subjective" worlds, Habermas is led to bracket the question of the disclosure, or the possibility, of these worlds themselves. But what precisely do we mean by "world disclosure"? While the pragmatic theory of meaning presupposes the orientation of a subject to other subjects, the world-disclosive conception (in a lineage that stretches back to von Humboldt and Herder) emphasizes, as Gadamer puts it, that "Language is not simply one human possession among others in the world, rather, on it depends the fact that human beings *have* a world at all."[43] The concept of "world" refers to the always already articulated, shared orientations and interpretations, independent of the individuals who come to be socialized in it.[44]

As Jay Bernstein has argued, while Habermas suggests that interpretation plays an important role in philosophy, namely through the mediation of the three spheres of value, he clearly privileges the *justificatory* discourses within these spheres. However, such a privileging rehabilitates the positivist claim that there can be no logic of discovery – that only justificatory discourses are rational. In other words, the validity claims raised within the spheres of art and morality are analogous to those of scientific truth, which itself, at least for Habermas, presupposes "nature as it *is*."[45] The marginalization of world disclosure places the emancipatory content of modernity – namely its time consciousness, its relentless need to generate its normativity out of itself, its need for a radically new beginning – in jeopardy. As becomes clear in his polemics against "post-structural" critiques of modernity, Habermas juxtaposes his own pragmatic conception of language with the world-disclosive conception. The central problem for the world-disclosive conception of language is: how can it account for the new? The most influential answer is provided by Heidegger, who suggests an account of the happening of truth (as *aletheia*) in the artwork.[46] The essence of Habermas's disquietude with the post-structural appropriation of the Heideggerian conception of world disclosure is, as suggested above, that it is erected upon the ontological difference: the happening of truth that discloses the world is a mysterious, supra-mundane dispensation of Being, rather than a result of intra-mundane action and learning processes. In other words, the concept of world disclosure imperils the possibility of problem-solving in the world itself. As I have already suggested, central to Marcuse's critique of technology, albeit without its fullest linguistic implications, is an understanding of technology as a mode of world disclosure. Yet it is one that, contrary to Habermas's suspicions, does not extinguish the possibility of agency, though it does, to be sure, render it more fraught. By emphasizing the world-disclosive dimension of Marcuse's critique of technology, it becomes possible to defend him from Habermas in such a way as to expose some of the central limitations of the communicative paradigm.

We might say, then, that the very strength of Habermas's critique of the normative pre-eminence of the production paradigm in Marcuse is its weakness. Habermas is right to take issue with Marcuse's attempt to ground his critique of technological reason in the paradigm of production.[47] Such a critique of the paradigm of production, however, can be undertaken without accepting the premises of the communication paradigm.[48] As I have already suggested, the production paradigm sits uncomfortably with Marcuse's appropriation of phenomenology because it rests on an understanding of the production of meaning analogous to the productivity of labor power. While I am unable to develop this point further at this time, suffice it to say that this would mean that tradition, as accumulated meaning, is as susceptible to re-appropriation as are accumulated forms of "dead labor." However, as Marx recognized, tradition cannot simply be construed in these terms. As I shall argue below, Habermas must privilege validity over meaning in order to differentiate communicative reason from the philosophy of the subject.[49] In contrast, Marcuse can be redeemed if we read his phenomenology of technology as anticipating, if not actually carrying through, the following insight: that in art, as in the other spheres, including science and technology, there exists an irreducible moment of world disclosure – what Adorno calls "constellations" or what Wittgenstein calls "aspect seeing." Moreover, far from subverting rationality ("the acquisition and use of fallible knowledge"), the moment of world disclosure in fact makes such rationality possible. Marcuse's insight is that the "yes or no" positions that speakers take up in relation to other speakers presupposes a prior understanding of the world. Any theory that fails to elucidate the manner in which the world itself is possible must reify the symbolic structures of the *Lebenswelt* and, therefore, short-circuit the possibility of their transformation. In contrast, a considerable merit of Marcuse's theory is to show how validity and meaning exist in genuine tension.

While it does indeed appear that Marcuse's critique is, as Habermas suggests, ambivalent, an attentive reading of the chapter devoted to technology in *One-Dimensional Man* shows that this critique is not quite as contradictory as it might at first appear. The crucial concept that Marcuse, drawing on phenomenology, explicates in this context is what he calls the "technological a priori" under which both science and technology stand in late modernity. The technological a priori appears as the culmination of the process of rationalization and disenchantment that Marcuse delineates in his critique of Weber and his appropriation of Husserl. As rationality comes to be defined in terms of objective laws of motion (for example, in Hobbes' displacement of the Aristotelian question of the "Good Life" by that of the "continuance of motion," in a political theory explicitly modeled on physics) values become subjective, that is to say, non-verifiable. The obverse side of this process lies in the fact that, with the mathematization of nature, the objective world comes to be more dependent in its objectivity on the subject. The effect of this double movement is that, theoretically, the transformation of humanity and external nature is freed from all limits, except, of course, from the "brute factuality of matter," and becomes a "(hypothetical) system of instrumentalities." The elaboration of such a system becomes more than simply the development of all forms of particular technical organization; rather, it is their precondition. Marcuse argues, "proved in its effectiveness, this conception works as an *a priori* – it predetermines experience, it *projects* the direction of the transformation of nature, it organizes the whole."[50]

To return to the example cited at the beginning of this essay, the automobile functions as a technological a priori. The very judgment that the automobile is the most effective means of traveling from point A to point B structures in advance the visible and the invisible, what can be seen and what cannot. The most effective means of achieving a desired end, in this case reaching a destination, itself is a moment of world disclosure. Albert Borgman views the modern highway system, along with symbolic logic and architecture, as exemplifying the essential features of technology. Like the other two forms of technological practice, that is to say, as an "embodied calculus," the highway system is not simply instrumental but also *paradigmatic*. Thus, "in technological practice formal features are discovered in the concrete phenomena of our world. Such discoveries lead to the construction of formal models that cover a certain domain of the concrete world. These models form a hierarchy from concrete and limited realizations at the bottom to more abstract and encompassing models in the higher reaches of the hierarchy." In the process, technological practice "delimit(s) in rigorous form the space of all the possibilities of the domain that they cover,"[51] the result of which is that the "world in its historical coherence and its actual and singular presence recedes."[52] As Marcuse puts it, "The country-side is shaped and organized by the highway."

Viewed in light of the concept of the technological a priori, the seeming contradiction between technics, as neutral, and technology, as value-laden, dissolves. The technological a priori functions at the level of what Marcuse terms "technology," while technics are the actual productive forces that are, in a strict sense, neutral. Technics, the productive forces, represent learning processes that are, indeed, legitimately viewed as irreversible. Their ethical-political meaning comes to light on the horizon of the semantic structures through which the world takes shape. By formulating the problem of technology through Husserl, Marcuse takes up the understanding of technology as a manner of "revealing beings," without, at the same time, placing world disclosure, or the ontological, beyond the pale of what Heidegger disparages as the merely ontical realm of history. The technological disclosure of the world thus is not a mysterious "sending" of Being, but rather is produced and reproduced through historically situated human decisions and practices. Therefore, the question of whether technics can serve as the basis for human freedom or the opposite can only be answered historically (rather than in terms of *historicity*). Indeed, it is precisely the very productivity of technics – the productive forces – that makes it possible to imagine the objective possibility of a radically different set of social arrangements, or what Marcuse calls the "pacification of existence."[53] This does not, of course, mean that the appearance of such an imaginary *is* its realization. What I am suggesting, then, is that Marcuse offers the possibility of understanding the relation between technology (the technological a priori) and technics as the relationship between meaning and validity, respectively. While technics can be judged in terms of the criterion of success, that is to say, as the capacity for achieving a pre-given end, the sense of "success" itself would have to be understood in terms that lay beyond the narrow provenance of technics itself. Such a criterion would have to make reference to a wider set of assumptions, orientations, and commitments that cannot, ultimately, be understood as independent of the languages in which they are expressed.

Viewed in this way, it becomes possible to defend Marcuse's conception of technology from Habermas's charges of irrationalism. In direct opposition to the critique of the type lodged by Habermas, Marcuse explicitly rejects the idea of a qualitatively different form of science, a "qualitative" physics for example, as "obscurantist." Rather, transformations in scientific methodologies and technics would hinge upon corresponding transformations of perception through re-descriptions of their object domains. The technological a priori functions in much the same way as Kuhn's conception of paradigm, although, of course, stripped of its empirical-psychologistic presuppositions. Hence, the technological a priori would run parallel to the basic background assumptions employed by scientists engaging in "normal sciences," although its logic would ultimately be grounded in the social *Lebenswelten* in which they are embedded. Indeed, far from inhibiting the problem-solving and learning processes *in-the-world* that Habermas is so anxious to protect, paradigms actually make these activities *possible*. Such assumptions provide scientists with prisms through which the world takes shape and, in the process, enables them to engage in scientific research by posing and solving problems. According to the now familiar account of "revolutionary science," set forth by Kuhn, paradigms break down by virtue of an accumulation of immanently generated anomalies. When this accumulation eventually reaches a breaking point – the point at which problem-solving becomes no longer possible, the point at which research can no longer go on – then a new optics and a new language must be found that enable their solution.[54] Here, the faculty of imagination plays an irreducible role. In the most radical instances, of course, the map of the object domain, the grandest vision of the universe or its most minute, subatomic structure, must be turned on its head, as in the Copernican revolution or in the development of quantum physics, respectively. As Kuhn has convincingly shown, scientists do not seek relentlessly to falsify their hypotheses *pace* Popper; rather, they seek to solve problems within an object domain that is pre-given, disclosed in advance. What is at stake here, then, is not the taking up of "yes or no" positions through a dialectic of what Popper called "conjecture and refutation" concerning a world that remains more or less fixed and stable, but, rather, the mode through which the world itself appears.[55] Far from simply being confined to scientific or philosophical questions, then, a conception of world disclosure is indispensable to the historical critique of social institutions.[56]

Notes

1 I wish to thank John Abromeit and Raj Gandesha for their helpful comments on previous drafts of this essay. I am especially grateful to John for his encouragement of my participation in the conference.
2 Max Horkheimer, "Traditional and Critical Theory," *Critical Theory: Selected Essays*, trans. M.J. O'Connell *et al.*, New York: Continuum, 1986, pp. 233–4.
3 "Some Social Implications of Modern Technology," in A. Arato and E. Gebhardt (eds) *Essential Frankfurt School Reader*, New York: Continuum, 1990, p. 143.
4 Barry Katz, *Herbert Marcuse and the Art of Liberation*, London: Verso, 1982, p. 64. Of course, this stems from the four years Marcuse spent working with Heidegger at the University of Freiburg between 1928 and 1932, culminating in his *Habilitationschrift* on Hegel. How far Marcuse's work was influenced by Heidegger after the fateful year of 1933 is an open question. Nonetheless, *One-Dimensional Man* exhibits the unmistakable influence of Heidegger.
5 See "Ideas and Trends: The Latest Fashion: Fear-of-Crime Design," *New York Times*, 23 July 2000.

6 One thinks here of Ford's slogan that every assembly-line worker must be a consumer. For an elaboration of the Benjaminan concept of "dream image," see Susan Buck-Morss, *Dreamworld and Catastrophe: The Passing of Mass Utopia in East and West*, Cambridge, Mass.: MIT, 2001.
7 See Samir Gandesha, "Der Letzte Mensch am Ende Geschichte [The last man at the end of history]," *Perspektiven Internationale Zeitung*, no. 36 (June 2000), pp. 11–12.
8 See David Harvey, *The Condition of Postmodernity*, Oxford: Basil Blackwell, 1990.
9 As Moishe Postone has indicated, such recent history undermines the notion of a non-contradictory form of post-liberal capitalism. See Moishe Postone, *Time, Labor, and Social Domination: A Reinterpretation of Marx's Critical Theory*, Cambridge, UK : Cambridge University Press, 1993, p. 105.
10 "An der Einheit der Produktion soll der Freizeitler sich ausreichten. Die Liestung, die der kantische Schematismus noch von den Subjekt erwartet hatte, nämlich die sinnliche Mannigfaltigkeit vorweg auf die fundamentalen Begriffe zu beziehen, wird von der Industrie abgenommen" (Max Horkheimer and Theodor Adorno, *Dialektik der Aufklärung: Philosophische Fragmente*, Frankfurt: Fischer, p. 132).
11 Ludwig Wittgenstein, *Tractatus Logico-Philosophicus*, trans. C.K. Ogden, London: RKP, 1988, p. 31.
12 Marcuse, "Industrialization and Capitalism in Max Weber," *Negations: Essays in Critical Theory*, Boston: Beacon, 1968, p. 215.
13 *Ibid.*, p. 204.
14 *Ibid.*, p. 207.
15 *Ibid.*, p. 207.
16 *Ibid.*, p. 214.
17 Marcuse, "On Science and Phenomenology," in Arato and Gebhardt (eds), *Essential Frankfurt School Reader*, New York: Continuum, 1990, p. 469.
18 *Ibid.*, p. 472.
19 *Ibid.*, p. 473.
20 *Ibid.*, p. 470.
21 Marcuse, "Industrialization and Capitalism in Max Weber," p. 215.
22 Cf. Lukács, "Preface to the New Edition [1967]," *History and Class Consciousness: Studies in Marxist Dialectics*, trans. R. Livingstone, Cambridge, MA.: MIT Press, 1971, p. xxxv.
23 Such a conception comes very close to the early Sartre's slogan, "Existence precedes essence." Cf. Sartre, *Existentialism and Humanism*, trans. P. Mairet, Brooklyn, NY: Haskell House, 1977.
24 Marcuse, "Foundations of Historical Materialism," *Studies in Critical Philosophy*, trans. J. de Bres, Boston: Beacon, 1973, p. 45.
25 The actual originality of the project is open to question, given, as David Carr notes in his introduction to the English translation of the *Crisis*, the often Hegelian idiom of this text ("Translator's Introduction," *Crisis of European Sciences and Transcendental Phenomenology*, Evanston, IL: Northwestern University Press, 1970, p.xxxiii). See also, for example, Part I of this text in which Husserl writes of "humanity struggling to understand itself" (p. 14).
26 Marcuse, "Industrialization and Capitalism in Max Weber," p. 223.
27 *Ibid.*, pp. 223–4.
28 Marcuse, "Some Social Implications of Modern Technology," p. 138.
29 See also Horkheimer, "Traditional and Critical Theory," p. 232.
30 Marcuse, "Some Social Implications of Modern Technology," pp. 160–1.
31 Habermas, *Theory of Communicative Action, Vol. 1: Reason and the Rationalization of Society*, trans. Thomas McCarthy, Boston: Beacon, p. 249.

32 *Ibid.*, p. 249.
33 Habermas, "Technology and Science as 'Ideology,'" *Towards a Rational Society: Student Protest, Science and Politics*, trans. Jeremy J. Shapiro, Boston: Beacon, 1970, p. 92.
34 *Ibid.*, p. 92.
35 *Ibid.*, p. 86.
36 *Ibid.*, p. 87.
37 Interestingly, Peter Dews argues that the reduction of communication to the status of a natural process, which he finds at work in Habermas, is as unacceptable as the construal of nature through the concepts of communication. See P. Dews, "Naturalismus und Anti-Naturalismus bei Habermas," *Deutsche Zeitschrift für Philosophie*, vol. 49, no. 6 (2001), p. 871.
38 Habermas, "Technology and Science as 'Ideology,'" p. 89.
39 Habermas, *Philosophical Discourse of Modernity*, trans. F. Lawrence, Cambridge, MA: MIT Press, 1987, p. 312.
40 *Ibid.*, p. 314.
41 *Ibid.*, p. 314.
42 *Ibid.*, p. 314.
43 Cited in J. Bohman, "Two Versions of the Linguistic Turn: Habermas and Poststructuralism," in M. Passerin d'Entrèves and S. Benhabib (eds), *Habermas and the Unfinished Project of Modernity*, Cambridge, UK: Polity, 1996, p. 200.
44 *Ibid.*, p. 200.
45 Jay Bernstein, *Recovering Ethical Life: Jürgen Habermas and the Future of Critical Theory*, London: Routledge, 1995, p. 210.
46 Cf. Heidegger, "The Origin of the Work of Art," *Basic Writings*, ed. David Farrell Krell, San Francisco: Harper & Row, 1977, pp. 143–88.
47 As Marx famously argued in the *Eighteenth Brumaire of Louis Bonaparte* in the *Marx-Engels Reader* (New York: Norton, 1978, p. 437), "The tradition of all the dead generations weighs like a nightmare of the brains of the living." Hence, the revolution would have to draw its "poetry from the future and not the past." See Walter Benjamin's "Theses on the Philosophy of History" for a concept of historical materialism shot through with theological motifs that takes as its premise the understanding of tradition as a field of ruins.
48 Cf. Theodor Adorno, *Negative Dialectics*, trans. E.B. Ashton, New York: Continuum, 1987, pp. 189–92, and also Postone, *Time, Labor, and Social Domination*, pp. 123–85. For a deeply flawed critique of modernity based on the centrality of the reduction of human beings to animal laborans, see Hannah Arendt, *The Human Condition*, Chicago: University of Chicago Press, 1958, pp. 79–135.
49 Bernstein, *Recovering Ethical Life*, Ch. 7.
50 Marcuse, *One-Dimensional Man*, p. 152.
51 Albert Borgman, "Heidegger and Symbolic Logic," in Michael Murray (ed.), *Heidegger and Modern Philosophy*, New Haven, CT: Yale University Press, 1978, p. 20.
52 *Ibid.*, p. 21.
53 One could say that Adorno does something similar in his understanding of the rationalization of the aesthetic forces of production and the role such a rationalization plays in modern, that is to say, innovative forms of expression. For example, he argues that "Art is modern when, by its mode of experience and as the expression of the crisis of experience, it absorbs what industrialization has developed under the given relations of production" (*Aesthetic Theory*, trans. Robert Hullot-Kentor, Minneapolis: University of Minnesota Press, 1997, p. 34).

54 Cf. Thomas Kuhn, *The Structure of Scientific Revolutions*, Chicago: University of Chicago Press, 1970, pp. 66–77. Interestingly, Kuhn draws attention to the world-disclosive dimensions of paradigms by emphasizing their visual aspects. He says, for example: "paradigm changes do cause scientists to see the world of their research-engagement differently. In so far as their only recourse to that world is through what they see and do, we may want to say that after a revolution scientists are responding to a different world" (*ibid.*, p. 111).
55 Kuhn largely agrees with Popper's account of scientific activity, viewing it, however, as applicable only to revolutionary science. See *Criticism and the Growth of Knowledge*, ed. A. Musgrave and I. Lakatos, Cambridge, UK: Cambridge University Press, 1970, pp. 1–24.
56 Bohman, for instance, gives the example of the Civil Rights Movement's re-description of the Declaration of Independence. This, interestingly, raises the question of whether the relationship between world disclosure and immanent critique as the normative standards against which practices are immanently evaluated is also subject to interpretation and therefore transformation. See Bohman, "Two Versions of the Linguistic Turn: Habermas and Poststructuralism," p. 209.

11

THE FATE OF EMANCIPATED SUBJECTIVITY

Michael Werz

Critical theory was shaped by its experiences in America in a more thorough sense than is commonly assumed or is apparent at first sight. This is not only true with respect to the banal insight that the relation between the familiar and the strange is a constitutive factor of subjectivity. The transatlantic broadening of horizons during Horkheimer's, Adorno's, and Marcuse's first years in exile intensified their interest in the heteronomy of life. This concern was integral to their experience in the United States, where the multiple forms of alienation they experienced – alienation of being exiled, of being German Jews, of being "Marxists without a party" – were theoretically transformed. This process of intellectually transforming alienation into thought – a process one might call "emancipated homelessness" – meant lifting the awareness of being non-identical to one's environment up to the level of critical insight. At the first instance, it developed as the opposite of emancipation – simply out of the need to survive and adapt to new surroundings. Perceiving and processing new experiences in a foreign cultural climate demands continuous and intense revision of what one had assumed as binding and authoritative. It makes sense in this context to speak of a cognitive displacement that any émigré must undergo if he wishes neither to imprison himself in prejudice nor to deify his lost homeland. Adorno's aphorism, in which he ironically notes that in exile every German roast venison tastes as if the *Freischütz* had hunted it personally, thematizes the simultaneity of nearness and remoteness, of the intimate and the strange.[1] If one imagines the obvious necessity for the émigrés to write and communicate in English, the argument can be extended. The prospect of formulating one's own thoughts in a foreign idiom – especially for philosophers and sociologists who were not only deeply rooted in the traditions of European Enlightenment philosophy, but who also, as dialectical thinkers, depended upon the structure of the German language to express their antagonistic method of thinking – was fraught with ambivalence. If, in order to put one's thoughts to paper, one must reify them, the émigré experiences this reification doubly, as each translation is one of mind and self.

These problems already give a sense of the powerful moment of the non-identical that governs the experience of emigration. One can with justice speak of Marcuse's relation to America in terms of the experience of a doubled alienation – linguistic and social – which opened up possibilities for reflection upon the more general meaning of alienation. It is simply not possible to think adequately about Marcuse's experience – or that of the entire Frankfurt School – without reference to experiences of flight and migration, to the winding and tortuous ways they each followed from the German *Reich* to the United States. These experiences mediated the forms of reflection that became characteristic for the critical theorists, and, at the same time, they influenced the methodological alignment of the research projects they were to take up. Central to this was an intense concern with the problem of authoritarian structures of consciousness, which the Institute for Social Research discussed in the context of historical and economic developments. In a proposal for a systematic investigation of modern anti-Semitism, Theodor W. Adorno wrote that the central concern and promise of the investigation was that of understanding "the growth of National Socialism not only in terms of the social-economic forces that led to it, but also in human terms – in the terms of the human being, or rather, of the inhuman climate that had made it all possible."[2]

From the very beginning, the question of how the dimensions of humanity – its needs and forms of psychological reaction – could undergo the profound transformation that fascism seemed to represent was particularly important to critical theory. In the very first edition of the Institute's journal, Erich Fromm had already argued that "social-psychological phenomena" were interpretable as processes "of active and passive adaptation of the drive-apparatus to the socio-economic situation."[3] In light of the current crisis in the social sciences and humanities, these formulations prove fruitful once again – and can be potentially as productive as they were sixty-six years ago. Max Horkheimer articulated the difference between "traditional" and "critical" theory in his path-breaking essay of that name. By arguing that theory was never to be equated directly with practice, Horkheimer sought not only to protect the critical theory of society from the demands of immediate applicability that might be made upon it – whether those demands be placed by Social Democrats or by party Communists – but also to preserve the essential content of Marx's critique of society, focusing on the dialectic that ensues between alienation and the universality of the individual. Central to this issue was the specific way in which individuality is constituted within the division of labor of a competitive and internally antagonistic society. Marx understood the history of civilization as a process of radical alienation, of the splitting up of traditional needs, and of the permanent upheaval and transformation of social forms. The dialectic of progress and regression, of emancipation and subordination, determines the life process of individuals. As Marx points out in the *Grundrisse*, this process must be viewed with great ambivalence, for it encompasses and makes possible both "the basis as the possibility of the universal development of the individual, and the real development of the individuals from this basis as a constant suspension of its *barrier*, which is recognized as a barrier, not taken for a *sacred limit*."[4] It does not lie within the individual's power to decide whether they wish to exist within the universality and generality of social relationships; these are the necessary and, in every case, historically particular conditions of everyday life, of consciousness, and of reflection. The universality of the individual is "not an ideal or imagined" one, Marx wrote, "but the universality of his real and ideal relations."[5]

Though these relations of course changed considerably beyond the form they took as part of their initial articulation in the *Grundrisse* – the notebook draft of *Capital* – one can plausibly argue that these same notions of alienation and reification proved to be even more productive for the twentieth-century analysis of modern ideology than they had for the analysis of nineteenth-century social forms. It is worth asking whether many of Marx's concepts have actually acquired substantiality with the decay of bourgeois society – and whether such a belated substantiality might not also be at work in the categories introduced by critical theory. Formulated just as radio was becoming a medium of mass communication (or, rather, was, in Germany, being actively shaped into this role in the form of the "people's receiver"), and well before the television became common, the prescient culture- and ideology-critique in the celebrated culture industry chapter of Adorno and Horkheimer's *Dialectic of Enlightenment* is as substantial as ever. The prognostic power of critical theory has, in the meantime, survived for more than fifty years, and has thus outlived the particular historical context in which it originated.

For this reason, it is no wonder that it was to the reading of the Marxian categories of reification that Marcuse returned in the early 1970s in order to interpret the social changes underway in the United States. One can reconstruct and understand these considerations by examining two unpublished typescripts, in which he took issue with contemporary political and social conflicts in the US. It was after Nixon's re-election in 1972, in the period before the end of the Vietnam War and during the conflicts in the Philippines and in Puerto Rico, that the text "The Historical Fate of Bourgeois Society" was written. Marcuse struck a highly critical note in this essay, accusing the US of having moved from being a "liberal-progressive into a reactionary-conservative society."[6] Although in retrospect his interpretations can certainly appear overstated – as, for example, when he warned against the danger of neo-fascism in the US – these analyses were not without a strong kernel of truth, noting as they did that, despite all the changes in Western societies, some of the basic social structures that had made authoritarian regimes possible remained in place: this is the basic theme of the limits of Enlightenment. The tenor of this critique of the US is surpassed in vehemence perhaps only by Sartre's wide-ranging foreword to Frantz Fanon's *The Wretched of the Earth*, written ten years earlier. Marcuse interprets the monopolistic economy as a return to the originary, primarily political nature of political economy in which "the spectre that haunts the capitalist metropole" is nothing other than the "world-historical prospect." In this context, "the insanity of the established system begins to affect the 'normal' behavior required for the continued, enlarged functioning of capitalism – the behavior at work as well as at leisure."[7]

Marcuse brought the Marxian critique up to date and, with the help of the concepts of alienation and reification, analyzed the decline of a liberal era; the end of the "Golden Age"[8] was already becoming apparent. No longer did domination rest upon direct violence; rather, it depended on the individual's ability to identify with and internalize external reality and pressures. The power of the government is based on "a large scale *identification* of the people with their rulers." He continues: "Rousseau is stood on his head; the general will is incorporated in the government, rather the executive branch of government. Dissent and opposition are free to the degree to which they are manageable."[9] The indifference of the individual, the coldness of the bourgeois subject, increasingly becomes the distinguishing feature of a middle-class society unconscious of itself: "bourgeois democracy has found a kindred instinctual foundation for its regressive and destructive development;" what began as the "constant pursuit of true and solid happiness" realized itself as unfreedom and repressive tolerance.[10]

Marcuse described the US as "Bonapartism without Bonaparte"[11] – and he had already used the aforementioned categories in 1965 for the title of an essay criticizing repressive and destructive tolerance. But in their second usage, they were much more directly applied to economic categories than in their previous usage. Marcuse perhaps needed this moment of heteronomy at that moment, because Marx's categories had for him always contained the imperative toward liberation and therefore could serve as a self-reflexive and constitutive component of critical analysis. In Marcuse's attempt to describe a form of everyday life in which ideology assumed real forms, but in which possibilities for overcoming these relations nonetheless remained in view, he once again reclaimed and recrafted the Marxian concepts. Even while rejecting, in the face of so-called "really-existing socialism," any notion that there were immediate alternatives to capitalism, Marcuse insisted that it was humanity itself that must bring reification to an end – that "the people *can* do something!"[12] – which is to say, that the possibility of emancipated subjectivity had not yet been entirely lost. This potential has remained, by and large, an immanent one.

Perhaps because Horkheimer's hope for the entirely Other was forced to seek shelter in negative anthropology and in a theory of history's negativity, readers of critical theory often overlook the fact that Marcuse never considered the people's identification with the dominant forces — their Bonapartism without Bonaparte — to be irreversible. To interpret the history of critical theory based on this first transition to negativity is to overemphasize the aporetic moment, and to fail to recognize Marcuse's rehabilitation of Marx's core concepts. This attempt cannot be understood without taking account of the American experience. Marcuse tried to cope with a tremendously dynamic society in which the prosperous years of the Golden Age had unleashed much potential for transformation. Precisely because Marcuse witnessed this turning point of the short twentieth century, he was able to develop materialist categories capable of grasping the ambivalence of what is occurring today. The social dialectic Marcuse recognized is, today as in the 1960s, a valid framework in which to sketch out historical developments. Given the unforeseeable changes since 1989, critical theory's concepts may prove their capacity to show how the new reappears in anachronistic forms: nation, religion, ethnicity.

A transformation of religion into ethnic nationalism is currently shaping much of the European continent and has already claimed many victims. This social dialectic propagates itself through the individual — the individual who experiences himself as a victim — and leads to a systematically distorted perception of social reality. The ambiguities of the English word "victimization" expresses this process precisely, because the concept can be read from both sides — from the perspective of the victimizer as well as the victim. The bi-directional dynamism of the concept of victimization expresses the truth of its increasing usage as a method of searching for identity in a world emptied of tradition. The German language has no equivalent means of expressing this process whereby both parties of exploitation become damaged, because both belong to one and the same ambivalent reality.

Unfortunately, the present has largely forgotten how to read concepts for their social content and, reciprocally, to understand society through the power of concepts. As early as 1930, Max Horkheimer criticized the shift in meaning that the Marxian concept of ideology had undergone after being translated into the language of the social, and he noted the tendency for society and social meaning to disappear in the concepts of contemporary sociology. With the final collapse of what had still, at the turn of the last century, called itself "bourgeois society," "the traditional concept of ideology had itself" lost its "object" — so Adorno and Horkheimer affirmed once again in a discussion held during the mid-1950s.[13] In the place of an ideology corresponding to social totality, there emerges, on the part of the individual, a kind of "faithless faith" in pure existence — a self-enclosed second nature, which never really enters into traditional concepts, and which evades being captured by these terms.

Marcuse reflected upon these new relations in his reinterpretation of Marx. Society, Marcuse argued, had constituted itself in new ways, due to the fact that the interplay between production and destruction, liberty and repression, power and submission (i.e. the unity of opposites which permeates the entire capitalist society today) has, with the help of technological means not previously available, created, among the underlying populations, a mental structure which responds to, and reflects the requirements of the system. In this mental structure are deep individual, instinctual roots of the identification of the conformist majority with the institutionalized brutality and aggression. An instinctual, nay, libidinal affinity binds, beneath all rational justification, the subjects to their rulers"[14]

and this affinity gives way to a new form of mediation between base and superstructure which cannot be wholly grasped by the traditional concept of ideology. For Marcuse, the danger of this tendency toward social adjustment lies in the "abandonment of the civilized restraints on destructive power."[15] Experiences of violence, repressive institutions, and the culture industry's production of everyday compromise – sports and music – constitute, according to Marcuse, a new normality whose inner principle is that of a collective escape from freedom. This "normality" constitutes a "sadomasochistic" syndrome, which, while rooted in identity-thinking, also draws strength from the desires of subjects living in a world where domination is taken for granted – and thus from the subject's own desire to assimilate a portion of the psychological appeal that domination exerts upon him.

This constellation transforms the psychological category into a political one. Although taking place at a higher level of abstraction in the process of social development, the process of the reification of human needs is perpetually reproduced – (as Marx described it) a dialectic of self-realization and self-denial, of the appropriation of subjectivity and the decline into bondage. Marcuse was capable of returning to Marx at this juncture and, in the spirit of social transformation, of envisioning a form of production that led beyond manipulation. As Marx argued in the *Grundrisse*:

> If individual A had the same need as individual B, and if both had realized their labor in the same object, then no relation whatever would be present between them; considering only their production, they would not be different individuals at all....Only the differences between their needs and between their production give rise to exchange and to their social equation in exchange; these natural differences are therefore the precondition of their social equality in the act of exchange, and of this relation in general, in which they relate to one another as productive.[16]

Marcuse holds fast to the Marxian point that the manipulation of needs is not really final and definitive – that needs are not eternally or absolutely instrumentalizable, for the act of reification is also tied to a specific social-historical context. Here, too, the critical theorist's point is not only one of aporia, but also of a social-historical dialectic. It is the totality of production that enforces what Georg Lukács referred to, in *History and Class Consciousness*,[17] as the contemplative attitude of individuals vis-à-vis the products of labor. Lukács' concept was consciously chosen and contains an association, through its affinities to the concept of contemplation in the Aristotelian sense, with the *intellectus speculativus*, which first established experience as a category of consciousness. Marcuse preserves this possibility of exploding reification from within, arguing that it remains possible precisely because it is in economic exchange that human consciousness first constitutes itself in its species being — because of the fact that, in economic exchange, each participant "reaches beyond his own particular need."[18] Nevertheless, this specific form of society constitutes itself in an unconscious way, for it "proceeds, as it were, behind the back of these self-reflected particular interests, behind the back of one individual's interest in opposition to that of the other."[19] Critical theory has interpreted this shift from objective to subjective reason as a form of the instinctualization of reason, the fusion of rationality with the unconscious. Marcuse explicitly posits himself as a member of this interpretive tradition when he writes that "the instinctual need, the desire for freedom, becomes concrete as a *negative*: a desire for liberation *from*..."[20]

This new, theoretical constellation that draws upon psychological and social analysis has a direct impact upon the possibilities for political change. If Adorno and Horkheimer articulated the need for a new concept of ideology, it was in the sense of a society formed and characterized by fear, of a society which longs for totality but lacks the sense of where to direct its rebellious impulses: a society in which — as Marcuse puts it — "the remoteness of conditions is being permanently reproduced, under which opposition had to be organized and thought."[21] Marcuse described the ambivalence of the New Left, which is "faced with the task of defending this democracy while attacking its capitalist foundations, that is so to say, to separate the political forms of capitalism from its economic structure," exactly because the "bourgeois democratic form lags behind the monopoly...structure."[22]

This differentiation between the political sphere and political economy — the fact that the political and economic spheres seemed no longer to be in phase with one another — allowed critical theory the possibility of bringing the analysis of fundamental social and social-psychological changes to the fore of theoretical work: it was in this differentiation that "the translation of the objective conditions into political consciousness" became possible.[23] In the draft proposal for the anti-Semitism project some years earlier, Adorno had explicitly discussed this shift as indicative of a transformation in the substance of individual character, and one can see how this single observation led to the type of rich and sophisticated investigation that one finds in

The Authoritarian Personality. What in modern mass societies is understood as an "identity problem," Adorno analyzed in terms of a Marxian negative anthropology: "It appears that in our epoch humans are undergoing transformations much more profound than can be explained by psychology." He continued: "It is as if the very substance of humanity had been transformed along with the foundations of society...Today, religious emancipation of the middle classes, with all of its manifestations of 'progressiveness,' has itself been revealed as a dehumanizing force."[24] The notion of incomplete secularization, of a failed emancipation from religion, is of central importance to the relation between social and psychological categories.

At the end of the short century, the unsuitability of traditional forms of ideology critique has become quite obvious, and several widely discussed debates and concepts testify to the need for a better method of grasping the problem of Enlightenment. At the moment, there is much talk of globalization, and while various "imagined communities" pop up here and there, there has been an ongoing rediscovery of "national spaces" – all leading to a number of divergent conceptual innovations. Space and its individual-psychological counterparts come to be viewed in terms of "collective memories," which are thought to bind together transnational spaces like so many nodes on a fiber optic network. The incessant culturalization of social conflicts, which are often simplified into "culture clashes," shows the degree to which much social reflection within the academy has been eroded.

The de-differentiation of complex questions – even within the branches of science that are supposed to study them in their complexity – and the increasing loss of social categories to deal with such complexity, must, partly at least, be interpreted in terms of the devastation of critical faculties and social categories so precisely described by Marcuse. This devastation, which has become increasingly evident since the end of the short century, has bequeathed to individual consciousness a legacy of alienation. The search for meaning and historical relevance has, in the last ten years, become considerably more intense – undoubtedly because of the genuine losses of tradition, long underway but concealed by the ideological polarization of the Cold War era. Today, one can observe an aggressive attempt to rehabilitate traditions that history itself has long abandoned – for example, the religious-cultural finger-pointing that constitutes *The Clash of Civilizations*.[25] With the visible differences between community and society eroding ever further, this phenomenon can hardly be ignored any longer. Yet because contemporary mass societies demand too great an adaptation of individuals; and because, at the same time, they offer individuals no spiritual or material points of connection that allow for reliable orientation in questions of everyday practice, the search for and ascription of "identity" (and identity conflict) becomes self-justifying.

Marcuse had already criticized this reduction of the category of the social to cultural and identity issues as a distorted reflection of the real social changes, and had attacked the New Left for their usage of the word community: "the concept of 'community' is ideological: it suggests a basic identity of interests cutting across class divisions."[26] The categorical shift of the opposition from class to "the people" was equally one-dimensional. "Power to the people," Marcuse writes – only to ask, "But who *are* the people?"[27] He interpreted these conceptual shifts primarily as a crisis of consciousness of social totality, as a parceling-out of thought that only redoubled the short century's own tendencies toward reification, and transformed society into an amorphous mass in search of identity and difference.

At the same time, Marcuse's specific critique of intellectual life is also closely bound up with the particular experience of migration. These two moments within Marcuse's intellectual life intersect, diverge, and combine – by means of the criss-crossing of emigration and alienation experience – to form a general critique of the various forms of social relations. Because secular society, in translating traditional religion into morality, has only partly overcome religion, unfulfilled needs persist, evidenced by a longing for meaning and for the completion of experience. Because of the anachronistic nature of this endeavor, however, all attempts to return to the past are artificial, merely reviving old falsehoods as contemporary truth. The true danger really comes, though, when these archaic models are called upon to serve as explanations for social realities – since, of course, social realities have long outgrown these models. The violence of repression translates into a tendency to see everything in terms of culture, and therefore becomes personalizable. The aggressions it produces are most easily projected onto those who can be recognized as strangers. Critical theory develops this category as a materialist one against the background of a critique of alienation and reification.

Georg Simmel described earlier the social-historical descent of the concept of the stranger quite powerfully. He noted:

> In the whole history of economy, the stranger always appears as a merchant, or the merchant appears as a stranger...insofar, that is, as people do not themselves go to foreign places in order to take care of necessary purchases...the merchant *must* be a stranger – there is no possibility for him to be anything else.[28]

As the representative of the developing system of circulation, the image of the merchant stands over and against that of the landowner; the former is the mediator and bearer of past and future changes, and is, for this reason, an unsettling figure. The stranger is, "according to his own nature, not an owner of land, by which land is understood not only in the physical sense, but also in the metaphorical sense of a substance of life, which, if not physically and spatially fixed, in any case occupies a definite place within a social environment." Because of his mobility, the merchant is a synthesis of near and far: "he who is absolutely mobile meets up at some point with every individual element, but he is organically bound up – whether it be through familial, local, or professional fixities – with no one."[29] His person embodies the experience of strangeness within commodity-producing societies, and, with this strangeness, the new structuring of space and time, belonging and difference.

Herbert Marcuse's theoretical work reflects upon this social-historical process. What is important, in his theory, is the conscious recollection of the loss of tradition in the light of tradition's irretrievability – the experiences of emigration thus reflect, in an individual way, the larger process of social alienation. It is a form of anticipatory recollection that Marcuse has in mind.[30] His arguments in the 1970s were conceptually well ahead of the contemporary theoretical mainstream.

The constitution of prejudice against strangers which Simmel described – the constitution of the projection of one's own experiences of alienation upon another person or group – goes along with the suppression of traditional religion. Yet traditional religion has not really been overcome; metaphysical scraps of it remain, scraps which can mutate into political dynamite under the conditions of a secular society. Ethnic-religious constructions of identity, no longer kept in check by medieval orders, religious ethics, or individual piety, give testament to the failure of emancipation. This displacement was a central theme of critical theory's critique of anti-Semitism; the concepts developed by Marcuse, Horkheimer, Adorno, and Löwenthal are as fruitful to analyses of global realities now as they were then.

Perhaps the emigrants' gaze was made more keen by their own, subjective experience – as, for example, when Herbert Marcuse came to see the category of individual concreteness as a dialectical counterpart to the abstract generality of the social. The break with European traditions they had experienced in the act of emigration did not just make them sensitive to the invasion of spirit and thought by the American culture industry; as late as the 1970s, Marcuse's work still drew on these experiences when he considered the degree to which the emancipatory movements of the time were formed by the objective conditions of capitalism in the twentieth century. In place of the *contrat social* or of public consent, which had been the principles of republican democracy and enlightenment, there now appeared processes of forced sublimation and internalization. Public and private were no longer differentiated as they had once been in bourgeois society – and this change, which transforms the self into the stranger, makes itself evident even in the rebellious slogan "personal is political."

In a further unpublished typescript, from the late 1970s, Marcuse took up this critique of reification yet one more time in order to analyze the advanced states of internalization which he observed in the US. The question was not easy to answer: anarchistic and communistic traditions had long suffered their downfall, while the only form of production that really remained intact in Eastern Europe was that of socialist ideology. At least since the time of his penetrating critique of the social system of the Soviet Union, it had of course ceased to appear to Marcuse as an emancipatory alternative.

Once again, the insight into the reciprocal relations between the individual and the objective universal helped Marcuse make a critical intervention against an economic regime that was alienated from human interests and needs, but which was "to originate in the individuals themselves."[31] Because the experience of the strange – that is to say, of estrangement and alienation – has become part of subjectivity, because it forms and accompanies the process of its constitution, existing society cannot simply be negated. Marcuse criticized the abstract negation of the existing as a historical construct, since the only possibility for liberation lay in viewing the stupidity and falsehood of contemporary society as the grounds for one's own actions and for the actions of others. When one reflects upon this state of affairs, possibilities open up for the realization of reason in history. The experience of migration is just such an example, and shows, moreover, that the truth of the universal social process is at the same time inscribed in the alienated particular. Marcuse's critique of the status quo that emerges from this line of thought was particularly attractive for the student protesters in the US and in Germany.

This connection makes evident the way in which the dialectic of enlightenment has played itself out in the most advanced Western societies, for Marcuse developed his critique of the status quo in the moment in which, on account of the student movement, the tension between democratic tradition and lack of alternative seemed to stand at the breaking point: the production of the conditions of social change affects the process of transformation itself. This occurs in connection with that contemporary social dynamic which Marx described as the self-negation and sublation – "*Selbstaufhebung*" – of the capitalist in the more advanced conditions of capitalist production. With the negation and sublation of the social bases of industrialized production, however, the antecedents of its change or "overcoming" are themselves transformed.

Such complicated reflections were, of course, only to be translated into political forms of practice in a very limited way, particularly since the new relations produced by advanced media societies considerably limit and qualify the critical power of a traditional concept of ideology. Against this background, and against the withering-away of the international student rebellions, Marcuse turned with renewed interest to Marx's *Economic and Philosophical Manuscripts of 1844* and to the *Grundrisse*. He set out on a search for the (human) basis of a complete reshaping of social relations, which are destined "to continue the inherited unfreedom *unless* the process of change finds, in the substratum itself, a basis for the total transformation."[32] It had long been the case that socialism could not be realized by the proletariat and thereby be brought into practice. The important thing, for Marcuse, was to rehabilitate subjectivity vis-à-vis the objective and general. Following the *Grundrisse*, he understood "the individual as the particular human being who, while a member of a class, still remains the 'natural', elementary agent of change, who, no matter how much he may be 'socialized', can never be 'dissolved' into [an] aliquot part of a class." Following this remark, then, comes the decisive sentence, in which Marcuse reaches back through Marx to Feuerbach's categories of the sensuous and meaningful content of experience. Marcuse writes: "His [the human's] concreteness resists abstract generalization."[33] One can speak of a utopian moment, which saves critical theory from an aporetic ending. Adorno had already formulated a similar argument in the mid-1940s in the second, unprinted part of the culture industry chapter of the *Dialectic of Enlightenment*: "The rationality of adjustment has already progressed to such a point that the slightest jolt would be sufficient to lift its irrationality to the level consciousness." And further:

> Through regression, the renunciation of resistance is ratified…But since it is the case that, as subjects, human beings remain the limit and the cutting edge of reification, so it is that mass culture must continuously re-ensnare them within its bad infinity: the unending and thankless effort required for this repetition provides the only glimmer of hope that this repetition might be in vain, and that human beings are not, after all, to be ensnared within it.[34]

Marcuse saw potential in this ambivalence – potential for a new anthropological concept of the basis of revolution, and thus for the transformation both of consciousness and of sensibility. His negative-anthropological readings of the *Grundrisse* touch upon this point: in order to make *Capital's* critique of political economy once again fruitful for modern mass societies, wrote Marcuse – in order, that is, truly to understand the categories of alienation and reification – the reading of the *Grundrisse* must precede a reading of *Capital*. Marcuse understands the roots of the concrete universal in the emancipation of sensuous experience (*Sinnlichkeit*), and, following Marx, he sees the realization of man *as* man as immanent within his existence as a species being. Yet the dialectic of enlightenment encodes human needs in a repressive everyday practice; and that which passes itself off as a kind of modern *ideae innatae*, as inborn ideas, are in reality the "repressed claims of the human senses, and their universality,"[35] which, "far from being a vague, rather abstract idea of humanity and humanism, would turn out to be a rather material, psychological condition."[36]

It is precisely at this point that Marcuse's insistence upon the social content of the Marxian critique of economy can be a guide for current confrontations. When it is understood how second nature presents itself as first nature, and how the repressed claims of the human senses leave behind the need for meaning and orientation which cannot be filled, then it becomes clear why any number of modern doctrines of predestination and transcendent identity, including nationalist exclusion, ethnic particularism, and the authoritarian character, are pushed toward this fault-line within subjective reason. Critical theorist Zarko Puhovski once described the essence of victimization, itself a form of modern ideology, as social amnesia – an amnesia that constitutes the kernel of nationalist "epistemology." This new ideology is no longer that of a bourgeois society, which always attempted to create an image of itself (albeit an ideological one) in history; rather, this version of identity formation is based upon forgetting. Nationalist particularism and ethnic or religious fundamentalism are always bound up with the experiences of historic defeats. In order to make the dialectic of failed secularization and reification more accessible, Detlev Claussen, continuing in the tradition of critical theory, has categorized these modern ideologies in terms of "the religion of everyday life."[37] The experience of social disintegration brings the "basic questions of social meaning back into everyday consciousness in a much more radical fashion" than ever before. The notion of the "religion of everyday life" is helpful for making opaque relations explainable in terms of polarities. For the believer, the religion of everyday life introduces and justifies – by means of a stylization of one's own *victimization* – the clear separation of friend from foe, and, as Claussen notes, supplies one with answers to all the central questions of social meaning that a society hungry for identity demands: "Who are we? Where are we coming from? Who is guilty?"[38] These are important points for building on Marcuse's writings and the writings of his fellow critical theorists in general. Their experiences of emigration led to the rehabilitation of the negative power of social theory. For, even into the 1970s, Marcuse continued to insist upon the centrality of determinate negation as a method of defining unrealized forms and of setting free emancipatory potential. In this sense, Marcuse remains a point of reference to contemporary social scientists. Adorno's endorsement of an idea of negative anthropology stands alongside Marcuse's reinvigoration of contemporary critical theory:

> In the phenomenon of radio, the authority of society consummately manifests itself, immediately and unopposed, behind every speaker, as it turns against those being addressed. If in fact the advance of technology largely determines the economic fate of society, then the technologized forms of consciousness carry premonitions of society's fate. They transform culture into a total lie, but this untruth divulges the truth about the [economic] substructure it approximates. The magical banners stretched up across the cities, superimposing their light over the natural light of the night, announce like comets the chilling natural disaster facing a society threatened with freezing death. Yet these projections do not come

from heaven. They are directed from earth. It all depends upon whether humanity wishes to extinguish them and to wake from the fearful dream – a dream that threatens to become real so long as human beings believe in it.[39]

Notes

This chapter has been translated from German by Eric Oberle.

1 Theodor W. Adorno, *Minima Moralia*, trans. E.F.N. Jephcott, London: Verso, 1978, p. 49.
2 Theodor W. Adorno, "Begründungsentwurf", Max Horkheimer Archive, Frankfurt am Main, VI.1D.94, p. 94.
3 Erich Fromm, "Über Methode und Aufgabe einer analytischen Sozialpsychologie," *Zeitschrift für Sozialforschung*, vol. 1, Leipzig: C.L. Hirschfeld, 1932, pp. 39–40.
4 Karl Marx, *Grundrisse*, trans. Martin Nicolaus, London and New York: Penguin, 1993, p. 542.
5 *Ibid.*
6 "The Historical Fate of Bourgeois Society," *Towards a Critical Theory of Society: Collected Papers of Herbert Marcuse*, vol. 2, ed. Douglas Kellner, London and New York: Routledge, 2001, p. 165.
7 *Ibid.*, p. 166.
8 See, for example, Eric Hobsbawm, *Age of Extremes: The Short Twentieth Century 1914–1991*, London: Michael Joseph, 1994, Ch. 9.
9 Marcuse, "The Historical Fate of Bourgeois Society", p. 167.
10 *Ibid.*, p. 167.
11 *Ibid.*, p. 8.
12 *Ibid.*, p. 13.
13 Theodor W. Adorno and Max Horkheimer, "Ideologie," in T.W. Adorno and Walter Dirks (eds) *Soziologische Exkurse. Nach Vorträgen und Diskussionen*, Frankfurt: Europäische Verlagsanstalt, 1956, p. 176.
14 Marcuse, "The Historical Fate of Bourgeois Society," p. 17.
15 *Ibid.*, p. 20.
16 Karl Marx, *Grundrisse*, p. 242 (translation amended).
17 Georg Lukács, *History and Class Consciousness: Studies in Marxist Dialectics*, trans. Rodney Livingstone, Cambridge, MA: MIT Press, 1971.
18 *Ibid.*, p. 243.
19 *Ibid.*, p. 244.
20 Marcuse, "The Historical Fate of Bourgeois Society", p. 27.
21 *Ibid.*, p. 34. The off-putting quality of Marcuse's English here can be overcome if one takes into account that Marcuse was struggling, as the author has argued above, to translate the idioms of critical theory into English. A paraphrase of the sentence that takes these translation issues into account might read: "As the process of production increasing incorporates a distancing process into labor, whereby the conditions of labor seem more remote to the workers, so the idea of opposition to these conditions must be rethought, politically and theoretically" (translator).
22 *Ibid.*, p. 43.
23 *Ibid.*, p. 46.
24 Adorno, "Begründungsentwurf", p. 94.

25 Samuel Huntington, *The Clash of Civilzations and the Remaking of the World Order*, New York: Simon & Schuster, 1996.
26 Marcuse, "The Historical Fate of Bourgeois Society", p. 53.
27 *Ibid.*, p. 9.
28 Georg Simmel, "Der Fremde," *Das individuelle Gesetz. Philosophische Exkurse*, Frankfurt: Suhrkamp, 1968, pp. 64ff.
29 *Ibid.*, pp. 64ff.
30 See "Anamnestic Totalization: Memory in the Thought of Herbert Marcuse," in Martin Jay's still thought-provoking work, *Marxism and Totality: The Adventures of a Concept from Lukács to Habermas* (Berkeley and Los Angeles: University of California Press, 1984, pp. 234ff.).
31 Herbert Marcuse, "Cultural Revolution," *Towards a Critical Theory of Society*, p. 124.
32 *Ibid.*, p. 125.
33 *Ibid.*, p. 127.
34 Max Horkheimer and Theodor Adorno, "Das Schema der Massenkultur," in Theodor W. Adorno, *Gesammlte Schriften*, ed. Rolf Tiedemann, vol. 3, Frankfurt: Suhrkamp, 1969, p. 331.
35 Max Horkheimer and Theodor Adorno, *Dialectic of Enlightenment*, trans. John Cummings, New York: Continuum, 1991, p. 80.
36 Marcuse, "Cultural Revolution," p 129.
37 See, for example, Detlev Claussen, "Über Psychoanalyse und Antisemitismus," *Psyche. Zeitschrift für Psychoanalyse und ihre Anwendungen*, vol. 41, pp. 1–21, or "Die Banalisierung des Bösen. Über Auschwitz, Alltagsreligion und Gesellschaftstheorie," in Michael Werz (ed.) *Antisemitismus und Gesellschaft: Zur Diskussion um Auschwitz, Kulturindustrie und Gewalt*, Frankfurt: Neue Kritik, 1995, pp. 13–28.
38 Detlev Claussen, "Mißglückte Befreiung. Zur Ethnisierenden Auflösung des Realsozialismus," in Nenad Stefanov and Michael Werz (eds) *Bosnien und Europa: Die Ethnisierung der Gesellschaft*, Frankfurt: Fischer, 1994, p. 62.
39 Horkheimer and Adorno, "Das Schema der Massenkultur," p. 335 (translation altered).

Part III

MARCUSE AND CONTEMPORARY ECOLOGICAL THEORY

12

MARCUSE'S DEEP-SOCIAL ECOLOGY AND THE FUTURE OF UTOPIAN ENVIRONMENTALISM

Andrew Light

This essay will briefly address the relationship between Marcuse's work and contemporary environmental political theory (which is often called "political ecology"), both as a body of theory but also as a set of practices by environmental activists. In particular I focus on the possible contribution that Marcuse's scant work on environmental issues can make to the dominant conflict in political ecology of the 1980s and early 1990s, the deep ecology–social ecology debate. I will first describe this debate, and then follow with a summary of my previous attempts to use Marcuse's work as a possible bridge between these two theoretical positions. I conclude with some brief remarks on the utility of utopian theory for political ecology today.

In the mid-1980s, the more radical end of the American environmental community was being wooed by two competing sets of theorists – deep ecologists and social ecologists. A watershed event in this dispute was the 1987 first National Greens Gathering in Amherst, Massachusetts. At that meeting, social ecology and deep ecology publicly clashed, and various figures in both camps made appeals to the hearts and minds of the assembled green activists. Following this meeting, Murray Bookchin, the principle theoretician of social ecology, began to write in earnest against deep ecology, most notoriously claiming that members of the deep ecology movement held fascist views. The resulting debate was interesting, to say the least, and occupied the time of many theorists and activists over the following decade.

In bare-bones terms, deep ecology refers to a body of work that originated with the thought of Norwegian philosopher Arne Naess. The first paper Naess published on this topic, in 1973, was entitled "The Shallow and the Deep, Long-range Ecology Movements."[1] Fairly quickly, however, one was able to distinguish between deep ecology as a body of theory and as a political movement. What is common between the theory and the movement is that both try to articulate some sense of how the self needs to be reformed in order to make environmental sustainability possible, or in order to create a world which is more environmentally responsible. With Naess, the idea is that we should go out into the world and have special kinds of phenomenological experiences in nature. The point of going into nature is to realize that one's self is indistinguishable from nature on an ontological level. As a body of theory picked up in America and later in Australia, the thrust of the need for these phenomenological experiences became wilderness-oriented. Only in the wild would we experience our indistinguishability from nature. What we wind up getting with this view is not so much an environmental ethic or political ecology, but rather an ontology with normative implications. The rules, obligations, or duties one has toward the environment are, in a sense, obligations toward one's self – in this case, though, an extended sense of one's self as an indistinguishable part of nature. Humans come to dominate nature when they fail to recognize their ontological connection to nature. The most extreme form of deep ecology's ontological claim is expressed in the work of the Australian deep ecology activist John Seed, who puts it this way: "I try to remember that it's not me, John Seed, trying to protect the rainforest. Rather I am part of the rainforest protecting myself, I am that part of the rainforest recently emerged into human thinking."[2] Such a claim is curious, to be certain, but is actually meaningful given the presumed ontology of deep ecology.

In opposition to deep ecology, social ecology is a body of anarchist political theory that evolved almost exclusively out of the work of Murray Bookchin, although there is some work now (primarily by John Clark) which claims that social ecology has roots in the works of Peter Kropotkin and Elisee Reclus. Bookchin's work, at least, completely rejects the kind of philosophical foundations for environmental responsibility that we see in deep ecology.

The key to understanding Bookchin's views is to realize that for him, the notion of domination, as applied to nature, is incoherent; one makes a category mistake when one says that humans dominate nature. Rather, "domination" is a human–human relationship. Bookchin maps from prehistory to the present different forms of hierarchy that have evolved over time – gender, race, class, age, etc. He then claims that at some point in the history of human–human domination (to perhaps unfairly paraphrase a much more complicated argument) a "spill-over" effect ensues which creates a society incompatible with environmental sustainability. Because this view is grounded in a larger social theory about the evolution of human society, Bookchin, in contrast to the deep ecologists, winds up focusing much more on the city, instead of the wild, as an important sphere of environmental concerns.

Bookchin's views are much more concerned with the role of humans in relation to nature, not as indistinguishable from nature, but rather in a kind of a relationship with nature. Humans, like the rest of nature, are driven, shaped, and formed by evolution as "first nature," but we also have a different "second nature" – our self-conscious ability to create the world around us. Hierarchy arises as we grow more and more distant from our original altruistic first nature. Social structures gradually evolve out of the systems enabling one human to dominate another. The justification of Bookchin's anarchism becomes in part the environmental consequences of decreasing state power and in turn dismantling institutions that enable domination. Given his approach, Bookchin focuses more on the reform of material conditions of society as the path toward environmental renewal, and not the reform of the self.

The rhetoric of the deep ecology–social ecology debate escalated through the 1980s and 1990s. Early on, Bookchin described deep ecology charitably as "vague and formless." Later, responding to the sometime outrageous claims made by a few deep ecology activists – that starvation in Ethiopia was a natural and acceptable process; that "Northern European" American culture was in danger of "Latinization" from Central and South American immigrants; and that AIDS was a self-regulating process to stem world population growth – Bookchin threw down the gauntlet by labeling deep ecology "the same kind of ecobrutalism that led Hitler to fashion theories of blood and soil that led to the transport of millions of people to murder camps like Auschwitz."[3] Bookchin's main target was the deep ecology-inspired organization, Earth First!, a group that is much less influential today than it once was. In opposition to such groups, Bookchin organized social ecologists into a small, now defunct, assemblage called the Left Green Network. At the time the struggles between these two groups were both theoretically and practically important.

Many attempts have been made to describe, theorize, and cajole a rapprochement between the various positions and groups associated with the deep ecology–social ecology split. My own contribution was, in standard philosophical fashion, to try to step back from this particular debate, and the ascerbic character it had assumed, and find some middle ground. Accordingly, I tried to more broadly characterize the kinds of views into which these two theories fit. My hope was that if one could fairly describe deep ecology as part of a broader theoretical category, and then describe social ecology as part of another broader theoretical category, then there would be discernable overlaps between the broader categories where we could find some room for connection between deep and social ecologists. Such a broader terrain of analysis might also give us a place from which to theorize political ecology in a more sober atmosphere.

In service of this strategy, I came up with a distinction between two broader kinds of political ecology which might capture the sorts of general approaches advocated by deep ecologists and social ecologists. I argued that social ecology was a form of "environmental materialism" (not a materialist ontology, but, rather, simply a thin materialism which focuses on material conditions in its analysis of environmental change), and that deep ecology was a form of "environmental ontology." But what distinguishes these broader types of views?

I defined environmental materialists as those political ecologists who saw the preferred response to environmental problems as primarily involving an analysis of the organization of human society through the material conditions of capitalist or state capitalist economies, and the social and political systems that sustain those economies. Pertinent material conditions include such considerations as who owns and controls the technological processes that are used to stimulate economic growth, expand markets, and consume natural resources. The best radical political ecology will push the boundaries of these systems and champion a change in the material organization of society as a whole, as its primary path to a more sustainable society. Bookchin's social ecology fits squarely within that description, though is not exhaustive of all forms of environmental materialism. Another environmental materialist might be grounded in socialist political theory rather than Bookchin's anarchism.

In contrast, environmental ontologists see more potential in diagnosing environmental problems as primarily involving the human self in relation to nature, rather than originating in our social, political, and material systems. The primary cause of environmental problems is our psycological or spiritual disconnection from nature. For ontologists, the principal location of solutions to environmental problems is to be found in changing the "consciousness," for lack of a better term, of individual humans in relation to the non-human natural world. Theorists embracing this broadly identifiable view argue that humans should be identified with nature, not as a separable organism or set of organisms, but as an integrated part of a larger life system.

While, it may sound like I am describing these broader views as co-extensive with deep ecology and social ecology, actually this is not the case. There are many other political ecologies which fit these two broader categories. In addition to my comments above concerning other environmental materialists, one can find environmental ontologies in several forms of religious-based environmental views. Many of these views are also focused on reform of the self. My first published article was a comparison between Martin Buber and Arne Naess, arguing that Buber has something like an environmental ontology. This is found especially in the postscript to *I and Thou* concerning the possibility of an I–Thou relationship with nature. One could find a more contemporary version of an environmental ontology in David Abram's *The Spell of the Sensuous*.[4]

In trying to negotiate the deep ecology–social ecology debate, the materialist–ontologist distinction serves a useful purpose. It more generally describes the grounds upon which these two schools of thought disagree. Furthermore, if Bookchin's argument with deep ecology can be situated along the more general materialist–ontologist divide, then we may be able to get a better perspective on the territory covered by social ecology and deep ecology. If it were the case that other materialists, with whom Bookchin shares some common ground, took seriously the claims of an environmental ontology, then perhaps social ecology, as a form of environmental materialism, could be argued to be closer to deep ecology than Bookchin is willing to admit. Or, more modestly, perhaps the philosophical underpinnings of these views are not so far apart as to warrant the necessary exclusion of the concerns of deep ecology from the program of social ecology.

Marcuse, I have argued, is just such a bridge figure between environmental materialists and environmental ontologists, and hence also serves as a possible bridge between deep ecologists and social ecologists. Marcuse's environmental views belie a commitment to environmental materialism, while at the same time demonstrate a strong predisposition to the importance of an environmental ontology. The clear ontological dimension to Marcuse's work can be seen, for example, in *Counterrevolution and Revolt*.[5] There, Marcuse argues that the transformation of technology from its repressive forms in advanced industrial capitalism occurs within a framework that includes an ontological dimension – specifically, the idea of a shared revolutionary subjectivity of humans and nature. For Marcuse, a combination of views is needed to articulate a viable radical alternative to the existing technological society.

I should note, however, that this is exactly the part of Marcuse's work that many, such as Steven Vogel in this volume, have problems with: remember, for Marcuse, "nature, too, awaits the revolution!" How are we to understand the notion of nature as a subject, let alone a revolutionary subject? Whatever one thinks of this view, though, Marcuse's ontological sense of the subjectivity of nature is absolutely necessary for his vision of a better environmental future. But even with these sorts of intuitions in his work, Marcuse does have certain materialist priorities. Ultimately, in his critical theory, changes in the material conditions of society cause further changes in individual consciousness, which consequently lead to more changes in the material conditions of society. For example, Marcuse suggests in *One-Dimensional Man* that ontological change may be achieved through individual participation in a radical aesthetic, but the causes of alienation that motivate such an aesthetic are the debilitating material conditions of society.[6]

I do not have the space here to flesh out how I make the argument for Marcuse as a bridge figure between social ecology and deep ecology given his combined materialist and ontologist approach. The details are in my chapter on Marcuse and Bookchin in my edited collection, *Social Ecology after Bookchin*.[7] Oddly enough, the hardest part about prosecuting this argument was not demonstrating Marcuse's ontological commitments, but rather the claim that Marcuse and Bookchin have enough in common to both be considered environmental materialists, or, indeed, enough in common to be considered anything in the same category. This had nothing to do with the particular theoretical difficulties in reconciling their texts at some level. It was more the fact that Bookchin refuses to allow a comparison between his work and any other work. For example, in the first version of the paper just mentioned, and even more so in the updated version which appeared in the book, I spent a lot of time trying to make this comparison work. I compare the work of Marcuse and Bookchin on a variety of topics, including the self-negation of technology, aesthetics, and the thesis of false needs. The result of all of these endeavors, however, was to invite a forceful attack by Bookchin on this comparison with Marcuse. In his original reply to my piece, Bookchin went so far as to accuse me of being a deep ecologist (which, for Bookchin, is tantamount to accusing me of being an environmental fascist), apparently simply for making a comparison oriented toward reconciling deep and social ecology.[8] Interestingly enough, the reception on the other side was much more positive, perhaps because some deep ecologists, especially Naess, have been pushing other deep ecologists for some time to develop the materialist side of their theories, calling for more political economy, more political theory, and more traditional critical theory. In the end it was the deep ecologists who were much more willing to bridge the gap between the two sides of this debate.[9]

My conclusion from this endeavor is that despite the relative lack of attention given by Marcuse to environmental issues, as compared to the other political ecologists I have mentioned, when read through the materialist–ontologist distinction, Marcuse may have the richest and most pluralist voice in political ecology so far. While Marcuse did not anticipate these debates in political ecology, he completely avoids any implication in the contemporary divides because of the complexity of his views. The fundamental pluralism of Marcuse's work (seeing, as he does, the complex necessity of both broad categories of ecological theory for a robust political ecology) provides a sober view of the varieties of changes that would have to happen in order for us to move toward a truly sustainable society. One can also read *Counterrevolution and Revolt*, for example, as anticipating several important moves in contemporary political ecology and environmental ethics, especially concerning the ascription of a subjectivity to nature. Marcuse's attribution of a radical subjectivity to nature is what we would call today a "non-anthropocentric view." And if one looks at the current work that has been done in environmental ethics on non-anthropocentric theory (which, in normative terms, is essentially the argument that the proper focus of environmental ethics is one which describes the value of nature in terms outside of the human appreciation of that value), Marcuse's notion of radical subjectivity provides the strongest ground on which to claim the basis for duties, rights, and obligations toward nature (even if it is in fact a very contentious ground). Marcuse's notion of the subjectivity of nature anticipated much of contemporary non-anthropocentric environmental ethics well before most figures in the field had articulated such views. Still, many in environmental ethics now go back to figures like Aldo Leopold for the origins of non-anthropocentrism, but then skip over everything until we get to Naess's "Shallow and the Deep" or Richard Sylvan's "Do We Need a New Environmental Ethic?" (also published in 1973). Marcuse's work is too often left out. Clearly, more work needs to be done to demonstrate the relevance of Marcuse to contemporary work in environmental theory.

But even with such conclusions, in closing these remarks I will end with a problem. While I think Marcuse's work represents a high point in the development of political ecology, in many ways overcoming the principal debate that has shaped political ecology in recent decades, it is no longer clear to me that we really should be working out a revolutionary or utopian political ecology at all, be it a better form of social ecology, deep ecology, or even an environmental critical theory. Of course, I understand in general why utopian and revolutionary theorizing is important, and how it is clearly possible to take a long-range view of social transformation and combine it with short-range achievable goals. Nonetheless, I now have both philosophical and political worries about the utility of spending much time today on utopian theories. I have in fact given up any further work on materialist- and ontologist-style theories, and am quite comfortable leaving the project I set out for myself ten years ago to bridge the gap between these sorts of views to others. I now think that the deep ecology–social ecology debate did little good at all in advancing the cause of environmentalism. What was produced was more heat than light, more grandstanding than actual theoretical, let alone practical, progress.

This sense of the futility of the deep ecology–social ecology debate was further compounded by my evolving views on the current state and necessity of environmental philosophy and political theory. What, after all, is environmental philosophy for? To me it seems clear – and this has been the principal direction of my work in developing a pragmatist environmental ethic of late – that the point of environmental philosophy and political theory is to make a philosophical contribution to the resolution of environmental problems. I mean by this actual solutions to these problems, not theoretical constructs about how these problems could be solved given utopian notions of the possibilities of reform of society or reform of the self. I think that given the pressing and critical juncture that we face at present concerning environmental problems, we need to focus more on making a contribution to forming better environmental polices than on the other theoretical endeavors which have been the priorities of most environmental ethicists and political ecologists. To make a contribution to the formation of better policies, we need to pay attention to those forms of argument that will morally motivate people. This means formulating arguments for more environmentally responsible policies in language that is compatible with the everyday moral intuitions of most people. The moral intuitions of most people, I think, are not non-anthropocentric but, rather, anthropocentric. These intuitions, while not at all revolutionary, can still serve as the basis for profound changes in environmental policies. For example, basing arguments for better environmental policies on obligations to human future generations has in the past led to the adoption of some of our most important environmental legislation in the US. Why is this the case? Because many people care about the welfare of either their own children or other children and are motivated in their everyday lives to protect children and preserve certain things for them. But we have not yet, I will maintain, seen the full extent of what a recognition of such obligations can justify in the environmental arena. What we need to do, then, if we take seriously the claim that the point of environmental philosophy is to make a contribution to today's environmental problems, is to work harder on more fully extending our ordinary sense of morality to justify the means to resolve these problems.[10]

In that context I have the following two difficulties with Marcuse's work on the environment: (1) Philosophically speaking, I am not convinced that achieving long-term environmental sustainability actually requires the assertion of a subjectivity to nature, let alone a revolutionary subjectivity. Nor am I convinced that a revolution must presage the conception of such a subjectivity. For reasons different from those articulated by Vogel in his contribution to this volume (see Chapter 14), I think that there is a very practical sense in which nature is indifferent to the revolution and always will be. Or, at least, I do not think we need to spend much time trying to figure out whether nature awaits the revolution as a premise for reforming society on ecological grounds. (2) Politically (or maybe materially), I am not convinced that achieving environmental sustainability requires a radical break with current material structures or forms of political organization, as Marcuse and Bookchin would have us think. In the end, this may be an empirical question. Actually, I am much less certain about this last point given the work of thinkers such as Jim O'Connor on the second contradiction of capitalism. Nonetheless, absent a real revolutionary hope, if environmental philosophers and political theorists are to do more than just provide interesting theories for each other to read, then perhaps we should direct more of our attention toward more achievable transformations. There is a lot that can still be done, to take just one example, inside the market system to try to relieve some of the current anthropogenic stresses on the environment. Are these only short term, band-aid solutions? I do not think so, unless one wants to take the implausible position that some of our strongest environmental legislation passed in the West so far has been only palliative.

In some respects I hope that someone can talk me out of my current skepticism toward utopian theorizing. When I was working on the deep ecology–social ecology debate, I was fully committed to working through such problems in a utopian model of theorizing. But I quickly became dissatisfied with such a model given the task at hand: to respond to the very real, very present, environmental crisis. In that sense, the publication of *Social Ecology after Bookchin* is something of an anachronism in my present work: the concerns of the book are no longer the concerns of my current work. To retreat into theory, which is what I see happening in the lingering debates over social ecology and deep ecology, is to act irresponsibly as an environmental citizen. Or, at least, to spend all of our time talking about the revolutionary potential of or for nature is to abandon the reasons why most of us work on environmental problems in the first place.

Notes

1 Arne Naess, "The Shallow and the Deep, Long-range Ecology Movements," *Inquiry*, vol. 16 (1973), pp. 95–100.
2 Quoted in Joanna Macy, "Awakening to the Ecological Self," in Judith Plant (ed.) *Healing the Wounds: The Promise of Ecofeminism*, Toronto: Between the Lines, 1989, p. 202.
3 Murray Bookchin, "Social Ecology Versus Deep Ecology," *Socialist Review*, vol. 18, no. 3 (July–September 1988), p. 13.
4 David Abram, *The Spell of the Sensuous: Perception and Language in a More-Than-Human-World*, New York: Pantheon, 1996.
5 Herbert Marcuse, *Counterrevolution and Revolt*, Boston: Beacon, 1972.
6 Herbert Marcuse, *One-Dimensional Man*, Boston: Beacon, 1964.
7 Andrew Light, "Reconsidering Bookchin and Marcuse as Environmental Materialists: Toward an Evolving Social Ecology," in Andrew Light (ed.) *Social Ecology after Bookchin*, New York: Guilford Publications, 1998, pp. 343–84.
8 See Murray Bookchin, "Response to Andrew Light's Bookchin and Marcuse as Environmental Materialists," *Capitalism, Nature, Socialism*, vol. 4, no. 2 (June 1993), pp. 101–12. For my own reflections on this exchange, see Andrew Light, "Bookchin as/and Social Ecology," in Light (ed.) *Social Ecology after Bookchin*, pp. 1–23.
9 For Naess's comments on the need to move more toward political economy and away from the excessively spiritual side of deep ecology, see Andrew Light, "Deep Socialism? An Interview with Arne Naess," *Capitalism, Nature, Socialism*, vol. 8, no. 1 (March 1997), pp. 69–85. It is important to also note that Naess included substantial (though somewhat haphazard) discussions of technology, economics, and politics in his opus, *Ecology, Community, and Lifestyle* (Cambridge: Cambridge University Press, 1989).
10 For more detail on this view, see my "The Case for a Practical Pluralism," in Andrew Light and Holmes Rolston III (eds) *Environmental Ethics: An Anthology*, Cambridge, MA: Blackwell, 2003, pp. 229–47, and "Taking Environmental Ethics Public," in David Schmidtz and Elizabeth Willott (eds) *Environmental Ethics: What Really Matters? What Really Works?*, Oxford: Oxford University Press, 2002, pp. 556–66.

13

MARCUSE'S ECOLOGICAL CRITIQUE AND THE AMERICAN ENVIRONMENTAL MOVEMENT

Tim Luke

My talk, first, will articulate how I understand Marcuse, particularly his approach to environmental issues, and, secondly, will indicate why I think he continues to be very useful for those seeking to answer pressing environmental questions today. For me, many key insights about how Marcuse sees the environment, ecology, and nature can be found in his *Counterrevolution and Revolt*. In this text, Marcuse suggests that in the established networks of social control, Nature itself, as it becomes ever more effectively administered, has become another means for the control of man. How the environment is managed, in turn, reveals the cultural, economic, and political tools being used to guide the strategies of extended social control as well as the tactics behind the deployment of this power. When one talks about the question of revolutionary change, then a radical transformation of nature, as Marcuse suggested, becomes an integral part of the radical transformation of society.

Plainly, the thing that has always impressed me about Marcuse is the complexity and subtlety with which he approached these difficult questions. He does not get caught up in a very simple conceptual division between "nature" and "society," where one either has to side, on the one hand, entirely with the agendas of social rationalization and the conservation of nature to promote economic production, *or* one must step entirely, on the other hand, over into the camp of nature to advocate wildness, greenness, and other "authentic" natural qualities. Marcuse admits how completely interwoven nature and society actually are. Most importantly, he stresses how the domination of nature always leads to the domination of people. What is also striking about Marcuse is how fully he realizes how our "inner nature," or psychosocial agency, always expresses itself, at the same time, in the relationships of society with "outer nature," or the planet's ecology.

These insights are what are most striking in Marcuse's thought: the sophisticated combination of a critique of psychosocial identity, the operations of technology as total environment, and this embeddedness of nature inside of the economy, society, and state. The one thing that we should take away from Marcuse's approach to ecology is how concretely and critically he analyzes the destructive ways in which any advanced industrial society works: in particular, the mobilization of technological rationality to generate short-term material surpluses to cultivate popular interest in the prevailing operational establishment – or the state, corporate capital, and technoscience – by distorting the desire for human liberation with the enjoyments of a stupefying culture, consumeristic waste, and false needs. All of these interlinked ties between production and consumption seem to create some sense of positive progress for the general population, but they actually create very little that is progressive or positive.

Another point worth mentioning is Marcuse's acknowedgment of an ongoing struggle between the death instinct, or an impulse to destroy other living things in nature, and the life instinct, or the will to protect and enhance life itself, in all human activities. The political dynamics of structuring psychosocial identity are reflected in how advanced capitalism's relationships with nature mediate this balance of instincts. In many ways, the struggle to realize a more pacified, harmonious, or right relationship with nature through the life instinct cannot proceed until the conflicts and contradictions of a death instinct in capitalist exchange, which deeply distorts individual psychosocial identity, are addressed with some finality.

Most centrally, Marcuse correctly identifies how technology itself becomes a pernicious form of social control and domination through the practices of abstraction, calculation, formalization, and operationalization. As these normalizing techniques become congealed in technological artifices, things themselves make possible the domination of human beings as people use them in their economic and technical exploitation of nature. Technology cannot simply be seen as an empty operational imperative. When technics are treated in this fashion, they can always become enrolled in an almost perfectly working model of social control. It is important for critical theory to look at how the black boxes of technology are constructed, blackened, and then moved around. One must open them up, and discover that they never contain purely engineering imperatives. Instead, their mechanisms are also the motive pieces of larger political conflicts, social crises, and cultural contradictions.

Consequently, Marcuse gets us thinking, albeit maybe not as effectively as some would want, about how we must re-imagine our relationships with nature by articulating a new aesthetic sensibility that could begin to reintegrate the things that now seem to be so disintegrated and dissociated, such as labor and leisure, science and art, work and play. This change must be made by mobilizing the powers of aesthetic imagination, because these forces can help us chart a more emancipatory relationship between humans and nature. Ecology, environmentalism, or analyses of nature become very useful foci for questioning advanced capitalism when we talk about our relationship with the life and death instincts, particularly the nature of social needs, and political agendas embedded in culture. Turning to the aesthetic dimension allows one to talk about this system of urban development or that mode of industrial production as destructive strategies that self-serving elite interests use to define and satisfy false needs. Counterpoised to distorted ways of life, the aesthetic dimension can also propound alternative utopian visions of living. Those utopian visions should develop the programs for how we can transcend false needs with real truths tied to a minimum of toil, creative labor, abundant free time, and a more pacified style of social existence. In many ways, Marcuse comes quite late in the 1960s to what has been developing as the modern American environmental movement, but we cannot really dissociate much of what he has written from the movement's ecological critiques.

Indeed, there is an unusually deep concern with the environment and technology in Marcuse's writings, whether one looks at *Eros and Civilization*, *One-Dimensional Man*, or even his very early works. Even in texts such as *Soviet Marxism* he is talking about how, or under what conditions, collectives of people and things in technological relationships of production shape our psychosocial identities within the built artificial and the unbuilt natural environments in which we live. While he does not talk about these collectives in an overtly ecological fashion until the 1970s, when this issue becomes far more central to public debates in the media, universities, and government, it is very difficult for me not to see those works as studies in environmental philosophy. While there may not be many citations of Marcuse in the writings of some environmental groups and many ecological thinkers, there is a vivid anticipation of their values in much of what Marcuse is arguing.

Social ecology's analyses of society, for example, have a very clear sense of what this technological problematic is. And Marcuse articulates how much social change has to occur before anyone will attain a more ecological, emancipatory, and liberatory technology. Like this radical school of ecological criticism, he asserts that the domination of human beings can only end when the domination of nature ends. Like many ecofeminists, Marcuse sees many environmental crises being tied to the performance principle. In turn, the connection of performance principles to the death instinct as well as the impulse for domination by male agents within society are objects of his critique. Like deep ecology, Marcuse is very apprehensive about the domination of nature by overdeveloped technological systems. He is aware of the peculiar kind of anthropocentrism that is centered upon a technological despoliation of nature to sustain capitalist exchange. While he wants a "pacified existence," I think that he also appreciates some measure of sublime wildness in nature. Of course, Marcuse's thinking about how existence might be pacified always moves within modern frameworks for thinking about controlling nature, but he respects a degree of its otherness.

Like some soft path technologists, Marcuse believes in a rational form of emancipatory technology. Once humanity has those tools, it can deal with the questions of material scarcity that continue to be postponed as we accept false needs, instrumental rationality, and oppressive vested interests which misdirect the economy and misapply scientific rationality. By pushing for a different aesthetic agenda in technological action, the reunification of a liberatory imagination with technological invention becomes his preferred means of dealing with what we now consider to be the environmental crisis. Aesthetics can overcome, Marcuse maintains, the purposeful production of waste by advanced industrial societies. Like some advocates of voluntary simplicity, Marcuse was very disturbed about excessive overdevelopment. The corrosiveness of complexity, resting at the heart of the current mode of everyday life, only amplifies what makes it most difficult to see the harmonies, the beauties, or the transcendental qualities of life reflected in how nature works. Like many nature poets or writers, Marcuse also definitely wants to develop a new sensibility of nature. This new sensibility is conceivably more erotic, liberatory, feminist, aesthetic, and life-affirming, because it is pitched against a sensibility that reproduces one-dimensional forms of destructive technological rationalization.

Even though we must often engage in a series of archaeological excavations when we return to his texts, one can find moments when Marcuse talks about the environment and ecology. These topics definitely interested him later in his life, especially during the 1970s. While they are spare, I think he outlines some expansive notions of what "the environment" is, and a sophisticated sense of how "ecology" actually ought to work to account for the full range of human interactions in nature. The concern for how humanity works upon nature is also found in those writings that are not explicitly addressed to ecological concerns. Texts that appeared earlier, during the 1950s, such as *Eros and Civilization*, or, in the 1960s, *One-Dimensional Man*, are implicitly ecological treatises that anticipate most of the critical themes he touts more directly in much more environmental works during the 1970s. Most importantly, Marcuse puts on the table, and then critically takes apart, the conditions of those psychosocial relationships that mingle technology and society in the contradictions of science and imagination, labor and leisure, work and play, and art and engineering. This theoretical contribution brings us some real innovations, and it must continue to anchor our thinking about capitalist society's use and abuse of nature.

14

MARCUSE AND THE "NEW SCIENCE"

Steven Vogel

Marcuse, of course, was the great philosopher of everything being possible. He thought that things really could be radically different than they are, and that we could think about other ways of living. He wanted us to see that what we take for granted as eternal and as *natural* – and I use that word on purpose, because I want to talk about nature – is not so eternal and is not so natural and could be transformed, and perhaps should be transformed. Marcuse represents that kind of thought, and it is hard to go back to that nowadays when for so many of us a kind of exhaustion has set in, a sense in our lives that this is the way it is, that it has to stay this way, and that there is nothing much we can do about it, like it or not. I am inspired by those thoughts of his.

I want to talk about Marcuse and environmental theory, and his influence. I agree with a lot of what Tim [Luke, in Chapter 13 of the present volume] has said. I think Marcuse's influence on environmental issues is very great, both in acknowledged ways and in unacknowledged ways. He represents a way of thinking about nature that, as Tim pointed out, has been influential throughout environmental theory. But one of the reasons I think Marcuse is very important (and in this he is at one with the older traditions of Marxism going back to Marx and Engels) is because of his insistence that there is a deep connection between *critical social theory* on the one hand, and a *theory of nature* or a theory of the physical environment that humans live in on the other. If you are a materialist, then somewhere, if not at the core then at least very close to the core of your critical social theory, has got to be a theory of the actual physical world in which we live and of what the relationship is between humans and that world – the way in which we live in that world, the way in which we transform it or do not transform it, and so on.

And such a theory is *part* of political theory: Marcuse sees this. I have the sense that too often nowadays political theory does not pay much attention to those sorts of questions. That is true of general mainstream political theory, but I am thinking here also of Habermas, who is part of the same tradition as Marcuse but who fairly explicitly says that he does not want to provide a theory of nature; that is someone else's department. But Marcuse's insight goes both ways, because it also means that you cannot have an environmental theory that is not at the same time a critical social theory. I think that too much of what passes for environmental philosophy nowadays forgets this – it does not see that the questions associated with environmental philosophy are fundamentally political and social questions and have to be understood as such.

I think that Marcuse and the tradition to which he belongs are very good at recognizing these connections between society and nature. The "tradition" here of course is that of the Frankfurt School, and especially of Horkheimer and Adorno in *Dialectic of Enlightenment*. The Frankfurt School and Western Marxism in general broke with orthodox Marxism over a number of issues, but one of them certainly had to do with a suspicion of natural science and technology, which was obviously not characteristic of, say, Marx or Engels. Such a suspicion makes sense given the historical experiences of people like Horkheimer, Adorno, and Marcuse – with the culture industry, with the technologized horrors of Nazism and the Second World War, and so on. They believed that natural science itself, and technology itself, had to be interrogated, and might indeed be complicit in the crises of modernity. What you get, already in Horkheimer and Adorno, is a critique of enlightenment or of modernity for, among other things, the way it treats nature, for its "disenchantment" of nature – for the way in which any kind of value or meaning in nature is systematically removed from it. Nature appears to enlightenment as merely a kind of meaningless matter for instrumental manipulation. It is no longer something with any kind of intrinsic meaning or value or certainly anything like rights. What is characteristic, Horkheimer and Adorno argued, of science and technology is the attempt to dominate nature, to master nature, which ends in the destruction of nature. This is also paradoxical because the project of enlightenment is a project oriented precisely toward improving human life and making human existence better and increasing human happiness: but of course, humans themselves are natural beings, and if enlightenment destroys nature, it thereby also destroys humanity. Humanity itself then loses its value and loses its meaning. The project of enlightenment is thus subject to a kind of fatal dialectic.

We have already heard a lot of talk today at the conference about pessimism and optimism, and of course in Horkheimer and Adorno this conception of enlightenment leads to a very deep pessimism. But in Marcuse, at least toward the mid- to late 1960s, that pessimism begins to lift. He is complex and ironic, of course, but fundamentally, if you read a work like *An Essay on Liberation*, there really is a sense that there is some kind of hope. Marcuse began to see in the 1960s, in the counter-culture, in the New Left, in Third World liberation movements, in the Black liberation movement, possibilities of another way of interacting with nature, of a new sensibility, as we have heard mentioned a couple of times today. The radical idea was that a revolution would not merely be a kind of political or economic overthrow, but rather a fundamental transformation of *world-view* – which would also mean, at least in Marcuse's most utopian moments, a fundamental transformation *in nature itself*. Nature as he says would be treated as another subject by us; it would no longer be something to be dominated but rather something with which we could interact as a partner. This new sensibility would move beyond anthropocentrism, and would indeed be a liberation of nature. There is a great line in *Counterrevolution and Revolt* where Marcuse says: "Nature too awaits the revolution!" The revolution is not just for humans; we are doing it for nature's sake as well. And this involved, at perhaps its most radical moment, a notion of a kind of new science and a new technology, which Marcuse, at least at certain places, suggests is a real possibility. A science whose hypotheses, "without losing their rational character, would develop in an essentially different experimental context (that of a pacified world); consequently, science would arrive at essentially different concepts of nature and establish essentially different facts."[1] This is a wild thing to say, and a very intriguing thing to say – the idea that there really could be a fundamentally different sort of science, a fundamentally different sort of technology that would treat nature in a fundamentally different way.

This idea has been widely criticized, not least by Habermas who argues against what he sees as romanticism in Marcuse, and who thinks that on this point Marcuse is simply wrong. *There is no such thing* as a new science, *there is no alternative* to the science and technology we have, because these are associated with a fundamental project of the human species, and not one that is socially variable. It is a project that is built in (as Habermas says) "quasi-transcendentally" into the structure of what it is to be human at all: science and technology, he argues, derive from the fundamental interest of the species in predicting and controlling the natural world, based on work and on labor. It is a transhistorical project of the species. But this project, Habermas also argues, is distinct from another equally significant, equally fundamental and "quasi-transcendental" species project, associated with language and with the attempt to achieve mutual understanding. These are two separate, distinct, equally fundamental projects – the one associated with production and control of nature, the other with languages and mutual understanding. This allowed Habermas to reformulate the old Frankfurt School critique, not as a critique any longer of instrumental or technical rationality as such, but rather of the *misapplication* of technical rationality – which, in fact, is perfectly appropriate when applied to the realm of nature – to a realm where it *does not* apply: the social or ethical realm.

Thus Habermas offers a critique of the scientization of politics. He criticizes the notion that you can apply categories associated with prediction and control – such as categories of efficiency, for example – to political material so that you no longer really need democracy, and it becomes simply a matter of getting experts to make decisions about how to organize society. But then very interestingly he turns around and says Marcuse's romanticism involves making the same error in the opposite way. Whereas scientism on the one hand takes categories appropriate to nature and misapplies them to the social realm, what happens in Marcuse is that categories appropriate to the social realm get misapplied to the natural one. Thus it is simply a category mistake, Habermas argues, to talk about "dominating" nature or "liberating" nature. Domination and liberation are *ethical* categories that have to do with relations between people, and nature is not a person. We do not engage with nature in the kinds of relations with which we engage in the social realm. Therefore Marcuse is making an error that is the flip side of the scientistic error.

There is a lot that I like in Habermas's account, especially the rejection of scientism and the strong link that he draws between language and the ethical realm. But the one thing that I think is really wrong with it, and want to defend Marcuse on, is the strong dualism it asserts between nature and the social, and its implicit claim that nature is somehow outside the ethical and political realms. This is associated especially in Habermas with the idea that the only theoretically fruitful approach to nature is a scientific one oriented toward prediction and control, which is an asocial and ahistorical project of the species. I think this way of putting it will not work (and actually I think Habermas may have figured out that it will not work, which is why in his later writings he has never come back to the idea). Habermas was operating with a very old-fashioned, logical positivist, monological notion of what science is; but in fact I think the whole trajectory of the philosophy of science over the last thirty-five years has been precisely to show the ways in which the scientific project is a *social* project, is a *historical* project, and that therefore conceptions of nature and ways of interacting with nature are socially and historically variable, so that, to put it bluntly, *nature is a social category*. The way that nature appears and is conceptualized will radically change from society to society. Once you acknowledge that, it seems to me, the notion of a new science and technology becomes possible again. In a different society, it is plausible there might indeed be a different way of interacting with nature and a different kind of science and perhaps a different kind of technology. I think recent work in cultural studies of nature, and especially in environmental history, all really go to show that nature is social, that in a certain sense it is indeed socially constructed. And I think these kinds of ideas help to make Marcuse's notions of a new sensibility and a new science more plausible. (Although I have to say I do not share any longer his optimism that this change is imminent; I think we may have longer to wait.)

And yet, having said that in Marcuse's defense, I think there is a problem in his work, or at least a palpable tension. He is quite clear, on the one hand, that nature is a social and historical category, that what counts as natural is historically variable, including the nature of natural science. Yet at the same time, when you look in works such as *Counterrevolution and Revolt* and elsewhere about what he imagines this "new sensibility" as being like, he starts to betray a kind of naturalism that seems inconsistent with the sense of nature as socially constructed. I have some quotations here from *Counterrevolution and Revolt*. The new sensibility "would be nonviolent, nondestructive: oriented on the enhancing, sensuous, aesthetic qualities inherent in nature."[2] It is the word "inherent" that I want to question. Marcuse talks about "the ability to see things in their own right, to experience the joy enclosed in them, the erotic energy of nature – an energy which is there to be liberated; nature, too, awaits the revolution."[3] Marcuse wants "to help nature 'open its eyes' " – and here he is quoting Adorno, who says he wants to help "the poor Earth to become what perhaps it would like to be."[4] There is constantly this kind of trope in Marcuse, according to which the new sensibility would involve "letting nature be." This would be a kind of *passive* relation to nature, in which it is allowed, for the first time, to be what it really wants to be, to achieve its *telos*. But this does not make any sense if nature is socially constructed, because there is not anything *inherent* in nature. That is the point about the sociality of nature. If something is a social category, then talking about allowing it its autonomy makes no sense at all because there is no "it" there. I think Marcuse is caught in this kind of inconsistency. It is complicated because there are a lot of places where he does not talk in this way. He talks elsewhere of the new sensibility as involving a kind of *reconstruction* of reality, a new formation of the world. In *An Essay on Liberation*, Marcuse asks for a "reconstruction of reality" and "a science and technology released from their service to destruction and exploitation, and thus free for the liberating exigencies of the imagination." He wants to see a "rational transformation of the world [which] could then lead to a reality formed by the aesthetic sensibility of man," and adds that "the aesthetic universe can emerge only in a collective *practice of creating an environment*."[5] So here he is obviously talking about an active relationship that *makes* the environment. But then he says that it is an environment that encourages "the nonaggressive, erotic, receptive faculties of man." And I do not see how in such an environment human faculties can actually be "receptive." What Marcuse is talking about here is in fact the *active* practice of transforming the environment. That is the only way I can understand these claims about the social character of nature: that our relationship to nature is fundamentally a transformative one. So it makes no sense to talk about "letting nature be" or allowing "it" a certain kind of liberation.

Marcuse, I think, betrays here a desire which is all too common in the environmental movement today, one which conflicts with his own epistemological sophistication. It is the desire somehow to be able to read off from nature the answers to political or social questions, questions about how we ought to live. But you cannot read off the answers to political and social questions from nature because we have no access to what nature is like in itself. Any account that we give of nature is going to be one already infused with our own views of nature, and therefore already infused with our own social and political ideas. So our own social answers get smuggled in at the end. What follows from this for me is that nature has to be seen as a social category. The questions as to what the environment is and what the environment ought to be are political questions to be answered only by *us*; nature cannot answer them.

The trouble with the social world today, and with its relation to the environment, is that these questions – What ought the environment to be? What sorts of transformative practices ought we to be engaging in? – do not get asked. Instead, they are "answered," so to speak, by leaving them up to the operations of the market, that is to say, to individuals who make decisions *by themselves* about the kinds of transformative practices in which they are engaged. (This is, of course, a traditionally Marxist argument.) There is no space for a *communal* decision about what kind of transformative practices we want to engage in. Instead, these practices are left up to the anarchic, nature-like workings of the market – a "second nature" in which individuals do not and cannot acknowledge any global or communal responsibility for their actions. Thus to take seriously the idea of a "new science" or a "new sensibility," it seems to me, would involve the idea of a science or worldview that was *conscious*, that *self-consciously acknowledged human responsibility for the environment*. I mean "responsibility" here both in a causal and a moral sense: that the world we live in is fundamentally a world affected by our practices. This seems to me the possible significance of Marcuse's ideas to contemporary environmental thought.

Notes

1 Herbert Marcuse, *One-Dimensional Man*, Boston: Beacon, 1991, pp. 166–7.
2 Herbert Marcuse, *Counterrevolution and Revolt*, Boston: Beacon, 1972, p. 67.
3 *Ibid.*, p. 74.
4 *Ibid.*, p. 66.
5 Herbert Marcuse, *Essay on Liberation*, Boston: Beacon, 1969, p. 31.

Part IV

RECOLLECTIONS

15

HERBERT MARCUSE'S "IDENTITY"

Peter Marcuse

What was my father's "identity?" He was clearly a philosopher by training (although his first degree was in German literature), and by occupation (although he was also employed as a political analyst during the war, and lectured on a wide variety of topics in his later life). He was politically active all his life, although he would have disclaimed the description "activist." That was something he admired and supported in others; he saw his own role as supportive and engaged, but hardly as leading a charge.

But the question I want to examine is that aspect of identity so often taken to be its main substance: ethnicity, or nationality. Was my father German, or American (we nationalistically use the term as meaning from the US), or Jewish, or what? Our family came to this country [the US] when my father was 35, and I 5 years old. We were certainly Jewish; we would never have been in the U.S. otherwise. My father was bar mitzvah'd, and to my knowledge his parents were relatively observant. But he himself was strictly secular. I remember at home hearing Jewish jokes, a smattering of Yiddish, Jewish friends, a Jewish intellectual circle – no doubt we were Jewish; but I remember no religious observance, no going to *schul* or services, even on the High Holy Days. At least before we arrived in the US, I suspect he never felt any contradiction between being German and being Jewish; his father refused to believe that, as a good German, he could possibly be the subject of discrimination or persecution, and refused to consider leaving Berlin until the very last moment before the war broke out, and then getting out only at substantial risk and cost. We of course were luckier (or read the political signs more accurately – political understanding does after all sometimes have some direct personal use!).

My father's identity, one would think, was well formed by then; mine perhaps not. I had to learn English here and was put in a private school for one year to help the process; but thereafter I went straight through public school in New York City and then in California. I never had any doubt, as a grown-up, that I was American, even though, as late as college, friends made fun of one or two remaining quirks of foreign accent. I first went back to Germany on a visit in 1976, when I was 47, and had to struggle to regain my German.

But my father spoke fluent, indeed both eloquent and, when he wanted, very colloquial, German all his life. When he lectured there, everyone recognized him as German-born. They did in the US, too; even after he had been here thirty years, his German accent was clearly recognizable. I sometimes kidded him that he kept it on purpose to go with his philosopher's persona. But I don't think that was quite fair. He really was "German" in many ways. His cultural tradition was German; he had not only studied German literature, but had the complete Goethe prominently on his bookshelf, and could quote German poetry from all ages. When I was studying German literature at college, he would write me regular commentaries on what I was supposed to be reading – good stuff, too, which I wish I could still find, but I did not know then how good it was or how famous he would become!

When we first came to this country, our social circle was entirely German. My father met regularly with other friends from the Institute for Social Research who had come over at the same time. They played skat (a cross between bridge and pinochle, and a standard German pastime) with each other, went for Sunday drives in the country together, vacationed together. When we moved to California just before the beginning of the war, his circle was overwhelmingly of German émigrés: Brecht, Reichenbach, Günther Stern (later Anders), and of course the Institute crowd. He still needed and got help with putting *Reason and Revolution*[1] into English, and would occasionally pace up and down in his study looking for a word in Roget's Thesaurus, or even asking me or one of my friends.

But I think that identity changed when we moved to Washington, DC, and he began working for the government in the war against fascism. The Neumanns were still our closest friends, but conversations were as likely to be in English as in German, and his circle, both through the office, through the psychoanalysts he began to know in connection with his research on Freud, and socially, were American. My mother, who worked as a statistician at the Department of Agriculture, was in an entirely American environment. And so was I, at school, at summer jobs, and then at college in Boston. Ten more years, and there was no question my father was American – although also clearly of German extraction.

I do not think the change was entirely political, although politics certainly played a major role. We had relatives in England who had barely escaped Germany before the war began, in addition to my grandparents, including an uncle who swore never to set foot in Germany again. My father of course went back many times, but he always refused to buy (or have his wife buy, since he did not drive) a Volkswagen, because of its association with Nazism. He was also always very much in with the German Left opposition, had many German friends all through his life, visited often, and never had misgivings about doing so. I think he felt no more or less at home there — and no more or less alien — than he did in the US.

More than the political, I think my father found the more informal and open atmosphere of the US more congenial than the more rigid and hierarchical relationships traditionally found in Germany. It was for a time a matter of amusement in the Research and Analysis section of the Office of Strategic Services, where my father and some others of his set, specifically Franz Neumann, also worked during the war, that they all addressed their American colleagues by their first names, but each other by their last. Even that issue is not exclusively cultural, but also partly political. I was surprised, during a visit to Frankfurt much later, that when my father was invited to a small house party at his publishers, he addressed everyone, and they addressed him, with the informal "Du," not the formal "Sie." Well, he explained, they were all on the Left, and addressed each other as comrades.

Other former colleagues from the Institute did of course return to Germany after the war, most notably Max Horkheimer and Theodor Adorno. Their politics only separated from my father's in the 1960s; during and immediately after the war, they remained close, both personally and politically. The correspondence in the first volume of the material we are publishing from the archives[2] is revealing of that relationship. But both Horkheimer and Adorno were stiff — what one might today call uptight — in their personal posture, Horkheimer to the point of pomposity. I remember as a little boy always being told to be on my best behavior when we went to visit Horkheimer and his wife. My father simply liked the American manner more than the German. While he enjoyed giving lectures, which he always carefully prepared, he enjoyed even more the question and answer sessions that followed that were certainly more part of the American educational style than the traditional German. He simply liked living here better than living there. Perhaps there was a subtle change of identity involved, but it was a conscious one, an adaptation to a different environment that was found more acceptable than the old.

At the same time, my father had a much clearer view of political and social relations in the US than his former colleagues who returned to Germany after the war. In the famous exchange of letters about the war in Vietnam, Adorno makes the comment that, after all, "in America, everything is possible." My father knew better; *One-Dimensional Man* is, after all, one of the most trenchant analyses of the American way of life yet written. Unlike Adorno, who looked down on political activists (according to his analogy, they were like radio technicians, while serious political thinkers should be media analysts), my father took immediate political issues seriously, and was actively involved in campaigns around both foreign policy issues and issues of civil rights and civil liberties.[3] Not that he did not have his doubts about conventional parliamentary politics; in conversations with Rudi Dutschke, who he regarded as highly as anyone in the European Left, he continually warned about the difficulties a Green party would have in playing the conventional political game. But he was not interested in *"Flaschenpost,"* putting a message for the future in a bottle and casting it on the seas, hoping some day someone somewhere would find and heed it; he wanted to influence things today, because they so badly needed changing and possibilities were similarly so great. The situation is not so different today, and I am happy that what he said and wrote then may still be of some help to us in the here and now.

Notes

1 Herbert Marcuse, *Reason and Revolution: Hegel and the Rise of Social Theory*, New York: Oxford University Press, 1941. This was the first full-length study he published in the US.
2 Herbert Marcuse, *Technology, War and Fascism: Collected Papers of Herbert Marcuse*, vol. 1, ed. Douglas Kellner, London and New York: Routledge, 1998.
3 Of course, he was not a conventional civil libertarian, *vide* "Repressive Tolerance" [in *Critique of Pure Tolerance*, Boston: Beacon, 1965 – eds]. It was one of the few points on which I felt that he misunderstood the political situation in the US. I was then practicing law, and saw an important role for civil liberties in the US. He had a different perspective on the issue.

16

ENCOUNTERING MARCUSE

Carl E. Schorske

It is hard for those who came to know Herbert Marcuse after 1950, whether in person or through his works, to conceive of him as a US intelligence expert. Yet that is the role in which I first encountered him in the Office of Strategic Services (OSS) in 1943. He had joined the section of the Research and Analysis branch of the OSS that was charged with reporting on the political, social, and cultural developments of Nazi Germany that would be useful in the construction and/or execution of American policies toward its enemy. In one of those paradoxical inversions of hierarchy that war produces, young academics like me, fresh from graduate school, often occupied positions of authority over mature scholars who adapted their ways of work less readily than the young to collective intellectual production and to the practical requirements of their government consumers. Thus I often found myself as organizer and editorial critic of the work of intellectuals whose superiority in learning and analytic power was evident to all concerned. No one was embarrassed by the semi-carnivalesque inversion; each party was engaged in educating the other. The seniors provided the cultural substance and sometimes the methods of analyzing German developments; the juniors showed how to sharpen the focus of research projects and clarify the formulation of research results to maximize their practical relevance and persuasiveness.

For us younger Americans, it was both enlightening and enjoyable to attend the research strategy sessions of the Central Europeans. They would address collectively such major problems as providing social and political guidance for the future American occupation forces, or preparing the structural framework and administrative information for the American war crimes prosecution. Three of the four German émigrés who carried the greatest weight in the discussions were veterans of the Institute for Social Research, first in Frankfurt, then at Columbia in New York. They introduced their method of collective criticism in the development of research projects. Franz Neumann, political sociologist, was the natural leader of the group. Sharp in thought and in speech, dogmatic in style, though responsive to challenge, he knew how to steer broad-ranging enquiry toward practical political conclusions. Marcuse was at the furthest remove from Neumann in temperament, at his best in long-run analyses of social forces and their shifting ideological resultants, but avoiding political or policy choices where moral ambiguity was involved. Otto Kirchheimer, like Neumann a lawyer by training, had not only a judicial temper but also a juridical outlook especially useful in preparing for the war crimes trials. The historian Felix Gilbert, the fourth member of this group, had ties neither to the Frankfurt Institute nor to Marxism as an intellectual system. Quiet-spoken and subtle in his critical input, he enjoyed the deep respect of his colleagues for his empirical learning and his insightful approach to political behavior. Marcuse expressed his admiration for Gilbert by according him the title of "Preceptor Germaniae."

In the social dynamics of the Central European section's deliberations, Marcuse's ever-ready wit played a prominent part. He had the comic's critical spirit, the gift of deflating illusion. His voice, deep in pitch and gravelly in timbre, could rapidly convert gravity into mocking sententiousness. Where Neumann was the section's Faust, defining and pursuing specific projects with intensity of purpose and logical rigor, Marcuse was its Mephisto, the spirit of negation wherever what he saw as exaggerated optimism – especially with respect to the political order – appeared. His was a needed contribution, welcomed by Neumann and his colleagues for its intellectual substance as well as for the witty, sometimes anal, language in which it was conveyed.

The OSS has often been compared to a second graduate school for the young Americans like myself who were lucky enough to serve there during the war. I certainly learned much of substance and of method from the émigrés. But the form of education was unlike any prevailing in graduate schools then or now. Peculiarly in the OSS, the line between goal-oriented discussions interpreting war-time Europe and intellectual play, between collegial work and conviviality, was often impossible to draw. When Marcuse became engrossed in the French Left Catholic periodical *Esprit*, he drew me into his concern with it. He insisted that I read *Les Temps Modernes* and opened my eyes to existentialism as a new response of liberal individualism to the conditions of Nazi occupation with wide implications for the liberal heritage. Marcuse made me reconsider *Parsifal*, while Neumann and Gilbert were pushing me into Burckhardt's *Weltgeschichtliche Betrachtungen*[1] and Hölderlin respectively. As these examples suggest, it was no academic education, but a general intellectual and cultural one that the intelligence workshop of the OSS offered the young. The émigrés were Europeanizing the minds of us Americans, even as we who benefited from their culture helped to orient them in the ways and outlook of their adopted country and its new generation. In this exchange, Marcuse stood out for the ease and generosity of his intellectual friendship.

I had my second encounter with Marcuse when I began teaching after the war. This time I became engaged not with the man in the flesh but with his printed word in *Reason and Revolution*. The works that followed Marcuse's turn to Freud in the early 1950s have long overshadowed *Reason and Revolution* of 1941, a study still conceived under the primary impact of Marx. This is not the place to discuss the contents of the work, but to acknowledge my debt to it as I tried, in teaching intellectual history, to break through what seemed to me an Atlantic wall in America's academic culture in the late 1940s and 1950s. The Nazi domination of Europe had created a kind of continental blockade that divided the Anglo-Saxon empirical rationalist tradition from the German idealist and dialectical one. Immediately after the war, American philosophy, which had been eclectic in its acceptance of both idealist and positivist elements, embraced English analytic school philosophy as a new orthodoxy. By extruding the continental idealist tradition from its place in American philosophy, and reinforcing the behavioralist turn in the social sciences, the new scientific positivism strengthened the Atlantic wall of separation in the post-war era. In the universities, fields like mine – intellectual history – became the residuary legatees of continental philosophic thought as philosophy departments jettisoned it.

Marcuse, vigorous anti-positivist though he was, placed the problem of Europe's divided philosophic legacy in a unifying historical perspective. In *Reason and Revolution*, which he had conceived in a historical spirit not unlike that of Engels' *Socialism Utopian and Scientific*, he offered a nationally differentiated framework for the history of the European Enlightenment tradition and its modern fate. It was a real eye-opener for me. It provided an analytical approach and a phraseology for thinking and teaching European intellectual history, from Locke to Freud, in its national loci and its social-historical context.

Among the friends that both Herbert Marcuse and I made at the OSS was Norman O. Brown, a classicist and at that time a committed Marxist. After his day's work in the French section of the OSS, he spent the evenings preparing for publication his first fine work of mythological analysis, *Hermes the Thief*. Brown took a position at Wesleyan University at the war's end, where, doubtless thanks to his initiative, I was soon invited to join the faculty. Our friendship was deepened by politics, for both of us belonged to the small minority who sought to stem the drift into the Cold War by working for the candidacy of Henry Wallace in 1948. Shortly after the Wallace debacle, Brown began to plunge into the study of Freud. In so doing, he participated in a widespread turn of academic intellectuals across the political spectrum in the 1950s – one thinks of Lionel Trilling and the historian William Langer – a turn from the social to the psychological as the key understanding of the human condition.

In this moment of intensifying political pessimism and heightened consciousness of the irrational that the Cold War brought in its wake, Brown invited Marcuse to visit him at Wesleyan. Both came to our house for dinner. Inevitably the question arose: "What are you working on?" Brown stated that he was into Freud. Marcuse indicated that he was too. It was a surprise to both friends. I do not remember the substance of the conversation, but Marcuse received Brown's announcement as a competitor's transgression, and the discussion grew quite frosty. The revelation, happily, did not poison the well of friendship between the two, but it was the harbinger of serious intellectual discord to come as each fleshed out his conception of psychoanalysis, Marcuse to transmute, Brown to transcend the legacy of Marx in which both had their roots.

After I left Wesleyan for the University of California at Berkeley in 1959, I saw nothing of Marcuse for several years. In the autumn of 1964, I became engaged in the Berkeley free speech crisis and the anti-Vietnam War movement that overlapped with and reinforced it.

One day – it must have been in the spring of 1965 – I received a call from Marcuse, recently established in the University of California at San Diego. He had learned of an anti-war protest march that was planned for the next day at Berkeley. Could he and Inge come to participate and stay with us?

The march was to form at the Berkeley campus and proceed to the Oakland Army Terminal, the major port facility for the shipment of military materiel to Vietnam. There the demonstration would reach its climax. The Terminal was strongly guarded. The route, too, it was feared, would be heavily policed. Oakland's police were notoriously tough – much more so than Berkeley's. The organizers, determined to avoid violence, provided monitors with strict instructions to maintain discipline among the demonstrators.

Herbert, Inge, my wife Liz, and I set out on foot from our house in South Berkeley to join the march on its route just short of the Oakland boundary. There the intersection of two broad avenues formed a large space. When we arrived at it, we found the procession halted. It was a remarkable scene. At one end of the plaza-like intersection a dense line of Oakland police, massed like a faceless Roman phalanx in their forbidding riot gear, stretched menacingly across the avenue. For their part, the demonstrators, their road blocked, had sat down on the pavement to wait for the road to clear. Their mood was cheerful and relaxed. Some had broken out guitars, others their lunches. Children scampered about in the sun.

Marcuse was enchanted by the spectacle. "Carrrl," he said to me in the unforgettable warm bass tones of his Berlin English, "it's beautiful!...the unification of the political prrrinciple with the pleasure prrrinciple..."

Alongside the police barrier, another player, more threatening because less predictable, appeared unbidden: a squadron of Hell's Angels. Marcuse wanted to go up to inspect them face to face. Liz, with whom Herbert was walking slowly through the crowd, urged against such a course of action. She remembers what she said to him: "Inge would kill me if anything happened to you!" He dismissed her concern with the remark that he knew how to behave; he had been in the street fighting in revolutionary Berlin ... No harm came to Marcuse from his close inspection of the enemy ... With the negotiation of a passage through the police barrier, the cheerful demonstrators that had so captured his philosophical heart resumed their peaceful march.

My encounters with Marcuse in California were few and far between: rare exchanges of visits between San Diego and Berkeley, or common visits to the Browns in Santa Cruz. The different roads that the two friends took to find in and through Freud some substitute for the utopian promise of Marx ultimately destroyed their intellectual common ground. In *Eros and Civilization*, Marcuse turned to Schiller to find in sensuous play and art his guide to human fulfillment. Marcuse conveniently forgot that Schiller developed his ideas of building a citizenry through aesthetic education in disillusioned recoil from the French Revolution and its terror. In his *Letters on Aesthetic Education*, Schiller was advising a prince on how to create a *Rechtsstaat*[2] by reform rather than face revolution. In *Life against Death*, Brown, taking his clue from Nietzsche's piercing breakthrough to the primacy of instinct, adopted the downside of Freud – anality – to develop a new critique of capitalism and post-Reformation culture. Where Marcuse regrounded civilization through a new sublimational vision, Brown subverted it by means of a de-subliminating exposure of anality's powerful presence.

The differences here were deep, but as nothing compared to the gulf which opened up when Brown published *Love's Body* in 1966. In it, Brown turned aside from using Freud's thought as a critical instrument against repressive civilization. Instead, he adapted it to provide a center in sexual theory for the poetic elaboration of a metaphysic of human communion. For the presentation of his new message, Brown devised a new form, at once academic in its erudite marshalling of cultural authority and prophetic in its aphoristic utterance. Marcuse responded to both the content and the style of the book with outrage. In an article in *Commentary*, "Love Mystified" (February 1967), Marcuse attacked Brown on several levels, of which the basic one was his surrender to the ghosts of religion. Symbols had become reality for Brown. In such concepts as eucharist, resurrection, mystical union, and renewal, Marcuse maintained, Brown had gone beyond metaphor to the restoration of the sacred, betraying the affirmation of this life. "You have revealed the latent, the true content of politics [in *Life against Death*]," Marcuse apostrophized his friend in the peroration of his review, "...you know that the political fight is for the whole: not the mystical whole, but the very unmystical, antagonistic whole of our life and that of our children – the only life that is." Brown's response was controlled but unyielding: "The idea of progress is in question; the reality of Marx cannot hide the reality of Nietzsche [eternal recurrence]." "Yes, indeed, there was a God that failed; that mortal God, the great Leviathan [i.e. the political state]; discovered to be not only mortal, but dead, an idol. From literalism to symbolism: the lesson of my life. The next generation needs to be told that the real fight is not the political fight, but to put an end to politics. From politics to metapolitics." "From politics to poetry....Poetry, art, imagination, the creator spirit is life itself; the real revolutionary power to change the world; and to change the human body."

In this exchange, the two friends recognized the radical divergence of their intellectual positions that had occurred since the day when they first discovered their mutual turn to Freud at the Wesleyan dinner table. In their first post-Marxist works of the 1950s, each harnessed Freud to somewhat different though related purposes. In *Eros and Civilization*, Marcuse sought to strengthen the positive, utopian element in Marx with explorations in Eros and art. In *Life against Death*, Brown deepened the negative, social-critical aspect of Marx with Freud's ideas of infantile psychology and anality. In the 1960s, while both continued to pursue "the unification of the political principle with the pleasure principle" that Marcuse had so happily recognized in the Berkeley anti-war demonstration, the two men changed the priority of their commitment to each. Marcuse's *One-Dimensional Man* (1964) is political criticism first and foremost, a critique of the modern liberal-capitalist order. The redeeming role of art and play, so central to *Eros and Civilization*, is explored primarily in its distortions in the existing repressive system of domination. Brown in *Love's Body* expanded the implications of Eros (and Thanatos!) beyond all politics, in his utopian search for a New Man. Small wonder that he called forth Marcuse's wrath.

The differences between the two friends did not prevent the student movement of the 1960s and 1970s from embracing both Marcuse and Brown with enthusiasm as intellectual guides, even as idols. As the movement expanded its scope from political to cultural – especially sexual – revolution, the two aspects seemed to the participants part of the same emancipatory thrust. But as the movement met reverses, especially in California, the cultural rebels withdrew from the political struggle, sometimes into urban drug culture, sometimes into utopian communes. Marcuse increasingly became the political activist and patriarchal spokesman. He employed the utopian aspect of his thinking essentially to strengthen alienation and the negation of the existing order. Brown spoke to a narrower circle, the cultural radicals, who sought community in nature and in withdrawal from society and present politics.

From teach-ins to sit-ins to be-ins to love-ins: in this trajectory of the 1960s generational movement, Marcuse, ever more politicized, remained in the first two stages; Brown, ever less the activist and more the philosopher of culture, felt a sympathy for the last two that Marcuse could not share.

The intellectual differences that surfaced with *Love's Body* in 1966 grew deeper with the years, as Brown, inspired by John Cage and other deeply American cultural radicals, pursued his philosophic-poetic quest into fields where Marcuse could not follow. Yet as far as I know, controversy between them was never resumed. Although the intellectual gulfs were unbridgeable, the personal ties remained unimpaired.

My last encounters with the Marcuses were always at the Brown's in Santa Cruz. The conversations, a natural part of picnics in fields above the sea, were as wide-ranging and riveting as those we had had at the OSS thirty years before. Marcuse salted them still with his special mixture of dogmatism and skepticism, human warmth and sardonic wit, affection and aggressivity that made any encounter with "meine Wenigkeit,"[3] as he liked to call himself, an unforgettable experience.

Notes

1 Jacob Burckhardt, *Force and Freedom: Reflections on History*, New York: Pantheon Books, 1964.
2 Constitutional state.
3 My humble self.

INDEX

Abram, David, *The Spell of the Sensuous* 230
Abromeit, John 28
"Absolute", the 75
"actually existing socialism" 93, 212
"administered world", American experience of critical theorists 60
Adorno, Theodor 3, 9–10, 17–18, 28, 163, 175; America and 51, 63, 209; anti-fascism 45; anti-Semitism project and 215; critical theory 64, 218; Davis on studying with 47; Earth and 244; "faithless faith" in pure existence 213; Frankfurt School and 21, 43–4, 96, 163; fully administered society 153; historical transformation and 54; "identity problem" analyzed 216; music and 53; need for new concept of ideology 215; negative anthropology 221; observation of bourgeois society 64; Princeton Radio Research Project and 55–6; problem of European and American ideology 60; read by Americans (1960s) 184; Rorty and 183; science and 64–5; "Scientific Experiences of a European Scholar in America" 57; subjectivity 82, 94; "Thesis on Need" paper" 53; understanding growth of National Socialism 210; utopian moment 220; world disclosure "constellations" 202; WORKS: *Minima Moralia* 52, 63; *Negative Dialectics*, "missed moment" 52; "On Tradition" 57, 141; *Prisms* (1955) 53, 60; "Reflections on a Theory of Class" 55–6, "Thesis on Need" 53, see also *Dialectics of Enlightenment*

advanced capitalist societies, repressive sublimation and 122–3
Aeschylus 107
aesthetic, considerations 142; contentious critique 79; dimension 125, 238; education as form of praxis 6; education, new sensibility and 91; experience 120, 122; radicalism 78; reality 88
Affirmation of life, the essential and 77
affluent society 52
Agger, Ben, "Marcuse in Postmodernity" 5
Agnew, Spiro 3, 164, 183
al-Qaida 16
Alford, C.Fred, *Narcissism: Socrates , the Frankfurt School, and Psychoanalytic Theory* (1988) 4; *Science and the Revenge of Nature: Marcuse and Habermas* 4
alienation 119, 170, 173; double 209–10; experiences of emigration 218; individual consciousness of 216; Marcuse and Marxian critique 212; Marcuse's emigration experience of 217; radical 210
Altman, Dennis 180
American dream, utopian content 58
ancient craft, self-manifesting product 71
ancients, Being and 70
anthropology, of bourgeois era 153, 154–7; definition 159; from practical point of view 153, 157–61; scientific status and 156
anti-Semitism 61–2, 210
AOL Time Warner 94
Apollo and Athene, new law 108

INDEX

Arabs and Muslims, discrimination and racial profiling 17
Aragon, Louis, novel *Aurelien* (1945) 9
Aristaeus, Eurydice and 101
Aristotle, importance for Marcuse 166; *intellectus speculativus* and 215; notion of *nous theos* 87, 105; "Now-Time" (*Jetzt-Zeit*) 135
art 123, 201; center of Marcuse's theory 160, 184; general plea for humanity 124; "Great Refusal" and 85; subjective achievement 122; vulgar-Marxist position 123–4
Ashcroft, John 16
Austromarxist Workers' Movement, empirical social research 56
authenticity 135–6; Marcuse and latent consciousness of 154
Authoritarian Personality 177, 216
automobile, example of technological reason 189, 196, 203

Bachofen, Johann Jacob 26, 102–6, 110; *Mother Right* 105
Bahro, Rudolf 93; "Surplus Consciousness" 26, 92; work, *Die Alternative* 15
Baudrillard, Jean 94; "white obscenity" 125
beauty, Kantian aesthetic judgment 120
Beckett, Samuel 1
Being, ancients and 70
Being and human being, belongingness of 70
Being (*Sein*) 115
Bell, Daniel, "End of Ideology" thesis 173
Benhabib, Seyla 20
Benjamin, Walter 3, 14, 21, 43, 96, 114, 163; importance of hope and 176; quotation from by Marcuse 181
Berkeley conference, "Legacy of Herbert Marcuse" 6, 24
Berkeley free speech crisis, anti-Vietnam War movement 256
Berlin, failed revolution (1918) and Marcuse 131
Bernstein, Eduard 138
Bernstein, Jay 201
Bernstein, Richard J. 4, 133–4; *Philosophical Profile* 185
bicycle couriers, nihilism of sections of society 189

"Black Book of Communism" 62
Black liberation movement 241–2
Black Panther Party (1966) 47
Blackburn, Robin, review of MacIntyre's *Herbert Marcuse* 174
Bloch, Ernst 158
Bloom, Allan 4; *The Closing of the American Mind* 3
Bokina, John 2–3, 5
Bolsheviks 133
Bookchin, Murray (social ecology) 227–8, 230, 234; argument with deep ecology 231; environmental materialism and 232; role of humans in relation to nature 228–9
Bordieu, Pierre, "Cultural Capital" and 22
Borgman, Albert 203
Borradori, Giovanna 184; *The American Philosopher* 183
bourgeois society 54; America as radical 58; capitalism and 177; consistent ideology 53; critical theory and 63; disappeared into the "middle class" 52; ideology lost its object with collapse of 213; image of itself in history 221; Marx and decay of 211; Marx and Engles and 59; reason as actualization of individual autonomy 196; science and 65
Brandeis University 165
Brecht, Bertolt 54, 119, 250
Breines, Paul, "Revisiting Marcuse With Foucault: An Essay on Liberation meets History of Sexuality 180
Breuer, Stefan 153
Briffault, Robert 26, 102
Brown, Norman O. 29, 259; deepened negative aspect of Marx 258; response to Marcuse 258; study of Freud 255; writings: *Hermes the Thief* 255; *Life against Death* 257; *Love's Body* 102, 257, 259
Bundschuh, Stephan 28
Burckhardt, Jacob, *Weltgeschichtliche Betrachtungen* 254
Bush administration, military courts and 16

Cage, John (American cultural radical) 259
capitalism, corporate 110; developed 55;

INDEX

ecology, environmentalism or analyses of nature and 237–8; emancipatory movements and objective conditions 218; fascist and "real socialist" opponents and 59; functioning of 212; global restructuring and 94; impersonal and fateful quality 192; iron laws of 135; late 54, 124, 157, 199; liberal 191, 199; Marcuse's critique of 185; monopoly 191; only one aspect of problem 177; organized to disorganized 189; perhaps cannot "deliver the goods" 189; Pollock's conception of state 54, 190; post-liberal 199; proletariat assimilated will not initiate revolution 181; relationships with nature 237; rejecting notions of alternatives 212; second contradiction of 234; technological despoliation of nature and 238–9; West accepted name after Cold War 52–3
Carmichael, Stokely (Kwame Toure) 47
Chicago School, European migration and 55
civic privatism, *political economy of narcissism* 102
Clark, John 228
Clash of Civilizations, The 216
classes, constituted out of individuals 57–8
Claussen, Detlev 25, 51–66; "The Religion of Everyday Life" 221
Cobb, W. Mark, "Diatribes and Distortions": Marcuse's Academic Reception" 28–9
Cold War 2, 5, 52, 216; idea of "One World" and 59; minority who sought to stem drift into 255–6; staved off global society 65; totalitarian horror as aspect 61
"collective memories", bind transnational spaces 216
Commentary, article "Love Mystified" Marcuse attacked Brown 257
Communist Manifesto 6
concept of class, historical understanding of social being 56
concept of truth (*phos*), life focus on *human* existence 116
"concrete universals" 120, 126n.86
consciousness, authoritarian structures of 210; concept making a comeback 62; critical 94; *Dasein's* of the past and the future 135; experience as category of 215; historical 123; human 215; individual and alienation 216; latent of authenticity 154; surplus 26, 92
contemporary sociology, disappearance of society and social meaning 213
contrat social, processes of sublimation and internalization 218
Cooper, David 47
corporate capitalism, welfare state to warfare state 110
Coulanges, Fustel de, *The Ancient City* 105
Counter-Revolution and Revolt (1972) 91, 216; ecology and environmental ethics 232, 236; "Nature Too Awaits the Revolution" 242, 244; new anthropology and 152; ontological dimension of Marcuse and 231; reaction to demands of May (1968) 13; transformation of nature and society 23
critical consciousness and oppositional subjectivity, forces of domination and 94
critical social theory, connection between *theory of nature* 240
critical theorists, America as "radically bourgeois" country 57–8; concept of revolution 55; concept of totality and 54; intersection between materialism and idealism 56; looked at Europe with Americanized gaze 64; migration that influenced methodological alignment 210; utopian content in writings of 58; writings contain sense of the ontological 60
critical theory 81; (1942) conference and 54; advanced Western social forms 59; attempt to preserve Marxian obstinacy 169; changes since (1989) 213; critique of anti-Semitism 218; European experience of failed revolution 55; Marcuse and 163–4, 168; Marcuse's reinvigoration of 221; National Socialism or Stalinism and 51; program (1937) 118; reconstructive 94; shaped by American experiences 209; shift from

INDEX

objective to subjective reason 215; social transformation and 57; strangers and alienation and reification 217; *sui generis* of totalitarianism 61; tools of critical self-reflection and 63; US after new Deal 52
critique of ideology, illusion and reality 118; understanding of critique of reality 155
Cuba 49
culturalization of social conflicts, "cultural clashes" 216

Dasein 18–19, 73, 76, 115, 133; being-*in*-the world 132, 140; Heidegger and full significance of 135–6; Marcuse and 134
Dasein's motality (*Bewegtheit*), mere movement (*Bewegung*) 135
Davis, Angela Y. 2, 5, 15, 18, 24–5, 43–9
Davis, Mike 3
death instinct, struggle with life instinct 237
deep ecology 227–8; form of "Environmental Ontology" 230
deep ecology-social ecology debate, materialist-ontologist distinction 230; utopian theory and 235
Deleuze, 184; *Nietzsche and Philosophy* 184
delusion (*Verblendungszusammenhang*), fictionality and 117
Demeter 103, 106–8
Derrida, Jacques 182–4; *Spectres of Marx* 184
Descartes, René, *cogito* 81, 133, 140, 166; dualistic form 132; Foucault's *History of Sexuality* and 182; historical time and 135
destiny (*Schicksalsgemeinschaft*) 133
desublimation of reason, self-sublimation of sensuousness 121
Détienne, Marcel 103
developed capitalism, network of "socialization" and 55
"development" question 75
Dialectic of Enlightenment (Adorno and Horkheimer) 9–10, 45, 67; "American experience" 65; culture industry chapter of 211, 220; Frankfurt School influence 241;

historical experience in 61; images of ideal man 156; rationality in 175
"dialectical anthropology", Horkheimer and Adorno 156
"difference feminism" 91
differentiation, political sphere and political economy 215
Dilthey, Wilhelm 6, 20, 135, 139–40
disastrous social developments, "false thinking" and 62
domination and liberation, *ethical* categories 243
domination of nature, overdeveloped technological systems and 238
drug-induced experience, opposition between reality and fiction 122
Dutschke, Rudi (European Left) 49, 251–2

earth, self-sufficient 108
Earth First! 229
Eastern Europe, socialist ideology 219
"Ecofascists and Cyberpunks" 5
Economic and Philosophical Manuscripts of 1844, Marcuse and labor 194
Eisler, Hans 54, 160
"emancipated homelessness" 209
emancipation, sensuous experience (*Sinnlichkeit*) 220; withdraws into illusion 122
emigration, moment of non-identical that governs 210; rehabilitation of negative power of social theory 221
émigrés, Europeanizing minds of Americans 254
end of age of ideology 53
Engels, Frederick 102, 105, 169, 199, 240; *Origin of the Family, Private Property and the State* 105, 110; *Socialism Utopian and Scientific* 255
Enlightenment, the 67; human capacity for thought and knowledge (*Erkenntnis*) 58; improving human life and 241; limits of 212; MacIntyre on shortcomings of 175; philosophy, European 209, 255; problems of 216; radical rationalism of 196; science as heir of 65
environmental issues 227, 236, 239–40
environmental movement, subjectivity and 91
environmentally responsible policies, arguments in language 233–4

INDEX

Erinyes old law 107
Eros, Marcuse's conception of 4; Marcuse's focus and critique of "sexual revolution" 180; predominates over Thanatos 18, 154; sexuality part of 179
Eros and Civilization (1955) 4, 19, 46, 122; aesthetic dimension of rationality 114–15, 117; alternative patterns of human behavior 160; ambivalence towards technology 196; Auschwitz references 10; concern with environment and technology 238; critique by MacIntyre 171–2; dialectics of liberation 121; dual anthropology 154; ecological treatise 239; emphasis on life in 76; Freud and 10, 22; imagination and 26; Marcuse turned to Schiller 257; Marcuse and utopian element in Marx 258; Marcuse's treatment of erotic utopianism in 2, 178; "Polymorphous Sexualities" and 179; re-reading of 83–9; role of gender 91; subjectivity 82; utopian theory 100
Eros and Thanatos, expanded implications in *Love's Body* 258
Esprit (French Left Catholic periodical) 254
Essay on Liberation (1969) 6, 13; aesthetic imagination in 115; alternative patterns of human behavior 160; case for a new anthropology 152, 154; character of autonomous art 14; continuation of *Eros and Civilization* 122; Marcuse and "Reconstruction of Reality" 244; New Left and 91; passage from 49; passage on language 48; some kind of hope in 241; utopianism and 178
essence (*eidos*) 69, 75
essence or nature of man 154
Euripides 107
European continent, transformation of religion into ethnic nationalism 213
European proletariat, fascism and 177
Eurydice 103
"Everyday Religion" 62, 66n.12
exploitation, German language and 213
expressive language 200

Fahrenbach, Helmut 158
family, defender of tradition, pursuit of happiness 58
Fanon, F.O. 49; *Wretched of the Earth, The* 212
Farias, Victor 27
Feenberg, Andrew 4–5, 25
female, stripped of metaphorical otherness, defective male 109
feminine *sporium* (womb), representation of Demetrian mystery 106
feminism, criticism of Marcuse 92; subjectivity 82, 91, 94, 96
Feuerbach, L.A. 29, 152, 220
Fichte, J.G 140
Fordism 189
Foucault, Michel 29, 83–4, 94, 165, 183–4; discourse on sexuality 182; docile bodies and Eros weakened 180; foray into Freudo-Marxism 176–83; Nietzschean individualist 182; power relations and 182; sexual discourse coercive and regulated 179; sexual revolution and 177–8; work, *History of Sexuality* 176, 180
Frankfurt conference 6
Frankfurt School 1, 3, 21, 25, 76, 96, 165; critical assimilation of psychoanalysis 102; experiences of flight and migration 210; Habermas and 242; influence on cultural studies and 163; MacIntyre and 175; Marcuse in 1960s and 1970s 43; subjectivity and 81–2, 94; thinkers and anti-fascist -theoretical work 44; tradition of 241
"Freedom Summer" (1964) 12–13
Freud, Sigmund 4, 10, 25, 75, 81; *Anthropology of Liberation* and 86; feminist theory and gender studies 22; final theory of drives 121; genital sexuality mature sexuality 179; instinct theory 76, 84, 86, 96; Marcuse and 18, 22–3, 73, 143; Marx's utopian project and 100; metaphysics of 124; notion of Nirvana principle 87; Orpheus/Narcissus myth and 103; paternity theory 102; patrilineage and matrilineage conflict 105; "phantasy" 85; repressive content of Western civilization 83–4, 177;

264

INDEX

subjectivity 83; suppression of memory 84; theory of human nature 85; WORKS: *Beyond the Pleasure Principle* 101; "On the Two Principles of Mental Functioning" 101; *Totem and Taboo* 105
Freudo-Marxism, concerned with freedom and revolt 178
Fromm, Erich 94, 96, 102, 210

Gadamer, Hans-Georg 183–4, 201
Galileo, science and 193
Gandesha, Samir 27
gay liberation movements (1960s) 180
Genoa conference 6
Germany 55, 60, 62, 64, 133, 134, 219
Gide, André 193
Gilbert, Felix 254
globalization 59, 93, 189, 216
Golden Age of short twentieth century 57–9, 212–13
Great Refusal, art and 85; Foucault's critique 180; Marcuse and 13, 18, 161, 181; no longer represents mere utopia 122; radical subjectivity 90; repression important part of 180
Green Party, Marcuse's warning about politics and 252
Guatanomo Bay, treatment of prisoners 16
Guevara, Che 2
Gulf War 5
"Gynema Effect" 110

Habermas, Jürgen 3, 26, 86, 163, 183–4; critique of Marcuse 197–200, 201, 242; critique of Marcuse's conception of technology 190, 193, 199, 202; critique of scientization of politics 242–3; linguistic turn 15–16, 190; "nature as it *is*" 201, 241; nature of language 200; separate Marcuse's sociology from his technology 199; subjectivity and agency 94–6; Vogel and 27; WORK: "Psychic Thermidor and the Rebirth of Rebellious Subjectivity" 4
happening (*Geschehen*) 135
Harowitz, Gad, "Psychoanalytic Feminism in the Wake of Marcuse" 5
Hegel, G.W.F 2, 8–9, 25, 49, 75, 81, 105, 166; Absolute Spirit 201; concept of class and 56; concept of "doing" (*Tun*) 142; concept of life 139; "End of History" 70; ideal of spirit 87; life is process of movement 76; logic, privileging of 152; Marcuse and 138, 169; Nazi's irrational policies and 143, 151n.61; WORKS: *Phenomenology of Spirit* 20, 117, 139–40, 170, 195; "Philosophy of History" 56–7; *Philosophy of History* lecture 117, 138; *Philosophy of Right* lecture 117, 139; *Science of Logic* 75, 139, 170
Hegelian-Marxist negation of the negation 114
Heidegger, Martin 6, 20, 25, 165; active subjective moment 132; ancient craft and 74, 77; authentic existence 135; catastrophe of modernity 75; concept of essence 69–70; concept of historicity 137; conception of world disclosure 202; *Dasein* and 76, 115, 132–3, 135–6, 142; ethics and 78; German idealism (1920s) 139–40; individuality as response to death 79; key concepts and Marcuse 141–2; Marcuse and 8, 19, 26, 28; National Socialism and 27–8, 133, 142, 144; Nazi phase 73; phenomenology and 134, 143–4; reifies fear 160; *Seinsvergessenheit* (forgetting of being) 9; subordinate moment in each era 71; technology and 67, 71–2; theory of historicity and Marcuse 134–5, 139; WORKS: *Being and Time* 8, 73, 76, 115, 132, 135–7, 140; *Kant and the Problem of Metaphysics* 115; "Question Concerning Technology, The" 68, 73, 78
Heracles story 104
Herbert Marcuse Archive 9; "Historical Fate of Bourgeois Democracy, The" 17
Herbert's Hippopotamus: Marcuse and Revolution in Paradise (film 1996) 5
hetarism, before matriarchy yielded to patriarchy 106–7
heteraic sexuality, reverse of patriarchal order 109
"Historical and Social Labor" 195, 198
historicity 115, 134, 137, 153–4, 191;

ontological determination (*Seinsbestimmung*) 117
Historikerstreit (the historians' debate) 62
history, genesis of present out of the past 57; (*Geschichte*), succession of events (*Geschehen*) happening 115
Hobsbawm, Eric 2; the "Golden Age" 57, 59, 64
homosexuality 179
Horkheimer and Adorno, enlightenment, deep pessimism 241; friendship with Marcuse 251
Horkheimer, Max 3, 9–10, 21, 175; America and 51, 209; anti-fascism 45; behavior necessary in capitalist era 155; conflicts and protest movements 52; critic of Heidegger 28; critical theory and 15, 188, 218; critical theory and "one world" 59; difference between traditional and critical theory 210; "Faithless Faith" in pure existence 213; Frankfurt School and 44; historical transformation and 54; hope for entirely Other 212; letter to Löwenthal about "Elements of Anti-Semitism" 61; letter to Löwenthal about *social science* 64; Marcuse's correspondence with 6; need for new concept of ideology 215; new version of Communist Manifesto 59; pessimism and negative dialectics 17–18; rejection of philosophical anthropology 157; returned to Germany 17; severed critical theory and notion of an addressee 60; shift in Marxian concept of ideology 213; studied in 1980s and 1990s 43; subjectivity 82; truth had become utopian 118; WORKS: "Egoism and Freedom Movements" 153, 154–5; "On the Anthropology of the Bourgeois Era" 153; "Remarks on Philosophical Anthropology" 155; "Thesis on Need" paper 53; "Traditional and Critical Theory" 8, 241 *see also Dialectics of Enlightenment*
Hoy, David, *Foucault: A Critical Reader* 182
human beings 70, 74, 157, 193, 216, 237–8
human consciousness, constitutes itself in its species being 215

human happiness, obstacles of pain and death 161
humanity, transformation of fascism and 210
Husserl, E.G.A., phenomenology 81, 132–3, 166–7; scientific rationality 192–4; "transcendental subjectivity" 198
Huxley, Aldous 60; "*Brave New World*" 53

I-Thou, relationship with nature 230
idealism, empty "metaphysics" 132
"identity", concept 62, 216; what was Marcuse's? 249
illocutionary language 200
illusion, indistinguishability of real and fictional 122
imagination, *aesthetic* 115–17, 123, 237; *cognitive* and *aesthetic* 26; collective universal force 101–2; constitutive function 122; contaminated 119; function of 118; *Geist* is 117; historical 26, 115, 122, 125; imprisoned 120; irreducible role of 205; liberatory with technical invention 239; limits of prescribed by technology 118; male which privileges parthenogenesis 104; Marcuse and 184; negative dialectics of 119, 124; problem of emancipation and 123; process of reification and 119; productive 125; reason and 118; role in theory 171; status of 123; theory of 119; transcendental 115–17, 123, 140; trivialization of 121; utopian 105, 109; will become central category of knowledge 160
"imagined communities" 216
IMF 94
industrialization 85, 91; logic of the "iron cage" 192
industrialized production, negation and sublation of social bases 219
Institute for Social Research 3, 6, 142, 253; authoritarian structures of consciousness 210; colleagues of Marcuse and 25; conference on Aldous Huxley in Los Angeles 53; critique of pragmatism 15; debates by which social subject constituted 55; essays by Marcuse 20;

Horkheimer and Pollock and critical theory 65; Marcuse and 137, 168, 250; relocation to New York 51, 142; *Zeitschrift für Sozialforschung* journal 8–9, 53–4
interaction, definition 198, 200
"is", "ought" 74

Jameson, Fredric 5, 184
Jay, Martin 4, 61, 105, 117; *The Dialectical Imagination* 165
Juutilainen, Paul Alexander (film maker) 5

Kant, Immanuel 28, 49, 78, 139, 166; aims of anthropology 160; concept of transcendental imagination 140; distinction between *cognitive* and *aesthetic* imagination 26; distinguishes metaphysics from anthropology 159; practical-constitutive ideas in practical philosophy 159; schematism of the pure understanding 190; subjective moment 132; two sciences of man (physiological and pragmatic) 159–60; WORKS: *Anthropology from a Pragmatic Point of View* 153; *Critique of Judgment* 23, 115–16, 123; *Critique of Pure Reason* 115–16, 123, 140
Kantian "as-if" 159
Kātz, Barry, unity of the "essential" 189; work, *Herbert Marcuse and the Art of Liberation* 4
Kautsky, Karl "orthodoxy" 133–4; scientism, groundwork for Lenin 134
Kellner, Douglas 6, 44; *Herbert Marcuse and the Crisis of Marxism* (1984) 4, 167; "Marcuse and the Quest for Radical Subjectivity" 25–6; "Marcuse renaissance, A" 5
Kermode, Frank, *Modern Masters* series 165, 174
Kierkegaard, S.A. 18–19; Marcuse discussion of in essay 132
Kimball, Roger, Marcuse's Critical Theory and 4; WORKS: "Gender, Race and Class" 3; *Tenured Radicals: How Politics Has Corrupted Our Higher Education* (1990) 3
King, Martin Luther 58
King Melisseus, daughters of 103

Kirchheimer, Otto 9
Korsch, Karl 138
Kuhn, Thomas 56, 204–5

labor concept 141–2
Laing, R.D. 47
Langer, William 255
Lash, Christopher 102
Latour, Bruno 72
lawful marriage (*Thesmophoria*) 103
Lazarsfeld, Paul 56
leaders of bourgeois revolts, magnified versions of average bourgeois 155
Lebensphilosophie 115, 122, 132
Lebenswelt 90, 195, 198, 201, 203, 205
Left Green Network 229
Lenhardt, Christian 105
Leopold, Aldo 233
Lettau, Reinhard 5
liberation, impossibility of 122
"libidinal rationality" 88
life, fulfillment as *Geist* 117
Light, Andrew 27, 234; Bookchin and 232; comparison between Martin Buber and Arne Naess 230; *Social Ecology after Bookchin* 231, 235
"Logos of Gratification" 87
London conference, "Dialectics of Liberation" 47
Löwenthal, Leo 51, 60, 218
Löwith, Karl, Heidegger and concept of historicity 137
Lukács, George 138; active subjective moment 132, 134; reification of consciousness 135; Weber and 194; work, *History and Class Consciousness* 131, 215
Lukácsian terms, "art against alienation" 6
Lukes, Timothy J. 5, 27, 240; *Flight into Inwardness* (1985) 4
Lyotard, J.F. 94, 184

Macey, David. *Lives of Michel Foucault* 182
MacIntyre, Alasdair 29, 165; academic fireman act 175; "analysis" is object in reification 170; attitude to Marcuse's *Soviet Marxism* 172; critique of Marcuse's "Repressive Tolerance" 173; discussion of Marcuse's *Reason and Revolution*

INDEX

169–70; Marcuse really a Hegelian 167–8, 172; philosophy of education 174; questions Marcuse's conception of philosophy 166; WORKS: *After Virtue* 165–6, 175; *Herbert Marcus: An Exposition and Polemic* 165, 167, 174

Maine, Henry, *Ancient Law* 105

Male philosopher, site of metaphorical reproduction 109

Man; center in philosophy as species being 153

Manichean, dualism 132; friend-foe logic 16

manipulation of needs, not final and definitive 214

Mann, Thomas, letter to Ulbricht (1951) 54

march from Berkley campus to Oakland Army Terminal 256–7

Marcuse: Critical Theory and the Promise of Utopia anthology 4

Marcuse, Herbert 58, 218; aesthetic is historical 78–9; aesthetics 21–2; agrees with Horkheimer on anthropology 157; Anglo-American reception of critical theory 1–6; anthropology and 152–3, 159; the bourgeoisie and 8–9; bridge between environmental materialists and ontologists 231; critical Marxist 133; critique of technological reason and 191–7; deficit in democratic theory 24; Dilthey's concept of "Life" 140; ecology 23–4, 227–35, 237, 239; emigration to New York 8, 51; erotic utopianism 178; example of automobile 188–90; faith in significance of philosophical discussion 79; feminist movement 26; first years in America 209; Frankfurt School and 163; freedom of man must be realized 160; Freud and 86, 102–3, 105, 255; government service in US 4, 6, 60, 250, 254; Great Refusal and 13, 18, 85, 161, 181; on Hegel 138–9; Hegelian-Marxist 28; Heidegger and 77, 131–2, 140–1, 143, 149n.46, 152; historical transformation 54; history of philosophy 19–20; impact of Heidegger's *Being and Time* 131–4, 137, 143; importance for gay liberation 180; impressed by *History and Class Consciousness* 132; lecture "Marxism and Feminism" (1974) 91–2; leftist émigré scholars and 9; London conference 47; Marx and 23–4, 73, 76, 133, 141, 152, 163, 169; Marxian critique of economy and 220; materialist theory of subjectivity 16, 232; *memory* 84–5; myths of Orpheus and Narcissus 103; "new sensibility" 90; new *techne* would enhance life 75; nothing outside of capitalism 54–5, 59; opposition to fascism 44–5; overview of life and work 6–15; paper on Huxley's "*Brave New World*" (1942) 53; phantasy and 85; play impulse, aesthetic function and 88; politics 16–19; possibilities of utopia 45; post-technological era and 70; protest movements 122; psychoanalysis 22–3; "quality of life" 78; radical critic of US 17; rationality a social construct 83; read by Americans (1960s) 184; rejected sectarian violence 17; relevance to contemporary discussions 15–16; repressive hypothesis 176–7; reservations about phenomenology 137; role in 1960s and 1970s 48; Rorty and 183; student protesters in Berlin (1967) and 54; subjectivism in Marxist theory and 10; subjectivity 81–4, 86, 88–9, 93–6, 140; support of student movement and New Left 6, 43–4, 52; survived fascism and Nazism with hope intact 178; technology 20–1, 67, 72, 74, 77, 190; theory of historical subject-object mediation 125; transformative oppositional possibilities and 44; US denazification policy after the war 44; utopia and 75, 102, 110, 114, 118, 158, 160–1; utopian project is scientific 157; woman missing in account of Orpheus and Narcissus 103; WORKS: *Aesthetic Dimension, The* 6, 14–15, 26, 46, 114–15, 123–4; "Beyond One-Dimensional Man" 17, 122; "Beyond the Reality Principle" 154; "Contributions to a Phenomenology of Historical Materialism" 114, 143; *Counter-*

INDEX

Revolution and Revolt (1972) see separate entry; "End of Utopia, The" 158; *Eros and Civilization* see separate entry; essay on Marx's *Philosophic-Economic Manuscripts* 6; "Existential Judgment on Society" 188; "Foundations of Historic Materialism, The" 141, 167; *Hegel's Ontology and the Theory of Historicity* 8, 19–20, 76, 116–17, 138–9, 143; "Historical Fate of Bourgeois Society, The" 211; "Industrialization and Capitalism in Max Weber" 191; "Marxism and Feminism" 26; *Negations: Essays in Critical Theory* 168; "On Concrete Philosophy" 132, 134, 143; "On Hedonism" 20, 159; "On the Philosophical Foundation of the Concept of Labor in Economics" 141; "On the Problem of the Dialectic" 117, 138, 143; *One-Dimensional Man* see separate entry; "Philosophy and Critical Theory" 45, 118, 168, 169, 174; "Political Preface" 4; *Reason and Revolution* 9, 20, 117, 143, 169–70, 250, 255; "Repressive Tolerance" 4, 12–13, 24, 173; "Some Remarks on Aragon: Art and Politics in the Totalitarian Era" (1945) 46; "Some Social Implications of Modern Technology" 53, 196; *Soviet Marxism* 10, 172, 238; *Studies on Authority and Family* 8; *Technology, War and Fascism* 6; "Transcendental Marxism" 115–16

Marcuse, Peter, "Herbert Marcuse's Identity" 29, 249–52

Marquard, Odo 152–3

marriage, "sexual relation" once judicial relation 109

Marx, Karl 2, 6, 49, 81, 105, 240; all-encompassing market 78; concrete social theory and 138; dialectical method 133; history of civilization process of radical alienation 210; "icy waters of egotistical calculation" 192; liberal capitalism 199; Marcuse and 28, 166, 255; notion of communism as dream 70; self-negation and sublation ("Selbstaufhebung") 219; whole man in historical and social labor 194; WORKS: *Capital* 211, 220; *Capital: Critique of Political Economy* 154; *Economic and Philosophic Manuscripts of (1844)* 23, 141–3, 158, 167, 194, 219; *Grundrisse, The* 29, 211, 214, 219–20

Marxism, critiques in (1970s and 1980s) 93; female narcissism and maternal bonding/bondage 102; Heideggers theory of historicity and 134; Marcuse retains view of productive forces 196; Marcuse wanted to reinvigorate 169; Marcuse on weaknesses of theory 134; philosophy of Hegel and 138; theory of subjectivity 95

materialism and idealism, conflict must be dialectically transformed (*aufgehoben*) 56

maternal right (*Mutterrecht*) 102

matriarchal history, utopian phantasy and 105

matricide of Orestes and Alcmaeon 107

Melissa (Bee-Woman) 103

memory 62, 84–5, 100

merchant, landowner and 217–18

metaphysics, definition 159

Michael X 47

Microsoft 94

migration 55, 210, 217, 219

modern technology, raw materials in systems 71

moderns, role of human being 70

monopolistic economy 156, 212

Morgan, Lewis H., *Ancient Society* 105

"motility" of life 116

multiculturalism, subjectivity and 82

Naess, Arne 228, 232; "The Shallow and the Deep, Long Range Ecology Movements" 227, 233

narcissism, Marcus and Orphic character of 103

national Greens Gathering (Amherst, Massachusetts) 227

National Socialism, Adorno on Anti-Semitism and 210; failure of Weimar Republic to prevent 24; Hegel as precursor 9; Heidegger and 8, 27–8, 133, 137, 142; Horkheimer's feelings about 51; Marcuse, Neumann and Löwenthal in US intelligence 60; Neumann's critique of 16

"national spaces", rediscovery of 216
nationalist particularism, historic defeats and 221
natural science, crises of modernity and 241
naturalism, opposed to late capitalism 124
nature 240; control of man and 236; enlightenment and 241; erotic energy of 244; Marcuse and new sensibility of 239, 242; mediates balance of instincts 237; *social category* 243–5
nature and society, completely interwoven 236
"Nature Too Awaits the Revolution!" 242, 244
Nazi regime 13, 29, 253
Nazism 64, 241, 250, 253
neo-liberalism 64
Neumann, Franz 9, 16, 54, 60, 251, 253–4; prosecution of Nazis and 44, 254
New Deal, state intervention 54, 60, 64
New labour 64
"new language", "methodical reversal of meaning" 122
New Left 2–3, 91, 164, 241; defending democracy while attacking capitalism 215; Marcuse attacked for word community 217
"new rationality", new sensibility and 91
new science 243, 245
"new sensibility" 90–91, 99, 122, 125; another way of interacting with nature 242; Marcuse and 243–5
"new social movements" 91
Nietzsche, Friedrich 6, 81–2, 105; breakthrough to the primacy instinct 257; subjectivity in emphasis on the body 87; WORK, *On the Genealogy of Morals* 85
Nixon, Richard (1972) 17, 211; Marcuse's reference to law-and-order rhetoric 49

obstinacy, Marcuse and 45–6
O'Connor, Jim, second contradiction of capitalism 234
Oedipus Rex, guiltless guilt 124
Offe, Claus 4

Office of Strategic Services (OSS) 4, 29, 44, 251, 253–5, 259
"One World", at end of war (1945) 59; social divisions and 61
One-Dimensional Man (1964) 2–3, 14, 20, 191; ambivalence towards technology 196; categories Marcuse applied to advance countries 64; concern with environment and technology 238; critical theory offers no easy solution 181; ecological treatise 239; "fictional" history 124; foreclosure of possibility and 52; "Great Refusal" 13, 90; intentions in 157–8; Macintyre and 172–3, 175; ontological change, radical aesthetic and 231; political criticism first and foremost 258; protest rendered ineffective by one-dimensional society 181; reification and alienation are major themes 173; social interaction into aesthetic sphere 124–5; subjectivity 89–90; technology and 73; theory of historical imagination 26, 117, 119–22; total integration 29; trenchant analyses of American way of life 251
O'Neill, John 22, 26, 105
Orestes 107
Orpheus/Narcissus myth 103
"other", concept brought from Europe 55–6
otherness in nature 239
Ott, Hugo 27
Ovid, *Metamorphoses* (Book III) 103

"pacified existence" 204, 238, 242
"paradigm shifts" 56
Parsifal 254
paternity, triumph over chthonian-maternal principle 107
patriarchal principle, consanguinity inessential to patronymy 108
patriarchy, genealogical thread (*filo genealogico*) 106; mystical act 110; women and repression 177
peace movement, subjectivity and 91
people's identification, Marcuse never considered it irreversible 213
performance principle 87; domination of in bourgeois 155; environmental

INDEX

crises and 238; labor and 160; reality principle and 154; surplus repression and 171
Pericles 108
"personal is political" 218
phenomenology 81, 131–4, 137–8, 142–4, 166–7, 194–5, 202–3
Philippines 211
philosopher's persona, Marcuse and German accent 250
philosophical anthropology 156–7
philosophy, dependent on logical discourse 114; that which has neither nor ever will exist 57
physiological science, investigates what nature makes of man 159–60
physis, Being and 69
Pippin, Robert 4
Plato 76, 166, 171
Platonic doctrine of androgynous love, woman supplanted by man/woman lover 108
Platonism, paradigm of knowledge 193
pleasure principle 83, 85–6, 256
Plessner, Helmut 152
Plutarch, *Conjugalia praecepta* 103
political ecology. Marcuse and 233
political right, Marcuse and 4–5, 24
politics of *gynesis* 105
politics of narcissism, family and 102
Pollock 51, 54, 190
Pope, the, opposition to Marcuse 164
Popper, Karl, "conjecture and refutation" 205
positivism, Habermas and logical 241; nineteenth century 74, 134, 166, 190; scientific in America 255
Post-Fordism 189
post-structuralism, subject and 81–2, 84, 86, 88–9, 93–4, 96
postmodern dream of security, advertisement for vehicle and 188–9
postmodernism, subject and 81–2, 93–4
power, resistance and 182
power of government, scale *identification* of people with rulers 212
"practical", utopian dimension in Marcuse's theory 157
pragmatic anthropology, not concerned with all dimensions of human being 159
pragmatic science, what man can make of himself 160

Pravda 164
problem-solving, world disclosure imperils 202
production paradigm, Marcuse's appropriation of phenomenology and 202
productive forces, differentiated from relations of production 197
pseudo-concreteness, phenomenology and 137–8, 142
psychoanalytic theory, strict truths and 100–1
Puerto Rico 211
Puhovski, Zarko, essence of victimization 221
"purposiveness without purpose" 23

racism 48
radio 211, 221–2
Radio City and Hollywood 53
rationality, defined in objective laws of motion 203; instrumental 239; libidinal 88; scientific 192, 239; speech act theory and 201; technical-scientific 189; technological, mobilization of 237; world disclosure and 202
rationalization 190–2, 198; *Lebenswelt* 198; Protestantism central to process 197; societal 197; solidification into an iron cage 194
Raulet, Gérard 26
Reagan, Ronald 3, 5, 164, 183
reality principle 83, 85, 87, 124; Logos of 87; performance principle and 154; pleasure-ego and 121
reason 120, 125, 192, 198
Reed, Ishmael, *Japanese in Spring* novel 174–5
Reich, Wilhelm 177–9
Reichenbach, Hans 250
reification 135; categories 220; émigré and 209; exploding from within 215; human needs and 214; humanity must bring it to an end 212; Marcuse (1970s) and 218; Marxian categories of 211–12; short century's tendencies toward 217; tied to specific social-historical context 215
Reitz, Charles, *Art, Alienation and the Humanities: A Critical Engagement with Herbert Marcuse* (2000) 6
religion 101, 216

religious emancipation, dehumanizing force 216
religious fundamentalism, historic defeats and 221
"responsibility", meaning 245
repressive tolerance 212
repression 4, 17, 171, 177, 179
repressive desublimation 120, 125, 180
repressive hypothesis 176–7, 179, 182–3
Rio de Janeiro conference 6
Robinson, Paul 180
Roman patriarchal system 106
Rome conference 6
Roosevelt, Franklin D. 51
Rorty, Richard 29, 94, 165, 183–5; admirer of French post-structuralism 184; American intellectuals and philosophy (1960s) 184; interview with Giovanna Borradori 183
Rousseau, Jean-Jacques 212
Rumsfeld, Donald 16
Russia, failed revolution 55

Said, Edward, *Culture and Imperialism* 164
salvation through revolution, administered world and 60
Sappho's poetry 105
Sartre, Jean-Paul 212; "project" and 193; writing, *Being and Nothingness* (1948) 9
Scheler, Max 152; philosophical anthropology 156
Schiller, Friedrich 21, 78; aesthetic education and play 87–8, 257; *Letters on Aesthetic Education* 257
Schmidt, Alfred 4; "Existential Ontology and Historical Materialism in Herbert Marcuse" 115
Schmitt, Carl 16
Schoolman, Morton, *Imaginary Witness, The: The Critical Theory of Herbert Marcuse* 4
Schopenhauer, Arthur, restless ever-striving will 87
Schorske, Carl E. 20, 29
science, *Aufhebung der Lebenswelt* 193; different concept of nature 242; European, continuous process 195; heir of the Enlightenment losing *raison d'être* 65; revolutionary 205; sociology of 56; subject to drive to forget 55
science and technology, attempt to dominate nature 241
search for meaning and historical relevance, losses of tradition 216
Second International 133–5, 138
Second World War 241
Seed, John (Australian deep ecologist) 228
self-consciousness, technical subject and 77
self-realization, embodiment of *logos* 193; self-denial 214
senses, currently socially constrained 90
"sensuous order" 89
September 11 (2001) attack 16–17
sexual repression, role of political power 179
sexuality, part of Eros 179
shift from class to "the people", one-dimensional 217
Simmel, Georg, concept of the stranger 217–18
Sinnlichkeit 88
social analysis, "consciousness" and "subject" 62
social classes, component of a material society 57
"social constructions" 55
social ecology 227–8, 230
social sciences 61–3, 191
socialism, proletariat and 219–20
"socialization", ensnaring people in network of 55
society, constituted in new ways Marcuse argued 213–14
Socrates, *Phaedrus* 108–9
Soviet Union 10, 219
speeding truck, allegorizes restiveness of organized labor 189
"stagflation" 189
Stalinism 51, 64
State Department service, Marcuse and 4, 44
state intervention, New Deal and 54
Stern, Günther (later Anders) 150
Steuernagel, Trudy, "Marcuse, the Women's Movement and Women's Studies" 5
stranger, the 217–18
student movement (1960s and 1970s) 6, 43–4, 52, 54, 219, 258

INDEX

subject, character of 62; crisis of 95–6
subject and agency, problematics of 94
subject and history, problematization 94
subjective moment 132
subjectivity 81, 92; abstract concepts of 133, 140, 143; active human 132; appropriation and decline into bondage 214; demands participation and fulfillment 93; embodied 26; environmental movement and 91; estrangement and alienation part of 219; Great Refusal and 90; initiated by Descartes' *ego cognito* 140; Marcuse notion of radical to nature 232; Marcusean 88–9; multiculturalism 82; of nature 231; normalized of technological society 89; objectivity correlated with 193; ontology of 121; problematics of 96; rehabilitation important for Marcuse 220; social movements and 91; unreconciled 122; validity 122
subjectivity and agency 89, 93, 95
"surplus consciousness" 26, 92
Sylvan, Richard, "Do We Need a New Environmental Ethic" 233
syncretic world society 65

techne, definition 68; Marcuse and Heidegger 74; modern incorporates ethics and aesthetics 73; new environmentally aware 75; technology and 67, 72
technical reason, concept ideological 195
technics, (neutral) 204; social control and 237
"technological a priori" 203–5
technological reason 189–91; *aufgehoben* 195; Marcuse's critique of 200
technology 67–8; decontextualizing and 72; historical-social *project* 195; ideological nature of 200; "Instrumentalization Theory" 72; Marcuse's ambivalence toward 191, 195, 198; Marcuse's phenomenology of 202; mode of world disclosure 202; ontological account 69; relationship with technics and 204; *techne* and 77, 200–5; that would treat nature in different way 242; value-free 72, 77

technology and technics, Marcuse and 197
television advertisement, sports recreational vehicles 188–9
Temps Modernes, Les 254
terrorism, interpretation of in critical theory 61
theory, able to recognize truth 56
thesmophoros (a ritual bee) 103
Third International 133
"third way" 114
Third World liberation movements 183, 241
"Traditional and Critical Theory" 52
traditional religion, alienation and suppression of 218
Trilling, Lionel 255
"true" thing, manifests its own essence 74

understanding (*Verstand*) 140
University of California at San Diego (UCSD) 5, 184, 256
US, bourgeois society without feudal vestiges 59; critical theory and 51, 209; deep ecology and social ecology 227; detentions of al-Qaida suspects 16; focused on sexuality instead of Eros 179; influence of Frankfurt School 163; Marcus described it as "Bonapartism without Bonaparte" 212; Marcuse on internalization in 218; Marcuse, Neumann and Löwenthal in intelligence 60, 183; Marcuse warned about neo-fascism in 211; Marcuse's critique of status quo and student protesters 219; more congenial life for Marcuse 251; people and Marx 183; political right and Marcuse 3; social science has complex tradition 55; study of disappearance of bourgeois society 64; *syncretic world society* 65
US Department of Agriculture, Marcuse's wife as statistician 250
utopia 45–6, 101–2, 158, 160
utopian theory, Light's skepticism toward 234; Marcuse's *Eros and Civilization* and 100; Marcuse's utopian moments 220, 242; political ecology and 227

273

Valéry, Paul 103
validity 198–9, 201, 203
Veblen, Thorstein, Adorno and 53, 60
Vico, Giambattista 106; *The New Science* 105
victimization concept 213, 221
Vienna Circle 166
Vietnam War 48–9, 211; Adorno and Marcuse, letters about 251; Horkheimer and 51
violence of repression, strangers and 217
Virgil, *Georgics* (Book IV) 103
Virilo 184
Vogel, Steven 27, 231, 234

Wallace, Henry 255
Webel, Charles P. 4
Weber, Max 4, 81, 190, 198; account of modernity and *Zweckrationalität* 198; concept of rationalization 191–2; conflation of reason with *rationalization* 199; Marcuse's critique of 194; political context of Wilhelmine Germany 191; societal rationalization and 197; technological reason identification 195
Weimar Republic 53; crisis-ridden 131; critical theory and 51; failure to prevent national Socialism 17, 24; Heidegger and 136–7, 142

welfare, transformation into "welfare" state 5
Werz, Michael 29
West, Cornel 3
Western capitalist countries, anthropology of damaged life to come 157
Western civilization, antagonism between subject and object 86–7
Western philosophy, Marcuse appreciation of 143
Western rationalist tradition, Marcuse critical of 10
Western societies, authoritarian regimes and 211; dialectic of enlightenment and 219; environmental legislation pallative 234
Wiggershaus, Rolf, *Frankfurt School: Its History, Theories and Political Significance* 167
Wittgenstein, Ludwig 190, 202
woman, function 106, 108
work, definition 198, 200
world, logocentric or objectivistic concept 200–1; ontologically (*seinsmässig*) 116–17
World Bank 94
world disclosure 201–2, 204–5
WTO 94

eBooks – at www.eBookstore.tandf.co.uk

A library at your fingertips!

eBooks are electronic versions of printed books. You can store them on your PC/laptop or browse them online.

They have advantages for anyone needing rapid access to a wide variety of published, copyright information.

eBooks can help your research by enabling you to bookmark chapters, annotate text and use instant searches to find specific words or phrases. Several eBook files would fit on even a small laptop or PDA.

NEW: Save money by eSubscribing: cheap, online access to any eBook for as long as you need it.

Annual subscription packages

We now offer special low-cost bulk subscriptions to packages of eBooks in certain subject areas. These are available to libraries or to individuals.

For more information please contact webmaster.ebooks@tandf.co.uk

We're continually developing the eBook concept, so keep up to date by visiting the website.

www.eBookstore.tandf.co.uk